ARCHAEOLOGY AND MEMORY

edited by
Dušan Borić

Oxbow Books
Oxford and Oakville

Published by
Oxbow Books, Oxford, UK

© Oxbow Books and the individual authors, 2010

ISBN 978-1-84217-363-3

This book is available direct from:

Oxbow Books, Oxford, UK
(Phone: 01865-241249; Fax: 01865-794449)

and

The David Brown Book Company
PO Box 511, Oakville, CT 06779, USA
(Phone: 860-945-9329; Fax: 860-945-9468)

or from our website

www.oxbowbooks.com

*Cover image: Bernardo Bellotto, The ruins of the old Kreuzkirche in Dresden, 1765
(reproduced with permission from Kunsthaus in Zürich).*

A CIP record for this book is available from the British Library

Library of Congress Cataloging-in-Publication Data

Archaeology and memory / edited by Dušan Borić.
     p. cm.
  Includes bibliographical references.
  ISBN 978-1-84217-363-3
 1. Archaeology--Research. 2. Archaeology--Philosophy. 3. Archaeology--Methodology. 4. Memory-
-Social aspects--History. 5. Mnemonics--History. 6. Social archaeology--Eurasia--Case studies. 7.
Prehistoric peoples--Eurasia. 8. Eurasia--Antiquities. 9. Eurasia--History. I. Boric, Dušan.
  CC83.A69 2010
  930.1072--dc22

                              2010002772

Printed and bound in Great Britain by
Short Run Press, Exeter

Contents

Contributors

MRDJAN BAJIĆ
Birčaninova 28b
11000 Beograd
Serbia
Email: mrdjan@EUnet.rs

DUŠAN BORIĆ
Cardiff School of History and Archaeology
Cardiff University
Humanities Building, Colum Drive
Cardiff CF10 3EU
UK
Email: BoricD@Cardiff.ac.uk

ANNA BOOZER
Department of Archaeology
University of Reading
Reading RG6 6AB
UK
Email: A.L.Boozer@Reading.ac.uk

VICTOR BUCHLI
Department of Anthropology
University College London
14 Taviton Street
London WC1H OBW
UK
Email: vbuchli@yahoo.com

PAOLA FILIPPUCCI
Department of Social Anthropology
University of Cambridge
Free School Lane
Cambridge CB2 3RF
UK
Email: pf107@cam.ac.uk

ADAM GUTTERIDGE
Institute for the public understanding of the past
University of York
York YO10 5DD

UK
Email: ag591@york.ac.uk

BRYAN HANKS
Department of Anthropology
University of Pittsburgh
#3113 WWPH, 230 S. Bouquet St.
Pittsburgh, PA 15260
USA
Email: bkh5@pitt.edu

ANDY JONES
Department of Archaeology
University of Southampton
Avenue Campus, Highfield
Southampton SO17 1BF
UK
Email: amj@soton.ac.uk

RUTH TRINGHAM
Anthropology Department
University of California Berkeley
232 Kroeber Hall
CA 94720-3710
USA
Email: tringham@berkeley.edu

LINDSAY WEISS
Department of Anthropology
Columbia University
New York, NY 10027
USA
Email: lw2004@columbia.edu

ALASDAIR WHITTLE
Cardiff School of History and Archaeology
Cardiff University
Humanities Building, Colum Drive
Cardiff CF10 3EU
UK
Email: whittle@cardiff.ac.uk

1. Introduction: Memory, archaeology and the historical condition

Dušan Borić

In thousands of languages, in the most diverse climes, from century to century, beginning with the very old stories told around the hearth in the huts of our remote ancestors down to the works of modern storytellers which are appearing at this moment in the publishing houses of the great cities of the world, it is the story of the human condition that is being spun and that men never weary of telling to one another. The manner of telling and the form of the story vary according to periods and circumstances, but the taste for telling and retelling a story remains the same: the narrative flows endlessly and never runs dry. Thus, at times, one might almost believe that from the first dawn of consciousness throughout the ages, mankind has constantly been telling itself the same story, though with infinite variations, to the rhythm of its breath and pulse. And one might say that after the fashion of the legendary and eloquent Scheherazade, this story attempts to stave off the executioner, to suspend the ineluctable decree of the fate that threatens us, and to prolong the illusion of life and of time. Or should the storyteller by his work help man to know and to recognize himself? Perhaps it is his calling to speak in the name of all those who did not have the ability or who, crushed by life, did not have the power to express themselves.

(Andrić 1969)

…Sir, everything that is not literature is life, History as well, Especially history [6]…So you believe, Sir, that history is real life, Of course, I do, I meant to say that history was real life, No doubt at all…[8]

(Saramago 1996)

Will it not then be the task of a memory instructed by history to preserve the trace of this speculative history over the centuries and to integrate it into its symbolic universe? This will be the highest destination of memory, not before but after history.

(Ricoeur 2004, 161)

Prelude

Next to my bedside, there is a black and white sepia-toned family photo (Fig. 1.1). The photo shows my grandmother holding my great uncle's son, my other great uncle feeding a horse, the boy sitting on the horse in his impeccable formal navy-like school-boy uniform, this anonymous horse standing still and an equally anonymous kitten in the arms of the boy. The year is 1936. It is the summer on the family farm in the region of Srem, Vojvodina, the northern province of the Kingdom of Yugoslavia. The tranquillity of the atmosphere on the photo may indicate a *belle époque* of a kind, a perfect, happy moment of a family reunion, only a few years before the official start of the second big war in the same century. The photo was taken five years before the peaceful facial expression disappears from the face of my, at the time 23-year-old, grandmother whose father and brother met their deaths before the firing squad of

Figure 1.1

the pro-fascist NDH *Ustašas* state. But trying to trace the inner consciousness of my grandmother on her face, on this photo, she is calm and happy. Yet, despite the tranquillity of the moment that the photo conveys we know that the photo captures time only two years after King Alexander of Yugoslavia was assassinated in Marseille, France, and already eight years after the Croatian delegate Stjepan Radić was shot dead in the assembly of the Kingdom of Yugoslavia, which later led to the abolishment of parliamentary life in the country. Both gruesome events, with the benefit of the hindsight, on the plane of political history, could have given uncanny hints of the direction in which the world events were going, slowly creeping into the fragile peace of this family's lives. Once the war broke out, my great uncle, the father of the boy on the photo, who is behind the camera, had to flee the Croatian city of Zagreb, leaving his business behind. He hid in a German train under the threat of the *Ustašas* militia, and escaped to the family estate in the village of Erdevik, somewhat of a safe harbour during these hard war years. In this village, German neighbours (*Volkdeutsche*) who had lived in this region along with other ethnicities for

centuries, often protected local Serbs from fascist militia persecutions.

Narratives surrounding this photo about the events that my grandmother passed on to me years ago still live in my memories. And, even more vivid are my childhood memories of exploring the attic in the family house that had been the hiding place during the Second World War. Here, among other things, in the dark, secretive and awe-inspiring space criss-crossed by sun-rays that illuminate unreal, floating dust, a large merchant basket, brought to this house at the beginning of the war by my fleeing great uncle, survives as yet another mute material witness of these events. When the basket arrived at the house it was filled with *astrakan* furs that the great uncle managed to rescue from his Zagreb shop, and this fur load years later, after the war, saved him and secured the existence of his family. The visual image of this now abandoned and wrecked object, slowly eaten by termites that thoroughly channelled its entirety, feeds my memories in an imaginative way.

These images and memories in my mind are mine and yet not only mine; they are a mixture of my own memories and of conjectural evidence of traces, which were in turn endowed with narrative meaning through testimonies of others. I remember because I am part of a family history of those close to me. Equally so, my family and I remain tied to collective and historical frameworks and my and our memories and these recollections of the past are tied to the wider realm of history and politics, and to the consciousness of a collective entity. In turn, this collectivity, like any other, remembers in a public sphere by celebrating particular (usually violent) founding events. The commemoration of these events can be selective and common memories could be (and always have been) manipulated and abused through ideological projects when certain historical events become skewed and distorted or overemphasised at the expense of other suppressed events. In the last instance, we are confronted with a pathological condition of memory. This pathological condition can exercise its power of manipulation and distortion over individual apprehensions and perceptions of events, their meaning and significance. From private and inward dilemmas of our own remembering and reminiscing on the past as 'mine' and of those close to me, to the apprehension of a collective past of those others with whom we (myself and those close to me) share the same cultural or political belonging and (narrative) identity – all our lives are constituted through memories. Hence on an intuitive level, one can talk of an immanent pre-understanding of the significance of memory in the constitution of our lives. Yet this initial comprehension about the importance of memory is only a hint of the task that this introduction and this volume set out to achieve.

Sketching the task

While on the one hand this volume seeks to examine how the notion of memory can significantly structure the research efforts in the empirical field of archaeology on the basis of contributions that follow, certain aspects of archaeology and its particular take on memory, in turn, could be considered as important elements in defining the field of memory studies. First, the archaeological approaches offered will enable

us to explore the diversity of mnemonic systems and their significance in past contexts, examining what can be put under the heading 'past in the past'. This avenue of research has been the focus of recent interest in archaeology for memory studies (*e.g.* Borić 2003; Bradley 2002; 2003; Jones 2001; 2007; papers in Chesson 2001; Hastorf 2003; Hodder and Cessford 2004; Kuijt 2001; Meskell 2001; papers in Van Dyke and Alcock 2003; Williams 2003). These useful contributions have covered a number of regional case studies, indicating the importance of memory as a unifying umbrella term to cover a wide range of examples from various past contexts with regard to ways of appropriating and thinking of their own pasts. Such diachronic and cross-cultural perspectives can be used to understand meaningful constitutions and trajectories of particular context-specific mnemonic systems. The present volume provides a diverse set of regional case studies and focuses on a range of prehistoric and classical case studies in the Eurasian regional contexts (papers by Whittle, Borić, Tringham, Hanks, Jones, Boozer and Gutteridge), as well as on predicaments of memory in examples of the archaeologies of 'contemporary past' (papers by Filippucci, Weiss, Bajić and Buchli).

The diachronic depths inherent in the accumulative nature of the archaeological record on the scale of the long-term are unparalleled, and the following chapters will take advantage of this condition. In its dealings with the socially constitutive role of material culture, archaeology is well-suited to tackle the problem of the relationship between materiality and memory, through both discursive and undiscursive aspects of social life. Already, this question has been addressed explicitly in various ways by ethnography (*e.g.* Bloch 1998; Mines and Weiss 1997; Seremetakis 1994), art history (papers in Kwint *et al.* 1999), and architecture (*e.g.* Kwinter 2001) and one would think that archaeology has a lot to add to this facet of the memory/materiality debate (*cf.* Jones 2007; Meskell 2004; Miller 2005; also various papers in this volume). And finally, at a deeper level of 'foundational' tectonics, the importance of the epistemological grounding of archaeology as the discipline of conjectural testimonies and its metaphorical significance in evoking distance and temporal depths will be explored as fundamental to the phenomenology of memory in relation to our historical condition as human beings. Here, also, we shall emphasise the possible way for archaeology to re-define or at least to make explicit its epistemological status, engaging in debates centered around the main goal of historical disciplines, that of the representation of the past. In this way memory, from being the subject of recent archaeological interest, moves on to the plane at which the uses of memory and archaeological practice become confronted with each other, and we shall explore the consequences of this interplay.

In this introduction, I briefly survey, on the one hand, the foundational significance of memory as a philosophical phenomenon, and, on the other hand, the current state of this recently revived theoretical and intellectual currency in the various fields of humanities and social sciences from an archaeological perspective. The relatively recent growing interest in and preoccupation with the issue of memory, remembering and forgetting is a phenomenon in itself, with the outcome in a coincidental proliferation of published works that have as their focus memory across a wide spectrum of unrelated disciplines, in this way reflecting the wider condition of the present-day (see Buchli, this volume). This trend, to which the present volume can serve as an example along with numerous other memory-related recent works referenced throughout, started occupying not only the dominant discourses of disciplines such as sociology, philosophy, history, anthropology or archaeology, but, also, has disseminated into the wider public discourse of the late capitalist society and culture today. Such a condition may perhaps echo the phenomenon of a millenary experience, which 'has had melancholia itself as a theme of meditation and as a source of torment' (Ricoeur 2004, 71). This 'melancholic' aspect of reminiscing also coincides with an apparent 'obsession with commemoration' in our nation-state cultures (see Nora 1996; *cf.* Le Goff 1992). Yet, following Paul Ricoeur, we see the importance of memory in its

role as 'the womb of history' and not just as 'one of the objects of historical knowledge' (2004, 95–96). Memory thus encompasses both history and archaeology.

Archaeology can be seen as a discipline that contributes to the general field of historical knowledge. The production of both archaeological and historical knowledge is structured under the sign of the philosophical notion of our 'historical condition' as human beings, *i.e.* our 'historicity' (*cf.* Arendt 1958). In Heidegger's words, this problem is related to the ontological condition of *Da-sein*, *i.e.* of the human individual, since '… *this being is not 'temporal,' because it 'is in history,' but because, on the contrary, it exists and can exist historically only because it is temporal in the ground of its being*' (1962, 345, original emphasis). This fundamental grounding of human beings in their historicity can be used to overcome the criticism of deconstructionist provenience that underlines the modern condition as the necessary prerequisite for the existence of disciplines such as archaeology (most elaborately Thomas 2004). While one should certainly not downplay the specific social and cultural context of post-Enlightenment thought, *i.e.* the specifics of the social *milieu* and *epoché*, that provided the necessary conditions for a distinctive discipline of archaeology to emerge (with its own set of analytical tools that stemmed from the projects endowed with the Enlightenment spirit), we should be able to show that memory and the related concept of 'trace', *i.e.* seen as an imprint that *has been* left behind by a past agency and which remains in the present as its testimony (see below), may best evoke the historical conditionality of human existence that significantly precedes those processes that are epitomised under the term modernity. Such an understanding may allow the field of studies we call archaeology to exceed its modernity confinement by admitting that the grounding of the historicity of the human condition is more than just a heritage of a certain epoch (*sensu* Foucault). Some anthropological works coming from the deconstructionist camp may warn us of the history-centric view of the human condition just sketched and one should carefully examine these critiques.

Memory for us thus bears its significance on several interconnected levels. In the following section, first, I will examine the 'what' of memories and the 'who' of memories. These starting remarks about what memories are constituted of, as well as posing the question about the ownership of memories, are contextualised within the time-honoured tradition of Western philosophy that goes back to Plato and Aristotle. This long tradition is then complemented with important conceptual reformulations more recently provided in the fields of sociology and anthropology, challenging the conceptual frontiers of the Western episteme. Second, I examine the epistemological status of archaeology in relation to its method of using conjectural evidence in providing interpretations of the past, both as verbal and nonverbal, discursive and undiscursive expressions of human action and agency. At stake here is the importance that this procedure has for the question about the obligation toward the truthful representation of the past, the question fundamental to the ontological and epistemological status of archaeological/historical knowledge. Finally, I shall specify particular problems encountered in archaeological and anthropological dealings with certain aspects of remembering and forgetting, primarily related to the notions of materiality, temporal depths and (dis)continuities and narrative identities. The concluding part of this introduction tacks between issues related to the constitution of archaeological knowledge and representation of the past on the one hand and memory as a synonym for our historical conditionality on the other hand. The focus here in particular is on moral implications of remembering and forgetting.

Philosophy of memory

The following, partially chronologically ordered, survey of a diversity of philosophical positions from which a number of Western thinkers touched upon the issue of memory is limited in its scope, yet it provides a cross-section and a review of the genealogy of thinking about memory within the Western episteme. At the same time, memory itself has served as a proxy in philosophical debates to address fundamental questions of epistemological as well as ontological orders. Hence memory, in more or less explicit ways, has been invested both in the problematic of how knowledge is possible as well as in the question about the temporal and existential character of human beings, and this doubly coined structure of memory marks this discussion. In the following, thus, I will embark inevitably on both of these central sets of philosophical questions as well as those related to the ethics of memory, while still led by a presumption that memory as an overarching notion can usefully be recognised in its singularity and importance as an ever-present ontological capacity.

The Ancients: Plato, Aristotle

The first philosophical discussion of memory is found in the Greek heritage, and comes to us through Plato's (428/427–348/347 BC) dialogues *Theaetetus* and *Sophist* (see Krell 1990; Ricoeur 2004). In fact, the entire philosophical tradition of memory thinking, subsequently, has been framed around the questions, terminology and metaphors evoked in these early texts. It is in the moment when Socrates discusses the nature of knowledge with Theaetetus that the question arises about the relationship between what one experienced and the memory of this experience (166b). At this point Socrates develops a founding memory metaphor, that of a block of wax in our souls, visualising the process of remembering as imprints (marks, *sēmeia*) of signet rings into the wax. Thus, what is impressed in the wax, as long as the image stays in the mind, is what constitutes our knowledge (191d). Socrates in this part of his discussion puts a lot of emphasis on the question with regard to the faithfulness of memory established by different perceptions. Interestingly, distinguishing between good and bad memories, Socrates is of the opinion that the judgment, *i.e.* the connection of perception with thought, is to blame for false opinion, not memory as such. Another metaphor developed in this philosophical dialogue for memory and knowledge is that of the birdcage, *i.e.* 'aviary' – to reach for a particular 'memory-bird' does not relate only to the question with regard to the possession of memories, as much as to an active engagement in the process of memory search, or hunt. But similar to the metaphor of mistakenly trying to fit a new perception with a previous foot imprint, here too, one can mis-take (Ricoeur 2004, 10) a memory-bird.

Yet, it is in another of Plato's dialogue, *Sophist*, that we go to the initial question about the status of previous experience, formulated in the manner of a temporal aporia about the persistence of something absent in the mind as image, moving further from the imprint metaphor. The question that preoccupies the sophists (and Plato) is how to distinguish an image that is a product of a mimetic technique, as a 'faithful resemblance', from an image that is a simulacrum or appearance (*phantasma*). It is here that the crucial question of the danger of connecting memory to imagination arises, *i.e.* whether one can possibly have a truthful resemblance of the past experience, something that is later emphasised with regard to the distinction between historical and fictional narratives (see below).

In *De memoria et reminiscentia*, Aristotle distinguishes remembering that relates to affection (*pathos*) from recollection (*anamnēsis*), which can properly be called the work of memory through the act of searching. Throughout his treatise, Aristotle insists that 'memory is of the past', indicating the idea of temporal distance and distinguishing what comes before and what after as a uniquely human perception of time. Aristotle is interested in what makes something absent endure, and his solution is to suggest the notion of inscription. He is also at the head of the school that put emphasis on the notion of habit, and habit-memory (*e.g.* Bourdieu 1992; *cf.* Ricoeur 2004, 441).

Although the first philosophical discussion about memory has in its core Plato's epistemological concerns about the nature of knowledge, memory immediately reveals its doubly coined structure. It relates to the temporal aporia about the persistence of an absent thing in the mind as an image (*eikōn*). In this way the question with regard to memory immediately triggers a set of ontological issues, primarily related to temporality. The following section reviews a number of thinkers lumped together under 'the tradition of inwardness'

(Ricoeur 2004, 96). What brings these thinkers together is their interest in the constitution of the individual inner experience through various ways of temporal extensions 'in the mind'.

Between individual and collective memories: St. Augustine, Locke, Husserl, Halbwachs

> (…) it is in memory that the original tie of consciousness appears to reside. We said this with Aristotle, we will say it again more forcefully with Augustine: memory is of the past, and this past is of my impressions; in this sense this past is my past (Ricoeur 2004, 96).

Ricoeur (2004, 93–132) defines, following Taylor (1989), the 'tradition of inwardness' in philosophical dealings with memory. What is at stake with regard to this strand of thinking about memory is the connection between what is an ordinary experience of memory at a personal level and its connection to a collective consciousness and collective memory. This question appears among the Ancients with regard to the discussion about the soul and the city. St. Augustine (354–430) is seen as most clearly voicing the concerns of the tradition of inwardness, providing an original understanding of problems inherited from Ancient Greek philosophy. His discussion of memory is tied to the discussions about the aporias of time and an understanding that sees time as an extension of human soul (*distentio animi*) to include the present of the past or memory, the present of the present or attention and the present of the future or expectation. Yet, the acute problem here is how to connect this individual site of memory to the operations of collective memory. For Augustine uses the first person singular of memories as 'my' or 'mine'. Here one may speculate about the possibility of history or historical narratives as a third time, between phenomenological and cosmological time (Ricoeur 1988; 2004).

The next important author to be mentioned in this school of inwardness is John Locke (1632–1704), whose contribution to the invention of the concept of human consciousness is of utmost importance for all subsequent Western philosophical theories of consciousness. Different from Descartes's *ego* and *cogito*, Lockean self sustains a particular personal identity ('sameness with self') enabled by consciousness. This personal identity of the self endures in time, something that lacks in the Cartesian *cogito*. The self establishes the difference in relation to 'all other thinking things'. The question of personal identity and its maintenance through time in Locke is thus directly connected to the question of memory. It is necessary also to mention that the word 'person' here belongs to a particular, historically situated ethico-juridical field (Ricoeur 2004, 107). The forensic character of this word comes together with the concept of 'accountability' and 'appropriation'. In this context, the question of personal identity must be problematised in relation to two different interpretations of one's permanence in time: identity as sameness (*idem*, *même*, *gleich*) and (Lockean) identity as selfhood (*ipse*, *Selbst*) (Ricoeur 1991b). Identity as sameness refers to a material resemblance (finger tips, genetic code, etc.) while identity as selfhood concerns the narrative coherence of one's personal identity or what Ricoeur likes to call 'making a promise' (Ricoeur 1998, 90). The self-constancy is realised by the interplay of these two types of identity. It is exactly at this point that the question is opened about to whom this Lockean self is accountable. Thus, the discussion on personal identity and selfhood always already involves others than the self, opening again the question of the connection of one's memory and its coherence in relation to a group, a society.

The third author who dwells on the question of inner perception of time is Edmund Husserl (1859–1938) in his celebrated work the *Phenomenology of Internal Time Consciousness* (1964). Husserl's phenomenological philosophy responded to Kant's view of time as an unrepresentable category, as an *a priori* sensibility, reachable only through transcendental deduction. This author developed the model of Internal Time Consciousness, which is one attempt to solve the aporia of time conceptually. Time is in this analysis grounded in perception, and is immanent to consciousness and thus possesses a certain intuitive character. We have perceptual experience of fleeting moments of time. Thus, if the present moment as a source-point (*Quellpunkt*) is marked as B, a past moment (A)

sinks into the thickness of time leaving behind its retentions (A', A'', A'''…). And in the same logic, future moments (C', C'', C'''…) are anticipated as protentions. As C becomes a present moment, B is modified into retentions of the past moments (B', B'', B'''…) etc. In this way, memory and remembering are conceptualised as a perpetual flow of lived experience, accumulating a series of 'sunk' memories or gradual temporal 'shadings' (*cf.* Gell 1992, 222*ff.*; 1998, 237*ff.*). Yet, how can such 'extreme subjectivism' speak to the problematic 'of the simultaneous constitution of individual memory and collective memory' (Ricoeur 2004, 114)? Husserl responds to this question by opening the possibility of the 'communalisation' of experience that introduces 'higher order personalities' in his 'Fifth Cartesian Meditations'. This transition from transcendental idealism to the theory of intersubjectivity is not without difficulties: '…it is indeed as foreign, that is as not-me, that the other is constituted, but it is 'in' me that he is constituted' (Ricoeur 2004, 118). According to Husserl, the constitution of collective entities is made possible through intersubjective exchanges, *i.e.* through analogical transfers from individual consciousness and individual memory to the collective memory of communities that celebrate or mourn particular events.

It is interesting to note that this question about the ownership of memories was not raised in the Ancient Greek writings of Plato and Aristotle: mnemonic phenomena as affections and as actions can be attributed to anyone and to each one (Ricoeur 2004, 126). Yet, this does not reduce the problem of memories as singular, confined to the sphere of the self. Here, one may wonder whether the hierarchy of memory supposed by the tradition of inwardness in exploring the question of the passage of time and of memories as first being within a singular mind, as mine, and only then through experience shared by a group, is an adequate way to conceptualise the phenomenology of memory. Also, is this an irreversible process? A different order in bridging the individual mind and the collectively shared, intersubjective memory has been suggested by one sociologist, Maurice Halbwachs (1877–1945), who forcefully turned the question of who first remembers to society, in the best tradition of Émile Durkheim's sociology. In his works *The Collective Memory* (1980) and *On the Collective Memory* (1992), Halbwachs emphasises the intrinsic connection between memories and the existence of others, of a collectivity. Halbwachs's main thesis is that we are able to remember because we are part of the collectivity: 'a person remembers only by situating himself within the viewpoint of one or several groups and one or several currents of collective thought' (1980, 33). Authors, like Bachelard (1964), similarly have argued for the importance of socially marked places for remembering: the house, the attic, the basement being examples *par excellence* for cherished memories of one's childhood as places that punctuate the life of a family as the first social milieu within which a person remembers. Halbwachs's otherwise very useful account of the importance of the social for remembering, at points slips into a more problematic version of social constructivism when claiming that it is only an illusion that we are owners of our beliefs and memories, arguing for the primacy of social structures with 'a quasi-Kantian use of the idea of framework' (Ricoeur 2004, 123–124). Such a perspective may diminish the role of social actors in remembering who are those individuals who remember.

A realistic view might be to suggest an asymmetric tie between individual memory and collective memory in solving this problem of how to bridge the inwardness of the memory perceived by an individual and the way collectivities retain particular shared memories. Ricoeur insists on the term 'ascription' in relation to one's memory as self-ascribable that must always already be other-ascribable. These two ascriptions are 'coextensive' (Ricoeur 2004, 127). For this author, remembering is directly connected to narrativity (see below) for which one needs others, the public sphere. By extending phenomenology to the social sphere, as done by Alfred Schutz (1967), one connects contemporaries, predecessors and successors, while at the same time stressing the asymmetry between different possessors of shared memories who as contemporaries belong to the world of shared experience in both space and time. Ricoeur extends this complexity of who remembers what to an intermediary level between the self and a collective of others. He introduces a different kind of memory, what he calls 'close relations' or 'privileged others' (Ricoeur 2004, 131–132). These friends, or family, those closest to us keep a very particular memory of our lives as individuals that is neither personal nor collective. In this way, the full complexity of memory ascriptions is revealed.

Enduring images: Bergson

> We will assume for the moment that we know nothing of theories of matter and theories of spirit, nothing of the discussions as to the reality or ideality of the external world. Here I am in the presence of images … Yet there is *one* of them which is distinct from all the others, in that I do not know it only from without by perceptions, but from within by affections: it is my body (Bergson 1981, 17).

With these words opens Henri Bergson's (1859–1941) famous work *Matter and Memory* (1981). The most celebrated theses of this work stress duration as a temporal flow phenomenon (see above, Husserl) as well as the idea about an independent survival of the images of the past, *i.e.* representations as recollections of memory. Bergson also makes a distinction between 'habit-memory' and 'event-memory'. The 'habit memory' thus refers to something learnt by heart and remembered with no effort, similar to writing or walking. On the other hand, the 'event-memory' relates to an effort to reproduce an image of a particular memory. An 'economy of effort' to recollect and remember an image (secondary memory) from a simple retention of a particular habit (primary memory) is an important aspect of memory for archaeological case studies (see various papers in this volume).

These two types of memory in fact occupy very different domains: while the habit memory is possible without discursive awareness, secondary memory or recollection is arduous; it is even not presentation of that past moment that is gone but it always must be its re-presentation. What may remain problematic and discomforting in Bergson's writing for us is his position about the independent survival of images, as pure perception, arguing effectively for 'immateriality of memory' (*cf.* Ricoeur 2004, 50–51). Here, the problem of memory's relationship with imagination is opened up. The relationship between making an image visible through the effort of memory, imagination and its faithfulness to the real, *i.e.* perception, is directly relevant to all our efforts as archaeologists and historians to represent the past.

Deconstruction of metaphysics: Nietzsche, Heidegger, Derrida

Friedrich Nietzsche (1844–1900) sets the scene for philosophical discourses that deviate from the systemic and move toward aphoristic reasoning (Ginzburg 1989, 124), with Nietzsche as the *avant-garde* of anti-rationalist modernist thought (Habermas 1987). His rebellious pamphlet against monumental and antiquarian histories directly concerns us here with regard to the questions of (dis)continuities in history and the importance of history for life (Foucault 1984; Ricoeur 1988, 235–240). Nietzsche (1980 [1874]) first denounces monumental history as a celebration of progressive stages and great and powerful figures, and forgetting everything else while, at the other end of the spectrum, antiquarian history only mummifies the past maintaining uncritical preservation and reverence of everything, making the past dead and ineffective. Hence the need for effective and critical history (*wirkliche Historie*) that would do justice to the past through 'dangers of research and delights in disturbing discoveries' (Foucault 1984, 95) and 'critical exercise of judgement' (Ricoeur 2004, 290). What Nietzsche attacks is not historiography *per se* but historical culture: 'that life requires the service of history must be comprehended, however, just as clearly as the proposition that will subsequently be proved – that an excess of history is harmful for life' (Nietzsche 1980, 96).

Nietzsche insists on the theme of youth contrasted to old age, as 'a metaphor for the plastic force of life' (Ricoeur 2004, 292). One of the main issues with regard to Nietzsche's work is focused on the question of forgetting that is 'ahistorical' and 'suprahistorical'. As a precursor of Bataille's

later discussions on animality, Nietzsche in the essay compares, on the one side, blissfully ignorant ruminants, grazing and living in a perpetual oblivion and, on the other side, a human being who says 'I remember' and is thus determined by one's past, as a reminder 'of what his existence at bottom is – an imperfect that is never to be brought to completion' (Nietzsche 1980 cited by Krell 1990, 255–256). While Nietzsche understands forgetting as inherent in the human animal understood as a 'necessarily oblivious animal', memory becomes understood not as typography but as connected to those cases when 'a promise is to be made', as 'an active *willing* not to get rid of something' (*cf.* below Ricoeur's notion of debt). He also suggests that memory depends on what he calls the 'prehistory of pain', *i.e.* that '… in order for something to remain in memory: only what does not stop *hurting* perdures in memory' (Nietzsche 1969, 292–297).

This discussion that Nietzsche initiated with regard to the importance of forgetting for fundamental ontology is taken up by Martin Heidegger (1889–1976) who insists that 'life is historical in the root of its being' (1962). One of the most distinctive features of Heidegger's philosophical thinking is his understanding of the past as 'having-been' (*Gewesenheit*). He brings to the fore the feature of the forgetfulness with regard to the meaning of being, left covered-up in everyday preoccupations. Yet, forgetting for Heidegger does not only have a negative connotation, as on the level of being-in, but also a positive ecstatic mode of having-been, as the act of closing off Da-sein's thrownness in the world (*cf.* Krell 1990, 240*ff.*; Ricoeur 2004, 442–443; see Borić, this volume).

Heidegger suggests an ecstatic hierarchisation of temporal levels. These are the levels of primordial temporality, also referred to as 'deep temporality', historicality and within-time-ness. To start with the level of 'within-time-ness', it refers to ordinary representation of time as a series of 'nows', *i.e.* observed changes of passing of days and nights, and seasons. One of the most important contributions of Heidegger's philosophy is the assertion that this sequence of 'nows' does not refer to abstract moments of linear and neutral time but to *preoccupation* as an existential characteristic of the subject. This concept of preoccupation is grounded in the ontology of Care as a way of *reckoning with time*. However, only if this habitual time is detached 'from this primary reference to natural measures, saying 'now' is turned into a form of the abstract representation of time' (Ricoeur 1980, 174). Ricoeur's insertion of the significance of narrative at this temporal level, in this way amending Heidegger's analysis, refers to the constitution of public time that is narrative time (Ricoeur 1980, 175), including 'others' (see below).

The main feature of Heidegger's level of historicality is repetition or recapitulation, which is conceptualised as directed toward the future in a way that it retrieves those potentialities of the past that remained suppressed and without a realisation. It can be considered as a 'heroic quest' for new 'openings' or as a process of travelling or becoming, breaking out from an existing paradigm. It is described as an 'existential deepening' of time, as the repetition/recapitulation go deeper from the 'levelled off' surface of the within-time-ness toward the temporal stratum of historicality. The third and the deepest level so strongly proposed by Heidegger (1962) is the level of 'deep temporality' that relates to Da-sein's finitude of Being-toward-death, as the most authentic experience of temporality. Heidegger maintains the incommensurability of mortal, historical and cosmic time and does not provide a sufficient answer to the question of how we can bridge the gap between the phenomenological, *i.e.* ordinary time, and cosmological time. This question is unsolved by stating that the most authentic level of the temporality (the most radical temporality) of Da-sein is Being-toward-death (*cf.* Ricoeur 2004, 343*ff.*). It leaves little space for any characterisation of the way for history to be constituted as public (and narrated) time, or for memory. We shall later examine the solution offered by Paul Ricoeur in order to move away from Heidegger's (unhealthy) fascination with death (see below).

In his book *Of Memory, Reminiscence and Writing* (1990), David Krell distinguishes two different phases in thinking about memory in the

works of Jacques Derrida (1930–2004). The early works, according to Krell, are preoccupied with the question of memory inscription, trace and play or movement of differ*a*nce, while in Derrida's later works, the question of memory and mourning is actualised. Derrida's early works, thus, revolve around what Krell identifies as three models of memory: the *typographic* model that refers to marks left as traces of a certain (past) presence for a future recall (see above about the Ancient Greek notion of *tupos*); the *iconographic* model that refers to images and 'likeness' of absent persons or things (see above about the Ancient Greek notion of *eikōn*); and, the *engrammatological* model, which is related to the problem of re-presentation of the past thing, which creates a gap of difference between the original and a copy, and the solution of this problem through the medium of letters and scripture. For Derrida, trace and differance are related to what he calls arche-writing. Trace, for Derrida, is 'an originary nonpresence and alterity'. In fact, the agency that left this imprint, or 'disarrangement', is never present *as such*, or as Derrida notes: 'It is a trace of something that can never present itself; it is itself a trace that can never be presented, that is, can never appear and manifest itself as such in its phenomenon' (Derrida 1973, 154). There is a sense of an irreducible alterity in the trace as an involuntary testimony of the Other (*cf.* Lévinas 1972 cited by Ricoeur 1988, 124–125). Derrida suggests that trace is more 'primordial' from the phenomenology of presence (Derrida 1973, 67). It is conceived as a play of differences between a cause and an effect and is 'nonorigin', replacing the nostalgic search for origins as it 'becomes the origin of the origin' (Derrida 1974, 61); similarly as 'history always precedes history' (Ricoeur 1988, 247). Yet, Derrida's notion of trace is understood as being prior to typography: an absence that 'presents itself' as 'an irreducible absence within the presence of the trace' (Krell 1990, 173).

Differance is what brings about the fact that the movement of signification is possible only if each element that is said to be 'present', appearing on the scene of presence, is related to something other than itself, preserving to itself the mark of the past element and allowing itself from the outset to be hollowed out by the mark of its relation to a future element. The trace is related no less to what one calls the future than to what one calls the past; it constitutes what one calls the present by its very relation to what is not it – absolutely not it; that is to say, not even a past or a future as modified presents (Derrida 1982, 13/13 cited by Krell 1990, 183).

The core of Derrida's discussion here focuses on the problem of the presence of being or being's 'coming to presence'. Derrida's work *Of Grammatology* (1974) focuses on the engrammatological model of memory and examines the problem of the tension between speech and text. A question that could stem from such an examination may ask the following: 'If the principal enigma of memory is resolved always and everywhere in our tradition by an appeal to marks, signs, notations, and text, is not scription rather than speech the privileged place of presence?' (Krell 1990, 170). Through a genealogical account, Derrida identifies this position as the 'usurpation' of speech by writing. For Derrida, trace is differ*a*nce, and he recognises that 'there never was a pure presence uncontaminated by the exteriority and instability of the system of signs, no icon that was ever preserved intact' (Krell 1990, 174). Thus, Derrida questions the heritage of the Western intellectual tradition as logocentric in its search for a transcendental being that serves as the origin or guarantor of meaning. The suggested method of unpacking of this repressive bundle of discourses is what Derrida refers to as deconstruction. Relevant for our discussion about memory, Krell wonders about the usefulness of Derrida's project: '… if Derridean grammatology announces the closure of the metaphysics of presence, the mnemic model that promises to restore the presence of the past will itself be disengaged and set aside' (Krell 1990, 7). Yet, even Derrida preserves the sense of the modified past presence, a 'past present', or what he calls 'absolute past'. It marks the impossibility of preserving the evidence of an originary presence.

For Derrida (1974), the graphism of our culture and its interiority that has always accompanied orality is best exemplified in Plato's *Phaedrus* that presents the myth about the birth of the writing of history. *Grammata* are offered to the king as 'a potion (*pharmakon*) for memory and wisdom' (274e). Here one gets to the question about the relationship between memory and history. Is the writing of history a remedy or a poison for memory (Ricoeur 2004, 139*ff.*)? This question may also echo Nietsche's second *Unfashionable Observations* (see above). The myth insists that the true memory is written in soul, while writing is only seen as a memory aide, a reminder. In a similar fashion, Derrida sees writing as inferior to living memory and living speech.

In his later writings on memory, Derrida turns to the question of mourning and memory, being intimately tied to each other, similar to the way Freud (1989) connected melancholy and mourning. Derrida speaks of memory's finitude and of memory as always being the memory of the other. In the context of the living memory of committed crimes, Derrida discusses the notion of forgiveness, with its Abrahamic religious origin, as an exceptional act that can only be given unconditionally for the unforgivable:

> '[e]ach time that forgiveness is in the service of finality, be it noble and spiritual (repurchase or redemption, reconciliation, salvation), each time that it tends to reestablish a normalcy (social, national, political, psychological) through a work of mourning, through some therapy or ecology of memory, then 'forgiveness' is not pure – nor is its concept. Forgiveness is not, and it should not be, either normal, or normative, or normalizing. It should remain exceptional and extraordinary, standing the test of the impossible …' (Derrida 1999 cited by Ricoeur 2004, 469).

In the final part of this introduction, I will turn again to this question of 'guilty memory' and its material and immaterial spectres that abound.

Narrativity and the continuity of action: Ricoeur

Probably the most comprehensive discussion of the phenomenological approaches to time in Western philosophy to-date is presented in volume 3 of Paul Ricoeur's (1913–2005) *Time and Narrative* (volume I –1984a; volumes II–III – 1988; see Wood [ed.] 1991; Moore 1990). In this study, Ricoeur discusses phenomenological approaches to time at great length, with extensive borrowings from the phenomenology of time. His own position relies largely on narrative theory, or to rephrase the author himself, his position is cast through a long journey of a threeway conversation between history, literary criticism and phenomenological philosophy.

In *Time and Narrative* I, Ricoeur relies on a lineage of thought that reaches back to St. Augustine and his meditations on time in Book XI of *Confessions* (1961). In this volume Ricoeur uses St. Augustine's conceptualisation and hierarchisation of time as threefold present (past-present, present-present and future-present) in combination with Aristotle's poetic theory of mimesis and emplotment. He bases his argument on the presupposition that any theoretical conceptualisation of time fails to capture time, as shown by the initial phenomenological core present in St. Augustine' analysis that reaches an insoluble paradox, *i.e.* aporia (doubt about what to do). Henceforth the only answer to the problem of time is its treatment within a genre of poiesis, following Aristotle's theory developed in the *Poetics* (Ricoeur 1991a, 180–181). Only in this way, according to Ricoeur, can time be captured, at least temporarily, before it emerges 'victorious from the struggle, after having been held captive in the lines of the plot' (Ricoeur 1988, 274). Furthermore, through the analysis of narrative modes, *i.e.* different ways of telling, time not only becomes thinkable but Ricoeur states that the whole structure of the human experience of temporality becomes inextricably linked to the practice of telling, and becomes viewed as essentially narrative. This reckoning with time can be seen as uniquely human: '*... time becomes human to the extent that it is articulated through a narrative mode, and narrative attains its full meaning when it becomes a condition of temporal existence*' (Ricoeur 1984a, 52, original emphasis).

In this way, *telling* stories is the basic element of human ontological being in the world. One should note that Ricoeur's whole narrative project continues at the point where another large project related to the phenomenology of time stopped. This last point refers to Heidegger's (1962) *Being and Time*. In the literal translation of Ricoeur's *Time and Narrative* as it stands in its original French

title – *Temps et Récit, i.e.* 'Time and Telling', an allusion was made that connects 'Being and Time and Telling' (Vanhoozer 1991, 43). With such an emphasis on narration, Ricoeur employs narrative theory in order to mediate questions related to the human experience of temporality.

The possible connection between living and telling is treated differently by various literary theorists and historians alike (see Carr 1986). I find it useful to explicate here a specific answer developed by Paul Ricoeur on this matter that constitutes one of the main achievements of volume I of *Time and Narrative*. It relates to the concept of a threefold *mimesis*$_{1-3}$ that explicitly theorises this process of interdependence between narratives and human livelihood, emphasising their reciprocal relationship. The concept of mimesis is borrowed from Aristotle's theory of poetics where plot (*mythos*; the term emplotment is used complementarily, suggesting a more dynamic form) is seen as mimesis of actions. Ricoeur (1991a, 180–181) explains the affinity for the term mimesis as close to a group of terms ending in –*sis*, such as *poiesis, catharsis*, etc. that allude to the dynamic character of the process that is described. In the case of mimesis this is the dynamic process of imitating or representing something (Ricoeur 1984a, 31) through the circularity of prefiguration, configuration and refiguration.

Under *mimesis*$_1$ Ricoeur encompasses the pre-narrative understanding of life. This pre-understanding means that humans are already born in a world that is configured by narratives and that a structure of temporal experience can be described as prenarrative. This temporal level refers to being 'within time' with a preunderstanding of the 'repertoire' of the world (Ricoeur 1984a, 64). It also means that human action is 'always already symbolically mediated' (Ricoeur 1984a, 57) and articulated within a 'conceptual network'. One can assume a practical understanding of intersignifications between the members of a particular conceptual network, *i.e.* 'culture', society, etc.

Ricoeur assigns *mimesis*$_2$ a dynamic mediating function, not a simple succession of events, but a process of configuring inchoate elements of lived experience into a narrative structure in the act of 'grasping together'. In this way the episodic dimension of narrative, *i.e.* events as incoherent and heterogeneous elements of a story of one's life, are synthesised acquiring the structure of a plot. Lives become meaningful with the coherence of a story and yet the extent of this coherence always oscillates between a 'discordant concordance' and 'concordant discordance'. At this level, one needs to mention features such as the 'schematism of a story' with its synthetic function, and the 'traditionality' as a dialectic interplay of sedimentation and innovation, stemming from a productive imagination that opens up new paradigms.

Finally, *mimesis*₃ points to the process of prefiguring lived experience under the influence of narrative as 'application' and goes back to the beginning of the circle, *i.e.* to the level of *mimesis*₁: '*We are following therefore the destiny of a prefigured time that becomes a refigured time through the mediation of a configured time*' (Ricoeur 1984a, 54, original emphasis)

Moreover, it ought to be stressed that this process where *mimesis*₂ mediates between its two sides – *mimesis*₁ and *mimesis*₃ – should not be conceptualised as an endless spiral passing 'the same point a number of times, but at different altitudes' (Ricoeur 1984a, 72). To reinforce his main thesis of the resemblance between life experience and story, Ricoeur emphasises the entanglement of plots where 'the story 'happens to' someone before anyone tells it', alluding to untold stories of our lives (Ricoeur 1984a, 75). 'There is a continual dialectical relationship between lived experience, the narratives we organise it by, and the rhetoric through which those narratives are expressed' (Hodder 1993, 274; 1995, 168).

Ricoeur's narrative theory is directly related to his take on memory. Ricoeur emphasises an existing impasse in seeing retention as memory and points out a number of deficiencies related to Husserl's model of time modifications (Ricoeur 1988, 23*ff.*). For Ricoeur, a much more potent feature of memory as materialised effect relates to secondary remembrance, *i.e.* recollection that is contrasted to primary (perceptual) remembrance as retention. Recollection enables repetition or

reiteration of the past through free intentionality and is conceptualised as an endless process that transposes the past moments into a quasi-present (Ricoeur 1988, 31*ff.*). This *dis*placement of a past moment enables a free-floating and open state of memory. Seen as nonperception, recollection is closely linked to the concept of 'trace' (see below) as a useful feature employed in memory modelling.

Ricoeur utilises Heidegger's analysis in *Being and Time* (1962) that offers a temporalisation, *i.e.* hierarchisation of different temporal levels (see above). The episodic dimension of narrative as a sequence with an irreversible order is contrasted to the configurational dimension, as a reflective act of 'grasping together' in order to invert the time arrow. In this way, the inchoate events acquire a subsequent meaning, as a way of recapitulating a story. Furthermore, telling already means reflecting upon a sequence of events and in this way represents a way of connecting within-time-ness and the subsequent level of historicality, moving from "reckoning with' time' to 'recollecting' it' (Ricoeur 1980, 178).

> By reading the end into the beginning and the beginning into the end, we learn to read time backwards, as the recapitulation of the initial conditions of a course of action in its terminal consequences. In this way, the plot does not merely establish human action 'in' time, it also establishes it in memory. And memory in turn repeats – recollects – the course of events according to an order that is the counterpart of the stretching-along of time between a beginning and an end (Ricoeur 1980, 183).

While finding Heidegger useful to think with, Ricoeur suggests a different solution to the finitude of Da-sein.

> Does not narrativity, by breaking away from the obsession of a struggle in the face of death, open any mediation on time to another horizon than that of death, to the problem of communication not just between living beings but between contemporaries, predecessors, and successors? (Ricoeur 1980, 188)

One of the key features in order to communicate between these different temporal horizons is seen in the concept of trace (Ricoeur 1988, 104–126).

Trace is a mark, imprint or material disarrangement left in the passage of a past agency. Traces make reference to a past that really happened, putting a specific ontological weight to the constitution of human temporal experience. The notion of trace can be seen with a decisive role in the constitution of historical time and historic consciousness.

> [...] it is in the phenomenon of the trace that we find the culmination of the imaginary character of the connectors that mark the founding of historical time. This imaginary mediation is presupposed by the mixed structure of the trace itself, considered as a sign-effect. This mixed structure expresses in shorthand a complex synthetic activity, involving causal types of inference applied to the trace as a mark left behind and activities of interpretation tied to the signifying character of the trace as something present, standing for something past. This synthetic activity, which is well expressed by the verb 'to retrace', sums up in turn operations as complex as those at the origin of the gnomon or calendar. These are the activities of preserving, selecting, assembling, consulting, and finally, reading documents and archives, which mediate and, so to speak, schematize the trace, making it the ultimate presupposition of the reinscription of lived time (time with a present) (Ricoeur 1988, 183–184).

Ricoeur argues for a continuity in the construction of a historical mode of consciousness, seen as a hybrid time. He emphasises that the symbolic meanings in the course of human history are continuous, which itself creates the sense of historicality. In order to strengthen the notion of trace linked to the deep structure of historic consciousness, Ricoeur also introduces the notion of debt, related to the 'efficacity of the past' in the transmission of heritage. It primarily refers to the 'solidarity' between the living and the dead, where the living maintain the memory of the dead 'for whom history mourns', as these are the actual victims of history (Ricoeur 1988, 118, 156, footnote 42): 'And does this history in turn remain historical only if, going beyond death, it guards against the forgetfulness of death and the dead and remains a recollection of death and a remembrance of the dead?' (Ricoeur 1984a, 75).

Stemming from his previous discussion that synthesises different features of temporality, Ricoeur introduces a hyphenated expression Being-affected-by-the-past (Ricoeur 1988, 207*ff.*) in order to reify the insufficiency of connecting different levels of temporality in Heidegger's philosophy. However, in the last instance Ricoeur's answer to the aporetics of time admits the limit of narrativity in concurring time, which is powerful and enveloping.

> It has to do with the ultimate unrepresentability of time, which makes even phenomenology continually turn to metaphors and to the language of myth, in order to talk about the upsurge of the present or the flowing of the unitary flux of time (Ricoeur 1988, 243).

Yet, the process of both historical and fictional narration mirroring the life experience may be understood as 'a timeless human drama, that of humanity at grips with the experience of temporality' (White 1987, 183). An optimistic solution to this question Ricoeur finds in Hannah Arendt's celebration of the power of natality and the continuation of action (Arendt 1958; Ricoeur 2004, 486*ff.*). Arendt sees action outliving the mortal lives of the actors since it always wants to continue. This is a radical break from and protest against Heidegger's idea of Da-sein's finitude as being-toward-death. In this context, the importance is given to the moral and political dimensions of the notion of promise, of making and keeping promises. This is the memory of *ipseity*, of remaining faithful to the given promise, and is thus intimately tied to the notions of 'debt, fault, guilt' (Ricoeur 2004, 603, n. 39; *cf.* Ricoeur 1998, 119*ff.*).

Beyond the Western episteme

While on the previous pages, the particular Western philosophical genealogy of thinking about memory has been discussed, can we say that the same arguments and the same problems are relevant for the rest of humanity? Are Heidegger's notion of historicality or Ricoeur's insistence on the duty of memory and debt to the dead universally shared? The obvious way to tackle these questions is to look into ethnography of non-Western contexts or even to the past itself, thus evaluating the adequacy of the concepts developed thus far.

One of the criticisms has been raised in relation to the text and the dominance of textual analogies with memory compared to textual practice (Fentress and Wickham 1992, 6; Thomas 1996, 53) under the influence of the hermeneutic philosophical tradition (Ricoeur 1981; Moore 1990). Memory is recognised as similar to the interpretative practice of reading. Text is conceptualised as independent from the author's original intentions as it 'lives its own life'. Thus similar to text memory is never a 'completed work' but an on-going montage of 'scraps' and fragments of meaning. On the other hand, the hermeneutic approach and 'textual analogy' in the study of social memory – predominantly conceptualising memory as conscious archiving of documentary evidence – largely neglected less formal and less conscious aspects of mnemonic activities, such as the significance of routine incorporating bodily practices or 'techniques of the body' (Mauss 1979; Connerton 1989).

Further, following Connerton (1989), Rowlands (1993) suggests that frequent emphasis on monuments and monumental sites in discussions about memory could be identified as an inscribing principle. It may relate to a specific European affinity for a monumental material culture inextricably linked with an emphasis on the linear concept of time, having a long historical trajectory. However in various social, cultural and historical contexts, memory is not merely accumulated and 'stored' in monuments. Forgetting is sometimes an equally constitutive part of future remembering (*e.g.* Borić, this volume; Harris forthcoming; Taylor 1996). This 'negative' to remembrance related to forgetting, loss, foreclosure, exfoliation, defacement or destruction of either material mnemonic and monumental objects (Küchler 1996; 1999) or knowledge (Strathern 1991) has been emphasised as equally important in the constitution of memory. In this way the recombining of fragments of memory re-constitutes and re-creates one's identity, where power and creativity lie in the play of gaps or lacunae of meaning and remembering

with a general impression of 'scrappiness' (Buchli 1999; see Deleuze 1988). Powerful metaphors, such as defacement (Taussig 1999) or the place of buried memory (Küchler 1999) best capture this multidirectional and non-linear temporal working of memory. Küchler's example of *malanggan* carvings as part of commemoration practices of the dead in the north-west of Papua New Guinea points to the place of memory displaced from a commemorative, visually lasting monument with its memorial value (see also Gell 1998, 223). The physical disappearance of a monumental object therefore creates a possibility for memory to be implanted in new places.

One recent collection of papers focuses on the question of memory and change in a regional context of Amazonian lowland societies (Fausto and Heckenberger 2007). This region as a whole has previously been considered as one where past is intentionally obliterated from memory. This particular feature of Amerindian thought was famously used by Lévi-Strauss to draw a distinction between hot societies (with history and dedicated to change and innovation) and cold societies (without history, aiming to remain static and stable). Many ethnographic accounts coming from this region over the years thus stressed that across this vast region one encounters shallowness of genealogical time and ties and a general absence of the concept of ancestrality (*e.g.* Cunha 1978; Overing Kaplan 1977). For instance, among various groups, the existence of endo- (funerary) and/or exo-cannibalism indicated the need for an intentional erasing of the memory of one own's dead, or through a complex interplay of predator-prey relations between different figures of alterity (*e.g.* enemies, animals, spirits, the dead, etc.) of coming to terms with the departure of one's kin (*e.g.* Conklin 2001; Taylor 1993; Vilaça 1992; 2000).

One may say that in such a context, questions of the 'being-affected-by-the-past' or historicality (see above) of a particular group play out very differently than the previous discussion on memory and time perception that dominated Western thought at least since the time of the Greek *polis*. Confronted with the Amerindian ethnographic evidence one is forced to go beyond the preferred philosophical notions of the Western culture, such as the questions about historical consciousness and individual agency (Fausto and Hackenberger 2007). The particular Amerindian 'openness to the other' that Lévi-Strauss emphasised from the start, means that identity is not envisioned as a distinction and difference but is produced in relation to figures of alterity by appropriating, or to speak in terms of literal conduct, *cannibalising* the otherness in a predatory move. It is the notion of 'structural transformation' and the metamorphic capacity of the body that become foregrounded in this particular ontological universe. Here, the typical Western realisation frequently stressed in memory studies about the importance of identity seen as self-constancy over time is an oxymoron. The key concept is that of transformation.

This Amerindian 'symbolic economy of alterity' (Viveiros de Castro 1996) meant that within these societies an equation was born between the dead and many other Others, be it related to the construction of inter-ethnic, inter-species or inter-topological relations. While such an identification of the dead and alterity is widespread across Amazonia, new archaeological and historical research indicates that this particular feature might have been different in the past, and that the whole region was characterised by more diversity in the treatment and the conceptualisation of the dead, countering the usual assumption about 'genealogical amnesia' (Chaumeil 2007). New archaeological evidence may after all indicate that across Amazonia before the contact period existed more complex societies than those that were encountered by the first ethnographers. Such hierarchical and 'complex' societies showed signs of genealogical reckoning and memory construction, something that can be attested in the Upper Xingu where, for instance, one finds the importance of ancestrality (Heckenberger 2007).

In sum, the construction of social memory in relation to the production of identity, self-constancy and the issue of change over time, take different forms in non-Western contexts, sometimes by a complete inversion of the assumed meanings of these categories. Sometimes, forgetting becomes

an important element of social relatedness as well as systematic distancing, and othering of the dead. However, these examples do not relativise our previous discussions about the importance of memory for defining the historical condition of human beings. They rather point to the inherent flexibility for redefining the terms of relations with regard to these categories depending on a particular social and historical context.

Yet, such a conclusion in favour of inherent human historical conditionality cannot in itself be satisfactory in removing doubts with regard to the problematic position occupied by historians or archaeologists in their attempts to *represent* the past. How dependent are these fields of expertise on their modernist origins and the Western ethnocentrism of traditional history? How 'real' is the past that becomes narrated in historical or archaeological accounts, and what separates it from fictional narratives? Finally, what is the relationship between the past represented through these 'professional' narratives and collective/ individual memory? The answers for these not easily conquerable questions will be sought in the following section.

Traces, clues and symptoms: Archaeological epistemology and memory

> And, during a visit to an archaeological site, I evoked the cultural world gone by to which these ruins sadly referred. Like the witness in a police investigation, I can say of these places, 'I was there' (Ricoeur 2004, 40).

> Though reality may seem to be opaque, there are privileged zones – signs, clues, which allow us to penetrate it (Ginzburg 1989, 123).

> …the true archaeological activity, the one in which the archaeologist finds his true identity and is aware that no one can take his place to advantage, is certainly the 'establishment' of facts. In the most general and characteristic case, that of an excavation, it is when he notes a mass of rubble, locates one wall, then the others, and sees a plan forming (...) it is when he differentiates between discarded bones and a grave, between a simple hearth and a localized or generalized blaze; it is when he does this that he is accomplishing work that no one is

better able to do, that no one else can ever do again. (…) He knows that, if he makes a mistake, sees things wrongly, misunderstands, his conclusions will then be irremediably falsified and cannot but lead to other errors among those who use them (Courbin 1988).

In the past several decades, the discipline of archaeology has been thought through a plurality of theoretical and epistemological positions, some of which have been radically opposed to each other. From classic culture history descriptive approaches, through the scientistic paradigm of positivist thought and law-like generalisations of the so-called 'processual' or 'New Archaeology' to the influence of hermeneutical tactics, structuralist and post-structuralist approaches characterising what has become known as post-modern or, in a confrontational mood, 'post-processual' tradition of archaeological thought: archaeology has sought its voice. It has been orienting itself in relation to the conceptual theoretical vocabulary available in the wider field of philosophy, social sciences and humanities. The present cacophony of thought in our discipline is a reflection of a similar condition in all other fields of human sciences where 'granting agencies function as gatekeepers' only with a limiting effect while 'different interpretive 'federations,' or simply clusters, coalesce around different questions, different methods, different standards of evidence, different types of argumentation, different career patterns, different sources of symbolic capital, differential placements within the cultural, economic, political, and social fields' (Rabinow 2003, 5).

In the midst of such a condition, here, I use the opportunity to subject the discipline of archaeology to memory, understood as a moral keeper of historical meaning, and to ask questions about the character of archaeological epistemology and rigour under which it should be practised and understood. This is done with a hope that on the level of elementary archaeological investigatory operations and with regard to the ontological weight of archaeological evidence in the constitution of the general historical knowledge a wider disciplinary consensus is possible.

I find the grounding for such an endeavour in the historian Carlo Ginzburg's essay 'Clues: Roots of and Evidential Paradigm' (1989). Ginzburg (1989, 96) here traces (and this is an intentional choice of the word!) 'the silent emergence of an epistemological model' or paradigm in human sciences. What he calls 'evidential' or 'conjectural' paradigm became a dominant practice in fields as diverse as divination, law, criminology, medicine, palaeography, meteorology, history, palaeontology or archaeology, which all rely on *particularities* of evidence of individual cases in providing clues about a condition that is being examined, be it for the purposes of interpreting the past or the future. It is also about gathering marginal details, information that the consciousness cannot hold, and 'infinitesimal traces [that] permit the comprehension of a deeper, otherwise unattainable reality' (Ginzburg 1989, 101).

While a clearer shape of this rarely recognised paradigm can best be gauged from the late sixteenth and the seventeenth centuries onwards, during the period that Ginzburg reconstructs in some detail, he convincingly argues that the origin of this type of human behaviour can be traced back to the time of hunter-gatherers and perhaps could be related to the idea of following *traces* of a particular prey in a hunt, or a chase, search for food: '[t]his knowledge is characterised by the ability to construct from apparently insignificant experimental data a complex reality that could not be experienced directly' (Ginzburg 1989, 103). Such an exercise required intellectual operations, such as analyses, comparison and classification (*cf.* Lévi-Straus 1966, *passim*). Importantly, Ginzburg suggests a hypothesis that such ability of compiling traces and their interpretation enabled narration as a way of putting incoherent elements into a meaningful sequence of events that comprises a story (on narrative and life *cf.* Ricoeur 1984; 1988; see above). The roots of this paradigm are then found also in Mesopotamian divination and legal texts (discussing concrete examples), or further in Hippocratic medicine in Ancient Greece, the latter maintaining 'that only by attentively observing symptoms in great detail could one develop precise 'histories' of individual diseases; disease, in itself, was out of reach' (Ginzburg 1989, 105). In Ancient Greece, this type of implicit knowledge became eclipsed by a more prestigious type of thinking developed by Plato.

In many ways, the ideas about the *trace* and *image* (Greek *tupos* and *eikōn*) can be connected to the invention of writing. As we have seen previously, such ideas constitute the core of memory-related discussions among Ancient Greek philosophers but can also be traced in Derrida's engrammatology and a recent philosophical memory synthesis by Ricoeur (see above). The invention of writing, for Ginzburg, could be related to the idea of following or 'deciphering' animal tracks. Here, there is a close connection between the very practice of divination and the task of deciphering messages. Ginzburg reminds us of the Chinese myth that writing was invented by observing bird tracks on a sandy shore (Ginzburg 1989, 103): '[e]ven a footprint indicates an animal's passing. In respect to the concreteness of the print, of a mark materially understood, the pictogram already represents an incalculable step forward on the road towards intellectual abstraction' (Ginzburg 1989, 104). And further, this process led 'to progressive dematerialisation of the text, which was gradually purified at every point of reference related to the senses; even though a material element is required for a text's survival. The text itself is not identified by that element' (Ginzburg 1989, 107; *cf*. Buchli 1995).

The evidential or conjectural paradigm can be put in sharp contrast to what Ginzburg calls Galilean sciences, which were formulated with the appearance of the Galilean physics. For what so sharply divides these two different ways of knowing is their different relation to the individual instance and sensuousness: while mathematics and the empirical method assume quantification of repetitive phenomena or law-like generalisations, human sciences are inherently qualitative and rely on individual instances, unique situations and particular events, or single patients. It is the image of anti-anthropomorphic and anti-anthropocentric natural sciences contrasted to a large body of loosely connected human sciences (Ginzburg 1989, 108). But in the course of the eighteenth-century, there was a need for such a heterogeneous group of conjectural disciplines or skills to achieve a scientific status. For medicine, for instance, it was particularly important to go beyond the 'uncertainty' and to become a respectful science with a 'written codification of conjectural knowledge' (Ginzburg 1989, 115). Ginzburg sees a decisive moment in the Counter-Reformation, and the encyclopaedic systematisation of knowledge, which was further facilitated by the invention of printing and a much easier distribution and availability of books. The experience of others became codified and available across the social classes. Towards the end of the nineteenth-century, this process was well under way and one should only quote the example of the popularity of what Thomas Huxley, publicising Darwin, called 'Zadig's method,' combining diachronic disciplines such as 'history, archaeology, geology, physical astronomy, and palaeontology, namely, the ability to forecast retrospectively' (Ginzburg 1989, 117). The rise in popularity of these disciplines lay in the fact that in order to study those things that cannot be experimentally reproduced, one needed to 'deduce them from their effects' (Ginzburg 1989, 117).

The described evidential or conjectural paradigm, which refers to a common epistemological model, cannot only be associated with the Enlightenment and modernity. In the eighteenth and nineteenth centuries, modes of conjectural knowledge only become codified, frequently striving to achieve a scientific status, similar to the Galilean natural sciences. This codification of the evidential paradigm happened due to, on the one hand, growing interest in detective stories and narratives about the animal and human past, and, on the other hand, the need for state control over individuals in industrial societies. To the latter, Ginzburg (1989, 118–123) quotes a fascinating example how an indigenous Bengalese conjectural knowledge of the uniqueness of fingerprints was appropriated by the British administration in order to become one of the critical means of control over the identity of colonial and other subjects. Yet, Ginzburg's paper discovers a fascinating complexity of numerous threads connecting different characters in his 'excavation' of this previously unrecognised epistemological model, for which he uses the metaphor of a (semiotic) carpet.

Surprisingly, there have been little mention and discussion of this seminal paper in archaeology (but see Shanks 1996, 39–40) despite its obvious importance for defining and defending the archaeological project. More recently archaeologists of deconstructionist provenience have primarily been occupied by denouncing archaeological (sinful) grounding in the project of modernity (*e.g.* Thomas 2004). While, such an identification remains useful and important for understanding various detailed aspects of disciplinary history of ideas and methodologies, perhaps we should not be blinded by modernity's proximity in our discipline. Ginzburg's essay, which is itself a detective story or an archaeological dig in identifying the development of particular ways about gaining knowledge about the unknown, is critical for reasserting archaeological epistemology. It may have the potential to bridge separate confederations within archaeology in order to sidestep unproductive positivist *vs.* post-modern positions still persisting in many quarters, or, at the very least, have the potential to spark discussions on the epistemological grounding of archaeological knowledge with a fresh perspective. But how is all this important for memory studies?

Killing two birds with one stone, Ginzburg's discussion of the evidential paradigm also reaffirms his dedication to microhistory and the study of details that are at the same time indications (or symptoms) of general phenomena (*e.g.* Ginzburg 1980). The microhistory project and discussion of variation in scales is not our primary purpose here (but see various papers in this volume). The notion of clue approximates the notion of vestiges and that of trace. The idea of vestiges, including archaeological ones, was highly valued by both the historian Marc Bloch (1964), who speaks of 'witnesses in spite of themselves' as a way of putting written testimonies under the historiographer's scrutiny, as well as by Robin Collingwood (1999) in his 'critical history'. The question that is opened here, thus, is that of trustworthiness of particular testimony, its relation to memory and the internal-external coherence of documentary proof (*sensu* Collingwood).

Our previous discussion about the epistemological grounding of archaeology (along with other similar conjectural diachronic disciplines) indicates that even if archaeological or historical facts come shorter of the empirical facts in natural sciences in their exactness due to their having an inherent and 'unsuppressible speculative margin' (Ginzburg 1989, 106), these facts can nevertheless be characterised in the Popperian sense as 'true' or 'false', 'refutable' or 'verifiable'. This means that it would not be possible to equate a historical (archaeological) narrative and fictional narrative. The past *really* took place – it really happened – and any attempt at relativising it inflicts great danger on what one could call the duty of memory (Ricoeur 2004, *passim*): [...] the mysterious aspect of the debt [...] makes the master of the plot a servant of the memory of past human beings' (Ricoeur 1988, 156). Here lies the importance for memory with regard to the previous discussion that firmly establishes the 'objectivity' of historical or archaeological knowledge. While this assertion may appear obvious, let us linger a bit longer on this issue and spell out why it is important to take seriously the idea about the 'truth element of the past' (*cf.* Ginzburg 2002).

In a short book with the title *The Reality of the Historical Past*, Paul Ricoeur (1984b) summarises one of the main points discussed in detail in several of his works: the idea that narrative about the historical past must be at any cost separated from fictional narratives. Using Plato's 'great classes' of the Same, the Other and the Analogue, Ricoeur discusses ways of representing the past: Collingwood's idea of re-enacting the past (through empathy and the movement of a historian's thought) in the present under the class of the Same; past seen as a foreign land and difference under the class of the Other, refusing the totalising view of history; and, a tropological approach to the past (such as the rhetorical theory employed by Hayden White (1978) through the tropes of metaphor, metonymy, synecdoche and irony) under the class of the Analogue. While Ricoeur has a preference for the class of the Analogue, *i.e.* the trace 'standing for' the past *such as it really occurred* (*sensu* Ranke), his critique touches on what he sees as a danger in

White's use of rhetorical theory, which 'runs the risk of erasing the dividing line between fiction and history' (Ricoeur 1984b, 33).

> Narratives are not something we choose or reject at will, nor are they linguistic artifacts we measure against a nonnarrative universe. Stories are what we live in, and in them we find both our worlds and our selves. We differentiate among them, we call some fairy tales and others true stories, and we tend to believe that our favorite tale is the one everyone else should adopt. But we do this from within narrative traditions we can interweave with others but never entirely escape. As our traditions change, so do our histories; as our histories change, so do our worlds; as our worlds change, so do our traditions. Saying that we live inside narrative traditions is not the same thing as saying that any story is as good as another (Klein 1997, 5–6).

There is a political reason for this kind of tacit but clear dividing line between history and fiction, and the frequently quoted example relates to the question of Holocaust victims (*e.g.* Ricoeur 1988, 187; 2004) as the most striking recent historical example. Moreover, in this context archaeology through its forensic side as part of the evidential paradigm becomes directly involved in the production of important, *true* facts that in the most obvious way must do justice to the past and those victims the memory of whom must be honoured at any cost (*cf.* Mitrović 2008; Filippucci, this volume; Weiss, this volume). Similarly this assertion applies to the question of subordinate groups and their rights to use the archaeological past as a way of becoming empowered in the present (Hodder 1991, 10). Such an empowering state, for archaeology, meant admitting the fact about the 'resistance of the past' (*cf.* Shanks and Hodder 1995, 18–22), and that archaeological data can be seen as being somewhat independent of archaeologists' assumptions (Wylie 2002, 161–167).

The very process of 'reading' and interpreting (archaeological) data in order to provide a 'historical' and not fictional account can be achieved by providing the 'guarded objectivity' for our historical/archaeological narratives (Hodder 1991, 10*ff.*). In archaeology, I. Hodder (1991; 1999, 32*ff.*) bases this methodological possibility on the theoretical footage developed within the tradition of critical hermeneutics, of which Hans-Georg Gadamer and Paul Ricoeur are the most prominent proponents. The 'guarded objectivity' of an archaeological inquiry relies on a) the autonomy of objects, *i.e.* configured independence of material culture, b) the notion of coherence in interpretation (following Collingwood), c) the necessity of 'translation' of the past Other and d) the critical stance against the prejudice of the analyst. Through a dialectic model of question-response, *i.e.* interrogation and response between the past and us, we reach a specific knowledge of the past that is not purely arbitrary or subjective. This procedure creates a necessary methodological balance regarding the specificity of historical and archaeological discourses when faced with the positivist demand that only empirically observed and scientifically described fact is real (*cf.* Ricoeur 1984a, 79). In Gadamer's phrase, the understanding reached through a hermeneutic dialogue can be seen as a *fusion of horizons* between the worlds of the reader and the 'text'.

In the previous discussion, it was suggested that if we understand archaeology as part of Ginzburg's evidential paradigm, it is an heir to an honourable epistemological line. Hence, a frequently justifiable insistence on its modernist 'guilt' should not deter us from admitting archaeology's genuine importance as a developed form of knowledge about past unknowns, which remain experimentally unverifiable, but for that reason not less 'objective'. Furthermore, traces, clues and symptoms that produce historical/archaeological facts about the past should be seen in terms of 'true' or 'false' statements in order to preserve the truth element of the past. This reality of the past is of primary importance for the moral obligation of keeping the memory of the dead, those victims of history, and for doing justice to the past when it comes to its *re-presentation*. Interestingly, the importance of keeping a firm dividing line between historical/archaeological narratives, on the one hand, and fictional narratives, on the other hand, becomes especially obvious when it comes to the testimonies of survivors of particular traumatic events, such as the Holocaust or more recent wars in the former Yugoslavia (see Mitrović 2008; Weiss, this volume). It seems that with the temporal distance of the observer from the object of study the emotional link is partly lost and the process of othering subconsciously and inevitably takes place (see Filippucci, this volume).

This gradation between emotional attachments and issues related to different pasts is possible to detect in the present volume when one moves back from the mentioned discussion of the most recent past where archaeological evidence is part of the criminal tribunal that shapes a particular version of history of most recent events relating to the 1990s Balkan wars (Weiss, this volume; *cf.* Bajić, this volume) to the discussion of the Western front and the archaeology of the First World War (Filippucci, this volume). The latter example still produces an uncanny element of discomfort of instances that are still within the horizon of survivors, awakening all too familiar and carnal feelings. Yet, it already slowly fades into the 'past past', endowed with a particular temporal distancing, admittedly midway between the instances of 'contemporary past' and older pasts discussed in papers found in the first part of the book. In the next section of this introduction, I turn to questions about the political dimension of memory.

Our historical condition and guilty memory: Spectres and angels

> It never happened without blood, martyrdoms, sacrifice, whenever human beings found it necessary to form a memory (Nietzsche 1969).

In this section we move to a wider understanding of memory as part of our historical condition as human beings. It rests on the assumption about the continuity of human action over time and its meaningful constitution. In this way, it incorporates the strands of thought previously discussed, such as the nature of archaeological knowledge in particular as part of general historical knowledge, the scales of investigatory explorations, the material experience of life and the persistence of narrative identity through time. As previously

admitted, the understanding of memory is here strongly influenced by Arendtean and Ricoeurean notions about the vitality of life and the power of natality of which memory is a constitutive element. Hence these closing remarks on the connection of memory and archaeology are under the sign of the discussion recently put forward by Ricoeur (2004) with regard to the morality of memory.

What happens when the object of love becomes lost? When good times are gone, and when all that remains is reminiscing on the past? What about nostalgia, and how is it expressed? Already Aristotle mentions that those who cannot stop recollecting turn into melancholics. Only by shattering 'the mirror of memory' can nostalgia be extinguished, says philosopher David Krell (1990, 22). In his short essay 'Mourning and melancholy', Freud (1989) uses the tradition-laden term 'melancholia' and compares this condition to mourning (*cf.* Buchli, this volume). As a medical condition melancholy produces sleeplessness. It revolves around the issue of the lost object and the object *cathexis*, as the loss of a love-object compels that the ambivalence in the love relationship comes out in the open. We become prisoners of our memories. As one of the characters in Jean-Luc Godard's 2001 film *In Praise of Love* says: 'I don't know how memory can help us reclaim our lives'. Reacting negatively to *Schindler's List* and its totalising gaze as well as to Hollywood's cannibalisation of the history of others, in the movie Godard colours the past and leaves the present in the shades of grey, reversing the logic of *Schindler's List*. He evokes resistance as a factor of memory and invites understanding of the complexity of historical events, objecting to the way such complex events and memories enter into the public imagination through ephemeral information technologies.

It is as if the past can never disappear against Nietzsche's best advice. Freud was convinced about the indestructibility of the past once experienced (*cf.* Ricoeur 2004, 445). Furthermore, how does one reconcile the experience and testimonies of the survivors of traumatic historical events (*cf.* Weiss, this volume)? Here arises the problem about the boundaries imposed on the historical representation of such limit experiences: 'A further reason for the difficulty in communicating has to do with the fact that the witness himself had no distance on the events; he was a 'participant,' without being the agent, the actor; he was their victim' (Ricoeur 2004, 176).

In order to rectify somewhat this situation, Paul Ricoeur suggests the term representation in the work of historians. What he aims to accomplish by the use of representation instead of the *Annales* school's notion of mentality has to do with the historiographical operation that emphasises 'a mimetic relation between the operation of representing as the moment of doing history [by historians], and the represented object as the moment of making history' (Ricoeur 2004, 229). This is also close to Clifford Geertz's (1983) idea of self-understanding as being immanent to a culture. Such an emphasis on the notion of representation may help liberate history and the *representation* of the past from the historical determinism of totalising history and 'retrospective illusion of fatality' (Aron 1961, 183). Ricoeur insists on the semantics of the word re-presentation in order to give the voice to the social agents in the past. Historians or archaeologists can rely on the resistance of a particular type of past reality that is in this way being represented. Such a perspective may appear 'liberating' to archaeologists in their attempts to understand a particular material culture rhetoric represented in the archaeological record.

In the book of philosophical and theological conversations with Paul Ricoeur made in the late 1990s, *Critique and Conviction* (1999), this philosopher reveals two orders of motivations for his more recent interest in memory and especially with regard to the issue of the duty of collective memory and duty of justice in relation to memory. Ricoeur explains that the first order of motivations is related to the events of Ricoeur's generation that are still within the living memory of the survivors of the Second World War and the memory of Holocaust. The second order of motivation, he relates to events in Europe after the fall of the Berlin wall and communism where 'it is almost as though [people] had been taken out of deep-freeze. They seem to display at times an excess, at times a

lack of memory' (Ricoeur 1999, 125). Perhaps this extremely unstable condition of collective memory can best be treated through the artistic mode of irony that is seen as freedom in negativity (Kafka) by negating personal and cultural ideas through humour (Bajić, this volume).

So, for example, what is one to make out of this excess of history per square mile in the Balkans, a thesis frequently repeated in the wake of the 1990s conflicts in the former Yugoslavia? How does one move away from such resurgence of the past in fragments that triggers destructive political action? Here, we could think of different versions of history that may have some consequences for the political action. This type of understanding of history would be closer to the archaeological method of Michel Foucault (1972) than to the history understood as progress, continuity and the accumulation of knowledge or search for origins. This is a move away from *total history* (*cf.* Ricoeur 2004, 240), which draws all phenomena around a single centre (a principle, a meaning, a spirit, a world-view, an overall shape). Instead, Foucault's *general history* deploys the space of a dispersion. Foucault's genealogies 'are intended, *inter alia*, to articulate political possibilities in the present by telling alternative histories of the present and by producing a historical ontology of the present – one that reveals fissures and breaks in its production, thereby interrupting a seamless narrative of the past that yielded a seamless architecture of the present' (Brown 2001, 168). These are histories that emphasise the diversity while drawing on unrealised possibilities. Paul Ricoeur (2004) reminds us that it is our debt to the 'victims of history' to revive all those possibilities and crossroads of projects that could have been otherwise. These attempts, apart from their therapeutic value of collective 'working through' in psychoanalytic terms, should open space for political action that can build on particularly potent sites of history in a responsible way: '[r]edemption of past suffering and retrieval of past possibility both become possible in the project of forging a future' (Brown 2001, 168).

In one of the chapters of her book *Politics Out of History* (2001), Wendy Brown compares such puzzling visions of the past as expressed in the writing of two authors: Walter Benjamin and Jacques Derrida. In the opening discussion she maintains that 'the relation of the present to the past is most often figured through idealisations and demonisations of particular epochs or individuals on the one hand, and reparations and apologies for past wrongs on the other' … 'Once guilt is established and a measure of victimisation secured by an apology or by material compensation, is the historical event presumed to be concluded, sealed [as cast], 'healed,' or brought to 'closure'?' (2001, 140; see above on Derrida's view about forgiveness). This 'economy of debt', however, seems to be more complex. In fact, do images of past traumas ever disappear? Or can we identify a particular feature of melancholia that a particular loss awakens? It is the feeling of missed opportunities and political formations related to the notion of progress that can haunt both individual and collective experience. One of Walter Benjamin's *Theses on the Philosophy of History* emphasises this aspect of loss. He describes 'the melancholic's investment in 'things' and in precepts of stories that acquire thinglike form' (Benjamin 1968 cited by Brown 2001, 170).

These haunting images of the past that one cannot break free from and which remain and resurge in the present is what Benjamin emphasises in his *Theses on the Philosophy of History* when he describes Klee's painting 'Angelus Novus' as the angle of History. Here is what Benjamin says:

> A Klee painting named 'Angelus Novus' shows an angel looking as though he is about to move away from something he is fixedly contemplating. His eyes are staring, his mouth is open, his wings are spread. This is how one pictures the angel of history. His face is turned toward the past. Where we perceive a chain of events, he sees only single catastrophe which keeps piling wreckage upon wreckage and hurls it in front of his feet. The angel would like to stay, awaken the dead, and make whole what has been smashed. But a storm is blowing from Paradise; it has got caught in his wings with such violence that the angel can no longer close them. This storm irresistibly propels him into the future to which his back is turned, while the pile of debris before him grows skyward. This storm is what we call progress (Benjamin 1968, 257–258).

This is a powerful and inspiring metaphor in our musings on the theme of the images of the past and their relations to the present. Such a view goes against 'a fundamental premise of progress, namely that more just and felicitous times have steadily displaced more impoverished ones. For Benjamin, the past is not an inferior version of the present but an exploitable cache of both traumatic and utopian scenes' (Brown 2001, 157; see Bajić, this volume). Benjamin's powerful image of wreckages of history piling up in their omnipresence removes a possibility of a comfortable and secure position of the *past* past. We are within history that cannot disappear, whose images are everywhere, haunting the present and the future. In the positive sense, this conceptualisation of history means that all the possibilities are always open as historical memory can be used to undo the inevitability or the givenness of the present. On the negative side, this means that the archive of disturbing possibilities is present around us and can be triggered at any particular moment, in an opportunistic move. Such a position in both empowering and disempowering (see Buchli, this volume; Connerton 2009).

Jacques Derrida's work *Spectres of Marx* (1994) can be compared to the Benjaminian vision of the angel of history. As Wendy Brown has put it succinctly, 'Deities, angels, spectres, and ghosts … what are we to make of these creatures arising from the pens of radical thinkers in the twentieth century as they attempt to grasp our relation to the past and future …' (2001, 142). Derrida's imaginative readings of Marx produced this work at the end of one history, the history of Marxism. But he maintains that spectres of Marxism still live among us. This particular reading of Marx focuses on Marx's own famous words from the first sentence of the Manifesto: 'All the powers of old Europe have entered into a holy alliance to exorcise this spectre …' (Marx and Engels 1978). Yet, Derrida's real aim when suggesting the discipline of 'hauntology' is to show in what way the past remains among us and in what way the dead affect the living, the way the past lives indirectly in the present.

These views of Benjamin and Derrida have a double message for us. On the one hand, they are the reminders of the unfinishedness and latent presence of various historical processes, something that became violently obvious in the 1990s with the dissolution of the former Yugoslavia. At that time, suppressed and for many spectators unimaginable atrocities were being committed. It was thus highly naïve to ask the question how this all happened out of nowhere. How was it possible for things to come back? What followed these events was an essentialisation of the peoples of the former Yugoslavia as having something inherently corrupt within them (*cf.* Todorova 1997). This distancing from the Balkans and similar 'corrupt' 'Others' is a naïve way to preserve the comfort of progress and a coherent past and present.

On the other hand, the anti-progressive historiography brings the possibility to draw on historical memory as an archive of potent images to configure responsible historical consciousness that would debalkanise memories. By unearthing buried memories of shared pasts one interprets, explains and understands present cultural differences that could infuse and perpetuate conflicts and intolerance. Penetrating through layers of constructed histories and identities is a possible therapeutic way to curing and reconciliation for diverse collectivities to come to terms with their overlapped pasts, heritage and memories.

Material engagements and memory

Finally, before we turn to particular archaeology-related case studies in this volume, it remains important to turn to the question of what appears as one of the central issues for archaeologists when dealing with memory – the issue of its relationship with the materiality of the world. Recently, archaeologists have been deeply embroiled in discussions about materiality (*e.g.* papers in Buchli 2002; Jones 2007; Meskell 2004; papers in Miller 2005; Renfrew 2001), regaining confidence on the grounds of their familiarity with the world of material culture that archaeologists routinely come to grips with. Similarly, many of the papers in this volume explicitly or implicitly address the issue of materiality in their archaeological case studies. But is this insistence on materiality and the celebration

of its importance for past actors perhaps an apology for late capitalist consumer society? Are we perhaps again caught up in the snares of our own historical positioning?

Tim Ingold criticises this recent emphasis on material culture, 'which has gained a new momentum following its long hibernation in the basements of museology' (Ingold 2007, 5). Ingold argues that instead of a too abstract notion of materiality, we, as archaeologists and anthropologists, should rather learn how one can practically engage with the properties and qualities of the materials that the world is made of. Thus, it is not only the material culture that is made into finished objects but everything that surrounds us, and our approaches should explore the consequences of such a perspective. In one of his previous essays, Ingold (1993), for instance directly relates the experience of an archaeologist digging in a particular landscape with the type of testimony about the past that is produced in the process:

> … *the practice of archaeology is itself a form of dwelling.* The knowledge born of this practice is thus on a par with that which comes from the practical activity of the native dweller and which the anthropologist, through participation, seeks to learn and understand. For both the archaeologist and the native dweller, the landscape tells – or rather *is* a story. It enfolds the lives and times of predecessors who, over the generations, have moved around in it and played their part in its formation. To perceive the landscape is therefore to carry out an act of remembrance, and remembering is not so much a matter of calling up an internal image, stored in mind, as of engaging perceptually with an environment that is itself pregnant with the past. To be sure, the rules and methods of engagement employed respectively by the native dweller and the archaeologist will differ, as will the stories they tell, nevertheless – in so far as both seek the past in the landscape – they are engaged in projects of fundamentally the same kind (Ingold 1993, 152–153, original emphasis).

This explicitly takes us to the idea of remembering and memory by inhabiting and physically dwelling in a certain landscape (*cf.* Schama 1985), even if only for a short period, during an archaeological field season. The testimonies we bring from such experiences are not only those of meticulous recording of archaeological facts, but are also of the experience of practical engagement with a particular physical environment inhabited by people in the past. Actively remembering this type of experience and using it in our accounts becomes of vital importance for our project as archaeologist (see Tringham, this volume). In this way, we stop disengaging and distancing from the object of our studies, and become a sort of *quasi-witnesses* along with the evidence we excavate.

Perhaps this example helps us to suggest collapsing the notion of habit-memory, on the one side of remembering, and, recollection, on the other, or undiscursive and discursive distinctions (Whittle, this volume), that have informed us in the previously discussed philosophical musings. While such distinctions were analytically necessary, I am interested in suggesting the way to use some of the previously discussed philosophical notions in conceptualising the way people were remembering and forgetting in the past through their practical engagements in the world and within a particular landscape, or through particular materials they were surrounded by and which they transformed. Yet, I would suggest three more abstract concepts that may be applicable to various case studies with regard to both the processes of remembering as well as forgetting but that also have very practical applications. These concepts are also clearly laden with layers of meanings added upon them by various theorists, philosophers or artists. I (Borić 2003) suggest the notions of trace, citation and repetition/recapitulation.

Trace

The notion of trace has been used by various authors, including Freud, Heidegger, Lévinas, Derrida and Ricoeur (see above), either as a conceptual tool or metaphor, with different and yet complementary and cross-referential understandings. The epistemological status of historiography and archaeology is significantly related to the routine use of traces in a rather intuitive manner, claiming a pre-understanding of their significance. However, the problematic aspect of the ontological status of trace comes with an enigmatic paradox. Paul Ricoeur sums it up by saying that 'the passage no longer is but the trace remains' (1988, 119). For Derrida the agency that left this imprint, or 'disarrangement', is never present *as such*. There is a sense of an irreducible alterity in the trace as an involuntary testimony of the Other (Lévinas 1972 cited by Ricoeur 1988, 124–125). It 'becomes the origin of the origin' (Derrida 1974, 61) in a similar way that 'history always precedes history' (Ricoeur 1988, 247). As already emphasised, Ricoeur (1988, 199*ff.*) recognises the importance of the concept of trace as a possible tool in bridging phenomenological and cosmic time by the constitution of hybrid time – historicality and historic consciousness. Seen as objectified nodes and marks in the passage of a past agency, traces can be quarrying sites in the constitution of meaningful narrative plots. In other words, the physical resistance of trace is subject to interpretation and questioning in the present. Trace is open for endless individual subversions and re-figuring (see Borić, this volume).

Citations

The concept of citation is very prominently found in the work of Walter Benjamin. Arendt (1968) argued that for Benjamin searching into the depths of the past, one could rescue those fragments that in the process of decay do not simply become a ruin of time but instead crystallise into new 'pearls and corals' (*cf.* Gutteridge, this volume). By rearranging such fragments, a citation 'starts to look back at its original self in new ways' (Taussig 1999, 45). A similar underlying principle can be seen in artworks of Marcel Duchamp, who made explicit references to and citations of his previous artworks, forming a unique *oeuvre* by the use of temporal duration as an active component of artworks' production. Simultaneously, it represents and *is* the network of stoppages by citing and embodying *material* layers of Duchamp's previous works. It is a sketch of the fourth dimension in its attempt to incorporate the dimension of time (see Gell 1998, 242–251).

This 'art of quotation' (*cf.* Taussig 1993, 109) can be further complemented by the concept of citationality that comes from Judith Butler (1993). Butler writes about conceptualising and 'constructing' perpetual performativity of sex and gender through historically contingent 'regulatory schemes'. For Butler, the derivative power of our practices, without an originating will, comes from citationality, *i.e.* reiterated acting without fixed effects (Butler 1993, 13). In other words, citation mirrors and produces itself rather than some anterior ideal. The concept of citationality here is intrinsically linked to the concept of repetition.

Repetition/Recapitulation

Repetition/recapitulation refers to iterability and is tied to concepts of citation and trace. The concept is used by Heidegger, who in speaking about a 'grasping moment of vision' says that '*repeating is handing down explicitly* – that is to say going back to the possibilities of the Dasein that has-been-there' (1962, 437 quoted by Ricoeur 1988, 76, original emphasis). In this moment of vision, something that is inherited as having-being-there is synthesised with fresh and free possibilities to choose repressed and neglected aspects of what is now abolished and yet still present (*i.e.* trace). This process is seen as a recovered anticipatory resoluteness of an innovational moment of change. A potential for innovation and change is thus created as repetition 'opens up the past again in the direction of coming-towards' (Ricoeur 1988, 76). This gap of creativity means that the concept of tradition and its transmission assumes both sedimentation and innovation as its constitutive features (*cf.* Ricoeur 1984, passim). Materialised effects that are achieved by reiteration of practices become inevitably confronted with the movement of *différance* as 'by virtue of this reiteration gaps and fissures are opened up as a constitutive instabilities in such constructions' (Butler 1993, 10; see also Strathern 1991).

These notions are dependent of each other and can be variously applied to the evidence of archaeological case studies. Their dynamic interdependence should be seen as reflecting the workings of memory, from its presence as trace, through the active search for it (citation) and its necessary iterability seen not as conservatism but as

a way of opening up new possibilities (repetition/recapitulation).

Papers in this volume

This collection of papers arises from the conference 'Excavating Memories: The Archaeology of Remembering and Forgetting' held at the Center for Archaeology at Columbia University in the City of New York, April 26th–27th, 2003.[1] Not all of the papers presented at the conference reached this volume and there are also several contributions that were not presented at the conference and were additionally included here. On the whole, papers are organised in the chronological order of the case studies examined, although there are some adjustments to the 'ascending' temporal order in those cases when the arrangement of particular memory topics necessitated some re-shuffling of the coordinates of the absolute chronological time.

Whittle's paper on diversity of memory opens the volume to different case studies. Whittle argues that archaeological arguments can and should draw upon our own experiences, our own memories, and that it is allowed to evoke disparate sources in order to imagine the past and the ways people might have structured the sense of their own past. Whittle illustrates his point about remembering with two different European Neolithic cases studies, both relating to the first Neolithic communities, one on the Great Hungarian Plain and the other in southern England. Both case studies rely on a higher chronological resolution than expected for prehistory thanks to the application of the Bayesian statistical modelling with regard to the radiometric evidence from these regions. Such a chronological precision helps to locate the memory of the past closer to the individual projects of people who dwelt at the discussed sites, exploring diverse scales of remembering and their interdependences: from day to day activities to generational continuities. Yet, Whittle questions whether our own experience allows us to comprehend the possibility of a much longer term memory that prehistoric case studies sometimes suggest.

Borić's paper continues the discussion about

different scales of remembering and further addresses the question about interdependencies between memory and forgetting in the Danube Gorges region of the Balkans during the Mesolithic period and in the course of the transformation of the Mesolithic foragers affected by the 'Neolithic' ways of being-in-the-world. The paper explores the importance of forgetting along with memory, or even as the precondition of memory. This argument evokes Nietzsche's and Heidegger's ideas about the double valence of forgetting by examining how the arrangement of the material remains of individual human bodies drew on the narrative coherence of a social body by eclipsing the dismembered individuality of its members. Similar to Whittle's paper, this paper questions the realistic nature of long-term continuities often seen in the prehistoric record along with the problematic assumption about the stability of meanings in a diachronic perspective.

While Tringham's paper remains within the domain of prehistoric case studies, the period specialisation is subsidiary to the author's interest in the recording of archaeological data through digital media, and especially with regard to the visual record, following Susan Sontag and John Berger. Through an abundant use of photographs and images in the form of *bricolage*, Tringham draws on a plenitude of colourful biographical examples of her own archaeological fieldwork, seen as a personal depository or trigger of archaeological and other memories, to walk us through the development of digital technologies that have been available to archaeologists in the past 50 years or so. She indicates a rapid pace of changes in the way we record the archaeological evidence in the field. These fascinating reflections expose the dynamic of what in our field experience as archaeologists becomes recorded and discursively remembered and those experiences that are left to the mercy of chance remembering through 'work shots'. Tringham argues that instead of 'public', 'official' and 'dehumanised' photographs of the archaeological record, the digital record (*e.g.* photographs) can be put to a much better use by producing 'private' records that preserve in a transparent way the memory of a particular

archaeological process and the wider context of its making. While fully embracing the need for reflexivity that the new digital technologies offer to archaeologists, the author warns us that it would be naïve to think that the era of digital recording will completely save us from oblivion as recording technologies continue to change at an increasing pace. Such ephemerality and immateriality of the current state of affairs echoes certain concerns also raised in Buchli's paper in this volume.

Jones focuses on the relationship between memory and acts of concealment, defacement and secrecy (following Taussig 1999), which he identifies as tropes that might have characterised the Early Bronze Age Britain, and in particular the evidence of Early Bronze Age Scotland that he discusses in his paper with regard to the mortuary record as well as in relation to practices of structured deposition of metal objects. The author sees homological relations between these different practices. Jones focuses on two different regions of Scotland during the Bronze Age with similarities in the type of mortuary architecture and the presence of prehistoric rock art but with marked differences in the patterns of metal object deposition. During this period there is an emphasis on the containment of bodies either in urns or stone cists and monuments. On the other hand, metal objects (frequently fragmented) are put out of the circle of use and buried, frequently close to dramatic landscape features. One also finds the practice of layering or 'wrapping' over bodies or even of monument complexes themselves either by materialities of surfaces (decorated and undecorated pots and stones) or complex (apotropaic?) designs. In this way, the content is guarded from onlookers, while at the same time 'in memorial terms, the act of forgetting through burial creates a trace to be remembered'. The emphasis on secrecy, Jones connects with the need to control the supply and circulation of metal objects at this time. Acts of deposition, either of bodies or metal objects, might have been intended as spectacles that triggered dramatic memories in the eyes of onlookers.

In a similar vein, exploring further the idea of socially situated remembering, Hanks discusses the construction of a particular warrior identity in the course of the Bronze and Iron Ages, with a focus on the region of Eurasian steppes. The memory of these buried warrior heroes became inscribed in monumental form across vast landscapes through the practice of creating spectacular burial mounds, *kurgans*. Here again a form of public secrecy trope can be recognised. Hanks discusses in particular examples of burial mounds dated to the first millennium BC, some with preserved traces of rich imagery in the form of complex body tattoos or object decoration, as in the case of the Pazyryk tombs. The emphasis on the decoration of body surfaces as well as interfaces between human and animal skins (*e.g.* saddles) through the use of the so-called 'animal style' imagery, reveal the embodied practices that drew on the potency of the past (heroic) acts and mythical animals. Through tattooing, the body of each of these warriors might also have been inscribed with memories of particular events, creating a particular individual identity. Since many of these tattoos were not openly displayed, as clothes frequently covered tattooed parts of the body, one may suggest that such personal memory props were not always publicly shared. Embodied and narrated memories and myths about the discussed warrior lifestyles persisted over long spans of time and survive even in our cultural imaginary thanks to narratives recorded in Classical times.

Boozer turns our attention explicitly to another facet of identity construction in relation to memory, namely social strategies within the context of urban Roman Egypt, where particular individuals were coping with the constraints of the imperial and colonial rule. She is interested in tracing intertwined aspects of memory and identity at a micro-scale level and examines a recently excavated household in the Roman city of Amheida. Here, the household is seen as the emblem of a particular social standing. Moreover, since Proust many authors have emphasised the importance of houses with regard to memories that are intimate or belong to our 'close relations' (see above). In the case Boozer describes, the interior decoration and the choice of Homeric mythological scenes depicted on the house's preserved walls indicate that the inhabitants of

this building at Roman Amheida aspired to the Hellenistic ideal of alliances. These citations of a deep mythological past depicted on the wall scenes expose a complexity of memory work oriented toward a common Roman past, which was embraced on the basis of narratives that were being promoted as desirable for a particular (upper) social class in the city. However, that identity memories are hardly fixed and uniform in such colonial contexts is amply shown on the basis of another excavated house that Boozer mentions. In a different area of the city, a family of a moderate social status left traces suggesting that their identity was clearly referencing an Egyptian heritage by drawing on the potency of locally grounded memories of the past.

While in the previous case study one finds a particular Roman provincial councilor evoking a deep mythological past by painting Homeric scenes on the walls of his house at the edge of an Egyptian desert, by the way of contrast, Gutteridge's paper takes us to the centre of political power of the Roman Empire, to the city of Rome at the time of the emperor Constantine, the period roughly contemporaneous with the previous example. This paper looks into a particular practice that especially characterises the period of Late Antiquity, that of *spolia*, which consists of the often intentional use of both figurative and non-figurative material fragments of older buildings and monuments that become dismembered and reused by recombining and embedding them in newly built buildings or monuments. In this way new meanings were forged. Gutteridge reviews the scholarship that has looked into decisions that, it turns out, were carefully made in choosing particular spoliated reliefs (from at least three older monuments) when building the Arch of Constantine in AD 315. It was the action of intentional reusing of the past. Gutteridge is interested in the way particular elements of these spoliated reliefs were meant to rearrange the coordinates of linear time. This was not done by a widespread practice of *damnatio* (defacement) but instead through a reverence of the past in the act of disfigurement, achieving the effect of a bricolage. Moreover, in building such a spoliated monument, the message that is conveyed is not about the biographical events in the life of Constantine, but about the timelessness and accumulation of all previous glorious triumphs, achieving a temporal elision and conjoining cosmic and biographical time. This choice of composition of spolias, Guterridge defines as trans-temporal. In the final instance, the author metaphorically compares the Arch of Constantine to the practice of archaeology in its constant struggle to reshuffle past fragments in pursuit of meanings that would guard us from threatening forces of oblivion.

The memory that Filippucci's paper evokes takes us to a very different setting, one where uncanny familiarity creeps into our discussion about memory by referring to the horizon of lived memories of our grandparents, memories that also impinge on our own personal memories through narratives about the First World War. By discussing recent archaeological excavations of the Western Front sites, Filippucci discloses the inbetweenness of this particular past – it is not completely gone from the horizon of living memories nor is it within our experiential reach. As a social anthropologist, in the archaeological process she studies Filippucci takes the role of a participant observer. She interestingly connects the archaeological experience, seen as a material engagement in a particular landscape, with the position that one may call that of quasi-witnesses or second-hand witnesses, in which the materiality of archaeological practice re-enacts experience of soldiers that fought on these grounds, in this particular landscape (*cf.* Ingold 1993; see above). She further draws a contrast between, on the one hand, the practices of commemoration and memorials, and, on the other hand, the production of archaeological narratives that 'bring the war past into the present as a reality that to some extent resists incorporation, troubling and disturbing us'. In this way, the 'matter-of-factness of the past' is underlined, while the archaeological process becomes a tribute to the dead, a debt and an obligation on the part of the living, as a dedication to the Fallen.

Weiss's paper develops further the theme that the previous paper triggered, that of the role of materiality of landscapes. She takes an archaeological perspective when dealing with the traumatic consequences of recent atrocities committed in the 1990s Balkan wars. The author introduces a new dimension to our dealings with memory and the construction of knowledge about the past: the role of international criminal tribunals and the judicial body. These tribunals, such as the one for the former Yugoslavia in the Hague, are 'as much about legitimating historical narratives as [they are] about prosecuting criminals at large'. This court practice and the judicial procedure followed invite constant references to the Holocaust trials after the Second World War. Weiss argues that, in these most recent trials, material evidence is still subsidiary to the witness testimonies, and she is determined to show that it is exactly by comprehending the physicality of evidence and the materiality of particular landscapes in which atrocities were committed that a more encompassing perspective can be forged, especially with regard to truth and reconciliation committees. She illuminates this point with examples from the trial of the late Serbian president Slobodan Milošević in the Hague. In doing so, one reveals the dark side of studying the role of landscapes previously largely considered in phenomenological accounts as 'felicitous sorts of lived spaces'. Understanding how crime could become inscribed over a landscape in the form of Seremetakis's 'islands of historicity' or Foucault's 'heterotopias', along with the immediacy evoked by material evidence, connects intimately the work of memory and the archaeological practice.

We continue to linger in the topic of the past that does not pass when entering into the maze of significations built by Bajić in his virtual Yugomuseum, located in the constructed imagination of the author's birth place, the city of Belgrade, the former capital of a now non-existent country – Yugoslavia. Bajić, who is an artist, connects to the archaeological practice of collecting and ordering materialities that symbolise particular events. He juxtaposes various material symbols and images from the 70-year-long (or short) history of Yugoslavia. While the tone may seem nostalgic, the underlying procedure is that of irony, seen as a powerful trope of humour for achieving freedom in the negativity. Messages sent by Bajić in his meticulous play of associations may, however, to some extent remain opaque to those unfamiliar with the history of Yugoslavia and events that followed its break-up at the beginning of the 1990s. Yet, such varying degrees of opacity with regard to particular objects and their meanings vividly evoke the complexity and historical situatedness of collective memories. The whole project could be seen as an experiment in re-enacting multiple theatres of social memory. By reordering images and symbols, Bajić 'works through' (*sensu* Freud) the memory of a particular collectivity in order to enable the healing of repressed and accumulated traumas (what he calls 'the malignancy of the era') by exposing the absurdity and banality of their adherence to particular objects and images. Bajić's museum can be compared to the previously discussed image of the site of historical wreckages evoked by Benjamin. In the case of Yugomuseum, accumulated materialities are confronted in an attempt to come to terms with these vivid reminders of a difficult past.

At the end, Buchli grapples with all those issues that have followed us on our journey through the complex labyrinths of memory's relation to archaeology: materiality, melancholy, the modernist emergence of archaeology as a particular field of study (a discipline!). Buchli attempts to describe the present condition of late capitalist society with its subtly elaborated ways of exercising control over individuals as obsessed with preserving everything, similar to the (melancholic) urge of historians or archaeologists for archiving documents or sherds of pottery. Yet, despite all of this, our present-day context is importantly structured by immateriality of information, their ever-changing digital formats, for example (see Tringham's paper above). Such a condition hinders the work of memory that depends on iterability, material and discursive. In the absence of such an anchorage in the context of the ephemeral superfluity of immaterial, fleeting information ('the tragic lightness of being'), the pathological condition of melancholy develops. Yet, Buchli insists throughout that this problematic state of affairs can both be empowering and disempowering, enabling and disabling. Archaeology, with its ability to dig through the layers of appearances in destabilising and challenging dominant settlements, should play a pivotal role in enabling the work of memory.

Notes

1   The conference was funded by the Center for Archaeology, Columbia University, and I would especially like to express my thanks to Lynn Meskell, Nan Rothschild and Terry D'Altroy for supporting the conference, and Lucas Rubin for his help in organising it. I am also grateful to a number of students who attended my classes about social memory and archaeology, and who stimulated and influenced my thinking about the subject. I am indebted to the Leverhulme Programme 'Changing Beliefs of the Human Body' based at the Department of Archaeology, University of Cambridge for supporting me in completing this work. For useful comments on an earlier draft of this chapter, I am grateful to Dani Hofmann and Alasdair Whittle.

Bibliography

Andrić, I. (1969) Speech at the Nobel Banquet at the City Hall in Stockholm, December 10, 1961. In H. Frenz (ed.) *Nobel Lectures, Literature 1901–1967*. Amsterdam, Elsevier Publishing Company.

Arendt, H. (1958) *The Human Condition*. Chicago, University of Chicago Press.

Arendt, H. (1968) Introduction. Walter Benjamin 1892–1940. In H. Arendt (ed.) *Illuminations*, 1–55. New York, Schocken Books.

Aron, R. (1961) *Introduction to the Philosophy of History: An Essay on the Limits of Historical Objectivity* (trans. G. J. Irwin). Boston, Beacon Press.

Bachelard, G. (1964) *The Poetics of Space*. Boston, Beacon Press.

Benjamin, W. (1968) Theses on the Philosophy of History. In H. Arendt (ed.) *Illuminations* (trans. H. Zohn), 253–264. New York, Schocken Books.

Bergson, H. (1981) *Matter and Memory*. New York, Zone.

Bloch, M. (1964) *The Historian's Craft* (trans. P. Putnam). New York, Vintage Books.

Bloch, M. E. F. (1998) *How We Think They Think. Anthropological Approaches to Cognition, Memory, and Literacy*. Oxford, WestviewPress.

Borić, D. (2003) 'Deep Time' Metaphor: Mnemonic and Apotropaic Practices at Lepenski Vir. *Journal of Social Archaeology* 3(1), 41–75.

Bourdieu, P. (1990) *The Logic of Practice*. Stanford, Stanford University Press.

Bradley, R. (2002) *The Past in Prehistoric Societies*. London and New York, Routledge.

Bradley, R. (2003) The Transition of Time. In Van Dyke, R. M. and S. E. Alcock (eds) *Archaeologies of Memory*, 221–227. Oxford, Blackwell Publishing.

Brown, W. (2001) *Politics Out of History*. Princeton and Oxford: Princeton University Press.

Buchli, V. (1995) Interpreting Material Culture: The Trouble with Text. In I. Hodder, M. Shanks, A. Alexandri, V. Buchli, J. Carman, J. Last, and G. Lucas (eds) *Interpreting Archaeology: Finding Meaning in the Past*, 181–193. London and New York, Routledge.

Buchli, V. (ed.) (2002) *Material Culture Reader*. Oxford, Berg.

Butler, J. (1993) *Bodies that Matter: On the Discursive Limits of 'Sex'*. London, Routledge.

Carr, D. (1986) *Time, Narrative and History*. Bloomington/Indianapolis, Indiana University Press.

Chaumeil, J.-P. (2007) Bones, Flutes, and the Dead Memory and Funerary Treatments in Amazonia. In C. Fausto and M. Heckenberger (eds) *Time and Memory in Indigenous Amazonia: Anthropological Perspectives*, 244–283. Gainesville, University Press of Florida.

Chesson, M. S. (ed.) (2001) *Social Memory, Identity, and Death: Archaeological Perspectives on Mortuary Rituals*. Archaeological papers of the American Anthropological Associations No. 10.

Collingwood, P. R. (1999) *The Principles of History: And Other Writings in Philosophy of History*. New York, Oxford University Press.

Conklin, B. (2001) *Consuming Grief: Compassionate Cannibalism in an Amazonian Society*. Austin, University of Texas Press.

Connerton, P. (1989) *How Societies Remember*. Cambridge, Cambridge University Press.

Connerton, P. (2009) *How Modernity Forgets*. Cambridge, Cambridge University Press.

Courbin, P. (1988) *What is Archaeology?: An Essay on the Nature of Archaeological Research*. Chicago, The Chicago University Press.

Cunha, M. Carneiro da (1978) *Os mortos e os outros: Uma análise do sistema funerário e da noção de pessoa entre os índios Krahó*. São Paulo, Hucitec.

Deleuze, G. (1988) *Bergsonism* (trans. H. Tomlinson and B. Habberjam). New York, Zone.

Deleuze, G. (1994) *Difference and Repetition* (1968). (trans. P. Patton). New York, Columbia University Press.

Derrida, J. (1973) *Speech and Phenomena. And Other Essays on Husserl's Theory of Signs*. Evanston, Northwestern University Press.

Derrida, J. (1974) *Of Grammatology*. Baltimore and London, The John Hopkins University Press.

Derrida, J. (1982) *Margins of Philosophy* (trans. A. Bass). Chicago, University of Chicago Press.

Derrida, J. (1994) *Spectres of Marx: The State of the Debt, and the Work of Mourning, and the New International*. London and New York, Routledge.

Derrida, J. (1999) Le Siècle et le Pardon. *Le Monde des Débats* (December).

Fausto, C. and Heckenberger, M. (2007) Introduction: Indigenous History and the History of the 'Indians'. In C. Fausto and M. Heckenberger (eds) *Time and Memory in Indigenous Amazonia: Anthropological Perspectives*, 1–43. Gainesville, University Press of Florida.

Fentress, J. and Wickham, C. (1992) *Social Memory*. Oxford, Blackwell.

Foucault, M. (1972) *The Archaeology of Knowledge* (trans. A. M. Sheridan Smith). London, Tavistock Publication.

Foucault, M. (1984) Nietzsche, Genealogy, History. In P. Rabinow (ed.) *The Foucault Reader*, 76–100. London, Penguin Books.

Freud, S. (1989) Mourning and Melancholia. In *The Freud Reader*, 584–589. New York and London, W. W. Norton and Company.

Geertz, C. (1983) *Local Knowledge. Further Essays in Interpretive Anthropology*. New York, Basic Books, Inc., Publishers.

Gell, A. (1992) *The Anthropology of Time. Cultural Constructions of Temporal Maps and Images*. Oxford/Providence, Berg.

Gell, A. (1998) *Art and Agency. An Anthropological Theory*. Oxford, Clarendon Press.

Ginzburg, C. (1980) *The Cheese and the Worms: The Cosmos of the Sixteenth Centuary Miller* (trans. J. and A. Tedeschi). Baltimore, Johns Hopkins University Press.

Ginzburg, C. (1989) Clues: Roots of an Evidential Paradigm. In C. Ginzburg, *Clues, Myths and the Historical Method*, 96–125. Baltimore and London, The John Hopkins University Press.

Ginzburg, C. (2002) *The Judge and the Historian* (trans. A. Shugaar). New York, Verso.

Habermas, J. (1987) *The Philosophical Discourse of Modernity: Twelve Lectures*. Cambridge, Polity Press.

Halbwachs, M. (1980) *The Collective Memory*. New York, Harper Colophon.

Halbwachs, M. (1992) *On Collective Memory*. Chicago and London, The University of Chicago Press.

Harris, O. J. T. (forthcoming) 'Blessed are the Forgetful': Social Tensions Between Remembering and Forgetting at Two Neolithic Monuments in Southern England. In R. Schulting, N. Whitehouse and M. McClatchie (eds) *Living Landscapes: Exploring Neolithic Ireland in its Wider Context*. Oxford, British Archaeological Reports.

Hastorf, C. A. (2003) Community with the Ancestors: Ceremonies and Social Memory in the Middle Formative at Chiripa, Bolivia. *Journal of Anthropological Archaeology* 22, 305–332.

Heckenberger, M. (2007) Xinguano Heroes, Ancestors, and Others Materializing the Past in Chiefly Bodies, Ritual Space, and Landscape. In C. Fausto and M. Heckenberger (eds) *Time and Memory in Indigenous Amazonia: Anthropological Perspectives*, 284–311. Gainesville, University Press of Florida.

Heidegger, M. (1962) *Being and Time* (trans. J. Macquarrie and E. Robinson). New York, Harper and Row.

Hodder, I. (1991) Interpretative Archaeology and Its Role. *American Antiquity* 56(1), 7–18.

Hodder, I. (1993) The Narrative and Rhetoric of Material Culture Sequences. In R. Bradley (ed.) *Conceptions of Time and Ancient Society. World Archaeology* 25(2), 268–282. London and New York, Routledge.

Hodder, I. (1995) Material Culture in Time, in I. Hodder, M. Shanks, A. Alexandri, V. Buchli, J. Carman, J. Last and G. Lucas (eds) *Interpreting Archaeology. Finding Meaning in the Past*, 164–168. London and New York, Routledge.

Hodder, I. (1999) *The Archaeological Process. An Introduction*. Oxford, Blackwell Publishers.

Hodder, I. and Cessford, C. (2004) Daily Practice and Social Memory at Çatalhöyük. *American Antiquity* 69(1), 17–40.

Husserl, E. (1964) *The Phenomenology of Internal Time Consciousness* (trans. J. S. Churchill). London, Indiana University Press.

Ingold, T. (1993) The Temporality of the Landscape. In R. Bradley (ed.) *Conceptions of Time and Ancient Society/World Archaeology*, 152–174. London and New York, Routledge.

Ingold, T. (2007) Materials Against Materiality. *Archaeological Dialogues* 14(1), 1–16.

Jones, A. (2001) Drawn from Memory: The Archaeology of Aesthetics and the Aesthetics of Archaeology in Earlier Bronze Age Britain and the Present. In C. Gosden (ed.) *Archaeology and Aesthetics/World Archaeology* 33(2), 334–356. New York and London, Routledge.

Jones, A. (2007) *Memory and Material Culture*. Cambridge, Cambridge University Press.

Klein, K. L. (1997) *Frontiers of Historical Imagination. Narrating the European Conquest of Native America, 1890–1990*. Berkeley, University of California Press.

Krell, D. F. (1990) *Of Memory, Reminiscence, and Writing. On the Verge*. Bloomington and Indianapolis, Indiana University Press.

Küchler, S. (1996) The Liquidation of Material Things. *Archaeological Dialogues* 3(1): 26–29.

Küchler, S. (1999) The Place of Memory. In A. Forty and S. Küchler (eds) *The Art of Forgetting*, 53–72. Oxford and New York, Berg.

Kuijt, I. (2001) Place, Death and the Transmission of Social Memory in Early Agricultural Communities of the Near Eastern Pre-Pottery Neolithic. In M. S. Chesson, (ed.) *Social Memory, Identity, and Death: Archaeological Perspectives on Mortuary Rituals*, 80–99. Archaeological Papers of the American Anthropological Associations No. 10.

Kwint, M., Breward, C. and Aynsley, J. (eds) (1999) *Material Memories. Design and Evocation*. Oxford and New York, Berg.

Kwinter, S. (2001) *Architectures of Time: Toward a Theory of the Event in Modernist Culture*. Cambridge, Mass, The MIT Press.

Le Goff, J. (1992) *History and Memory*. New York, Columbia University Press.

Lévi-Strauss, C. (1966) *The Savage Mind*. Chicago, The University of Chicago Press.

Lévinas, E. (1972) La Trace. In E. Lévinas, *Humanisme de l'autre homme*, 57–63. Montpellier, Fata Morgana.

Marx, K. and Engels, F. (1978) The Manifesto of the Communist Party. In R. C. Tucker (ed.) *The Marx-Engels Reader*. New York, Norton.

Mauss, M. (1979) Body Techniques. In M. Mauss, *Sociology and Psychology: Essays* (trans. Ben Brewster), 95–123. London, Routledge and Kegan Paul.

Meskell, L. M. (2001) The Egyptian Ways of Death. In M. S. Chesson (ed.) *Social Memory, Identity, and Death: Archaeological Perspectives on Mortuary Rituals*, 27–40. Archaeological Papers of the American Anthropological Associations No. 10.

Meskell, L. M. (2004) *Material Biographies: Object Worlds from Ancient Egypt and Beyond*. Oxford, Berg.

Miller, D. (ed.) 2005. *Materiality*. Durham and London, Duke University Press.

Mines, D. P. and Weiss, B. (1997) Materializations of Memory: The Substance of Remembering and Forgetting: Introduction. *Anthropological Quarterly* 70(4), 161–163.

Mitrović, S. (2008) Fresh Scars on the Body of Archaeology: Excavating Mass-Graves at Batajnica, Serbia. In D. Borić and J. Robb (eds) *Past Bodies: Body-Centered Research in Archaeology*, 79–88. Oxford, Oxbow Books.

Moore, H. (1990) Paul Ricoeur: Action, Meaning and Text. In C. Tilley (ed.) *Reading Material Culture: Structuralism, Hermeneutics and Post-Structuralism*, 85–120. Oxford, Basil Blackwell.

Nietzsche, F. (1969) *On the Geneaology of Morals and Ecce Homo* (trans. W. Kaufmann and R. J. Hollingdale). New York, Vintage Books.

Nietzsche, F. (1980) *On the Advantage and Disadvantage of History for Life*. Indianapolis and Cambridge, Hackett Publishing Company, Inc.

Nora, P. (1996) *Realms of Memory. The Construction of the French Past* (trans. A. Goldhammer). New York, Columbia University Press.

Overing Kaplan, J. (ed.) (1977) *Social Time and Social Space in Lowland South American Societies*. Paris, Peeters.

Rabinow, P. (2003) *Anthropos Today. Reflections on Modern Equipment*. Princeton and Oxford, Princeton University Press.

Renfrew, C. (2001) Symbol before Concept: Material Engagement and the Early Development of Society. In I. Hodder (ed.) *Archaeological Theory Today*, 122–140. Cambridge, Polity Press.

Ricoeur, P. (1980) Narrative Time. *Critical Inquiry* 7(1), 169–190.

Ricoeur, P. (1981) *Hermeneutics and the Human Sciences* (trans. J. Thompson). Cambridge, Cambridge University Press.

Ricoeur, P. (1984a) *Time and Narrative, Volume I* (trans. K. Blamey and D. Pellauer). Chicago and London, The University of Chicago Press.

Ricoeur, P. (1984b) *The Reality of the Historical Past*. Milwaukee, Marquette University Press.

Ricoeur, P. (1988) *Time and Narrative, Volume 3* (trans. K. Blamey and D. Pellauer). Chicago and London, The University of Chicago Press.

Ricoeur, P. (1991a) Life in quest of narrative. In D. Wood (ed.) *On Paul Ricoeur: Narrative and Interpretation*, 20–33. London and New York, Routledge.

Ricoeur, P. (1991b) Narrative identity. In D. Wood (ed.) *On Paul Ricoeur: Narrative and Interpretation*, 188–199. London and New York, Routledge.

Ricoeur, P. (1998) *Critique and Conviction. Conver-sations with François Azouvi and Marc de Launay* (trans. K. Blamey). Polity Press, Cambridge.

Ricoeur, P. (2004) *Memory, History, Forgetting* (trans. K. Blamey and D. Pellauer). Chicago and London, The University of Chicago Press.

Rowlands, M. (1993) The Role of Memory in the Transmission of Culture. In R. Bradley (ed.) *Conceptions of Time and Ancient Society/World Archaeology* 25(2), 141–151. London and New York, Routledge.

Saint Augustin (1961) *Confessions* (trans. R. S. Pine-Coffin). London, Penguin Books.

Saramago, J. (1996) *The History of the Siege of Lisbon* (trans. G. Pontiero). San Diego, A Harvest Book.

Schama, S. (1985) *Landscape and Memory*. New York, A.A. Knopf.

Schutz, A. 1967. *The Phenomenology of the Social World*. Evanston, Ill., Northwestern University Press.

Seremetakis, N. (1994) *The Senses Still. Perception and Memory as Material Culture in Modernity*. Chicago and London, The University of Chicago Press.

Shanks, M. (1996) *Classical Archaeology of Greece. Experiences of the Discipline*. London, Routledge.

Shanks, M. and Hodder, I. (1995) Processual, Postprocessual and Interpretive Archaeology. In I. Hodder, M. Shanks, A. Alexandri, V. Buchli, J. Carman, J. Last and G. Lucas (eds) *Interpreting Archaeology. Finding Meaning in the Past*, 3–29. London and New York, Routledge.

Strathern, M. (1991) *Partial Connections*. Savage, Md., Rowman and Littlefield Publishers.

Taussig, M. (1993) *Mimesis and Alterity. A Particular History of the Senses*. New York and London, Routledge.

Taussig, M. (1999) *Defacement. Public Secrecy and the Labor of the Negative*. Stanford, Stanford University Press.

Taylor, A. C. (1993) Remembering to Forget: Identity, Mourning and Memory Among the Jivaro. *Man* n.s. 28(4), 653–678.

Taylor, C. (1989) *Sources of the Self: The Making of the Modern Identity*. Cambridge, Mass., Harvard University Press.

Thomas, J. (1996) *Time, Culture and Identity*. London and New York, Routledge.

Thomas, J. (2004) *Archaeology and Modernity*. London and New York, Routledge.

Todorova, M. (1997) *Imagining the Balkans*. New York and Oxford, Oxford University Press.

Van Dyke, R. M. and Alcock, S. E. (eds) (2003) *Archaeologies of Memory*. Oxford, Blackwell Publishing.

Vanhoozer, K. J. (1991) Philosophical Antecedents to Ricoeur's *Time and Narrative*. In D. Wood (ed.) *On Paul Ricoeur: Narrative and Interpretation*, 34–54. London and New York, Routledge.

Vilaça, A. (1992) *Comendo como Gente: Formas do Canibalismo Wari'*. Rio de Janeiro, ANPOCS/Editora da Universidade Federal do Rio de Janeiro.

Vilaça, A. (2000) Relations Between Funerary Cannibalism and Warfare Cannibalism: The Question of Predation. *Ethnos* 65(1), 83–106.

Viveiros de Castro, E. (1996) Images of Nature and Society in Amazonian Ethnology. *Annual Review of Anthropology* 25, 179–200.

White, H. (1978) *Tropics of Discourse*. Baltimore, Johns Hopkins University Press.

White, H. (1987) The Metaphysics of Narrativity: Time and Symbol in Ricoeur's Philosophy of History. In H. White, *The Content of the Form. Narrative Discourse and Historical Representation*, 169–184. Baltimore and London, The Johns Hopkins University Press.

Wood, D. (ed.) (1991) *On Paul Ricoeur. Narrative and Interpretation*. London and New York, Routledge.

Williams, H. (ed.) (2003) *Archaeologies of Remembrance. Death and Memory in Past Societies*. New York, Kluwer Academic/Plenum Publishers.

Wylie, A. (2002) *Thinking from Things. Essays in the Philosophy of Archaeology*. Berkeley-Los Angeles-London, University of California Press.

2. The diversity and duration of memory

Alasdair Whittle

Sources

Does it matter where archaeologists get their theories from? We are often told that our own world and culture are bad guides to what went on in the past, and the desire to avoid ethnocentrism is obvious and understandable. This has, however, regrettable consequences, since it can lead to the creation of very general, if not rather abstract theory. Current interest in agency is a good case in point. John Barrett has presented some of the most important discussions of this central topic. An earlier study was centred on the case study of developments in the area around Avebury during the Neolithic period, from the perspective of the agency of knowledgeable actors (Barrett 1994). Other, more recent studies reinforce the central importance of agency (Barrett 2000; 2001). 'Agency is the means by which things are achieved. It therefore has the power to act and human agency operates knowledgeably and reflexively… Agents do not appear upon the historical stage as a given, rather they make themselves within and through their own specific social and cultural conditions' (Barrett 2001, 141; *cf.* Barrett 2000). This is a powerful statement, which repays consideration in the study of any period. It is, however, very general, lacking any engagement with specific archaeological examples. In being presented as a near-universal theory, it also tends to conceal the fact that it too is in the end based on specific, comparative studies, to be found ultimately in the work of Bourdieu and Giddens. Given that we are all agents in our own lives, it is surprising perhaps that there is not more use in our archaeological interpretations of reflection about how we go about the business of living ourselves. Certainly this could lead to modern bias, but it could also open important avenues in our approaches to agency. Agency so far has been a curiously bloodless matter, often seeming to lack motivation, values and emotion (Whittle 2001; 2003), despite general statements to the effect that 'practice draws upon memory, past experience, expectations and desires, and a communicative engagement with other co-inhabitants' (Barrett 2001, 152).

As the previous quotation indicates, memory and past experience are an inescapable part of the business of getting on in the world. Memory has quite recently become a popular topic in archaeology and other studies of material culture (*e.g.* Bradley 2002; Forty and Küchler 1999; Kwint *et al.* 1999; Sutton 1998; 2001). It has not, however, been much linked directly to agency. And it has often been treated as a series of separate kinds of remembering: material memories, the memory of food, the converse art of forgetting, and so on. Richard Bradley's studies present a compelling series of different kinds of memory, from the importance of distant origins to the legacies of more immediate pasts and the ways in which future memories can be created in the building of monuments and other practices (Bradley 2002). What is lacking in these wide-ranging case studies, however, is a sense of the simultaneous operation of different kinds of memory. Thus the LBK of the sixth millennium cal. BC is discussed with reference to distant pasts, or at least a perception of distant pasts, while the more immediate past is more a matter for the people of the Bronze Age (Bradley 2002, chapters 2 and 3).

In a way, this kind of separation may reflect the categorisations often imposed upon different domains of memory in the wider literature on the subject, which is obviously much older than its recent popularity in archaeology. I have noted elsewhere (Whittle 2003, chapter 5, and references) how these familiar distinctions – between oral and written, incorporated and inscribed, individual and collective, or habitual and conscious – never quite seem to capture what memory work is like in real life. And this is where some recourse to our own experience is useful as a check on the validity of general theory. I am not claiming, of course, that this is sufficient on its own. Practically any examples of different kinds of memory work in other cultures are enough to dispel this notion, such as the genealogical obsessions of the west African Tiv or the deliberate forgettings of some Melanesian and Amazonian people (Bohannan 1952; Küchler 1987; Taylor 1993). But we are ourselves constantly performing different kinds of memory work, and since this paper was first given as a lecture in America, where I had never been before, I want briefly to draw on two examples of how we have more sources of theory – construed as the basis for interpretation – at our disposal than we realise or admit.

Chomsky (1988, 159) has suggested that 'it is quite possible – overwhelmingly probable, one might guess – that we will always learn more about human life and human personality from novels than from scientific psychology'. In the spirit of Chomsky's quotation I should like to draw attention to the *Rabbit* novels of the American novelist John Updike. The evocation of remembering is at least as good as anything in Proust, and perhaps more immediate and with fuller impact because related to our own modern world. Thus to take just one example from *Rabbit is Rich*:

> The hot cracked sidewalks and dusty playground of Mt. Judge were summer enough, and the few trips to the Jersey Shore his parents organized stick up in his remembrance as almost torture, the hours on poky roads in the old Model A and then the mud-brown Chevy, his sister and mother adding to the heat the vapors of female exasperation, Pop dogged at the wheel, the back of his neck sweaty and scrawny

and freckled while the flat little towns of New Jersey threw back at Harry distorted echoes of his own town, his own life, for which he was homesick after an hour (Updike 1991, 498).

But there is more than mere evocation, since remembrance recurs throughout the novels, woven inescapably into the narrative of the crises, failures and partial successes of Harry Angstrom (or Rabbit). The life course of Rabbit is by no means only to do with memory, but it is incomplete without it.

On a personal note, the experience of my going to America for the first time was partly informed by memory. Like anyone else, I had expectations formed by books and films, by descriptions, images and imagination, and the experience of being there seemed to involve a constant comparison with these. The trip also evoked for me memories of my father and grandfathers. I flew over the North Atlantic in the daytime, looking down on waters where my father had served in the Second World War, and recollecting his own strong and difficult memories of that time. I still have a leather suitcase belonging to my maternal grandfather, complete with labels, who as a resident of Dunfermline in Scotland (birthplace of Andrew Carnegie) had gone by Cunard liner in the 1950s to visit the Carnegie Trust in New York. And before going, I looked up again old newspaper cuttings from the time when my paternal grandfather, based in Liverpool, worked in the cotton business in America, and won a gold medal for a long-distance walking race from Memphis to Collierville and back in March 1909, presented with gracious speeches on the floor of the Memphis Cotton Exchange. Where the medal is now I have no idea, and that grandfather died long before I was born. My other grandfather I knew well, and despite the leather bag and other material traces, I remember him best directly. Both grandfathers served in the First World War, my Whittle grandfather having enlisted with a Canadian regiment. Of those great events, only a brief recollection of his father's hatred of the first war came down to us in my own father's personal memoirs of the second. Trying to be objective, I would say that I only think of that generation from time to time, but on such occasions as my trip to

America we all perhaps make vivid use of such memories. And I am aware of, but have little direct personal sense of connection with, the generation before my grandparents.

This reflection on Rabbit and on my grandfathers may seem self-indulgent, but its serious point is to underline how inadequately we as archaeologists capture the diversity and duration of memory in our writing about the past. I have discussed in more detail elsewhere (Whittle 2003, chapter 5) some of the sources whose writings could help in such an enterprise, including Bergson (1911), Bartlett (1932) and Bloch (1998). From the first two comes a strong sense of the creativity of memory, Bartlett, for example (1932, 314), connecting it to 'that development of constructive imagination and constructive thought wherein at length we find the most complete release from the narrowness of presented time and place'. In his studies of Madagascar, Bloch has underlined how modes and styles of remembering vary according to different contexts and occasions. 'Adult humans construct a multiplicity of narratives of different types appropriate to different contexts and this very multiplicity ensures that their knowledge is not bounded by the narrative characteristics of any one of them' (Bloch 1998, 110).

Two case studies from Neolithic Europe

With this perspective, in the rest of this paper I want to look at two case studies. I am particularly interested on the one hand in how broad a sense of memory we might find in given situations, and what we could say about contexts and layers of remembering, and on the other hand in how long memories might be said to have lasted. The relationship between the diversity and duration of memory is also pertinent. I have briefly explored the first question above, but that of duration needs a little more of an introduction. Bartlett's view of memory was partly based on famous experiments in recollection; his student subjects were unable to maintain quite simple narratives in their original state. This strongly implies little fixity of memory. On a more generous timescale, Bradley (2002, 8) has suggested 200 years, based on historical comparisons, as the maximum likely duration of oral traditions in anything like their original form. Are there archaeological examples which might suggest longer chains of memory, 'great continuities of thought' as Foucault puts it (1972, 4), and if so, how would such remembering be transmitted across generations? Or is long memory in fact just a loosely connected series of much shorter-term rememberings? Have archaeologists in general exaggerated and over-emphasised the long term?

My two case studies come from recently completed projects. First, I use investigations of the Early Neolithic Körös culture occupation at Ecsegfalva 23, Co. Békés, on the Great Hungarian Plain, principally to examine the range of memories that might have been in simultaneous operation; these also have varying temporalities. Secondly, I use investigations of the Early Neolithic long barrow at Ascott-under-Wychwood, Oxfordshire, in southern England, principally to consider the varying durations of memory, but I also examine the range of references which the long history of the site may imply.

Ecsegfalva 23: an Early Neolithic occupation on the Great Hungarian Plain

At some time around 5800–5750 cal. BC, people came to occupy a small levée or ridge beside a great still-water meander, a former course of the nearby River Berettyó, which flows south-west to join the Körös river system; that in turns runs into the Tisza. From about 6000 cal. BC people had begun to occupy these flat lands in the northern part of the Carpathian Basin, in a way not visible in earlier periods. They may have come in large part from the south, but it is likely too that people of indigenous stock from regions roundabout were also involved, as the study of lithic traditions and technology strongly suggests (Mateiciucová 2001; 2004; 2007; Starnini 2001; Starnini and Szakmány 1998). The place occupied at Ecsegfalva was on the northern limits of the Early Neolithic Körös culture, to which it belongs, a restriction in distribution which has still fully to be explained. The place was merely one of a large number known principally along the varying watercourses of the southern half of the Great Hungarian Plain (Ecsedy *et al.* 1982; Jankovich *et al.* 1989; Kosse 1979). However, although the distribution maps look busy, it is possible that a situation like that beside the Ecsegfalva meander was characterised by relative isolation, with people living much of the year in a small social unit. The site consists of small clusters of concentrated occupation remains, including abundant animal and other bones, profuse sherds from numerous pottery vessels, and burnt daub from built structures: facilities, shelters or even houses (Carneiro and Mateiciucová 2007). Here, as seemingly in most other Körös culture occupations so far investigated, people appeared to have ranged widely across their taskscapes and landscapes, reflected on the one hand in the range of bird, game and freshwater shellfish species present on the site, and on the other in the lithics imported from distances of up to 150 km to the north and east. Yet their principal activity appears to have been concentrated on raising and tending herds of sheep, and maintaining the intensive cultivation of small gardens for cereals. People may have been here much of the year if not year-round, suggested by the evidence for autumn sowing of cereals, the range of bird species, spring or early summer fishing, spring or early summer and autumn collection of freshwater shellfish, and so on (Bartosiewicz 2007; Bogaard *et al.* 2007; Gál 2007; Gulyás *et al.* 2007; Pike-Tay 2007; Pike-Tay *et al.* 2004). However, it is an open question whether all inhabitants were permanently resident. Hunting and lithic procurement would have taken people away from the site, and study of sheep teeth strongly suggests slaughter in autumn and winter, with the clear implication that at least some of the animals were moved elsewhere in the middle part of the year (Pike-Tay 2007; Pike-Tay *et al.* 2004). Spring or early summer flooding might have been one of the conditions in which animals were shifted elsewhere. The abundance of pottery might also be to do with seasonal or periodic aggregations, rather than simply the recurrence of domestic activity. The Ecsegfalva 23 site, finally, probably lasted for only some seventy to eighty years, down to the mid-57th century cal. BC (Bronk Ramsey *et al.* 2007).

Several different kinds and temporalities of memory can be suggested in the ways in which people dwelled in this setting (*cf.* Ingold 2000). Much of life may appear to have been carried on in an immediate present: building structures, herding animals, tending crops, procuring raw materials, interacting with co-residents, neighbours and others, and attending to the level of floodwaters when they came. Yet all these activities rely on working knowledge or memory of the affordances of the taskscape and the social landscape. Each of these activities also has a greater time-depth. It appears from the stratigraphy of the site that there was probably a cycle of occupation, certainly involving the burning and rebuilding of structures, and perhaps punctuated by short (or longer) periods of abandonment. To move animals to best advantage and to give full attention to flood waters and other dynamic features of the taskscape, people presumably relied on past experience. Intensive plots for cereal cultivation were probably built up over time, gardens coming to embody the investment of labour by several generations (Bogaard 2005; Bogaard *et al.* 2007). And people have to keep track of social relations and alliances, and remember where to go on long-distance trips.

Some activities may have had a further dimension which could have connected them to a more distant past, as well as to a wider social field. I have already drawn attention to the possible significance of sheep in the context of the Körös culture. These were animals from the south, perhaps not very well suited to the conditions of the river systems of the Great Hungarian Plain (Bartosiewicz 2007), and presumably distinctively recognisable by people – whatever their origin or descent – as being unlike any of the native fauna, in terms of appearance, behaviour, size and even sound. While they may have been taken for granted on a day-to-day basis by a date of 5750–5650 cal. BC, it remains possible that they also represented a living embodiment of part of an older history of origins and arrival. In tending to sheep, people lived with the sight and sound of their past. At the same time, sheep were quite routinely killed and consumed, and it is goats and deer which were selected for occasional representation on pottery (Kalicz 1970). The procurement of obsidian, limnoquarzite, radiolarite and hard stone such as hornfels from distant sources to the north, west and east (Mateiciucová 2001; 2004; 2007; Starnini and Szakmány 1998) could also have connected people to a sense of their past and varied descents (including, as already mooted, from among indigenous people in the region), and the wide range of sources used does indeed suggest that more than mere practicality was involved. Finally, the styles of pottery used daily and in periodic aggregations must have connected people to some sense of a wider social field, given the broad distributions of similar, though not identical, wares throughout the northern part of the Balkan Early Neolithic, in the Körös-Starčevo-Criş orbit. These were perhaps in sum less specific orientations than those suggested for the LBK in the period after 5500 cal. BC (Bradley 2002), but these connections and memories may still have been powerful aspects of identity for all that.

As in the cases reviewed in the opening part of this paper, memory may have thus have operated in different ways and at different times, in varying contexts. The treatment of the dead is a useful last example here, not least since it gives another point of comparison with the second case study. The sample of evidence for mortuary practices in the Körös culture is small, and virtually all excavations have been of more or less limited extent. But a trend has been observed for more female and child than male burials (Chapman 1994; Trogmayer 1969). At Ecsegfalva 23, only scattered human bones can be assigned to the Körös culture occupation (Guba *et al.* 2007); at Endrőd 119 to the south-west in the Körös valley itself, there are certainly infant burials belonging to the occupation, and at least one adult, though sex is not yet established (Makkay 1992, 132). I have questioned elsewhere (Whittle 1998; 2001; 2003) whether conceptually the Körös female was in some way more closely linked to place, and the Körös male to the wider surroundings. Mortuary ritual may have been in part a final settlement of connections, perhaps even often involving the deliberate forgetting of men. In the case of Ecsegfalva 23, the one intact

burial recovered proved to date to the succeeding AVK phase (Bronk Ramsey *et al.* 2007; Guba *et al.* 2007), the site being left perhaps now to spirits and ghosts, while occupation shifted some 300–400 m to the next high point eastwards along the meander.

Life was therefore carried forward here through and with a range of rememberings. Daily life was predicated on memory, but also drew in memories of older times and practices. As part of the immediacy of daily existence, people dwelled literally on top of the structures and residues of their forebears, some of their bones included. How long and in what fashion people were remembered as individuals after death (and indeed the nature of their individualism in life: Whittle 1998) remains an open question.

The Ascott-under-Wychwood long barrow: longevity of place and the duration and range of memory

At some time around 4000 cal. BC people in southern Britain began to turn to new practices: herding animals, tending cereals, making pottery, and making increasing use of stone and flint axes from distant sources. Unlike in the Great Hungarian Plain, this was not previously a largely empty landscape, but one long inhabited by foragers, though these were not necessarily ubiquitous. The descent of the people of the Early Neolithic in southern Britain is just as much disputed as elsewhere. Here we may have to do again with a combination or fusion of people from outside with indigenous population. A case might be made for greater movement of people from the outside into southern Britain compared to western Britain (Cummings and Whittle 2004), but the evidence remains ambiguous (see papers in Whittle and Cummings 2007). This remains, however, an absolutely central issue, since it affects our interpretation of the chains and kinds of memory that partly constitute changing worldviews, bringing in the possibility of the discontinuities stressed by Foucault (1972).

It has been conventional to link discussion of the beginning of new practices and worldviews with the emergence of various kinds of public architecture or monuments, including in southern Britain the long barrows and long cairns with their contents of collective remains of the dead, often taken as some kind of anonymous or generalised ancestors. The Ascott-under-Wychwood long barrow, my second case study, is one of those monuments. It lay in the upper Evenlode valley, a tributary of the upper Thames. It is part of the broader distribution of Cotswold long barrows, and locally one of a number scattered across the upper reaches of the Evenlode (Darvill 2004; Saville 1990, fig. 1). It is a substantial, trapezoidal barrow, edged with a stone façade, and contains two opposed sets of paired cists or small chambers, each probably originally with an outer passage connected to the long sides. With the exception of the outer cist on the north side, these – and the small space between the pairs of cists – contained a substantial deposit of human remains (Benson and Whittle 2007).

An extended programme of radiocarbon dating and the interpretation of its results within a Bayesian statistical framework, however, suggest that the monument was probably constructed in the 38th century cal. BC (Bayliss *et al.* 2007a; 2007b). The very similar Hazleton long cairn (Saville 1990) may have been built not long after Ascott-under-Wychwood (Meadows *et al.* 2007a), and there is no certain evidence that any other such barrow or cairn construction in southern Britain was begun before the 38th century cal. BC (Whittle *et al.* 2007). It has therefore begun to be possible to situate Ascott-under-Wychwood and similar constructions in much more precise chronological contexts. A variety of temporalities and kinds of memory seem to emerge.

The barrow and its contents were not the first things that constituted this place. The barrow overlay an occupation of the Early Neolithic, including a probable midden or area of more concentrated deposition, and one larger or two smaller timber structures. The southern cists cut into this midden, thereby linking the history of the barrow with an older history of the use of this place (McFadyen 2007), but very probably after a turfline had formed over the midden and the buried soil (McFadyen *et al.* 2007a; 2007b), and

very probably after an interval of not less than 50 years (Bayliss *et al.* 2007a; 2007b). The pre-barrow occupation can be dated to the 39th or 40th centuries cal. BC, and the midden was conceivably a short-lived episode within that (Bayliss *et al.* 2007a; 2007b). Occupation and midden, as in the rather different setting of the Great Hungarian Plain, testify to a range of activities: the tending and consumption of animals, including cattle and again sheep, the use of a range of wild game, the use if not manufacture of pottery, the working of flint, and the burning of fires or hearths (Barclay and Case 2007; Cramp 2007; Mulville and Grigson 2007).

Alongside the implied attachment to place and forays into the taskscape beyond, go again a series of relationships and knowledges that rely on working and other memories. Perhaps the most striking feature of this pre-barrow Early Neolithic phase is the concentration of finds into what has come to be called a midden. It could be that this is just the result of a small occupation, base camp or settlement. But it is at least as likely that this is some kind of deliberate and conscious accumulation of material, perhaps over a short period of time, which acted in turn as a mnemonic for what took place here: an active recognition perhaps of the differences of life in the 40th or 39th centuries cal. BC compared with what had come before. Such a view would imply a longer span of memory, and assumes a population of basically indigenous tradition (which is of course much disputed). There had, however, been similar middens in the Mesolithic period elsewhere in southern Britain (Pollard 2004; 2005), and such longevity of view is *prima facie* plausible. The immediacies of existence are once again probably linked to a sense of the past.

This can be further supported in the specific case of Ascott-under-Wychwood because, in turn, there is an even older history of use of this place, in the form of Mesolithic occupation under the barrow. This principally consists of scattered hearths and pits, and a flint assemblage. The bulk of the microliths in the flint assemblage have been identified as of earlier Mesolithic style, perhaps of eighth millennium cal. BC date (Cramp 2007) and the environmental evidence from stratified tree-throw pits (Evans *et al.* 2007; Evans 1972) also suggests that the sequence could go back into the earlier Mesolithic. There were only a few microliths of identifiable late style, and a couple of radiocarbon dates indicate some late fifth millennium cal. BC activity. The story may have been a punctuated one, with beginnings as a base of some kind or as a place chosen for repeated visits, followed by an episode of woodland regeneration somewhere in the middle of the Mesolithic, and then by sporadic further visits in the late fifth millennium.

The Mesolithic timescale is potentially over three or more millennia. Memory over such periods of time is hard for us to conceive (see Borić, this volume). The null hypothesis must be that such successions are merely the result of coincidence, but some linkage may have been made possible by generalised senses of place and remembering. Openings in the trees, tree-throw pits themselves, the texturing of the ground with hearth debris, stone tools and waste, and animal bone might all have left visual clues (a point I owe to the late John Evans). It is easy to 'explain' the Mesolithic choice of location by reference to a single activity (a good place to hunt) or outlook (a good viewpoint), but the place may have been valued for a combination of reasons, including its cumulative oldness.

The link between Mesolithic and Neolithic use of the place can now be measured over a much shorter, but unfortunately still imprecisely defined span of time. Similar sequences have of course been found at other Cotswold-Severn barrows and cairns, including Hazleton (Saville 1990) and Gwernvale (Britnell and Savory 1984). Did people in the 40th or 39th centuries cal. BC come again to the Ascott-under-Wychwood place because of memories and tales of predecessors doing the same thing, or were there still visual and material clues to earlier presences? In this case, there is even the intriguing possibility that people in the early fourth millennium cal. BC were conscious of the encounter with a very old place – the earlier Mesolithic occupation – because the microliths from it seem non-randomly concentrated in the midden (McFadyen *et al.* 2007a).

There was therefore already a long, though punctuated, history by the time that the monument came to be built in the 38th century cal. BC, very probably after an interval of not less than fifty years after the occupation and midden. Monuments of this kind have often been taken to be quick constructions (though that view has been challenged [McFadyen 2003]), while by contrast their jumbled human contents have often been seen as the result of extended processes of accumulation and sorting, which come to stand for anonymous ancestors and the idea of a collective past. In the event, both construction and deposition seem, on the basis of fresh analysis and modelling of radiocarbon dates, to have been rather rapid, probably over a timescale of three to five generations, taking a generation for the sake of argument to be twenty-five years long (Bayliss *et al.* 2007a; 2007b).

The barrow itself certainly has two major constructional phases, the eastern end being extended some 17 m beyond a plain stone façade to create a final horned, blind façade. At this late point in the building history, the long sides were probably linked by single façade walls (McFadyen *et al.* 2007b). The cists may have been one of the very earliest elements to be created, and from their position a long axial line defined by stakeholes, coursed stone and stacked turves was set out. From this offsets, variously defined by further stakeholes and small stone walls, created bays reaching to the eventual edges of the barrow. The central long axis was renewed along with the eastwards extension of the barrow. The bays were infilled by a complex process of placing earth, turf and stone; some bay walling did not extend through the whole height of the barrow, and the whole construction gives the impression of a series of small-scale events, combining probably rather rapidly to form the monument which we recognise today as a Cotswold barrow. It is estimated that the primary barrow was extended probably within a generation, with the last depositions being made probably in the 3640s to 3630s (Bayliss *et al.* 2007a; 2007b).

Earlier analysis of the human remains at Ascott-under-Wychwood proposed excarnation and redeposition of uniformly disarticulated remains as the main rite (Chesterman 1977), a view which is certainly not sustainable (Benson and Clegg 1978). Fresh analysis has both considerably reduced the likely number of people involved (in the six deposits, minimum numbers of from one to five people, with a probable combined minimum total of twenty-one) and highlighted the recurrence of articulated or articulating body parts, observable despite the demonstrable succession in most of the deposits (Galer 2007; Whittle *et al.* 2007b). There was, however, considerable diversity of rite and treatment.

From this new research, a rather different kind of perspective emerges. Though the physical barrow itself was an architecturally complex affair, its plan shows coherence and symmetrical form, which was surely planned from the start, and its execution was relatively rapid. The deposition of human remains not only involved a relatively small number of people, but was completed in three to five generations. This new set of interpretations has important implications for the kind of memory work going on in and at this barrow and others like it. While the human remains could have come to be regarded by subsequent generations or by outsiders as anonymous ancestors, for those involved in their deposition, they would have been adult men and women, juveniles and children, whose identities and personalities would have been intimately known. It is hard not to think of the cists as the locus for scenes of emotion and grief, even if particular corpses were deposited a little while after death. We have no easy way of telling how long such intimate memories would have been maintained, but it is possible that, like in the modern-day example I explored from my own family history earlier in the paper, they were really quite short-lived.

This presumed intimate and short history was attached, however, to a construction which perhaps stood for something much longer-lasting. Several aspects are important. First, the idea of the long barrow as some sort of evocation of the memory of the LBK longhouses starting in the sixth millennium cal. BC in central and western Europe has long been held (Bradley 2003; Whittle 2003; and references). While histories varied across this broad area, the last substantial longhouses in regions more adjacent to southern Britain might have been built in the mid-fifth millennium cal BC, while the Ascott-under-Wychwood long barrow was not built before the 38th century cal. BC, and the span over which this suggested long memory could have been carried could be even greater than the several centuries suggested by this reckoning (see also Darvill 2004). Given the brief discussion above of the instability of oral traditions and memory, what was remembered by the early fourth millennium cal BC was very probably not any exact recall of late sixth or early to mid-fifth millennium cal. BC events. That only matters if memory is seen in the first place as a matter of precise recapture, and the approach of Bergson, Bartlett and Bloch noted earlier in the paper strongly suggests otherwise. We might here be more interested in the maintenance of a chain of remembering.

On the other hand, the gap between the last continental longhouses and the first southern British long barrows and long cairns is now so considerable (see also again Darvill 2004) that other sources of the barrow idea have to be entertained. These may now include the timber structures or halls which certainly date to an early phase of the Neolithic in Britain and Ireland, though few if any have yet been as precisely dated as long barrows or cairns. In this case, the evocation in barrow/cairn form may be partly to do with something older, certainly something of the past, even if only a recent past, but partly also as much to do with commemorating the socialities of new practice, including perhaps shared place taking, construction, gathering and feasting.

Both sorts of explanation have tended to take the fact of monument construction for granted, as though that was destined from the start of the Neolithic of southern Britain to be an inevitable expression of social practice and cultural identity. But why build at all in these ways? Emerging more precise chronologies (Whittle *et al.* 2007a; forthcoming) suggest that for some two centuries or so people did not. I have suggested that the phenomenon of barrow building can now be seen as part of a gradual development, with people taking stock and making sense of changed existence and sets of relationships (Whittle 2007). It is telling that evocation of the past was involved in this process, perhaps as much psychological as purely social, but there may have been no single past at stake. Some sense of the past may have been invented in the process of coming to terms with new senses of identity. For example, the complex process of building at Ascott-under-Wychwood might itself be seen as a recreation or again an evocation of a long history, one in some way recognised as consisting of a series of short-term events, layered and interwoven, and in this instance seen as revolving around the existence of a perhaps close-knit family or other small social group. Supposing that a bay stood for a generation, the opposed bays or at least the equivalent space which held the pairs of cists would cover two generations, an estimate compatible perhaps with the likely minimum number of individuals from fresh analysis of the human remains. There are then another thirteen bays in the first main phase of the barrow. At say twenty-five years per generation, this could stand for a history going back in our sense of time for some four centuries. In the Tiv case mentioned earlier, the normal focus of genealogical reckoning was three or four generations, but the founder Tiv himself was reckoned at seventeen generations back (Bohannan 1952). For the Lugbara of central Africa, genealogies graded into mythical accounts of the first heroes and creation itself (Middleton 1960). Speculatively, the bay divisions might have stood for a created sense of time depth – real or not – as both legitimation and psychological prop in a changing world.

Conclusions

I have discussed just two sites in detail in this paper: a settlement of the earlier sixth millennium cal. BC on the Great Hungarian Plain, and a long barrow in southern Britain of the earlier fourth millennium cal. BC, built on a place used several times before, over a timescale of millennia. Such places and monuments, often assigned separate meanings and rather specific and restricted roles occupations

as the base for daily life, long barrows as the focus for generalised ancestral rites, might both better be seen as loci of diverse remembrance. In one sense, the sequences at both sites are uncannily similar – though the settings are worlds apart in most ways – since dwelling in various forms was succeeded by the places being left to the dead. In the case of the Great Hungarian Plain, the old place was presumably recognised, respected and therefore remembered – left to ghosts and spirits – as there is virtually no occupation contemporary with the AVK grave. In the case of the Cotswolds, the old place was surely remembered, but it was commemorated by further construction and the insertion of the dead. The dead here were few in number, and probably deposited over not more than three to five generations. If so, they were only a selection of the total population of the community or communities concerned. Did intense commemoration of some go hand in hand with the forgetting of others? And could we see this as something recurrent, since in the Körös world too there were probably forgettings of the men after their death?

If memory is both creative and fluid, there is much in these instances that is to do with the short-term immediacies of existence and active social and emotional bonds. But the diversity of memory shades off into longer timescales. Activities in the occupation on the Great Hungarian Plain evoke other connections and aspects of the past, while the southern British long barrow may also embed a narrative of personal relations in a deeper past. In this respect, however, the two situations are quite different. With the abandonment of one particular occupation beside a meander *c.* 5650 cal. BC, presumably settlement shifted to other locales nearby. Plenty are known from surface survey (Ecsedy *et al.* 1982; Jankovich *et al.* 1989) and on the basis of present knowledge life continued much as before; even in the succeeding AVK case, when longhouses certainly appeared in parts of the Great Hungarian Plain, the general tenor of existence was maintained, such that the Körös culture and the AVK constitute nearly a millennium of continuity. In the Cotswolds at Ascott-under-Wychwood, however, after an interval of not less than two generations after the cessation of the occupation and midden – long enough for a turfline to form (McFadyen *et al.* 2007a; 2007b) – a novel form of construction was initiated, here amongst the earliest we can presently suggest for southern Britain (Whittle *et al.* 2007a). People seemed to have used a mixture of pasts to come to terms with change. The literature has emphasised the role of the dead in this, particularly the collective and anonymous dead, but the Ascott-under-Wychwood study suggests that the known and personally remembered dead may have been of far greater concern. There were other themes too, perhaps including evocations of distant (in both temporal and geographical terms) pasts of longhouse worlds, in which memory merged into history and myth (*cf.* Hodder 2005), but also featuring references to immediately local histories of place and practice, for which material cues may have survived on the ground. There may also be an element of created or invented past.

Just two archaeological examples, when treated in detail, suggest to me that we have been too ready to set kinds of remembering into opposed and neatly defined categories. Our own modern experience does not equip us well to understand the longer timeframes explored here, though it could at least help us to recognise more fully the multiplicity of rememberings over the shorter term which constitute an element of our agency and which carry our lives forward.

Acknowledgements

I am very grateful to Dušan Borić and Columbia University for the invitation to take part in the New York conference. Dušan, Vicki Cummings, Ollie Harris and Lesley McFadyen helped with critical reading of earlier drafts of the text. I should also like to thank all those involved in the Ecsegfalva project, with whom it has been my privilege to work, and particularly here those whose research is cited in this paper: László Bartosiewicz, Joanna Bending, Amy Bogaard, Christopher Bronk Ramsey, Ângela Carneiro, Erika Gál, Zsuzsanna Guba, Sándor Gulyás, Thomas Higham, Glynis Jones, Inna Mateiciucová, Ildikó Pap, Anne Pike-Tay, Elisabetta Starnini, Pál Sümegi, Ildikó Szikossy and Anikó Tóth. The project from 1998–2001 was a cooperation between the Institute of Archaeology, Hungarian Academy of Sciences, Budapest; the Munkácsy Mihály Museum, Békéscsaba; and Cardiff University. I should like to thank Professor Csanád Bálint and Dr Imre Szatmári for all their help, Dr István Zalai-Gaál for his participation, and Dr Eszter Bánffy for her unfailing support. The excavations were funded by The British Academy, The Society of Antiquaries of London, The Humanities Research Board, The Arts and Humanities Research Board, The Prehistoric Society, and Cardiff University. I should like to thank all those involved in the Ascott-under-Wychwood long barrow publication project, carried out on behalf of English Heritage, and particularly here Alex Bayliss, the excavator Don Benson, Kate Cramp, the late John Evans, Dawn Galer and Lesley McFadyen. Jonathan Last of English Heritage gave unfailing support and guidance throughout. The site was excavated by Don Benson from 1965–1969 for the then Ministry of Works.

Bibliography

Barclay, A. and Case, H. (2007) The Early Neolithic Pottery and Fired Clay. In D. Benson and A. Whittle (eds) *Building Memories: the Neolithic Cotswold Long Barrow at Ascott-under-Wychwood, Oxfordshire*, 263–281. Oxford, Oxbow.

Barrett, J. C. (1994) *Fragments from Antiquity: An Archaeology of Social Life in Britain, 2900–1200 BC*. Oxford, Blackwell.

Barrett, J. C. (2000) A Thesis on Agency. In M.-A. Dobres and J. Robb (eds) *Agency in Archaeology*, 61–68. London, Routledge.

Barrett, J. C. (2001) Agency, the Duality of Structure, and the Problem of the Archaeological Record. In I. Hodder (ed.) *Archaeological Theory Today*, 141–164. Oxford, Blackwell.

Bartlett, F. C. (1932) *Remembering: A Study in Experimental and Social Psychology*. Cambridge, Cambridge University Press.

Bartosiewicz, L. (2007) Mammalian Bone. In A. Whittle (ed.) *The Early Neolithic on the Great Hungarian Plain: Investigations of the Körös Culture Site of Ecsegfalva 23, Co. Békés*, 287–325. Budapest,

Institute of Archaeology, Hungarian Academy of Sciences.

Bayliss, A., Benson, D., Bronk Ramsey, C., Galer, D., McFadyen, L., van der Plicht, J. and Whittle, A. (2007) Interpreting Chronology: the Radiocarbon Dating Programme. In D. Benson and A. Whittle (eds) *Building Memories: the Neolithic Cotswold Long Barrow at Ascott-under-Wychwood, Oxfordshire*, 221–236. Oxford, Oxbow.

Bayliss, A., Benson, D., Galer, D., Humphrey, L., McFadyen, L. and Whittle, A. (2007) One Thing After Another: The Date of the Ascott-under-Wychwood Long Barrow. *Cambridge Archaeological Journal* 17.1, supplement, 29–44.

Benson, D. and Clegg, I. (1978) Cotswold Burial Rites? *Man* 13, 134–137.

Benson, D. and Whittle, A. (eds) (2007) *Building Memories: the Neolithic Cotswold Long Barrow at Ascott-under-Wychwood, Oxfordshire*. Oxford, Oxbow.

Bergson, H. (1911) *Matter and Memory* (trans. N. M. Paul and W. S. Palmer, first published 1908). London, Allen and Unwin.

Bloch, M. E. F. (1998) *How We Think They Think: Anthropological Approaches to Cognition, Memory and Literacy*. Boulder, Westview.

Bogaard, A. (2005) 'Garden Agriculture' and the Nature of Early Farming in Europe and the Near East. *World Archaeology* 37, 177–196.

Bogaard, A., Bending, J. and Jones, G. (2007) Archaeobotanical Evidence for Plant Husbandry and Use. In A. Whittle (ed.) *The Early Neolithic on the Great Hungarian Plain: Investigations of the Körös Culture Site of Ecsegfalva 23, Co. Békés*, 421–445. Budapest, Institute of Archaeology, Hungarian Academy of Sciences.

Bohannan, L. (1952) A Genealogical Charter. *Africa* 22, 301–315.

Bradley, R. (2002) *The Past in Prehistoric Societies*. London, Routledge.

Britnell, W. and Savory, H. (1984) *Gwernvale and Penywyrlod: Two Neolithic Long Cairns in the Black Mountains of Brecknock*. Cardiff, Cambrian Archaeological Association.

Bronk Ramsey, C., Higham, T., Whittle, A. and Bartosiewicz, L. (2007) Radiocarbon Chronology. In A. Whittle (ed.) *The Early Neolithic on the Great Hungarian Plain: Investigations of the Körös Culture Site of Ecsegfalva 23, Co. Békés*, 173–188. Budapest, Institute of Archaeology, Hungarian Academy of Sciences.

Carneiro, Â. and Mateiciucová, I. (2007) Daub Fragments and the Question of Structures. In A. Whittle (ed.) *The Early Neolithic on the Great Hungarian Plain: Investigations of the Körös Culture Site of Ecsegfalva 23, Co. Békés*, 255–285. Budapest, Institute of Archaeology, Hungarian Academy of Sciences.

Chapman J. (1994) The Living, the Dead and the Ancestors, Time, Life Cycles and the Mortuary Domain in Later European Prehistory. In J. Davies (ed.) *Ritual and Remembrance: Responses to Death in Human Societies*, 40–85. Sheffield, Sheffield Academic Press.

Chesterman, J. T. (1977) Burial Rites in a Cotswold Long Barrow. *Man* 12, 22–32.

Chomsky, N. (1988) *Language and Problems of Knowledge*. Cambridge, Mass, and London, MIT Press.

Cramp, K. (2007) The Flint. In D. Benson and A. Whittle (eds) *Building Memories: the Neolithic Cotswold Long Barrow at Ascott-under-Wychwood, Oxfordshire*, 289–314. Oxford, Oxbow.

Cummings, V. and Whittle, A. (2004) *Places of Special Virtue: Megaliths in the Neolithic Landscapes of Wales*. Oxford, Oxbow.

Darvill, T. (2004) *Long Barrows of the Cotswolds and Surrounding Areas*. Stroud, Tempus.

Ecsedy, I., Kovács, L., Maráz, B. and Torma, I. (1982) *Magyarország Régészeti Topográfiája: a Szeghalmi járás IV/1*. Budapest, Akadémiai Kiadó.

Evans, J. G. (1972) *Land Snails in Archaeology*. London, Seminar Press.

Evans, J. G., Limbrey, S. and Macphail, R. (2007) The Environmental Setting. In D. Benson and A. Whittle (eds), *Building Memories: the Neolithic Cotswold Long Barrow at Ascott-under-Wychwood, Oxfordshire*, 55–77. Oxford, Oxbow.

Forty, A. and Küchler, S. (eds) (1999) *The Art of Forgetting*. Oxford and New York, Berg.

Foucault, M. (1972) *The Archaeology of Knowledge* (trans. A. M. Sheridan Smith). London, Tavistock Publications.

Gál, E. (2007) Bird Remains. In A. Whittle (ed.) *The Early Neolithic on the Great Hungarian Plain: Investigations of the Körös Culture Site of Ecsegfalva 23, Co. Békés*, 361–376. Budapest, Institute of Archaeology, Hungarian Academy of Sciences.

Galer, D. (2007) The Human Remains. In D. Benson and A. Whittle (eds) *Building Memories: the Neolithic Cotswold Long Barrow at Ascott-under-Wychwood, Oxfordshire*, 189–220. Oxford, Oxbow.

Guba, Z., Szikossy, I. and Pap, I. (2007) Anthropological Analysis of the Human Skeletal Remains. In A. Whittle (ed.) *The Early Neolithic on the Great Hungarian Plain: Investigations of the Körös Culture Site of Ecsegfalva 23, Co. Békés*, 461–467. Budapest, Institute of Archaeology, Hungarian Academy of Sciences.

Gulyás, S., Tóth, A. and Sümegi, P. (2007) The Zooarchaeological Analysis of Freshwater Bivalve Shells and their Relevance Regarding the Life of a Neolithic Community. In A. Whittle (ed.) *The Early Neolithic on the Great Hungarian Plain: Investigations of the Körös Culture Site of Ecsegfalva 23, Co. Békés*, 395–411. Budapest, Institute of Archaeology, Hungarian Academy of Sciences.

Hodder, I. (2005) The Spatio-Temporal Organization of the Early 'Town' at Çatalhöyök. In D. Bailey, A. Whittle and V. Cummings (eds) *(Un)settling the Neolithic*, 126–139. Oxford, Oxbow.

Ingold, T. (2000) *The Perception of the Environment: Essays in Livelihood, Dwelling and Skill*. London, Routledge.

Jankovich, B. D., Makkay J. and Szőke B. M. (1989) *Magyarország Régészeti Topográfiája: a Szarvasi járás IV/2*. Budapest, Akadémiai Kiadó.

Kalicz, N. (1970) *Clay Gods*. Budapest, Corvina.

Küchler, S. (1987) Malangan – Art and Memory in a Melanesian Society. *Man* 22, 238–255.

Kwint, M., Breward, C. and Aynsley, J. (eds) (1999) *Material Memories: Design and Evocation*. Oxford and New York, Berg.

Makkay, J. (1992) Excavations at the Körös Culture Settlement of Endrőd-Örgeszőlőg 119 in 1986–1989. In S. Bökönyi (ed.) *Cultural and Landscape Changes in South-east Hungary. 1. Reports on the Gyomaendrőd Project*, 121–193. Budapest, Institute of Archaeology, Hungarian Academy of Sciences.

Mateiciucová, I. (2001) Silexindustrie in der Ältesten Linearbandkeramik-Kultur in Mähren und Niederösterreich auf der Basis der Silexindustrie des Lokalmesolithikums. In R. Kertész and J. Makkay (eds) *From the Mesolithic to the Neolithic*, 283–299. Budapest, Archaeolingua.

Mateiciucová, I. (2004) Mesolithic Traditions and the Origin of the Linear Pottery Culture (LBK). In A. Lukes and M. Zvelebil (eds) *LBK Dialogues: Studies in the Formation of the Linear Pottery Culture*, 91–107. Oxford, British Archaeological Reports.

Mateiciucová, I. (2007) Worked Stone: Obsidian and Flint. In A. Whittle (ed.) *The Early Neolithic on the Great Hungarian Plain: Investigations of the Körös*

Culture Site of Ecsegfalva 23, Co. Békés, 677–726. Budapest, Institute of Archaeology, Hungarian Academy of Sciences.

McFadyen, L. (2003) *A Revision of the Materiality of Architecture: The Significance of Neolithic Long Mound and Chambered Monument Building Practice, with Particular Reference to the Cotswold-Severn Group*. Unpublished PhD thesis, University of Wales College, Newport.

McFadyen, L. (2007) Making Architecture. In D. Benson and A. Whittle (eds) *Building Memories: the Neolithic Cotswold Long Barrow at Ascott-under-Wychwood, Oxfordshire*, 348–354. Oxford, Oxbow.

McFadyen, L., Benson, D. and Whittle, A. (2007a) The Pre-Barrow Contexts. In D. Benson and A. Whittle (eds) *Building Memories: the Neolithic Cotswold Long Barrow at Ascott-under-Wychwood, Oxfordshire*, 23–54. Oxford, Oxbow.

McFadyen, L., Benson, D. and Whittle, A. (2007b) The Long Barrow. In D. Benson and A. Whittle (eds) *Building Memories: the Neolithic Cotswold Long Barrow at Ascott-under-Wychwood, Oxfordshire*, 79–136. Oxford, Oxbow.

Meadows, J., Barclay, A. and Bayliss, A. (2007) A Short Passage of Time: The Dating of the Hazleton Long Cairn Revisited. *Cambridge Archaeological Journal* 17.1, supplement, 45–64.

Middleton, J. (1960) *Lugbara Religion: Ritual and Authority Among an East African People*. London, Oxford University Press.

Mulville, J. and Grigson, C. (2007) The Animal Bones. In D. Benson and A. Whittle (eds) *Building Memories: the Neolithic Cotswold Long Barrow at Ascott-under-Wychwood, Oxfordshire*, 237–253. Oxford, Oxbow.

Pike-Tay, A. (2007) Skeletochronological Evidence for Seasonal Culling of Caprines. In A. Whittle (ed.) *The Early Neolithic on the Great Hungarian Plain: Investigations of the Körös Culture Site of Ecsegfalva 23, Co. Békés*, 331–342. Budapest, Institute of Archaeology, Hungarian Academy of Sciences.

Pike-Tay, A., Bartosiewicz, L., Gál, E. and Whittle, A. (2004) Body Part Representation and Seasonality: Sheep/Goat, Bird and Fish Remains from Early Neolithic Ecsegfalva 23, SE Hungary. *Journal of Taphonomy* 2, 221–246.

Pollard, J. (2004) The Art of Decay and the Transformation of Substance. In C. Renfrew, E. DeMarrais and C. Gosden (eds) *Substance, Memory, Display: Archaeology and Art*, 47–62. Cambridge, McDonald Institute for Archaeological Research.

Pollard, J. (2005) Memory, Monuments and Middens in the Neolithic Landscape. In G. Brown, D. Field and D. McOmish (eds) *The Avebury Landscape: Aspects of the Field Archaeology of the Marlborough Downs*, 103–114. Oxford, Oxbow.

Saville, A. (1990) *Hazleton North: The Excavation of a Neolithic Long Cairn of the Cotswold-Severn Group*. London, English Heritage.

Starnini, E. (2001) The Mesolithic/Neolithic Transition in Hungary: The Lithic Perspective. In R. Kertész and J. Makkay (eds) *From the Mesolithic to the Neolithic*, 395–404. Budapest, Archaeolingua.

Starnini, E. and Szakmány, G. (1998) The Lithic Industry of the Neolithic Sites of Szarvas and Endrőd (South-Eastern Hungary): Techno-Typological and Archaeometrical Aspects. *Acta Archaeologica Academiae Scientiarum Hungaricae* 50, 279–342.

Sutton, D. E. (1998) *Memories Cast in Stone: The Relevance of the Past in Everyday Life*. Oxford and New York, Berg.

Sutton, D. E. (2001) *Remembrance of Repasts: an Anthropology of Food and Memory*. Oxford and New York, Berg.

Taylor, A. C. (1993) Remembering to Forget: Identity, Mourning and Memory among the Jivaro. *Man* 28, 653–678.

Trogmayer, O. (1969) Die Bestattungen der Körös-Gruppe. *A Móra Ferenc Múzeum Évkönyve* 2, 5–15.

Updike, J. (1991) *Rabbit is Rich*. London, Penguin Omnibus edition.

Whittle, A. (1998) Beziehungen Zwischen Individuum und Gruppe: Fragen zur Identität im Neolithikum der ungarischen Tiefebene. *Ethnographisch-Archäologische Zeitschrift* 39, 465–487.

Whittle, A. (2001) Different Kinds of History: On the Nature of Lives and Change in Central Europe, c. 6000 to the Second Millennium BC. In W.G. Runciman (ed.) *The Origin of Human Social Institutions*, 39–68. Oxford, Oxford University Press.

Whittle, A. (2003) *The Archaeology of People: Dimensions of Neolithic Life*. London, Routledge.

Whittle, A. (2007) Building Memories. In D. Benson and A. Whittle (eds) *Building Memories: the Neolithic Cotswold Long Barrow at Ascott-under-Wychwood, Oxfordshire*, 361–364. Oxford, Oxbow.

Whittle, A. and Cummings, V. (eds) (2007) *Going Over: The Mesolithic-Neolithic Transition in North-West Europe*. London, The British Academy.

Whittle, A., Barclay, A., Bayliss, A., McFadyen, L., Schulting, R. and Wysocki, M. (2007a) Building for the Dead: Events, Processes and Changing Worldviews from the 38th to the 34th centuries cal BC in Southern Britain. *Cambridge Archaeological Journal* 17.1, supplement, 123–147.

Whittle, A., Galer, D. and Benson, D. (2007b) The Layout and Composition of the Human Bone Deposits. In D. Benson and A. Whittle (eds) *Building Memories: the Neolithic Cotswold Long Barrow at Ascott-under-Wychwood, Oxfordshire*, 137–188. Oxford, Oxbow.

Whittle, A., Healy, F. and Bayliss, A. (forthcoming) *Gathering Time: Dating the Early Neolithic Enclosures of Southern Britain and Ireland*. Oxford, Oxbow.

3. Happy forgetting? Remembering and dismembering dead bodies at Vlasac

Dušan Borić

… our celebrated duty of memory is proclaimed in the form of an exhortation not to forget. But at the same time and in the same fell swoop, we shun the spectre of a memory that would never forget anything. We even consider it to be monstrous.

(Ricoeur 2004, 414)

Introduction

This paper is a reflection on one of my previous accounts about social memory in the prehistoric past. The paper was forced into existence by the evidence that had come to light through a recent excavation of a site that previously I had been able to study only from archival data. New evidence triggered not only the question of remembering in relation to accounts of social memory but also the question of forgetting. While remembering may be crucial for the continuation of social institutions and identity construction as much for an individual as for a social group, how important or vital is forgetting for social existence? Moreover, if one can argue for 'happy memory' of a particular moment triggered by a sudden and unexpected awakening of the past from a reserve of memories (*sensu* Bergson), can we also have happy forgetting and a reserve of necessary forgetfulness? I aim to show that specific practices associated with the treatment of dead human bodies at the Mesolithic-Neolithic site of Vlasac in the Danube Gorges of the north-central Balkans left traces that indicate both processes of remembering and forgetting as constitutive of a particular way of existence. Furthermore, these series of material engagements in the treatment of whole and dismembered dead bodies bear homological similarities with the ways

in which architectural features were referenced, remembered and dismembered.

In 2003, I published a paper arguing for striking long-term continuities in the archaeological sequences of Mesolithic-Neolithic sites in the region of the Danube Gorges of the north-central Balkans (Borić 2003). At sites such as Lepenski Vir, the type site of the sequence, I was able to show that memory worked through a series of on-site material engagements that included the spatial referencing of much older features and burials by later inhabitants, who habitually dwelt in the same landscape as their forebears more than a thousand years before them. I argued that it is possible to characterise this sequence as an obsession with 'deep time' and their own past. By *citing traces* of the previous existence at the same locales, these groups might have been *recapitulating* their adherence to a particular way of belonging, or way-of-being and 'common destiny' (*sensu* Heidegger) grounded in the past. This regional group can even be seen as consciously re-creating their specific cultural 'identity'. But, immediate epistemological and methodological questions stemmed from these first impressions. First, how was this long continuity of practices transmitted?; second, to what extent were meanings associated with such practices changed over many centuries and many human generations?; third, how was the dynamic between remembering and forgetting playing out in everyday practice?; and, finally, is the notion of cultural 'identity' helpful, *i.e.* does it best serve us in discussing the evidence of this case study?

Before I examine the empirical evidence for this obsessive referencing of past practices and places in the studied sequence, first I discuss general issues related to the survival of memory and scales of remembering. What are appropriate methodological tools to qualify the type of memory encountered in a particular archaeological record? These considerations are followed by the presentation of the case study. Finally, I discuss the relationship between memory and forgetting by resorting to the field of phenomenological philosophy as well as by evoking some examples from the ethnographies of non-Western societies.

Scaling memory

Some recent archaeological approaches that deal with the issue of social memory in the prehistoric past addressed the question of how far back a collectivity can be expected to remember in the absence of written documents. Bradley (2001) suggested that we can hardly expect that people within traditional, pre-industrial societies, *i.e.* the type of societies we may expect in the prehistoric past, could have remembered particular events and individuals more than 200 years back in time. In their discussions about 'prehistoric histories', Gosden and Lock (1998) make a distinction between genealogical and mythical links to the past, *i.e.* about various levels on which social memory might have worked in prehistory: from explicit links through remembering particular forebears and more distant ancestors through various shades of more anonymous figures of mythical pasts, such as paradigmatic heroes and divinities. In the same vein, Mircea Eliade has claimed that historical memory can hardly survive more than 200 to 300 years without turning to societal archetypes.

> The recollection of a historical event or a real personage survives in popular memory for two or three centuries at the utmost. This is because popular

memory finds difficulty in retaining individual events and real figures. The structures by means of which it functions are different: categories instead of events, archetypes instead of historical personages. The historical personage is assimilated to his mythical model (hero, etc.), while the event is identified with the category of mythical actions (fight with a monster, enemy brothers, etc.). If certain epic poems preserve what is called 'historical truth', this truth almost never has to do with a definite persons and events, but with institutions, customs, landscapes (Eliade 1959, 43).

Stratigraphic and contextual analyses of the archaeological record coupled with a strategic absolute dating of particular contexts/features are relevant and common archaeological means in understanding the continuity and persistence of particular practices over time. In this way, one could show whether objects are used in a secondary context by being taken out of the context of their primary deposition and passed down and subsequently 'bricolaged' into temporally later contexts, perhaps as important heirlooms with some special significance attached to them or holding some specific meaning. It is quite another but related question whether such objects were understood in the same way as in their primary context, *i.e.* whether 'originary' meanings attached to them (assuming that even these 'originary' meanings are socially shared) have changed in this type of transformation from one temporal context to another. A philosophical aspect of this basic question of the persistence of something that is *of the past* and that survives into the present, as a *trace* of past agency, is discussed in the introduction to this volume (Borić, this volume). Although prehistoric archaeologists can rarely be certain of specific meanings when dealing with long periods of time over which numerous diachronic transformations took place, one could at least ascertain that particular materialities were kept for periods of time, or that there was a conscious referring to older settlement features in the spatial layout of architectural units, burials, etc. By comparing respective dates of such different features and their association with particular objects, one could estimate the duration of the use lives in the case of architectural units or burial locations (see below), or define differences between primary and secondary temporal contexts in which objects, or their parts, are found.

Another important distinction could possibly be made here when discussing archaeological means of accessing questions of memory and culture transmission over time. This distinction refers to the discursive *vs.* non-discursive character of daily practices. While discursive transmission of meaning over time depends on the conscious effort of making explicit and *meaningful* links to the past, non-discursive practices refer to repetitive everyday rhythms, which continuously re-produced ingrained ways of doing and acting in a particular way (see Bourdieu 1990; de Certeau 1984). It is such practices that are largely responsible for the creation of accumulative patterns in an archaeological record. For instance, through the continuing use of particular areas in settlements for middens or perhaps even building one house over another, repeating the same outline, the long continuities of such practices become rendered visible (*e.g.* Hodder 1998a). Such links to the past derive from everyday memory but do not utilise the past through a conscious act of remembering. The exact meanings of these practices are often not emphasised and practices are taken for granted, being prone to constant negotiation and appropriation since they can loose their 'originary' significance over time (*cf.* Buchli 1995). A frequently quoted ethnographic example of such a situation is given by the anthropologist Maurice Bloch in his discussion of the meaning of carvings on wooden pillars found among the Zafimaniry living in the eastern forest of Madagascar (Bloch 1998). One may in fact question to what extent any practice or particular objects inherited from the past could be said to have preserved their 'originary' significance and meanings.

On the other hand, a discursive way of remembering can be connected to the concept of the 'invention of culture' (Wagner 1981) or the 'invention of tradition'. Through such practices, even in the absence of written documents, re-shaped meanings connected to significantly old practices or materialities, whose form or aesthetics may remain constant and unaltered, can be transmitted over significant temporal distances. To some extent, discursive practices of cultural transmission also relate to the question of 'manipulation' of memory but not necessarily to the abuses of memory (see Ricoeur 2004, 448–452). The invention of tradition can be described as the intentional act of renewing certain practices and customs, sticking to particular material and aesthetic forms and objects with roots in the past in new spatial and temporal contexts. In such new contexts, these old-new practices can have a different function and significance and are associated with different meanings.

> The tendency of culture is to sustain itself, by inventing itself. [...] Culture is ambiguous [...] we cling to our Culture, its proud tradition, its powerful techniques, its history and literature, its impressive rows of Great Names, over and above all attempts to reinvent it (Wagner 1981, 60).

Yet, the instability of meanings aside, what makes these practices of invention different from those non-discursive practices of repeating ingrained routines of habitual memory, where the original meaning is lost with the passage of time, is the fact that the invention of tradition is a conscious and intentional use of the past potency by drawing on the past as a potent archive for future-oriented action. Through narrative elaboration and re-interpretation of past contexts in such acts of reinvention or renewal new meanings are evoked: '[t]he interpretation is completely dependent on the invention, and the invention is completely dependent upon the interpretation' (Wagner 1981, 58). Although it can be said that these acts of the invention of tradition are arbitrary, they do rely on the conscious effort of a community or particular groups to elaborate on what is picked up as relevant aspects of the 'real' past.

> All meaningful expression, and therefore all experience and understanding, is a kind of invention, and invention requires a communicational base in shared conventions if it is to be meaningful ... (Wagner 1981, 36).

Thus, in order to appear convincing and believable, such awakening of the past is objectified frequently through material engagements and surviving materialities. And it is exactly the 'promiscuous' nature of material culture (Thomas 1991, *passim*), freely passing from one temporal and social context to another, that may enable such processes of legitimisation. Such a role granted to material culture and its narrative configuring (*e.g.* through myths) in the process that goes under the rubric of the invention of tradition offers archaeologists means of examining such social phenomena that explicitly and consciously evoke recent or more distant pasts.

For a moment, one could leave separate the question of the continuity of meaning from the importance of showing in which cases past traces were referred to and what types of materialities were imbued with non-discursive and discursive aspects of past actions. A contextual analysis of different strands of evidence could offer clues to what certain practices might have signified in a particular context. In what follows, I will review aspects of memory construction in the Mesolithic-Neolithic context of the Danube Gorges by examining the evidence of both remembering and forgetting. In addition, the important aspect of this examination does not only bear relevance to the problematic of remembering and forgetting but also, through the examination of the attitudes toward a dead human body, is relevant for understanding in what ways the materiality of the deceased's body and its constitutive parts were conceptualised in terms of their potency and agency.

Remembering by citing: Architecture and burials in the Danube Gorges

A number of Mesolithic-Neolithic sites in the Danube Gorges of the north-central Balkans have become known since their rescue excavations in the 1960s and 1970s. The eponymous site of Lepenski Vir is well known for its buildings with trapezoidal-shaped bases covered with limestone plaster. There were rectangular stone-lined hearths in the centre of each building while ornamented boulder artworks were found on the floor level, usually around the hearth (*e.g.* Borić 2005; Radovanović 1996; Srejović 1972). There were also numerous

burials found at this and other sites (more than 500 burials from twelve sites) that show a great diversity of ways and contexts of interment: placed both over and beneath building floors, or buried as primary or secondary inhumations in the space between buildings in various parts of the settlement. The most prominent phase with trapezoidal buildings at Lepenski Vir is confined chronologically to a period of only several centuries (*c.* 6200–5900 cal. BC, Borić and Dimitrijević 2007; 2009), reflecting a rather specific historical moment in the diachronic trajectory of the population inhabiting this region.

The earliest dated evidence for the occupation of open-air sites along the Danube's banks can be traced back to the period after *c.* 10,000 cal. BC. At Lepenski Vir and the neighbouring sites of Padina and Vlasac, several burials as well as occupational residues associated with stone constructions can be dated back to this early period (Bonsall *et al.* 2000; Borić and Dimitrijević 2007; 2009; Borić and Miracle 2004). It seems that during this early phase various locales along the Danube were recognised both for their excellent positioning in specialised fishing but also as places imbued with some symbolic significance, which is reflected in continuous interments of selected individuals at these settlement sites.

Mapping seated burials onto architecture?
The most intriguing group among these early burials, found at all three aforementioned and several other sites, were those placed as seated burials with crossed legs in a lotus position, facing the River Danube (Fig. 3.1). Recently, three seated burials with crossed legs from these three sites have been dated and they are confined to the Early Mesolithic phase with the following ranges at 95 per cent confidence: 8286 to 7749 cal. BC (Vlasac, Burial 17, AA-57776, Borić *et al.* 2008), 8237 to 7761 cal. BC (Padina, Burial 15, OxA-17145, unpublished data) and 8170–7594 cal. BC (Lepenski Vir, Burial 69, OxA-11703, Bonsall *et al.* 2004, 2008) (see Fig. 3.2). At the sites where seated lotus burials appear only one such burial has been found per site with the exception of the site of Padina, where at least two

Fig. 3.1 Seated inhumation with crossed legs in the lotus position, Burial 17, Vlasac (8286 to 7749 cal. BC at 95 per cent confidence) (photo: Centre for Archaeological Research, Faculty of Philosophy, Belgrade).

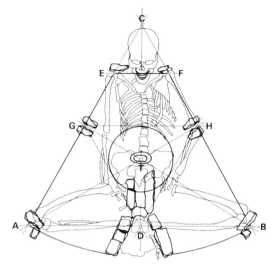

Fig. 3.2 Srejović's hypothesis about a meaningful correspondence between the lotus position of Burial 69 (c. 8200–7700 BC) from Lepenski Vir and the architectural shape of much later trapezoidal buildings dated to period c. 6200–5900 BC (after Srejović 1981: 40).

neighbouring burials were found in this position. The chronological positioning of this group of contemporaneous burials is of great importance for evaluating previous arguments that have implied the process of mapping of this body position onto architecture of trapezoidal buildings (Srejović and Babović 1983; for ethnographic analogies see Hugh-Jones and Carsten 1995, 42). According to this argument, the shape that the body takes when placed in this position was a metaphoric referent, *i.e.* template, for the construction of the architectural form of later trapezoidal buildings (Fig. 3.2). If this is to be the case, in the light of new dating evidence, a significant leap of remembering on behalf of builders of trapezoidal buildings has to be assumed and one needs to take this suggestion carefully into consideration.

The trapezoidal buildings, which became most elaborately built at Lepenski Vir and Padina after *c.* 6200 cal. BC, were more than a thousand years younger than the burials placed in the lotus seated position and such a chronological gap would exclude any reasonable connection between the burials and buildings. On the other hand, the prototypes of the Lepenski Vir trapezoidal buildings are most likely built from at least around 7000–6900 cal. BC as the radiocarbon dates from the site of Vlasac indicate (Borić *et al.* 2008). Yet, even with this reduction of the chronological gap between the date for seated burials and the first

experimentation with the trapezoidal building outlines, a minimum of 700 years must have separated these two types of features.

Persuasive and attractive as the connection between them may be, could we actually envision that a specific, and one may add a fairly limited burial practice, remained significantly present in the social memory or was revived and transmitted into a new architectural domain 700, and likely more, years after it had ceased being practiced? One could perhaps argue that the mythical significance might have been connected with these seated burials and that the importance of such a bodily position of mythical figures was transmitted through narrative forms although not reproduced any more in the mortuary domain. According to such a scenario, after several long centuries, due to the process that could be described as the 'invention of tradition' (see above), the shape of these burials from the mythical past with the complexity of associations they might have been surrounded with becomes reified in the shape of first trapezoidal buildings. Yet, if one is to make a more concrete and believable case out of this mere speculation primarily based on the evidence of absence, it would be necessary to find some material clues to connect the two phenomena. Perhaps one could argue by elimination. First, if looking for the material traces of the invention of tradition and metaphoric importance of the lotus position seated burials for the trapezoidal shape of later buildings, it would be reasonable to assume that there might have been a recognition of these early burials in later times through acts of exhumation and reburial. However, there is no evidence for such practices and it seems that all of the mentioned seated burials were left intact after their primary inhumation (see Fig. 3.1). Second, could one see a significant spatial relation between seated burials and later trapezoidal buildings? The seated burials with crossed legs from Lepenski Vir and Padina were found close to some trapezoidal buildings but there were other older burials placed equally close to some buildings, and this can hardly be a sufficient proof for a conscious referencing of these separate temporal contexts. At this point, one is forced to admit the limit in providing any firm material evidence in connecting the form of seated burials and architectural features in the Danube Gorges. As it will be indicated below, the shape of trapezoidal buildings could better be explained by a different act of resemblance – the one between a landscape feature and architecture.

Architectural citing and reinvention of tradition

> This invention … can be said to occur whenever and wherever some 'alien' or 'foreign' set of conventions is brought into relation with one's own (Wagner 1981, 10).

In contrast to the previous speculation about mapping architecture onto an iconic body position, perhaps a more convincing example of how social memory at Lepenski Vir might have worked over the long-term and through a series of material engagements relates to the example of intentional 'citing' of old and previously abandoned hearths by newly built trapezoidal buildings. This discussion owes a lot to new AMS dates obtained for these architectural features. On the basis of the current evidence, the earliest form of a more elaborate architecture recognised in the record of the Gorges' sites are rectangular stone-

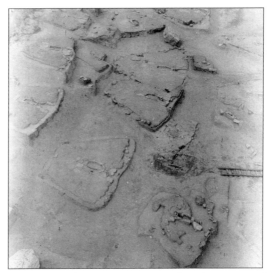

Fig. 3.3 Hearth 'a' (c. 7500–7200 BC) and superimposed Houses 41, 38, 37 (c. 6200–5900 BC) (photo: Srejović 1969: Fig. 10).

lined hearths. Before they became the integral and central feature of trapezoidal structures at Lepenski Vir, such hearths seem to have been either open-air features or central parts of a very light shelter with no elaborate furnishing of the living floor as seen in later trapezoidal buildings. It still remains insufficiently understood as to when such stone-lined hearths appeared as a recognisable local architectural feature for the first time. However, they can certainly be dated back to mid-eighth millennium BC if not earlier (Borić and Dimitrijević 2009).

One recently dated hearth from Lepenski Vir is particularly relevant in this context. Hearth 'a' is found next to a sequence of several partly overlapped trapezoidal buildings (Fig. 3.3). On the photograph showing this hearth, one can clearly recognise a dark oval surface around the hearth that seems to indicate the existence of an occupation zone. This zone was also associated with a concentration of animal bones left behind after the abandonment of this feature. There are two recent AMS dates associated with this hearth (Borić and Dimitrijević 2009). One is made on an animal bone from the concentration left next to the hearth, while the other date is made on an isolated human mandible Burial 22, found beside the hearth. The first date indicates that the hearth might have been connected to the period 7678 to 7593 cal. BC at 64 per cent confidence (7740–7587 cal. BC at 95 per cent confidence: OxA-16074). The second date, made on the human mandible, after the correction for the freshwater reservoir effect (see Bonsall *et al.* 1997; 2000; Cook *et al.* 2002), falls in the range 7526 to 7354 cal. BC at 64 per cent confidence (7580–7190 cal. BC at 95 per cent confidence: AA-57781). We may speculate that the later date for the mandible may indicate that its deposition in association with this feature might have been related to its abandonment, as an act of structured deposition. The dates obtained for this feature would put it into the late phase of the Early Mesolithic in this region, *i.e.* the later period of the Proto-Lepenski Vir phase at this site (Borić and Dimitrijević 2007; 2009).

The date of the mentioned Proto-Lepenski Vir hearth is of particular relevance when one examines the spatial sequence of placing later trapezoidal buildings at this location (Fig. 3.3). Thus, stratigraphically the earliest trapezoidal building, House 41, partly overlaps the oval zone around this hearth. Further, in the sequence of horizontal displacement spatially in the same direction, the floor of later House 38 overlaps the corner of House 41. Finally, the floor of House 37 cuts into the corner of House 38, damaging it partially. The latest building at this location, House 37, overlaps remains of an older fireplace found beneath the rear end of its floor and, also, cuts through an earlier building, House 42. The latest building, House 37, is now dated in the range 6048 to 5990 cal. BC at 64 per cent confidence (6071 to 5978 cal. BC at 95 per cent confidence: OxA-16082, Borić and Dimitrijević 2009). Such a date corresponds well with a representative series of dates recently obtained for a number of buildings belonging to the same phase – Lepenski Vir I–II (*c.* 6200–5900 BC). It is also likely that if one would attempt the dating of the earliest trapezoidal building in this sequence of overlapped buildings, House 41, the date of its construction/use would likely be around 6200 cal. BC, similar to other stratigraphically comparable and now absolutely dated buildings.

Such dating reveals a gap of at least a millennium between the dating of Proto-Lepenski Vir Hearth 'a' and the first building at this location House 41. Yet, it seems that the builders of House 41 recognised this old and, probably at the time of its building, long ago abandoned hearth.

This conclusion is also supported by the fact that in contrast to other neighbouring sites in the Upper Gorge of the Danube, such as Vlasac and Padina, at Lepenski Vir, the currently available series of sixty-seven obtained AMS dates indicates a gap in the occupation of this site during the regional Late Mesolithic period, *c.* 7200–6200 cal. BC (Borić and Dimitrijević 2007; 2009). The already mentioned date for Burial 22 found in connection with Hearth 'a' is presently the latest Early Mesolithic date for Lepenski Vir. The ensuing phase I–II at the site starts only around 6200 cal. BC, which is in turn the start date for the first Early Neolithic settlements across the Balkans. It is hard to exclude the possibility that future dating at Lepenski Vir would produce dates for the Late Mesolithic occupation and that the construction of trapezoidal buildings might have destroyed Late Mesolithic occupation zones. Yet, on the basis of the current data, one is forced to postulate a chronological gap of at least a thousand years between the Mesolithic occupation sequence and the phase with trapezoidal buildings.

This instance seems to indicate significant depths of memory in the Danube Gorges. There are more such instances at Lepenski Vir (Borić 2003) that indicate the intentional recognition of at the time almost millennium old features by the spatial placement of later phase buildings. It also seems that the practice of overlapping and physical touching of older by younger architectural features followed the same principle both when later trapezoidal buildings referenced a much older hearth feature and when younger trapezoidal buildings referenced older ones. As my further discussion will aim to show, there seems to be an underlying cultural principle in spatial patterning at work here that homologically connects the treatment and spatial positioning of architectural features with an analogous pattern of treatment when it comes to dead human bodies.

It is likely that the re-occupation of Lepenski Vir and construction of trapezoidal buildings in an elaborate way, unprecedented for the whole region of the Danube Gorges, related to the cultural shift that around 6200 cal. BC introduced a number of elements of the Neolithic world into the Danube Gorges forager communities. Among these elements were pottery, Spondylus beads and quite possibly new social, ideological and likely religious values (Borić 2007b). It seems that this old locale became the central place for the community that had inhabited the Upper Gorge of the Danube. By constructing a site such as Lepenski Vir at this time, they might have elaborated on old myths, recreating and building upon their own tradition in order to better fit into the newly emerged world of the Neolithic with its emphasis on the domestic area and the physical building – the 'house' as the central social institution (Borić 2007a; 2008). In such a historical moment, the Danube fisher-foragers developed the area around the central rectangular hearth at Lepenski Vir, as well as at the neighbouring site of Padina, in the form of a trapeze, covering the floor area with limestone of reddish-pinkish colour. The most elaborate construction of trapezoidal buildings took place at Lepenski Vir and it must have been directly related to the trapezoidal Treskavac Mountain found exactly across the Danube from Lepenski Vir. This remarkable landmark most clearly supplied this community with an amazingly durable blueprint of the building floor they started creating, thus symbolically and ideologically making a visual statement about the local grounding of this community. Hence the recognition of the importance of the spatial positioning of Lepenski Vir, followed by its reoccupation and flourishing as the focal point of this community during the phase with trapezoidal buildings (phase I–II), *i.e. c.* 6200–5900 cal. BC. At the same time, the community promoted the new 'house' ideology of the expanding Neolithic world by accepting/adjusting to new practices and materialities.

This very practice of building trapezoidal outlines covered with crushed reddish limestone for the first time appeared around 7000 cal. BC at the neighbouring site of Vlasac (Borić *et al.*

2008), perhaps as the echo of similar practices in the wider eastern Mediterranean world (Borić 2007a), and was then centuries later revived and further elaborated at Lepenski Vir around 6200 cal. BC with essentially the same and recognisable constructional elements. It seems that during the Late Mesolithic phase at Vlasac the practice died out but became relevant again and promoted at Lepenski Vir only at the time when historical and ideological constellations required such a reinvention of tradition. This reinvention relied on traces of previous occupation at Lepenski Vir that might have been imbued with mythical significance and related to narratives surrounding the history of this site. This referencing of a 'desirable' past might have been the reason for spatial referencing, *i.e.* citing, of old rectangular hearth features as in the case of Hearth 'a'. One cannot be certain whether the spatial 'citation' of this feature might have stemmed from an accidental recognition of its existence while levelling the ground during the construction of the first trapezoidal buildings here, or whether the terrain of the site *c.* 6200 cal. BC might have indicated the previous existence of particular abandoned dwellings and burials at this spot. Be that as it may, the very materiality of an old hearth must have played an important part in building this palpable link between the past and the present at Lepenski Vir, supplying the builders of trapezoidal structures with a believable, material trace that drew on the potency of the past by incorporating this feature into a build up of generational continuities.

The emphasis on building genealogical ties with the past that seems to have been taking place at this and other sites in the Danube Gorges is very similar to examples of practices that involved materialities of buildings in the Neolithic worlds of Anatolia and the Levant (see Hodder 1998b). I have previously connected such practices with the possible importance of house society social organisation described by Lévi-Strauss (1983; 1987). Such a social organisation might have been an important component of the Neolithic way-of-being and to a great extent might have contributed to the spread of this new Neolithic 'house ideology' (Borić 2007a; 2008). In the following, I describe a homological link between these architectural mnemonics and the treatment of burial remains at the site of Vlasac, where generational genealogies were similarly created in the mortuary domain chronologically overlapping with the phase of trapezoidal buildings at Lepenski Vir. The nature of the treatment of the old dead, however, prompts one to think not only about remembering but also about forgetting as a constituent element of such material practices.

Citation and dismembered memories: Mortuary practices at Vlasac

The site of Vlasac is situated three kilometres downstream from the eponymous site of Lepenski Vir. The current dating shows that both sites were contemporaneously if intermittently occupied in the course of the Early Mesolithic (Bonsall *et al.* 2004; Borić and Miracle 2004; Borić *et al.* 2008). Different from Lepenski Vir, where the Late Mesolithic phase of occupation from around 7200 to 6200 cal. BC is lacking (see above), the intensity of occupation at Vlasac peaked exactly during this period. A number of architectural features, including the first trials in constructing trapezoidal buildings, and almost 90 burials were uncovered at this site in the course of the rescue excavations in 1970 and 1971 (Srejović and Letica 1978). Renewed work at Vlasac started in 2006 after an unexpected discovery of still-preserved portions of the site despite the rise of the Danube that gravely damaged the remaining, upslope portion of the site after the construction of the hydroelectric plant (see Borić 2006; 2007b; Borić *et al.* 2008). This new work in 2006 brought to light an important discovery of a burial feature that suggests the continuous use of Vlasac from the Late/Terminal Mesolithic throughout the Early Neolithic, providing the first secure evidence about the contemporaneity of Vlasac and the phase of trapezoidal buildings at Lepenski Vir. In the following, I describe in what way this burial feature discloses the underlying structure of social connectedness between the living and their dead. Moreover, the same principle of referencing the place where the previous dead were buried is

Fig. 3.4 House 65 and Burials 54a–e, Lepenski Vir (c. 6200–5900 BC) (photo: Centre for Archaeological Research, Faculty of Philosophy, Belgrade).

found at the site of Lepenski Vir, where in several instances interments of individual burials on top of each other are recorded for the chronologically overlapping contexts (*e.g.* in the case of House 65 and Burials 54a–e, see Fig. 3.4).

The previous discussion about architectural features at Lepenski Vir has disclosed the importance of emphasising temporal continuities between old and new buildings in the Upper Gorge of the Danube in the period between *c.* 6200–5900 cal. BC through the spatial placement of new buildings in relation to earlier and abandoned features by repeating their outline and by the physical incorporation of earlier features in the build up of new ones. These principles of material *retaining* and *repeating* of past traces has strongly indicated the (very physical) attachment to the past cherished by the community at Lepenski Vir that promoted this emphasis on generational continuities and genealogical connectedness between physical buildings that possibly embodied particular social groupings. At Vlasac, a group burial feature, the upper portion of which overlaps with the temporal framework of trapezoidal buildings at Lepenski Vir, was discovered in 2006. A detailed excavation that carefully recorded the position of disarticulated human bones found in the burial fills and the way earlier burials were damaged and dismembered has also suggested the ambiguous nature of memory in this context. A particular pattern of treating physical remains of the old dead may suggest that the durability of a particular social unit, which this burial feature obviously embodied, surpassed any individual memory of a particular person and the importance of the integrity of its physical remains. In what follows, I reconstruct the sequence of events that took place at this burial location (Fig. 3.5).

The burial tomb found at Vlasac in 2006 was lying on top of an abandoned dug-in dwelling with a reddish burned floor surface, of which only the rear portion survived since the Danube had eroded away more than two-thirds of its front portion. It seems that after this feature had been abandoned, the floor was covered with sterile soil that levelled this area. A broken projectile point found at this level is dated in the range 6654 to 6484 cal. BC at 95 per cent confidence (OxA-16540) and likely represents a *terminus ante quem* for the occupation of the dwelling and a *terminus post quem* for the group burial. The first burial, H136, was interred above this rear part of the building in what possibly looked like a depression in the sloping terrace of the site, likely indicating the previous existence of a built feature. It is hard to be certain whether the group that abandoned this dwelling was related to the buried individual although one may suppose that it was. The individual marked as H136 seems to have been placed in extended supine position, parallel to the Danube and with the head pointing in the downstream direction of the river. Such a position and orientation was the dominant but not exclusive burial norm throughout the Late Mesolithic period in the Danube Gorges (see Borić and Miracle 2004; Radovanović 1996). Only articulated feet and the right tibia and fibula of this individual survived later disturbances at this location (Fig. 3.6). This burial is dated in the range 6775 to 6473 cal. BC at 95 per cent confidence (OxA-18865) after the correction for the reservoir effect and is roughly contemporaneous with OxA-16540. A larger cremation pit in which human and some animal bones were burned disturbed

the burial. There are several adjacent pits that contained such burned remains in this area and at this level, and it seems that they were in use over some time with several re-cuttings, perhaps indicating and containing a number of burning events (see Borić *et al.* 2009).

Another burial, H81 (adult male), was placed some 20 cm above burial H136 although with a slight displacement to the south, in the same position and with the same orientation as H136. After the required correction for the freshwater reservoir effect the date for H81 falls in the range 6639–6440 cal. BC at 95 per cent confidence (OxA-20762) (Borić *et al.* 2009, appendix 2). The articulated parts of this burial were less disturbed, consisting of the left pelvic bone, the whole left leg and the complete right leg below the knee. This burial was clearly disturbed by the interment of another, later, burial of H63 (adult female). The burial pit for the interment of H63 was cut in the same location, chopping off a large part of burial H81. Disarticulated bones of H81 ended up in the burial infill of H63 and even still later burial of H53. Larger cranial and long bones of earlier H81 must have been placed next to the body of H63 (Fig. 3.7 showing the complete humerus, proximal half of right femur and cranial fragments next to the feet of individual H63), while smaller, fragmented bones were found in the backfilled soil. H63 was less damaged than H81 and had completely preserved lower limbs below knees, which were partly covered by two flat stone plaques. This part of the burial saw no later disturbances. The head was missing from H63, and the practice of (most likely post-mortem) skull removal was common in the Mesolithic and Neolithic Danube Gorges, and it echoes similar practices found in the wider eastern Mediterranean region since the beginning of the Pre-Pottery Neolithic period (*e.g.* Kuijt 2000; Talalay 2004). H63 is after the correction for the freshwater reservoir effect dated in the range 6232 to 6018 cal. BC at 95 per cent confidence (OxA-16542), which is contemporaneous with the phase of trapezoidal buildings at Lepenski Vir, where one finds similar instances of headless burials (*e.g.* Fig. 3.4; see Radovanović 1996; Srejović 1972). Material culture evidence that supports

Dušan Borić

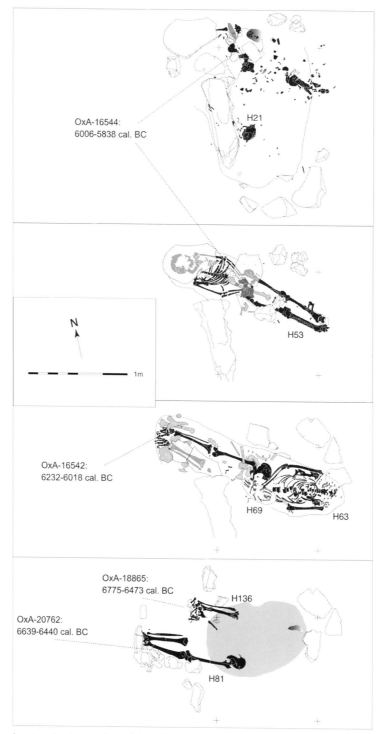

Fig. 3.5 Composite drawing showing overlapped burials excavated at Vlasac in 2006 (individuals H53, H60, H62, H69, H153/H21, H63, H81 and H136) (drawing: D. Borić).

Fig. 3.7 Lower level of the group burial at Vlasac. Headless adult female inhumation H63 (6232 to 6018 cal. BC at 95 per cent confidence) with child H153 and partly burned remains of juvenile individual H60 placed over the chest of H63; neonate burials H62 and H69 interred on the left side of H63, disturbing her left pelvis, left femur and lumbar vertebrae. Other disarticulated bones in the burial come from H81 (6639–6440 cal. BC at 95 per cent confidence), whose partly articulated remains were found beneath the level of H63; H81 was likely disturbed by the interment of H63 (photo: D. Borić).

Fig. 3.6 Remains of the earliest inhumation H136 (6775 to 6473 cal. BC at 95 per cent confidence) found in the group burial at Vlasac. Note a cremation pit (context 115) with burned soil that largely damaged H136 (photo: D. Borić).

such a dating comes in the shape of Spondylus beads associated with this burial (Borić 2007b; Fig. 3.7) that represent the first dated instances of the spread of the Neolithic Spondylus exchange network in Europe. A partially-burned articulation of a headless juvenile burial, H60, was found over the chest of H63 together with another smaller child below it, individual H153. Both H63 and H153 were damaged by yet another burial pit cut for the interment of two neonates, H69 and H62, placed one on top of the other, being buried likely at the same time. This burial pit for neonates clearly disturbed the lumbar vertebrae, left pelvic wing, left forearm and left femur of adult individual H63, as well as the right half of child individual H153.

The final interment at this location was the placement of extended articulated H53 (Fig. 3.8). Before it was placed in the burial pit at the same location, another burning/cremation event took place here. An oval area of burning lying on top of H60 (that significantly damaged this skeleton) and H63 contained remains of these two individuals' heads and other postcranial bones of H60. Such a practice strongly resembles similar burning of human bones observed in lower levels of this burial tomb, indicating the continuity of this particular mortuary practice (Borić *et al.* 2009). It is likely that this burning event took place

Fig. 3.8 The latest, complete inhumation burial H53 (c. 5950 BC) found in the group burial at Vlasac. Note that the left femur, left side of the pelvis and forearm bones of H63 (articulated inhumation found beneath H53) were placed in the burial fill of this last burial (photo: D. Borić).

immediately prior to the interment of H53 as the bones of H53 were practically lying directly on the burned deposit. Burial H53 was lying directly above earlier burial of adult individual H63. Yet, although the same orientation was respected, the body of this individual was interred not with the head pointing downstream the Danube, as with all other earlier burials at this location, but with its head pointing to the upstream direction. One could only speculate about possible reasons for this shift in burial orientation and a particular meaning of such change. As in previous instances, the disturbed bones of older burial individual H63 are now found in the infill of younger burial H53. The disarticulated left femur of H63 was placed along the body axis on top of the pelvis of H53, between her legs, while the left pelvic wing of H63 and lumbar vertebrae were found on top of the knees

of H53 (Fig. 3.8). Along the right side of H53, a stone plaque, similar to those covering the legs of burial H63 (see above), was leaning against this last inhumation, stuck in the ground, while on its outer side two ulnae and one radius were piled up in a stack together with a disarticulated child mandible. One of these ulnae and the radius belonged to the left arm of H63 earlier disturbed by digging the pit for neonates H62 and H69, while the second ulna probably comes from still older H81, and it must have been kept in the confines of the burial place over a considerable time. The last burial, H53, was covered by two stone plaques, which also might have been used continuously for covering earlier burials, acting as some form of burial furniture in the place that might have turned into a sort of burial chamber (there is no positive evidence to indicate the existence of a roof construction over this burial location although this possibility should not be excluded). The stone plaques covered the pelvic area and the head of H53.

On top of the stone plaque that was covering the pelvis of burial H53, a red deer skull with antlers was found, while at the same level and symmetrically placed in a structured manner, a disarticulated child's skull (H21) was found. It is likely that this skull relates to the partially articulated remains of child burial H153 found in the vertical sequence of burials, lying on top of H63 (see above). Numerous disarticulated human and animal bones were found in the burial fill that contained re-deposited dark, organic-rich soil with traces of burning and with numerous smaller burned and unburned bone fragments, possibly indicating several events of re-opening the burial chamber in order to either inter the remains of the newly deceased or, perhaps, to retrieve particular body parts. In this fill that was covering the burial place, there were also red and white limestone as well as Spondylus beads disturbed from their primary position of adorning the buried individuals. It is unclear whether the placement of the red deer's and the child's skulls took place immediately after the interment of H53 as part of the same ceremony (Fig. 3.9), although one could suppose that this is likely. This red deer skull has directly been dated in the range 6006

Fig. 3.9 Artist's reconstruction of the burial ceremony for individual H53 at Vlasac (drawing: J.G. Swogger).

to 5838 cal. BC at 95 per cent confidence (OxA-16544). After this act of consecrating the location that was for several generations used as the burial ground by a particular social group, large blocks of stone were placed over the tomb. It seems that soon after this burial/ceremonial event, the location might have been used again, since a number of Middle Neolithic Starčevo pottery fragments as well as river *Helix* sp. shells were found on top of stone blocks. After this, likely short-term, Middle Neolithic occupation/use of the site, the whole site was abandoned. A thick layer of hill-wash covered the Neolithic levels with no later human disturbances. Soon after, the forest vegetation stabilised the deposit of accumulated scree and prevented more intensive downslope erosion for millennia.

Remembering and forgetting: Complex interplays

There may be problems with any archaeological interpretation that ever assumes a stable core of meaning for any given set of practices that occur over a period of time. As poststructuralist critique has emphasised for several decades now, it is important to comprehend the unstable character of any meaning and its inability to adhere to particular objects, practices, etc. Meaning is always characterised by a mutation, loss and/or re-invention. Such a critique warns against the possibility to maintain a solid and unchanging transfer of meaning from the past to the present both in the presence and absence of written documents. For Foucault in *The Archaeology of Knowledge* (1972) the 'idea of the continuity of memory, and hence of the history of the subject, is an idealist illusion' (Ricoeur 1998, 79). If we accept this, such a perspective inevitably brings important ramifications to our project of studying the persistence of specific memory of the past in the past we study. It calls for an imperfect memory of the past, the one structured both by forgetting (*cf.* Harris forthcoming) and *re*-membering, *re-*

invention and *re*-construction, lacunas and new stories that fill the gaps.

The very core of any human conduct, according to the hermeneutic school of thought, is exactly a constant process of reinterpretation and reinvention of meaning on the basis of traces that remain as the consequence of past actions. Now, the notion of trace in such an understanding plays a fundamental role. It is the enigmatic ontological status of trace that enables any remembering. For Paul Ricoeur, the ontological status of trace is marked by an important paradox: that it is from the past and that it survives into the present. The whole human existence is structured by this process of following traces in which the human existence can best be described as *Being-affected-by-the-past* (1988), following a Heideggerean fashion of hyphenated notions. Ricoeur emphasises that the human temporal existence is structured by narratives and in this way he builds upon the foundations left by Heidegger in his insistence on *being* and *time*. Here Ricoeur adds: and *narrative*, creating an inextricably linked triad that marks the human condition. He points to the exceptional character of human existence that is not only temporal but also narrative. Trace, memory and narrative, which produce a historical consciousness for this school of philosophical thought, mark the human condition (see Borić, this volume).

Ricoeur (2004), in one of his last works dedicated to memory, history and forgetting, examines closely the relationship between memory and forgetting, and asks the question whether there can be a homology between 'happy memory', previously evoked by Bergson, and what one could possibly call 'happy forgetting'. Ricoeur argues that forgetting should not only be seen in terms of dysfunctions of memory, *i.e.* as distortions of memory and effacement of traces, but that we may be able to speak of 'the paradoxical idea that forgetting can be so closely tied to memory that it can be considered one of the conditions for it' (Ricoeur 2004, 426). Following Harald Weinrich (1997), Ricoeur discusses whether we can even speak of the *ars oblivionis* that would be on the equal footing with the *ars memoriae* of Frances Yates (1966).

In following this line of thought, Ricoeur's closest ally is Henri Bergson and his work *Matter and Memory* (1981). Bergson's work that emphasises the idea of an independent survival of the images of the past, *i.e.* representations as recollections of memory, serves to Ricoeur to expand Bergson's work in an original direction: he suggests establishing a connection between the wonder of happy-memory, *i.e.* the wonder of recognition through practical action, and forgetting.

> It is in this lived experience that the synergy between action and representation is confirmed. The moment of 'pure' memory, encountered through a leap outside of the practical sphere, was only virtual, and the moment of actual recognition marks the reinsertion of memories within the thickness of lived action (Ricoeur 2004, 439).

The self-survival of images from the past is directly related to the 'figure of fundamental forgetting', *i.e.* forgetting as a reserve (*oubli de réserve*) or a resource. For Ricoeur, this type of forgetting differs from the forgetting as effacement of traces. Forgetting as a reserve is in fact 'the perseverance of memories' through 'their removal from the vigilance of consciousness' (2004, 440). This idea that apart from the destructive forgetting through the effacement of traces, one could account with the forgetting that makes memory possible, can also be found in Heidegger (1962). He similarly talks of forgetting that does not have a negative but rather a 'positive' connotation, and is connected to the mode of 'having-been' (*Gewesenheit*) rather than to the mode of 'being-no-longer' (*Vergangenheit*) in thinking about the past. Heidegger sees it as inauthentic temporality of 'everyday modes of taking care of what is nearby' (1962, 317). He asserts that '… *remembering* is possible only on the basis of forgetting, *and not the other way around*. In the mode of forgottenness, having-been primarily 'discloses' the horizon in which Da-sein, lost in the 'superficiality' of what is taken care of, cannot remember' (Heidegger 1962, 312 [original emphasis]). Here, similar to Ricoeur's thesis, forgetting enables 'an immemorial resource' rather than being a destructive force. Furthermore, Heidegger (1962, 311) relates forgetting to repetition and subsequent retrieval of 'the being that is already there'.

This type of thinking about forgetting as complementing memory or even being the condition for remembering in the field of phenomenological philosophy can find some support in a number of ethnographic examples among non-Western traditional societies. One of the frequently quoted examples in anthropological literature when it comes to the figure of forgetting is Susanne Küchler's (1999) example of *malanggan* carvings as part of commemoration practices of the dead in the north-west of Papua New Guinea (see also Gell 1998, 223). Küchler's work points to the place of memory displaced from a commemorative, visually lasting monument with its memorial value. The elaborate making of *malanggan* is followed by the act of destruction. Yet, the physical disappearance of a memory object only creates a possibility for memory to be implanted in new places, and sustains its renewal.

Another striking ethnographic example that very much resembles Ricoeur's notion of forgetting in reserve that we previously discussed, comes from Anne Christine Taylor's (1993) interpretation of remembering and forgetting among the Amazonian group known as the Jivaro, found in eastern Ecuador and Peru. Amazonian groups in general are characterised by the absence of taste for commemoration of the dead and this is certainly true of the Jivaro. In fact, the Jivaro spend a lot of their time in eclipsing and obviating the individual character of their dead, or 'losing' them to use Taylor's words. But, as she clearly remarks right from the start: 'being nowhere in particular, not linked to a specific calendar period, they [the dead] are, potentially, everywhere all the time' (1993, 653). According to this interpretation of the work of mourning among the Jivaro that is dominated by forgetting, it is exactly the process of 'forgetting in reserve' that structures these practices of mourning. The dead are 'disremembered' in order to be available to the living, who through their disremembered dead have a finite pool of available names and 'unchanging set of faces'. After death, the disposal of the corpse depends on its gender: for example, adult men are sometimes exposed in the men's house or even in the forest on a constructed platform. This type of disposal of the dead is meant to accelerate the process of the physical decomposition of the corpse, which should disappear as quickly as possible. Through songs and chants that are parts of the mortuary rituals, 'the dead person is evoked simply by a pronoun (never by name or kin term) and his or her physical appearance is gradually ground into oblivion, through an obsessive and very graphic description of the rotting of the flesh and particularly the face' (Taylor 1993, 665). The image of the deceased must completely disappear, while due to the idea of a finite number of souls that constitute a particular group, the name of the deceased is passed onto a newborn. Through the work of mourning and disremembering, the deceased is transformed into an abstract singularity whose impersonal biography is the source of *arutam* visions, sought and experienced by men. For the Jivaro, 'the dead, being one-dimensional, are not credited with reflexivity. They are afflicted with a peculiar form of imbecility, for while they retain sensory perception as well as some kind of understanding, they are nonetheless entirely unselfconscious' (Taylor 1993, 664). By being forgotten and depersonalised in the course of the work of mourning, the dead become an important resource for the living.

In some other Amazonian groups, such as the Wari' of western Brazil, a similar process of forgetting the dead, *i.e.* their quick 'controlled' transformation, was very much being helped by the practice of funerary, compassionate cannibalism (Conklin 2001; Vilaça 1993; 2000). Among the Wari', this type of endo-cannibalism, always performed by the affines of the deceased, could not risk the survival of the corpse among the living. Such ritual cannibalism had an important psychological dimension for the close kin of the deceased in showing them that the corpse is no longer their relative, but that its change of status from a living to a dead body transformed the newly deceased into prey. The state of death turns the deceased into a figure of alterity, similar to enemies or spirits.

Thinking about remembering and dismembering at Vlasac

The previous discussion about the insights of phenomenological philosophy with regard to the interplays of remembering and forgetting can help us understand the complexity of the workings of memory that may significantly be structured by the notion of forgetting in reserve. This same structure has also been seen as conditioning empirical variations with regard to the works of memory and mourning seen in some of the discussed ethnographic examples. Yet, neither generalised philosophical notions nor some very remote ethnographic examples can be sufficient to account for the specificity of the case study under consideration. Hence, let us closely examine the main aspects of the described archaeological record.

In the Danube Gorges at the site of Vlasac, people buried their dead in the same location over several generations. There is a remarkable superposition of burials in the same place while respecting the same ritual observances. Such a record forces one to argue for the importance of genealogical links to the past, and perhaps the ancestral status of the dead in this community. This type of genealogical memory with the physical expression of links to the past has already been shown as the characteristic of the Danube Gorges fisher-foragers on the basis of an analysis of architectural features at the type-site of Lepenski Vir (Borić 2003). According to this analysis, I have suggested that the structuring of material memory can be abstracted in the following way: the past potency and memory were evoked by *citations* of past *traces* through physical attachment to previous architectural features, and, as seen now at Vlasac to earlier burials too, and, subsequently, by *repeating/recapitulating*, *i.e.* adhering to, the trace of past agency/actions. This type of practices both in the case of architectural features and burials produced either vertical superposition of architectural features and burial remains or horizontal displacement that involved only partial superposition: 'touching upon' the past remains by following and repeating the exact formal outline of older and 'cited' buildings or body positions of

older burials. The impression one gets from such material configurations evokes strict rules and closely-followed observances of the 'ancestral' ways and they suggest significant cultural conservativism or a lack of improvisational strategies.

Yet, a newly discovered group burial at Vlasac, excavated by careful recording and reconstructing of all visible and recognisable events in a vertical stratigraphic sequence of the tomb, opens up the space for discussing forgetting as a constitutive element of this specific cultural expression. While the same area at this site was repeatedly used for burying possible members of a single kin group (but this question of the biological relatedness of the deceased in the burial group remains to be elucidated further, *cf.* Borić 2007a), one observes relatively careless attitudes toward earlier burials. The body completeness of each burial is in direct proportion to its stratigraphic, *i.e.* vertical, position – more complete and articulated are younger burials at the top of this group burial and proportionally less complete articulated remains of older burials. Here one encounters in a material configuration what is theoretically suggested by Husserl (1964) in the model of time modifications that conceptualises a retentional sinking or 'shading off' of previous events into the thickness of time (see Gell 1992, 222; 1998, 237). This process may closely be connected to the previous discussion of forgetting evoked by Heidegger which according to him relates to the 'buried', inauthentic aspects of 'having-been' (see above).

Moreover, while bones of burials disturbed by opening this burial 'crypt' at Vlasac in order to inter the newly dead were *intentionally* kept within the confines of the burial place, there was often little care about keeping older burials undisturbed and articulated. The completeness of the old burial was obviously not an issue as long as one could keep the bones within the limits of the burial chamber and, very frequently, by incorporating these dismembered bones into new burials. Can one think then about these dismembered skeletal parts of older burials in younger burials as *citations* of the ancestral dead whose potency and *mana* were of some use to the newly deceased, or was this dismemberment of complete bodies meant to produce a lacuna in remembering, leading to the 'happy forgetting' of the old dead? Both of these options might have been at work. We have seen also that traces of earlier burials might have been further obviated by their cremation before the newly deceased was interred. Such events might have served to 'purify' the ground into which the new, complete body was being interred or to disempower a potentially malevolent agency of a particular dead person (Borić *et al.* 2009). At this point, one may conclude that perhaps the performative character of the burial ritual was of a much greater significance than the physical integrity of the body. Yet, burial rituals were not to take place just anywhere at the site, but at particularly chosen places, sometimes over several generations and centuries without significant alterations of burial norms.

Conclusions

The specificity of interplays of remembering and forgetting as seen at Vlasac through the evidence of burial practices, which bear homological similarities to the treatment of architectural features, may lay in their memory focus on a social unit rather than on a particular individual. The structuring of cultural practices in these communities at Vlasac, Lepenski Vir and other neighbouring sites in the Danube Gorges in the final phases of the regional Mesolithic and particularly strongly through the phase of transformation, when these communities were affected by the arrival of the Neolithic in the wider region of the Balkans, focused on the build-up of generational continuities through acts of physical superposition by *citing* and *recapitulating* past traces and actions. Such practices might have been politically motivated ways of proving allegiance to the expending Neolithic social networks and interest in successful and continuous lineages (Borić 2007a; 2008).

It seems that through actions of dismembering early burials by digging a new burial pit in the same place, or by burning the encountered remains, the memory of the dead might have been both recollected and then collaterally lost. The physical completeness of the already buried

dead did not matter much. After the burial, the dead, whose individuality and singularity might have been obviated and/or manipulated, were turned into a resource for the living. Practices of post-depositional skull retrieval and secondary burials might have been in large part about the depersonalisation of the dead, who increasingly must have lost their singularity with the passage of time. Most of the bones of the dismembered dead were still kept in the confines of the burial place or their body parts were incorporated into a new burial, sometimes in a manner that suggests an act of structured deposition. The evidence at hand largely indicates that these burial places might have related to the reification of particular social units, possibly of the 'house society' type described by Lévi-Strauss. The dismembered old dead in the described group burial at Vlasac can be seen as instances of 'forgetting in reserve' of the dead that helped maintain the memory and continuity of the social group that was obsessively touching upon and containing their physical singularities.

Acknowledgements

This paper was written during my postdoctoral appointment with the Leverhulme Research Programme *Changing Beliefs of the Human Body: Comparative Social Perspective* at the University of Cambridge. A version of this paper was presented at the session organised by Katina Lillios at the UISPP congress in Lisbon on September 8th, 2006. I would like to acknowledge the funding received for the archaeological excavations at the site of Vlasac in the Danube Gorges (Serbia) from the British Academy grants (SG-42170 and LRG-45589) and the McDonald Institute for Archaeological Research, University of Cambridge in the period 2006–2007. I am also grateful to Sofija Stefanović for her preliminary report on the sex determination of the human remains from the new excavations at Vlasac. I thank Leila de Bruyne, Oliver Harris, Daniela Hofmann and Alasdair Whittle for comments on earlier drafts of this paper.

Bibliography

Bergson, H. (1981) *Matter and Memory*. New York, NY, Zone Books.

Bloch, M. (1995) Questions Not to Ask of Malagasy Carvings. In I. Hodder, M. Shanks, A. Alexandri, V. Buchli, J. Carman, J. Last, and G. Lucas (eds) *Interpreting Archaeology: Finding Meaning in the Past*, 212–215. London and New York, Routledge.

Bonsall, C., Lennon, R., McSweeney, K., Stewart, C., Harkness, D., Boroneanţ, V., Bartosiewicz, L., Payton, R. and Chapman, J. (1997) Mesolithic and Early Neolithic in the Iron Gates: A Palaeodietary Perspective. *Journal of European Archaeology* 5(1), 50–92.

Bonsall, C., Cook, G., Lennon, R., Harkness, D., Scott, M., Bartosiewicz, L. and McSweeney, K. (2000) Stable Isotopes, Radiocarbon and the Mesolithic-Neolithic transition in the Iron Gates. *Documenta Praehistorica* 27, 119–132.

Bonsall, C., Cook, G. T., Hedges, R. E. M., Higham, T. F. G., Pickard, C. and Radovanović, I. (2004) Radiocarbon and Stable Isotope Evidence of Dietary Changes from the Mesolithic to the Middle Ages in the Iron Gates: New Results from Lepenski Vir. *Radiocarbon* 46(1), 293–300.

Bonsall, C., Radovanović, M., Cook, G., Higham, T. and Pickard, C. 2008. Dating Burial Practices and Architecture at Lepenski Vir. In C. Bonsall, V. Boroneanţ and I. Radovanović (eds) *The Iron Gates in Prehistory: New perspectives* (BAR Int. Ser. 1893), 175–204. Oxford: Archaeopress.

Borić, D. (2003) 'Deep Time' Metaphor: Mnemonic and Apotropaic Practices at Lepenski Vir. *Journal of Social Archaeology* 3(1), 41–75.

Borić, D. (2005) Body Metamorphosis and Animality: Volatile Bodies and Boulder Artworks from Lepenski Vir. *Cambridge Archaeological Journal* 15(1), 35–69.

Borić, D. (2006) New Discoveries at the Mesolithic-Early Neolithic Site of Vlasac: Preliminary Notes. *Mesolithic Miscellany* 18(1), 7–14.

Borić, D. (2007a) The House Between Grand Narratives and Microhistories: A House Society in the Balkans. In R. A. Beck, Jr. (ed.) *The Durable House: House Society Models in Archaeology*, 97–129. Carbondale, Center for Archaeological Investigations, Occasional Paper No. 35.

Borić, D. (2007b) Mesolithic-Neolithic Interactions in the Danube Gorges. In J. K. Kozłowski and M. Nowak (eds) *Mesolithic-Neolithic Interactions in the Danube Basin*, 31–45. Oxford, Archaeopress.

Borić, D. (2008) First Households and 'House Societies' in European Prehistory. In A. Jones (ed.) *Prehistoric Europe*, 109–142. Malden, MA, Blackwell Publishing.

Borić, D. and Dimitrijević, V. (2007) When Did the 'Neolithic Package' Reach Lepenski Vir? Radiometric and Faunal Evidence. *Documenta Praehistorica* 34, 53–72.

Borić, D. and Dimitrijević, V. (2009) Apsolutna hronologija i stratigrafija Lepenskog Vira (Absolute Chronology and Stratigraphy of Lepenski Vir). *Starinar* LVII(2007): 9–55.

Borić, D. and Miracle, P. (2004) Mesolithic and Neolithic (Dis)continuities in the Danube Gorges: New AMS Dates from Padina and Hajdučka Vodenica (Serbia). *Oxford Journal of Archaeology* 23(4), 341–371.

Borić, D., French, C. A. I. and Dimitrijević, V. (2008) Vlasac Revisited: Formation Processes, Stratigraphy and Dating of Vlasac (Serbia). *Documenta Praehistorica* 35, 293–320.

Borić, D., Raičević, J. and Stefanović, S. (2009) Mesolithic Cremations as Elements of Secondary Mortuary Rites at Vlasac (Serbia). *Documenta Praehistorica* 36, 247–282.

Bourdieu, P. (1990) *The Logic of Practice*. Cambridge, Polity Press.

Bradley, R. (2002) *The Past in Prehistoric Societies*. London and New York, Routledge.

Buchli, V. 1995. Interpreting Material Culture: The Trouble with Text. In I. Hodder, M. Shanks, A. Alexandri, V. Buchli, J. Carman, J. Last, and G. Lucas (eds) *Interpreting Archaeology: Finding Meaning in the Past*, 181–193. London and New York, Routledge.

Carsten, J. and Hugh-Jones, S. (1995) Introduction. In J. Carsten and S. Hugh-Jones (eds) *About the House, Lévi-Strauss and Beyond*, 1–46. Cambridge, Cambridge University Press.

de Certeau, M. (1984) *The Practice of Everyday Life*. Berkeley, University of California Press.

Conklin, B. (2001) *Consuming Grief: Compassionate Cannibalism in an Amazonian Society*. Austin, University of Texas Press.

Cook, G., Bonsall, C., Hedges, R. E. M., McSweeney, K., Boroneanţ, V., Bartosiewicz, L. and Pettitt, P. B. (2002) Problems of Dating Human Bones from the Iron Gates. *Antiquity* 76, 77–85.

Eliade, M. (1954) *The Myth of the Eternal Return*. New York, Pantheon Books.

Foucault, M. (1972) *The Archaeology of Knowledge* (trans. A. M. Sheridan Smith). London, Tavistock Publication.

Gell, A. (1992) *The Anthropology of Time. Cultural Constructions of Temporal Maps and Images*. Oxford/Providence, Berg.

Gell, A. (1998) *Art and Agency. An Anthropological Theory*. Oxford, Clarendon Press.

Gosden, C. and Lock, G. (1998) Prehistoric Histories. *World Archaeology* 30(1), 2–12.

Harris, O. J. T. (forthcoming) 'Blessed are the Forgetful': Social Tensions Between Remembering and Forgetting at Two Neolithic Monuments in Southern England. In R. Schulting, N. Whitehouse and M. McClatchie (eds) *Living Landscapes: Exploring Neolithic Ireland in its Wider Context*. Oxford, British Archaeological Reports.

Heidegger, M. (1962) *Being and Time*. New York, Harper and Row.

Hodder, I. (1998a) Creative Thought: A Long Term Perspective. In S. Mithen (ed.) *Creativity in Human Evolution and Prehistory*, 61–77. London and New York, Routledge.

Hodder, I. (1998b) The *Domus*: Some Problems Reconsidered. In M. Edmonds and C. Richards (eds) *Understanding the Neolithic of North-western Europe*, 84–101. Glasgow, Cruithne Press.

Husserl, E. (1964) *The Phenomenology of Internal Time Consciousness* (trans. J. S. Churchill). London, Indiana University Press.

Küchler, S. (1999) The Place of Memory. In A. Forty and S. Küchler (eds) *The Art of Forgetting*, 53–72. Oxford and New York, Berg.

Kuijt, I. (2000) Keeping the Peace: Ritual, Skull Caching and Community Integration in the Levantine Neolithic. In I. Kuijt (ed.) *Life in Neolithic Farming Communities: Social Organization, Identity, and Differentiation*, 137–163. New York, Kluwer Academic/Plenum Publishers.

Lévi-Strauss, C. (1983) *The Way of the Masks*. London, Jonathan Cape.

Lévi-Strauss, C. (1987) *Anthropology and Myth: Lectures 1951–1982*. Oxford, Blackwell.

Radovanović, I. (1996) *The Iron Gates Mesolithic*. Ann Arbor, International Monographs in Prehistory.

Ricoeur, P. (1998) *Critique and Conviction. Conversations with François Azouvi and Marc de Launay* (trans. K. Blamey). Cambridge, Polity Press.

Ricoeur, P. (2004) *Memory, History, Forgetting* (trans. K. Blamey and D. Pellauer). Chicago and London, The University of Chicago Press.

Srejović, D. (1972) *Europe's First Monumental Sculpture: New Discoveries at Lepenski Vir*. London, Thames and Hudson.

Srejović, D. and Babović, Lj. (1983) *Umetnost Lepenskog Vira*. Beograd, Jugoslavija.

Srejović, D. and Letica, Z. (1978) *Vlasac. Mezolitsko naselje u Djerdapu (I arheologija)*. Beograd, Srpska akademija nauka i umetnosti.

Talalay, L. E. (2004) Heady Business: Skulls, Heads, and Decapitation in Neolithic Anatolia and Greece. *Journal of Mediterranean Archaeology* 17(2), 139–163.

Taylor, A. C. (1993) Remembering to Forget: Identity, Mourning and Memory among the Jivaro. *Man* n.s. 28(4), 653–678.

Thomas, N. (1991) *Entangled Objects: Exchange, Material Culture, and Capitalism in the Pacific*. Cambridge, Mass., Harvard University Press.

Vilaça, A. (1992) *Comendo como Gente: Formas do Canibalismo Wari'*. Rio de Janeiro, ANPOCS/Editora da Universidade Federal do Rio de Janeiro.

Vilaça, A. (2000) Relations Between Funerary Cannibalism and Warfare Cannibalism: The Question of Predation. *Ethnos* 65(1), 83–106.

Wagner, R. (1981) *The Invention of Culture. Revised and Expanded Edition*. Chicago and London, The University of Chicago Press.

Weinrich, H. (1997) *Lethe: Kunst, und Kritik des Vergessens*. Munich, Ch. Beck.

Yates, F. A. (1966) *The Art of Memory*. Chicago, University of Chicago Press.

4. Forgetting and remembering the digital experience and digital data

Ruth Tringham

This paper grew out of a conversation about memories; about remembering my first Mac; what a sharp memory and a powerful event it was; and how all the memories of using computers and their peripherals in the field since then explode in its wake with ever increasing complexity and speed until the digital media engulf and revolutionise our field experience and we can hardly remember a time when experience in the field was entirely non-digital.

There are three threads of remembering and forgetting running in non-linear fashion through this paper:

Firstly, my starting point from Susan Sontag's (1977) and especially John Berger's (1980) discussion of how memory is connected to the creation of a visual record. The idea expressed by both is that photographs that are remembered are those that jog intimate memories in the observer, and that such 'intimate contexts of meaning' can be created even for apparently publicly published photographs.

Secondly, the transferring of some of these ideas from the non-digital technology of photography to digital technologies of image-making. I am especially interested in exploring the use of hypermedia, the embedding of metadata, and other digital tricks in order to keep the digital record of archaeological fieldwork alive, re-usable, and remembered, rather than buried, lost and forgotten.

Finally, I want to try to share with you the rapid explosion of digitisation of the archaeological record – how digital technology has helped us not only to record but also to *remember* what we did

in the field – as seen through the window of my own memory of experiencing it during the last thirty years.

There are many books that help us not to forget the efforts and thoughts of our intellectual ancestors. There are Histories of Archaeology, Archaeologies of Regions, even Histories of individual archaeologists and Histories of in-dividual archaeological projects. Introductory courses in archaeology always begin with the work of the ancestors. The aim of these (we hope) is to make the past research meaningful to the current practitioners, and thus keep it active in their minds. But how is the mass of archaeological data, field diaries, drawings and photographic records that were supposed to allow an archaeological field project to be remembered? How are they not to slip into oblivion? Has the digitisation of these records made a difference between remembering and forgetting them? I think I can show, from my own experience, that digitisation *per se* will not save archaeological records from oblivion.

I personally became aware of mainframe computers in the mid-1960s – mysterious black boxes, distant from me, used and manipulated by clever mathematical types such as David Clarke (1968). I would even argue that – as John Berger (1980, 52) pointed out for the development of photography – its use was somewhat ritualised as well as mystified. It took thirty years from the invention of the camera to its common usage in the public domain; likewise, it was at least thirty years after the Second World War before the Personal Computer brought the digital world into the public domain (Allan 2001; White 2005). As

REGISTERS
IMAGE

REMEMBERS
IMAGE

GIVES
MEANING
TO IMAGE

REGISTERS
IMAGE

FIXES
IMAGE

GIVES NO
MEANING
TO IMAGE

Figure 4.1

with photography, it took another thirty years before email, the Internet, digital photography and videography allowed digitisation to become a habitual and taken for granted way of 'capturing an experience' in archaeological field projects (as well as our personal lives). The question becomes, do we remember how this happened and does the digitisation help us to remember what happened in the field. The answer to the first question is 'no', but I would argue that the answer to the second question is a definite 'yes, in the last five years it has that potential'. To clarify the latter statement, I need to divert attention to the question of memory and image making.

Memory, the eye, the camera, and the digital kidnapper

Both the eye and the camera register images, but the camera captures the image and fixes it frozen in time (Berger 1980, 54). The image is preserved for the life of the film. It can migrate from one medium to another if, for example, it is scanned as a digital image. The person whose eye registers an image, on the other hand, does not fix the image

but treats it quite differently from the camera. He or she remembers the image incompletely, but along with the image is remembered meaning. And the image is given meaning as part of a person's history of experience, their narrative of life. The camera's image, by contrast, is removed from its meaning – its context. Like archaeological artefacts, it cannot speak for itself (Fig. 4.1).

So how can we take advantage of the fact that the camera's image is fixed and can be preserved and shared beyond the life of the original owner of the eye behind the camera's eyepiece? How could a photographic image at the same time be given meaning? John Berger's answer to this conundrum begins with the recognition that there are two kinds of photographs: 'public' and 'private' (Berger 1980, 56–60) (Fig. 4.2).

'Public' photographs are the ones that we as archaeologists publish, or are published for us, as in National Geographic magazine. Their aim is to create a spectacle of the subject, to illustrate a point, or to demonstrate a product (what the archaeologist has found). We know these as the dehumanised (*aka* scientific) photographs found in most archaeological reports (Hodder

PHOTO

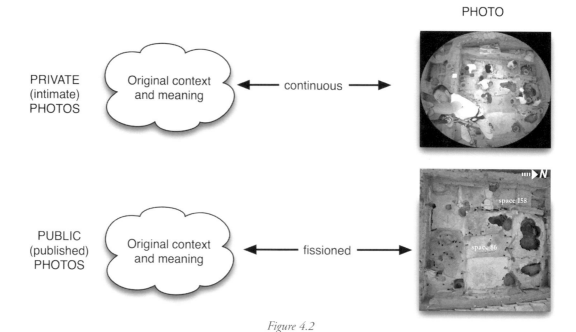

Figure 4.2

1999; Tringham 1991b). The memory of the original context and meaning is broken from the photograph and is not necessary for it to perform as spectacle. Public photographs do not contribute to a living memory, but rather create an eternal present of immediate satisfaction. Ultimately this leads to a limitation in their re-usability, and these photographs and their publication are abandoned and forgotten.

This is and will continue to be the fate of most of the photographic record of archaeology, whether analogue or digital. In fact, many of the spectacular 3D visualisations of past places that are being created often at great expense will, I believe, have this same fate, since their meaning and intention – even now – is quite obscure.

Creating an intimate ('private') context (memory) for images

Photographs that contribute to the memory of private experience of the photographer or those close to her/him retain continuity with the context of the original event. In a family photograph,

we know the people, we experienced the events; meaning grows out of the photograph and into it from other related memories.

> Photographs are relics of the past, traces of what has happened. If the living take that past upon themselves, if the past becomes an integral part of the process of people making their own history, then all photographs would re-acquire a living context, they would continue to exist in time, instead of being arrested moments (Berger 1980, 61).

During archaeological fieldwork, there are many private photographs being created by members of the team. But these are separated from the 'official' record of the excavation or survey and are not included in the database or publication. As I was working on my own personal collection of field photos for this paper, I became aware how few 'private' photos I took in the 1960s and 1970s of the archaeological fieldwork contexts. All the existing photographs are for publication – no people are included, nor are any extraneous personal objects or 'inappropriate' viewpoints. This is in marked contrast to my most recent field experience at Çatalhöyük in the late 1990s to the

Figure 4.3

present. Part of this could be explained as the effect of the lower cost of producing digital photographs encouraging a more frequent and less selective use of the photographic record. I believe, however, that it has more to do with a change in the 'use of photography' to use Berger's and Sontag's term.

Berger's idea of an alternative photography is to transcend the distinction between public and private uses of photography, and to provide public/published photographs with the same kind of context from personal, social and political memory that is provided for private photographs. An important suggestion by him – and one that would be quite radical for archaeological photography – is that the photographer thinks of her/himself as a recorder for those involved in the events rather than as a recorder for the world at large. Perhaps this would eradicate the dehumanised photographs of excavation areas that tend to pass for 'ideal archaeological photography'. Instead, the photograph becomes a memory of the constant ambiguity of archaeological data, rather than an illusion of a problem solved (Shanks 1991). I think that it is this use of photography that has come to characterize the 'style' of the photographic record in the Çatalhöyük project (Ashley 2002).

The reflexive methodology practiced at Çatal-höyük has put an emphasis on the voices of multiple individuals in creating the archaeological record (Hodder 1999). The multivocal practice goes beyond the archaeological team to multiple stakeholders in Turkey and globally, who – in theory – are encouraged to share their views through the Internet forum. One of the aims in the creation of the photographic record, therefore, is to use it to share not only the experience, but also the *memory*, of the archaeological process at Çatalhöyük. The aim has not yet quite caught up with the reality of sharing the full meaning of the photographs, according to Berger's suggestion of giving a private context to the photographs. But with the broad selection of subjects included in the published photographs, their 'privatisation' is poised to be accomplished.

Berger points out that memory is not created in a linear fashion. It is essentially non-linear – radial, in fact – with many different paths leading to the remembered event. The event that is remembered leads on to other memories of other events, and so on. So he suggests creating the context of a photograph in the same way (Fig. 4.3).

Both John Berger and David MacDougall have pointed out that memory is fragmentary, flexible and momentary. Doesn't this sound uncannily like the reflexive methodology of archaeology (Hodder 1997)?

David McDougall comments on the relationship of film and memory:

> Sometimes film seems even more astonishing than memory, an intimation of memory perfected. Memory is often apparently incoherent, and a strange mixture of the sensory and the verbal. It offers us the past in flashes and fragments and in what seems a hodge-podge of mental 'media'. We seem to glimpse images, hear sounds, use unspoken words and re-experience such physical sensations as pressure and movement. It is in this multidimensionality that memory perhaps finds its closest counterpart in the varied and intersecting representational systems of film (MacDougall 1998, 231).

The power of montage to create new meaning for images and sounds depending on their juxtaposition is a well-known art in film (Babash and Taylor 1997). Its effect can be seen in Figure 4.4 in which the images of the collage of Figure 4.24 have been re-arranged into a montage as in a film. Now, if I added some music.... (Fig. 4.4).

I would expand on MacDougall's idea and suggest that digital technology can allow us to approach more closely and more explicitly Berger's ideas of creating meaning and memory in photographs than with the paper media – words, signs and comparisons – that Berger (1982) suggests. If the image or film represents only the external signs or referents of memory, then the richer the repertoire of juxtaposed referents for the senses, the richer will be the expression of the remembered experience.

Digital images and non-linear digital editing of movies differ from images on photographic film in that 1) they can be manipulated very easily by the 'consumer': added to, changed, distorted, and 2) they can be linked to and embedded with other digital data. These features are a double-edged sword. The modifiability, especially, can challenge the authenticity of the image as well as the intellectual property ownership of the photographer. But the ability to permanently embed digital images with metadata such as authorship, reference to an original, actually enhances these aspects that cause doubt

(if they are taken advantage of); it encourages the re-purposing and re-combination of an image which, essentially, prolongs its life, its usability, and its memory (Ashley 2008; Kansa 2005, Shanks 2007) (Fig. 4.5).

The innovations in digital technology during the last ten years have all tended towards enabling the integration of data (including metadata) and the creation of non-linear narratives and research through various means: relational databases, embedding metadata, layering of imagery, juxtapositioning and scaling of images, animation and immersive contexts, as well as links to information and images distributed throughout the world within the searching distance of your therapeutic computer chair.

Remembering and forgetting the digital revolution in archaeological fieldwork

What you are reading is a 2-dimensional 'flat' paper representation of a theme that was originally presented live using Apple's presentation software Keynote. As I remembered my experience of the explosive evolution of digital technology in archaeological fieldwork contexts, I used hyperlinks and animation within the program to demonstrate the creation of intimate contexts for 'public' images. Each central image of the use in the field of the dominant digital technology of the time was given a more intimate memory through its links to other images, sounds, movies, and texts, along similar radial paths to those suggested by Berger (1980, 64). Berger's categories: personal, everyday, political, historical, and economic (that I have changed to 'computers') deepen and thicken the context of the central image.

A digital image – whether as photographic image or cinema – becomes much more than its digital representation; it is created by many associated data and memories, and itself leads to other context-rich memories. Metadata can be embedded about the context, authorship, and significance of the image – information that could be retrieved in a search for such data (see Figure 4.5). In this paper, however, I have expressed the Keynote hyperlinking by a two-dimensional

Figure 4.4

Figure 4.5

diagrammatic representation of Berger's idea of the radial paths from image to text. Alongside is a collage in which the eye starts with one image and travels to others, creating associations and memories (Figures 4.6–4.26). It is arguable, I believe, that this presentation of the images makes them less meaningful and less memorable than a digital version would be, although John Berger and Jean Mohr have managed to create a number of memorable narratives in this format (Berger and Mohr 1982).

Of great importance in this effort to make images meaningful and a means to remembering in a historiographic sense is the recent movement beyond hyperlinking to the creation of database narratives in which the multivocal and ambiguous memory of history can be expressed (Anderson in press; Manovich 2001). I have recently presented an analysis of this same debate, and a discussion

of the same history as that presented below, from a different viewpoint (Tringham, in press a).

Bylany 1963–68

The central image in Figure 4.6 is a photograph published in Stuart Piggott's book, *Ancient Europe*. It's a very 'public' photograph of a Linear Pottery house at the Neolithic site of Bylany in then Czechoslovakia. This was my first direct experience of digital representation in archaeology as a student participant in the Bylany excavations in 1962 (Pavlu 2000; Soudsky and Pavlu 1972). I definitely felt quite alienated from this process of quantification. I was studying the stone tools and had a set of hand-printed forms that bore no relation to the computer use. The only photograph I have is a murky one, with the conservator – Richard – peeking around a huge pot. The machine

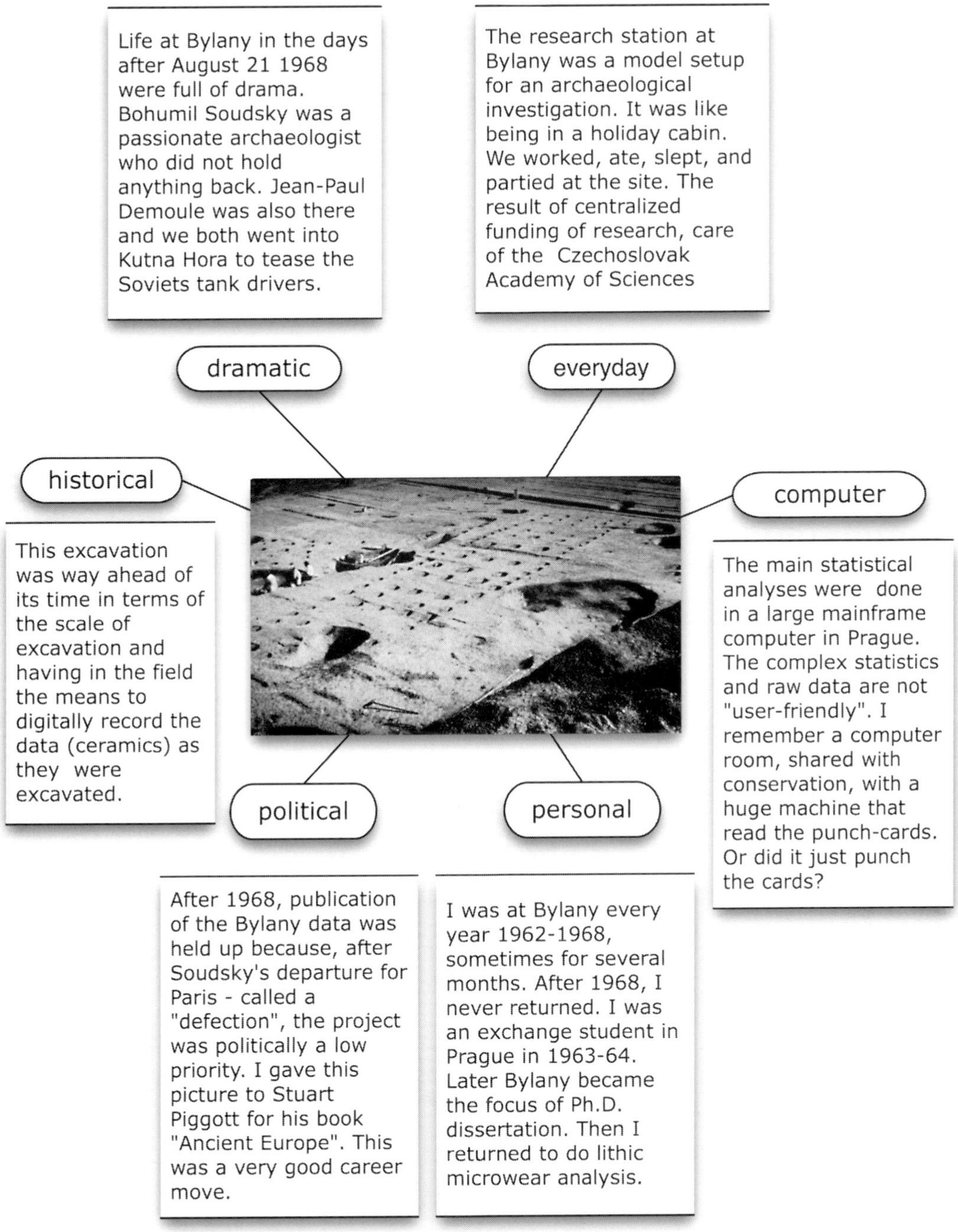

Life at Bylany in the days after August 21 1968 were full of drama. Bohumil Soudsky was a passionate archaeologist who did not hold anything back. Jean-Paul Demoule was also there and we both went into Kutna Hora to tease the Soviets tank drivers.

The research station at Bylany was a model setup for an archaeological investigation. It was like being in a holiday cabin. We worked, ate, slept, and partied at the site. The result of centralized funding of research, care of the Czechoslovak Academy of Sciences

dramatic

everyday

historical

computer

This excavation was way ahead of its time in terms of the scale of excavation and having in the field the means to digitally record the data (ceramics) as they were excavated.

The main statistical analyses were done in a large mainframe computer in Prague. The complex statistics and raw data are not "user-friendly". I remember a computer room, shared with conservation, with a huge machine that read the punch-cards. Or did it just punch the cards?

political

personal

After 1968, publication of the Bylany data was held up because, after Soudsky's departure for Paris - called a "defection", the project was politically a low priority. I gave this picture to Stuart Piggott for his book "Ancient Europe". This was a very good career move.

I was at Bylany every year 1962-1968, sometimes for several months. After 1968, I never returned. I was an exchange student in Prague in 1963-64. Later Bylany became the focus of Ph.D. dissertation. Then I returned to do lithic microwear analysis.

Figure 4.6

Figure 4.7

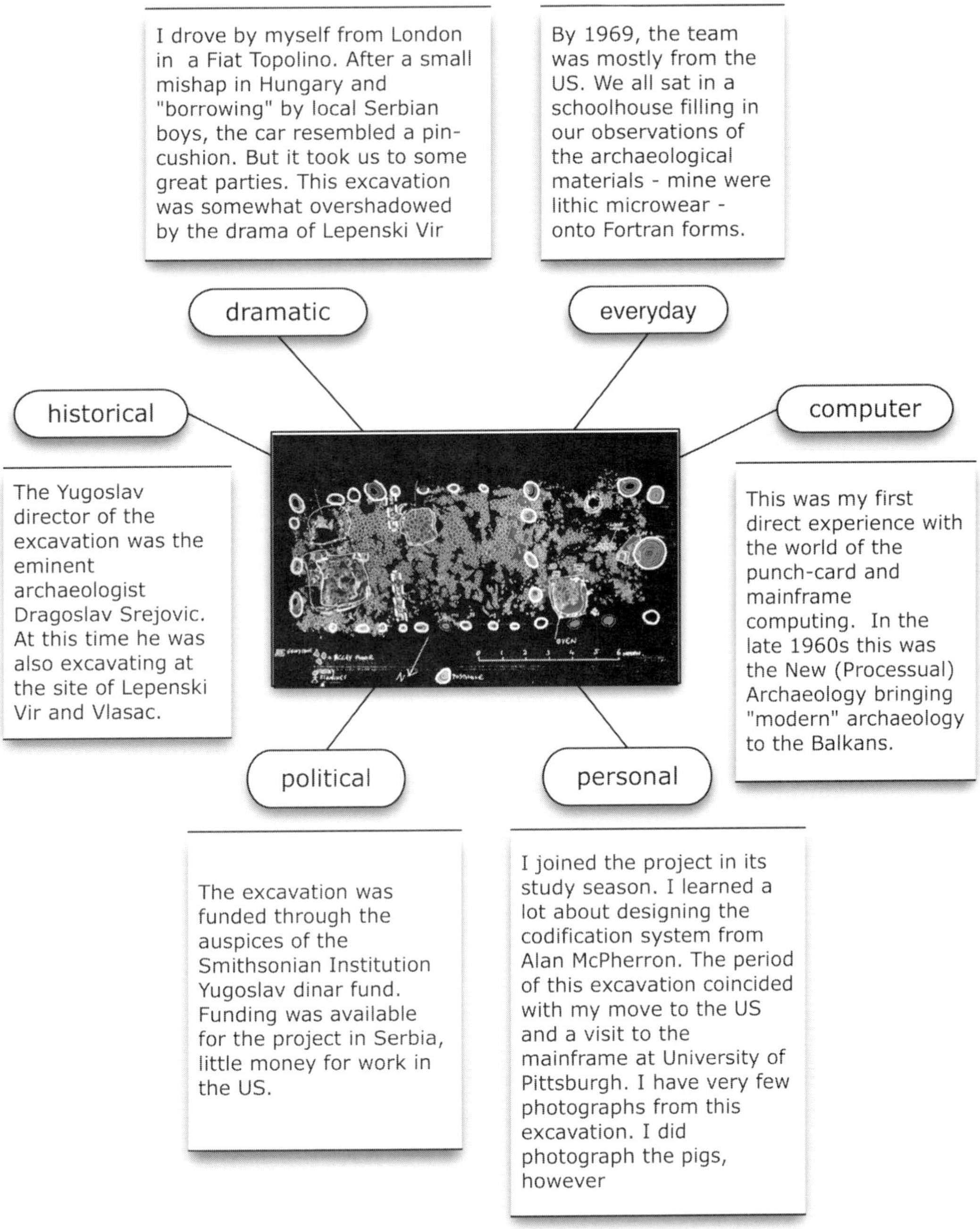

I drove by myself from London in a Fiat Topolino. After a small mishap in Hungary and "borrowing" by local Serbian boys, the car resembled a pin-cushion. But it took us to some great parties. This excavation was somewhat overshadowed by the drama of Lepenski Vir

By 1969, the team was mostly from the US. We all sat in a schoolhouse filling in our observations of the archaeological materials - mine were lithic microwear - onto Fortran forms.

dramatic

everyday

historical

computer

The Yugoslav director of the excavation was the eminent archaeologist Dragoslav Srejovic. At this time he was also excavating at the site of Lepenski Vir and Vlasac.

This was my first direct experience with the world of the punch-card and mainframe computing. In the late 1960s this was the New (Processual) Archaeology bringing "modern" archaeology to the Balkans.

political

personal

The excavation was funded through the auspices of the Smithsonian Institution Yugoslav dinar fund. Funding was available for the project in Serbia, little money for work in the US.

I joined the project in its study season. I learned a lot about designing the codification system from Alan McPherron. The period of this excavation coincided with my move to the US and a visit to the mainframe at University of Pittsburgh. I have very few photographs from this excavation. I did photograph the pigs, however

Figure 4.8

Figure 4.9

Close collaboration between the Anglo-American team and the Yugoslavs produced plenty of drama, passion, and poetry. The excavation of this figurine, for example, was dramatic and I am not proud of this photo - look carefully. My brother Oliver, who drove our Citroen Mehari, did much to allay the fears of the local farmers that we had come to repeat and surpass the Turkish occupation of 500 years. But our Yugoslav colleagues did think our archaeology was "unusual".

A large team from US and Yugoslavia. My team included veterans from Divostin and other US excavations in Yugoslavia. My director colleagues were from Belgrade. We lived and ate in the local school. There was an exchange of skills: excavation for quantification skills and vice versa.

dramatic

everyday

computer

historical

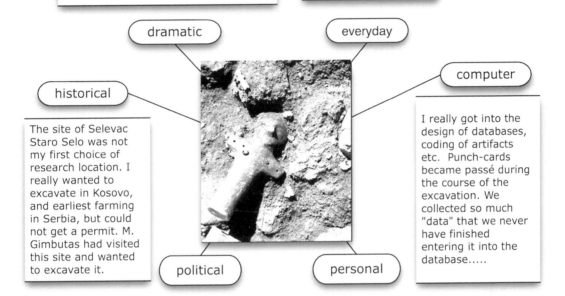

I really got into the design of databases, coding of artifacts etc. Punch-cards became passé during the course of the excavation. We collected so much "data" that we never have finished entering it into the database.....

The site of Selevac Staro Selo was not my first choice of research location. I really wanted to excavate in Kosovo, and earliest farming in Serbia, but could not get a permit. M. Gimbutas had visited this site and wanted to excavate it.

political

personal

We were funded by "hard" currency from NSF in US. This excavation was carried out at the height of the Yugoslav self-management euphoria and suspicion of the West, but anti-Soviet at the same time. But the authority of intellectuals and politicos was significant. I naievly saw this as very un-socialist.

This was the first excavation I directed, now from Harvard University. I was much more interested in the analysis of materials and inexperienced in Balkan excavation. My focus was on the intensification of resource utilization. "Microwear" had become "contact traces" and relevant to the use-life of all materials. By the time of the study season, I had moved on to UC Berkeley.

Figure 4.10

Figure 4.11

The joyous drama of finding Europe's earliest preserved fragment of textile contrasts with the awful tragedy of the Yugoslav Civil War at the end of our project. After our last season in 1989, it was impossible to get money to go back for a study season. I have not been back for more than short visits since 1989. Is this a pattern?

Our field lab was in the local schoolhouse but we lived scattered in houses in the town of Opovo. Many of the team continued from Selevac, overlapping with the team from Gomolava. The team included a Serbian ceramic analyst who was skilled in complex statistical manipulations, but something happened...

dramatic

everyday

computer

historical

From 1985 the Mac was in the field with us. The Mac allowed us to map spatially as well as register what we had found. But the mainframe was still needed for complex numerical analyses. We made full use of student data entry labor and the U.C. Berkeley Quantitative Anthropology Lab.

By the end of the excavation at Opovo in 1989, there were clear signs of growing nationalism in Serbia, and the break-up of the Yugoslav federation.

political

personal

We were funded from those Smithsonian sponsored funds in local Yugoslav currency that could not keep up with inflation. Opovo was in the Vojvodina, much more ethnically mixed (but no longer) than Serbia proper. I couldn't believe that the US would bomb Serbia, including Pancevo where our materials were stored.

This was to be the dream excavation where I would excavate in the way I wanted. Our focus was on the life-history of houses and the settlement, especially the issue of the widespread destruction of houses by burning. Mira Stevanovic and I put into practice a strategy of investigation we had developed at Gomolava

Figure 4.12

Figure 4.13

This photo is one of the interfaces of the Chimera Web, but only the introduction made it to the Web in 1995 in my first ever website, hosted by a hi-tech UCB computer group. Creating a hypertext/hypermedia narrative is like creating an opera with puppets. All around us at many different scales long-established barriers - not just the Berlin Wall were breaking down.

The Internet had started to impact our lives, but the lack of powerful search engines meant the impact was limited. But browsing can be fun too! There was not a lot of archaeology on the web - it was quite a mystery for me how you made a website and where it lived. Email was having a larger impact on our daily lives. At Berkeley, Meg Conkey, Rosemary Joyce and I answered every call for technological upgrades: scanners, printers, etc. We had early adopter status.

dramatic

everyday

historical

computer

The Internet in its various formats allowed the possibilities of safe self-expression and communication that I am sure paved the way for the breakdown of the Iron Curtain and general global democratization (globalization?), including the opportunities for the small dot-coms. How does the Gulf War and the bombing of Yugoslavia fit into this pattern of coincidences?

Windows based PCs were now everywhere. along with the windowed browsers for the WWW. Hypertext was the basis of web-browsing as well as some interesting innovations in literature. A common but never-achieved dream was for the ultimate database of all archaeological excavation materials in a standardized format.

political

personal

Although democratization was in the air, many "early adopters" in both education and archaeology saw the digital revolution of the Internet and CD publication as a means to gaining a monopoly on information and skills - maybe even profit. The aim was to embrace high tech - we were low-tech!

This was a very exciting time for me. Digital technology opened up possibilities that we only dreamed of before: expressing the elements of the feminist practice of archaeology including multiple lines of evidence; and architecture visualization with sound and movement, multiple voices and narratives. I felt like a mistress-pupeteer with my own digital world!

Figure 4.14

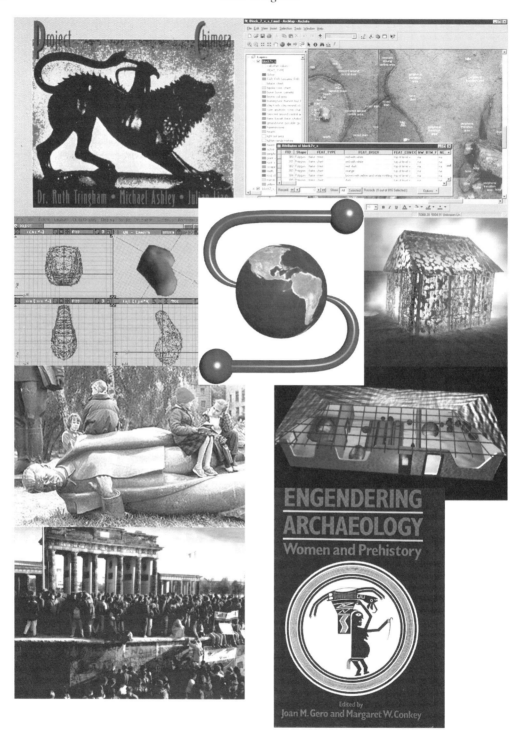

Figure 4.15

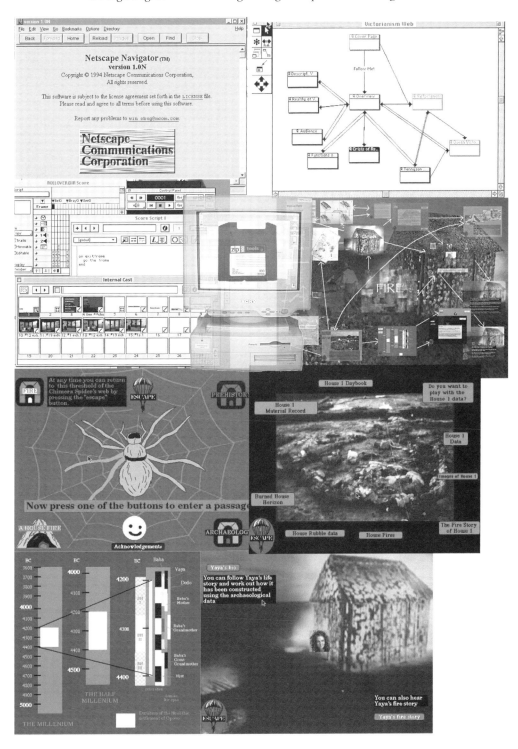

Figure 4.16

is somewhere there. Neither Figure 4.6 nor 4.7 can do justice to the complex story of my experience at Bylany, but I think the public/published card, code, and ceramics are made more memorable and meaningful by the surrounding images of their historical and intimate context, including a couple of images of the luxurious centre at Bylany – luxury that I would not experience again until Çatalhöyük; an image of Prague during my year as an exchange student; and an image of the invasion of Prague after the Prague Spring of 1968. I did not take this photograph; I was in Bylany with tanks around us and took no photographs. After 1968, I never went back to Bylany, and Bohumil Soudsky – the original excavator and my PhD dissertation mentor – left Czechoslovakia for Paris. Our meeting in a Bylany-like settlement in northern France in 1969 is the poignant image which is always my own starting point in this collage (Figs. 4.6 and 4.7).

Divostin 1969–72

For the first thirty years in archaeology, the use of computers in the field meant transforming observations of artefacts and context into coded numerical data on punch-cards or eighty-column sheets. The ritualised manipulation of these numerical data took place in a temple called the mainframe in a computer centre. I was gradually drawn into the coding and computerisation of field data by my participation in the American-Yugoslav excavation of a Neolithic site in Serbia – Divostin. My memories of the computer aspects of this project are mostly a feeling of being inadequate (what the hell is factor analysis), out of control (a huge gap between me, the data creator and the guys behind the central computer desk) and not happy. The worst was when you had to take your cards to the specialists at the mainframe who would punch them for you, or slot them into the reader for you, and what a pity if you had made a mistake. You would enter a 'programme' card that would have the instructions of what and how to manipulate the data. There was thus an enormous opaque gap between your observations in the field and the results you might (or might not) get as a

result of their analysis. This gap was epitomised by the separation of the US computer literate group who did the analysis and the Yugoslav team who did the excavation. At the same time, for the local Yugoslav audience, this was a minor excavation compared to the politically charged excavation of Lepenski Vir with its carved stone heads. As with Bylany, this was a difficult period to build into a photographic collage (Figs 4.8 and 4.9).

Selevac 1976–80

In keeping with the New Archaeology strategy, we tried to make observations on everything that we found and never rejected anything as irrelevant, even the mounds of burned architectural rubble. During the life of this project we went from the use of cards while I used the facilities of Harvard (1976–78) to the abandonment of cards in favour of direct data entry and tape storage when I moved to UC Berkeley and took advantage of the Quantitative Anthropology Lab. So the gap between field practice and digital record was beginning to close. However, the digitised data was all alphanumeric, mostly numeric, it was stored in a mainframe computer, and had to be manipulated by Unix commands by students or others trained to do this. The manipulation of numbers could then be interpreted. Numbers were not linked to visual imagery: photos, drawings, in any kind of database, except typed lists on paper were distinct from the numbers. These images are all from colour 35mm slides that have been digitised in 1997. In the late 1970s, possibilities for capturing images into a digital format, including satellite imagery, definitely existed, but not for archaeology. We had three photographers on this excavation, two from the United States and my brother Oliver from England. Between the three of them we got some remarkable photographs of people working in and around the project. Oliver and I plan to produce a book about Selevac similar to a John Berger and Jean Mohr collaboration (Figs 4.10 and 4.11).

Opovo 1983–89

The 1980s in addition to seeing the birth of post-processual archaeology saw an important revolution in the democratisation and commercialisation of computer technology. It was the decade when the innovation of the personal computer (PC) released us from the bonds of the mainframe 'temple', although at first they were quite limited compared to the latter. In the 1980s, the PC allowed the archaeologist to control data input and a certain amount of output in the lab and in the field. It allowed paperless copies of records, field diaries, letters, grant proposals, and reports to be carried back and forth in the field on floppy disks. In theory this eliminated the need to carry bulky paper records, a great advantage in faraway field sites. In practice, it was a long time before the 'soft' copies were trusted above 'hard' copies, a distrust that holds true even today for many archaeologists. The strength in the 1980s of the PC was in terms of text entry and spreadsheet data entry, so that gradually the PC replaced the typewriter (Figs. 4.12 and 4.13).

For me, 1984 was a huge year: I got my first Apple Macintosh and became a Mac person. Gene Hammel (founder of the UC Berkeley Quantitative Anthropology Laboratory) had negotiated a deal with Apple for us to receive some of the first Macs, for which I will be eternally grateful. The next year I took my Mac 512K to Opovo, a Neolithic site I was excavating in Yugoslavia. As soon as we could get the software – in our case Filevision and Macdraft – we started to digitise visual information beyond text and numbers. I used it for updating a daily map of the site, the distribution of spatial contexts, and Nerissa Russell created a database in which spatial data was linked to other information. For heavy-duty digital recording, however, we still relied on the 80-column sheets that were entered into the mainframe database in the QAL at Berkeley, using a version of SPSS software, with backup storage on tapes. Gradually, however, in the later 1980s we started to transpose some of this data to personal databases in Excel and Filemaker on our Macs.

At this time, photographic recording was exclusively on 35mm film. Digital imagery and associated data captured remotely from satellites became available to the public in the late 1980s. The capture of images to digital media became available to personal computer owners in the late 1980s in the form of flatbed scanners along with the development of software to edit and manipulate those images (Photoshop). This perhaps more than anything started the revolution in digital photography. 35mm slide scanners, however, which could transform colour transparencies – used by archaeologists to present their work – into digital media did not become commercially available until several years later in the mid-1990s and have remained expensive. In the mid-1990s we had all the 35mm colour slides scanned to PhotoCD commercially. By the late 1980s also, input devices for digitising spatial data, such as field drawings – digital tablets and pens – were being used by some archaeologists (not at Opovo) and replaced the only other form of image-making that archaeologists had recourse to – those ink-drawing machines (I've just remembered one in the QAL in Berkeley).

The images here include images of Mirjana Stevanović cleaning the house rubble, the topic of her PhD, started in Selevac and continued in Opovo. We got an 'earliest' at Opovo one morning at 6 am with the sunrise shining in our joyous faces as we excavate the earliest piece of textile from continental Europe – a single fragment that we never would have retrieved without the detailed excavation of these burned houses. Burning leads me then not to forget the published photographs of Pančevo burning after the US bombing in 1995, and Pero, our local worker who was killed in the early days of the Civil War that broke out immediately after our excavation at Opovo finished. Even while we were excavating, it was clear that this was the path down which Yugoslavia was being led.

The Chimera Project and the Chimera Web 1990–1995

The fifteen years since 1990 have seen the true revolution (that has been intensifying in the last five years) in digital data recording and computer literacy among archaeologists. It has also seen a revolution in the potential of what digital technologies can be used for by archaeologists with large and small budgets. In my opinion the greatest revolutions have been, firstly, in the communication and sharing of knowledge through the Internet (Okin 2005), and, secondly, in the production of digital audio-visual representation and the ever cheaper commercial availability of its technology (Ashley 2002; Forte and Siliotti 1997; Lock 2003). In this respect the democratisation of technology has been amazing.

During this period, starting in 1990, I entered with enthusiasm into this arena, partly as a response to the challenge of expressing the complex linking of multiple narratives and paths of interpretation that were part of the feminist critique of archaeology (Joyce and Tringham 2007; Tringham 1994; Wolle and Tringham 2000). It was also partly as a desire to use the new 3-D modelling abilities of computers to go beyond drawings and re-enactments to create visualisations of the interiors and exteriors of (pre)historic building that were occupied by people (Tringham 1991a; 1991b; 1995).

The first Chimera project was a collaboration between myself, an architecture graduate student Julian Liao, and undergraduate anthropology student Michael Ashley. Julian guided us through the intricacies of Alias on an expensive SGI workstation in visualising the Neolithic site of Opovo. This program, however, was not for the fainthearted or amateur, like myself. Michael Ashley used the visualised burning house of Opovo in his Senior Thesis project which dreamed of embedding real archaeological data in such visualised representations. This was a rather different concept from data embedded in digital spatial images as used in Geographic Information Systems software (Lock 2003). The latter's analyses developed out of the 1980s statistical manipulation of spatial data, such as Thiessen polygons. Although a more humanistic application of GIS was argued in the late 1990s (Curry 1998), at this time GIS was very different from the Chimera project in that the latter was based in computer-generated imagery rather than digitally generated spatial data (Figs. 4.14 and 4.15).

The Chimera Web that I developed out of Michael Ashley's Chimera Project took the idea of linking archaeological data (in my case again from Opovo) to its visualised and textual narratives of interpretation into the realms of hypertext and hypermedia construction (Barrett 1992; Joyce 1996; Landow 1992). Hypertext structure (used also in the Web browsers) offered the possibility of creating open-ended complex non-linear narratives in which we could express the multivocality, ambiguity and multiscalarity suggested by the feminist practice of archaeology. My colleague Rosemary Joyce had already embarked on a similar enterprise, using Eastgate's Storyspace to create a collaborative hypertext narrative *Sister Stories* (Joyce 2003; Joyce and Tringham 2007). I used Storyspace to map out the web of linked ideas, information, and narratives about the burning of the Neolithic houses of Opovo and then – using a new software Macromedia's Director – transferred it to a hypermedia-linked web of 'pages' or 'windows' that looked very similar to WWW-web pages of the time. The difference was that I wanted the Chimera Web to be a self-standing product, distributable on CD-ROM. As Rosemary Joyce and I have remarked, we were both nervous at this time of distributing our creations on the Web (Joyce and Tringham 2007). In addition, the technology and bandwidth could not have sustained the complex linking and imagery that I was using in the Chimera Web (Fig. 4.16).

Podgoritsa 1995

This was an excavation in which I had hoped to transfer some of the method and questions from our work in Yugoslavia, now an impossibility, to neighbouring Bulgaria, urged on by a colleague – Douglass Bailey – from Cardiff University, who shared many of the same interests. For three years we tried to get a permit to excavate the small fourth millennium settlement mound of Podgoritsa (Tringham 1996), and finally succeeded in 1995. In retrospect, it probably would have been better if we had not tried so hard. Bulgaria was still rocked by the break-up of the Soviet Union. Email was now a big part of our lives by 1995 and communication with colleagues in all parts of the world. However, I for one could not use it

This photo says it all!This project had a lot of drama, none of which related to what we found, except a faux prehistoric footprint!. The project was almost cancelled before it began. It was terminated dramatically on the last day. Afterwards we were accused of being spies

By this time email had become a commonplace habit. But in Bulgaria we were still very isolated. This was a new collaboration with Cardiff University and Bulgarian archaeologists. Douglass brought his field school. There were some familiar faces from Opovo. However, the lack of rapport with the Bulgarian team made life VERY difficult.We lived in houses scattered around the village, eating in a cafe with the worst toilet in the world.

dramatic

everyday

historical

computer

By the time of the Podgoritsa excavation, the Soviet Union had been dissolved, and its satellite countries (including Bulgaria) were looking towards capitalism - for example, Coca Cola - and the West as their future.

Michael Ashley and I devised a great database using 4D. We used some cool technologies: EDM, magnetometer, resistivity, off-tell survey with immediate results. At Podgoritsa, I had my first laptop computer in the field.

political

personal

This project was funded by an NSF grant. Political change did not always spell people change. We were in the middle of a struggle for power between Sofia - the center - and the regional archaeologists. There was huge tension between the Bulgaria and US-UK team created by our Sofia representative.

This is the only excavation where I have woken up with dread in my heart instead of eager anticipation. This excavation was not a happy experience. I just did want to be there. But I have remained close friends with the Cardiff team. And I remember a wonderful time with the bee-keeper....

Figure 4.17

Figure 4.18

Many dramas: the construction of our shelter; the Goddess and the thunderstorm who threatened it. Very active social life in a big team - fancy dress parties. News media coverage contributed to the sense of drama. Guards with guns; big dogs. The Dagger was our dramatic discovery in 1997, and the roof in 1998.

We lived in the luxury of the compound. Some of the team from Opovo and Podgoritsa were re-constituted here. We were quite isolated with intermittent phone line in the middle of the Konya Plain. We excavated in the luxury also of our shelter. This was a very "wordy" excavation - lots of talking and writing for the sake of "reflexivity"

dramatic

everyday

historical

computer

Çatalhöyük was a very famous site. The new project there started in 1993, directed by Ian Hodder. I came out in 1996 to look it over. Post-Processual Archaeology, reflexive methodology in action. We brought NSF funding to our project from Podgoritsa.

The project was well-endowed, and had a computer lab (PC dominated) and an on-line database. A digital video/New Media project from Germany was in progress. We brought our own Mac desktop and laptops. An experimental digital camera in 1998. A PC laptop for data entry.

political

personal

It was a coup for Ian Hodder and the British School in Ankara to get a permit to excavate Çatalhöyük, after 30 years of inactivity. Ian played the politician on site and talked with every level of Turkish administration. Few Turkish archaeologists on site except government representatives. The UK dominated the project. The Berkeley (BACH) project were the only Americans; there were also Greeks, interesting in view of Turkish-Greek political relations.

I had never before worked on a famous site. But I wanted to work here because of its methodology and my interest in house-life histories not for the fame. This was the perfect project and I have been very happy there. I appreciate every day the buffer that Ian provides with the government agencies and permit issues.

Figure 4.19

Figure 4.20

Jason and Michael climbing in full gear for aerial shots in our shelter created such dramatic shots as this one. National Geographic created their own dramatic - but over the top - images at night with spotlights. The drama of the total eclipse of the sun at Çatalhöyük complete with dancing on the mound with the Goddess tours. There is constant drama at Çatalhöyük: the Press; public visibility; important visitors - it's a famous site. The family of little owls provides limitless entertainment and drama

Limited email and phone cards. The Internet cafe is popular as email can only be received by team leaders. We are still using floppies for transfer from the email PC to our Macs. Our luxury compound breaks down: a water problem - 4 days without a shower. Our Turkish workers entered Building 3 and remark (unprompted) on what a very grand house it is.

dramatic

everyday

historical

computer

We are using Catal images as the basis for teaching the MACTiA courses of multimedia authoring. Ian announces publicly on Press Day that the Catal project will last another 20 years. In 1999 the main team is in the field for 6 months and prepares for publication, and 2000-2001 are study seasons. The BACH team is out of sync in this enterprise. In 2000-2002 we were the main Neolithic excavation on the East Mound.

Several laptops in the lab: Macs for BACH team, but Windows for data entry. Intensive photography and video with digital starting in 2000. CAD drawing but but as post-production of hand drawing. Wired network in labs

political

personal

Our team continues to include a contingent from war- and bomb-torn Serbia. We - like the main Catal project - now have to rely on private funding: but we have found an angel. The Greek team has dropped out, but a new team from Poland (Poznan) joins the project.

As we start to excavate deeper into the history of Building 3, I find the search for plaster floors and burial lids completely absorbing. But BACH team provides the lead currently in digital media recording and management (using cross-platform Portfolio). It is strange to come for a 2-month season to a site where people have already been working for several months - almost like being a visitor.

Figure 4.21

Figure 4.22

when away from home (i.e. in the field) because I refused to get on AOL! By now, we were used to the colour and WYSWYG of the World Wide Web. The great search engines had not yet got into their stride; Lycos and Webcrawler launched in 1994, but the first one I used – Altavista – did not launch until after our Podgoritsa excavation in late 1995.

The Podgoritsa excavation was an important digital revolution for me, not just because I had my first laptop with me (a Powerbook 145) but for the first time we had a database entirely independent from the mainframe and could enter our data directly into digital form. However, the truthful story is we didn't have enough laptops, so we still did need to enter the data on paper and transfer to desktop databases at home. Our digital relational database using 4thDimension, was designed by Michael Ashley, and included coded observations and measurements of the excavated materials as well as the textual daybook entries. It did not, however, link up with field drawings (hand-drawn) or photographs (35mm film). The latter were later digitised commercially in 1996 along with the Opovo slides.

The sub-surface reconnaissance (magnetometer and resistivity) data, however, was gathered and mapped electronically by the Cardiff team. The Electronic Distance Measurer (EDM) allowed us to produce a precise contour map of the mound in a fraction of the time with traditional survey equipment. Everything in the field began to be speeded up. The statistical manipulation of data was superceded by the promise of the flash and sizzle of the digital technologies to record and interpret the audio-visual experience of archaeology (Figs. 4.17 and 4.18).

Çatalhöyük 1996–2006

In the ten years that I have been working at Çatalhöyük, I have experienced significant developments in the application of digital technologies in archaeological fieldwork. In some cases, the technology existed earlier but did not become commonplace at Çatalhöyük until later in the project, for instance digital photography did not become common until 2002. In other cases, such as GIS technology and 3D laser scanning, the technology was developing fast on archaeological projects but was not applied at Çatalhöyük.

The technological developments can be monitored by the equipment that we brought into the field, seen in the collages of Figures 4.19–4.20. We started in 1997 with a Powerbook 3400, increased in 1998 by lugging a desktop (a Mac PC7200) and its CRT monitor to Turkey (it stayed in Turkey and went into retirement after 1999), and progressed to two Powerbook G3s in 2000, 4 PB-G3s in 2001, adding a Powerbook G4 (mine) in 2002, adding another PB-G4 in 2003, in 2004 4 Powerbook G4s networked wirelessly together. The peripherals developed alongside this sequence from floppies in 1997, Jaz and Zip drives and CD-ROM writer from 1999, scanner from 2001, DVD-writer and external hard drives from 2003.

The computers in these collages are Macintoshes of various kinds and reflect the fact that the BACH (Berkeley Archaeologists at Çatalhöyük) project within the main Çatalhöyük umbrella – like the MACTiA – was dominated by the Mac platform. The umbrella Çatalhöyük project, however, was dominated by the Windows platform which would have been perfectly compatible were it not for the fact that the database (including in-field data entry) was created using Microsoft's Access, a program that is accessible only through the Windows platform. We adapted to this by bringing with us PCs running Windows (but not always the correct version for the database). It was for this reason, also, that we brought the desktop at the beginning in which we installed a special card that would enable us to run Windows through emulation, much as VirtualPC later enabled us to do, though not very successfully, on our laptops.

Throughout our project, our lack of easy access to Access was an issue, sometimes on a joking basis, but often with much aggravation and grumpiness. In the last couple of years, it became an issue (still ongoing) for the larger team how to make the Access database compatible with the spatial data in image-rich context such as GIS, on the one hand, and the huge digital photographic and video record from the excavation, on the other.

The BACH team made full use of electronic digital measurements, providing a Leica Total Station – borrowed from the UC Berkeley Archaeological Research Facility – every season. This and the digitising of our field drawings using CAD software also demanded the use of Windows platform and left us somewhat at a disadvantage, relying as we did on PC laptops. In spite of this, however, our ultimate desire – as perhaps was that of the whole Çatalhöyük team – was to incorporate the digital imagery, whether 'photographic' (raster), 'drawing' (vector) or video, into the numerical/textual database through a GIS interface, or through a game engine interface. This is the challenge and dream for many archaeological projects at the beginning of the 21st century. How to make raw archaeological data meaningful and engaging for multiple audiences, from professional archaeologist to lifelong learner (Hodder 1999).

There are a number of arguments for archiving and migrating archaeological databases (Richards 2002) to make sure that data can be accessed long-term in the future. But it is usability – motivation for using the data, permission to re-contextualise them, and the fact that the data are meaningful – that ensures they will not be destined for the sea of forgetfulness. The fact that something is *accessible* does not ensure that it will be used. At Çatalhöyük, the database is still not fully accessible and usable (or re-usable), not because we lack the technology to access it, but the process by which you would use it is mystified and the data themselves are not made meaningful to more than a few. This is the challenge, then, to retain integrity and complexity, while ensuring that sharing is enabled over a broad spectrum of humanity (Tringham 2004; in press b; Wittman *et al.* 2007).

This period of fieldwork in Turkey coincided with the establishment and development of the Multimedia Authoring Center for Teaching in Anthropology (MACTiA) at UC Berkeley by myself as Presidential Chair for Undergraduate Education (1998–2001) and Meg Conkey. With Michael Ashley as research assistant and manager and – since being awarded his Ph.D. degree – its executive director, we taught courses that guided students in using digital technology to record

the archaeological process and to re-purpose digital data to create their own interpretations of archaeological research. We aimed to create media literate archaeologists (Ashley 2004). At the same time, the MACTiA server and personnel became the support group for digital imagery-making in UC Berkeley archaeological field projects, including Çatalhöyük.

At Çatalhöyük, the BACH/MACTiA team led the important transformations from film photography to digital photography, on the one hand, and, on the other, the use of digital video as an integral – rather than peripheral – part of recording the archaeological process (Tringham and Ashley in press). In our first three seasons (1997–99) all photographs were recorded on film and digitised commercially. Our Ricoh RDC-2 was used in 1998 and 1999 only as you might use a Polaroid camera – as a preview of the real record of film. In 2000 we brought our first mainstream digital cameras to Çatalhöyük: Nikon Coolpix 900s. With only 1.2 megapixels resolution, these cameras were still very inferior to our film cameras, so that we still relied on film photography for our permanent record. In 2001, this began to be reversed, since the technology had changed to make digital photographs of equal quality and much cheaper to use. We used Nikon Coolpix 950 (2 megapixels) cameras with special lenses. By 2002 we were using Nikon Coolpix 995 (3.1 mp). By 2002, our main visual database was entirely digital, although we used film photography as an archive, trusting the old hard copy. The Nikon D70 that we brought to the site in 2004 is a 6 megapixel camera and takes superb photographs.

We used a cataloguing program Extensis Portfolio to keep track of the digital and digitised images. The transition to digital photography entirely changed our attitude to 'the photograph' as well its documentation, since there was really no limit on the number of photographs that could be taken. In addition, metadata, such as date and time, were automatically embedded in each photograph allowing us to make a much fuller record, with a variety of contexts, both carefully prepared and spontaneous (Ashley 2002).

The Çatalhöyük project had a videographic

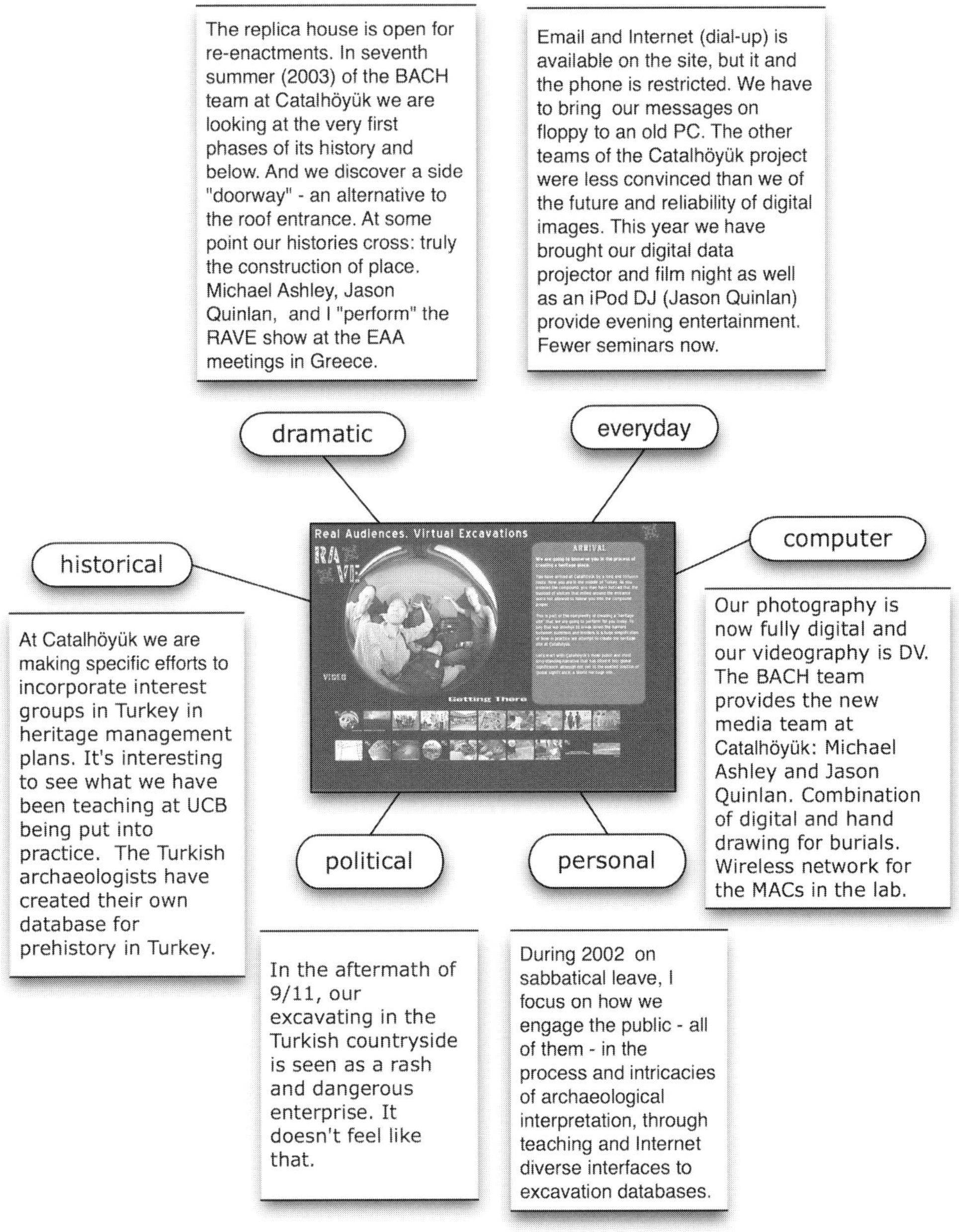

The replica house is open for re-enactments. In seventh summer (2003) of the BACH team at Catalhöyük we are looking at the very first phases of its history and below. And we discover a side "doorway" - an alternative to the roof entrance. At some point our histories cross: truly the construction of place. Michael Ashley, Jason Quinlan, and I "perform" the RAVE show at the EAA meetings in Greece.

Email and Internet (dial-up) is available on the site, but it and the phone is restricted. We have to bring our messages on floppy to an old PC. The other teams of the Catalhöyük project were less convinced than we of the future and reliability of digital images. This year we have brought our digital data projector and film night as well as an iPod DJ (Jason Quinlan) provide evening entertainment. Fewer seminars now.

dramatic

everyday

computer

historical

At Catalhöyük we are making specific efforts to incorporate interest groups in Turkey in heritage management plans. It's interesting to see what we have been teaching at UCB being put into practice. The Turkish archaeologists have created their own database for prehistory in Turkey.

Our photography is now fully digital and our videography is DV. The BACH team provides the new media team at Catalhöyük: Michael Ashley and Jason Quinlan. Combination of digital and hand drawing for burials. Wireless network for the MACs in the lab.

political

personal

In the aftermath of 9/11, our excavating in the Turkish countryside is seen as a rash and dangerous enterprise. It doesn't feel like that.

During 2002 on sabbatical leave, I focus on how we engage the public - all of them - in the process and intricacies of archaeological interpretation, through teaching and Internet diverse interfaces to excavation databases.

Figure 4.23

Figure 4.24

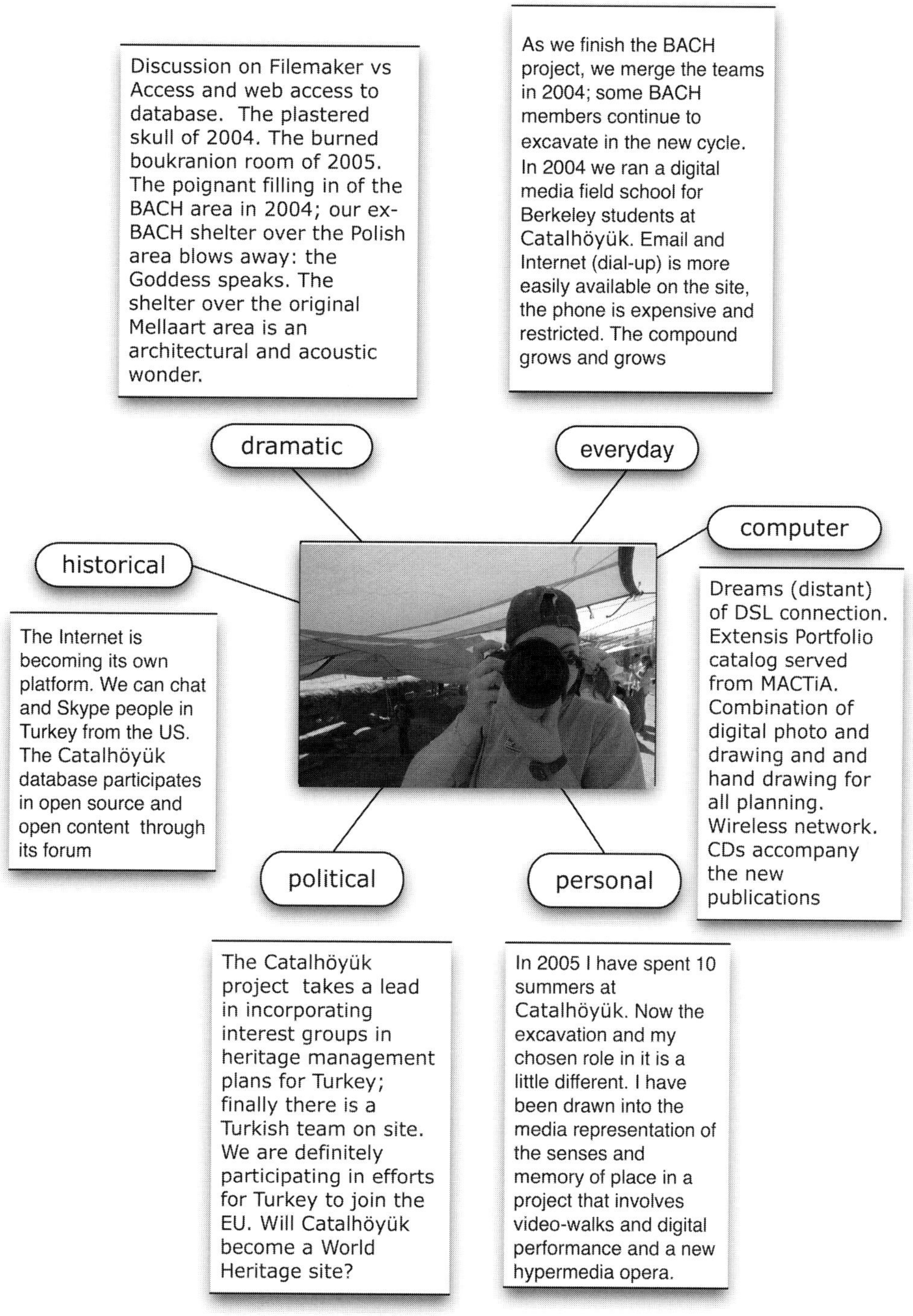

Discussion on Filemaker vs Access and web access to database. The plastered skull of 2004. The burned boukranion room of 2005. The poignant filling in of the BACH area in 2004; our ex-BACH shelter over the Polish area blows away: the Goddess speaks. The shelter over the original Mellaart area is an architectural and acoustic wonder.

As we finish the BACH project, we merge the teams in 2004; some BACH members continue to excavate in the new cycle. In 2004 we ran a digital media field school for Berkeley students at Catalhöyük. Email and Internet (dial-up) is more easily available on the site, the phone is expensive and restricted. The compound grows and grows

dramatic

everyday

computer

historical

The Internet is becoming its own platform. We can chat and Skype people in Turkey from the US. The Catalhöyük database participates in open source and open content through its forum

Dreams (distant) of DSL connection. Extensis Portfolio catalog served from MACTiA. Combination of digital photo and drawing and and hand drawing for all planning. Wireless network. CDs accompany the new publications

political

personal

The Catalhöyük project takes a lead in incorporating interest groups in heritage management plans for Turkey; finally there is a Turkish team on site. We are definitely participating in efforts for Turkey to join the EU. Will Catalhöyük become a World Heritage site?

In 2005 I have spent 10 summers at Catalhöyük. Now the excavation and my chosen role in it is a little different. I have been drawn into the media representation of the senses and memory of place in a project that involves video-walks and digital performance and a new hypermedia opera.

Figure 4.25

Figure 4.26

record 1995–98 created by a team from the Hochschule für Medienkunst in Karslruhe. Their aim was to integrate videos of the new excavations with Quicktime VRs of visualised scenes inside and outside the Neolithic houses, based on the early (1960s) excavations of James Mellaart. The finished product is a self-standing CD-ROM (Brill 2000; Emele 2000), that was obtainable as a demo in 2000, but now sadly will not work on recent operating systems and is destined to be forgotten unless migrated soon. The video record created by the Science Museum of Minnesota in 1999–2001 as part of their exhibit and website on "the Mysteries of Çatalhöyük" is available as a DVD and on-line (http://www.smm.org/catal/activities/video_tours_and_interviews/). It is the latter that allows this project to have some long-term sustainability and the fact that the videos can be downloaded and re-purposed without restriction (Shane and Küçük 2000; Wolle and Tringham 2000).

In 1998 I brought our first digital camera to Çatalhöyük – a Ricoh RDC-2 that could also record sound (Tringham and Ashley in press). I thought of this as the next best thing to a video camera (which we did not have at that time) rather than a digital camera to replace film. We used it primarily as an audio-visual diary in 1998–99 (Stevanović 2000). Unfortunately, it could not be saved in any non-proprietary format and cannot be migrated to any current operating system, so this valuable record will definitely be soon forgotten! In 1999 we brought an analog Sony Hi8 camcorder into the BACH area and started our own video record. In 2000 we had two of these recording our diaries and especially weekly observations. The limitations on creating the video record included the cost of tapes and our inability to digitise them in the field. In 2001, Jason Quinlan, who later became the project videographer, brought his own Sony DV camera that used mini-DV tapes which could be purchased much more cheaply than Hi-8 tapes, and could be digitised (captured) directly, complete with time-code. In 2002 we had two such (Sony 3CCD TRV 900 Mini-DV) camcorders. In 2001–2003, our use of video doubled, recording daily audio-visual

diaries, discussions, specialist visits, and informal gatherings. We keep track of the contents through an indexing system using CatDV; archives are created with duplicate tapes. Those of us preparing the BACH project for publication, have found the video record an invaluable jog to remembered and textually described observations. We have also found limitless opportunities to re-contextualise the video footage as new creative products about the archaeological process and the experience of Çatalhöyük (http://www.mactia.berkeley.edu/features/rave/default.html) (Figs. 4.19, 4.20, 4.21, 4.22, 4.23, 4.24).

The impact of the digital revolution in communication and the dissemination of information have finally in the last five years begun to reach archaeological fieldwork. Part of this has to do with thickening of the network of land cables and bandwidth of electronic communication enabling large amounts of data to be exchange very quickly by people who are willing and able to pay. It is also partly due to the expansion of the network of satellite wireless cells so that, with a cell phone, we are not dependent on the landlines which can be more expensive, or more restrictive. In the last ten years, I have experienced this breaking down of the technological barriers to communication to the point in which in Turkey I now almost never use the expensive telephone but instead rely on email. At Çatalhöyük, however, as in many parts of the world, it is not quite the dream of instant linking with your server at home, or the ability to exchange large data files. There is no DSL or Cable connection yet. This means that Instant Web publishing is not yet possible. But it will come soon.

And on its heels will come the more immense social revolution in terms of Internet communication that is so prevalent in the industrialised countries of the world. The Internet in the early 1990s when it was first conceived was a way to browse through images and texts, perhaps to search for information through those texts. Many of the websites and portals to that information have become forgotten or defunct, like ArchaeoNet. The Internet now comprises sites that are hubs of quickly updated information and dynamic databases. It is a townhall of forums, blogs and wikis to exchange opinions, helpful hints, creative pieces, images of experience, and often valuable information. That's the positive side … Still on a positive note, it is the dynamism of the social software of the Internet and the idea of re-purposing all that is found there that is what keeps the data and its utilisation alive and not forgotten. The archaeologists of Çatalhöyük have just caught on to this with their new website that contains a forum (http://www.catalhoyuk.com/) (Figs. 4.25 and 4.26) We are currently creating a dynamic on-line version of the final report of the BACH project at Çatalhöyük that utilises many of these so-called web 2.0 formats, but at the same time creates digital data for the long-term (Ashley *et al.* 2009).

Remembering digital technology

As an archaeologist, when I or one of my team take a photograph of a house – *e.g.* Building 3 at Çatalhöyük or House 2 at Opovo – we are not just capturing and fixing a trace of the architectural remains, but we are creating a memory of the context – why then, why that view, what were we imagining, theorising. Who was the projected audience of this photo or video? (It's well known that a photographer from outside will capture a very different image.) The image is not a crutch for that memory, as much as a vehicle in which to embed that memory. This is very hard and cumbersome to do in paper publication, but can be done elegantly and accessibly in a digital format through being searchable with metadata (keywords, photographer, date, image context, how the photo has been used by others). As you look at the images in this two-dimensional paper representation in their different formats, and read the text that seems to go along with them, ask (in your head or by email) these same questions of me. These are my personal statements as I remember the experience of digital technology in the different field contexts, but I created them to be able to share those memories with you. If I have not succeeded in sharing, then at worst the exercise is one of self-indulgence. But I hope the exercise has awakened your own memories, shifting your role from audience to engaged participant.

Transparency and embedding memory digitally

My hope is that the images have achieved the transparency of intentionality that Susan Sontag sought in photography and Ian Hodder seeks in the reflexive methodology carried out at Çatalhöyük (Hodder 1997; Hodder 2000). I believe that the effect would have been more powerful if it had been able to take advantage of digital technology. Look for this in the future. Nevertheless, the transparency I have tried to achieve takes away the false authority of the image but allows it to become meaningful for different audiences and to be re-used and remembered, rather than, as was the fate of the Ark of the Covenant in Raiders of the Lost Ark to be abandoned and forgotten in some hidden basement, whether real or virtual.

Bibliography

Allan, R. (2001) *A History of the Personal Computer: the People and the Technology*. Allan Publishing.

Anderson, S. (in press) Past Indiscretions: Digital Archives and Recombinant History. In M. Kinder and T. McPherson (eds) *Interactive Frictions*. Berkeley, CA, University of California Press.

Ashley, M. (2002) Real Webs and Virtual Excavations: a Role for Digital Media Recording in Archaeological Site Management. In *UNESCO World Heritage Center Virtual Congress, Mexico City, 2002*.

Ashley, M. (2004) Beyond Trowels and Pickaxes: Intergenerational Teaching and Stewardship in the Digital Age. In *5th International Symposium on Virtual Reality, Archaeology and Cultural Heritage, VAST, Italy, 2004*.

Ashley, M. (2008) Deep Thinking in Shallow Time: Sharing Humanity's History in the Petabyte Age. In *Digital Heritage in the New Knowledge Environment: Shared Spaces and Open Paths to Cultural Content*. Athens, Greece: Hellenic Ministry of Culture.

Ashley, M., Tringham, R. and Perlingieri, C. (2009) Last House on the Hill: Digital Remediating Data and Media for Preservation and Access. Paper presented at the Proceedings of 10th International Symposium on Virtual Reality, Archaeology and Cultural Heritage, VAST 2009, Malta.

Babash, I. and Taylor, L. (1997) *Cross-cultural Film-making [electronic resource]: A Handbook for Making Documentary and Ethnographic Films and Videos.* Berkeley, CA, University of California Press.

Barrett, E. (ed.) (1992) *Sociomedia: Multimedia, Hypermedia, and the Social Construction of Knowledge.* Cambridge, Mass, MIT Press.

Berger, J. (1980) *About Looking.* New York, Pantheon Books.

Berger, J. and Mohr, J. (1982) *Another Way of Telling.* New York, Random House Books.

Brill, D. (2000) Video-Recording as Part of the Critical Archaeological Process. In I. Hodder (ed.) *Towards Reflexive Method in Archaeology: The Example at Çatalhöyük by Members of the Çatalhöyük Teams,* 229–234. Cambridge, UK, McDonald Institute for Archaeological Research.

Clarke, D. (1968) *Analytical Archaeology.* London, Methuen.

Curry, M. (1998) *Digital Places: Living with Geographic Information Technologies.* London and New York, Routledge.

Emele, M. (2000) Virtual Spaces, Atomic Pig-Bones, and Miscellaneous Goddesses. In I. Hodder (ed.) *Towards Reflexive Method in Archaeology: The Example at Çatalhöyük by Members of the Çatalhöyük Teams,* 219–226. Cambridge, UK, McDonald Institute for Archaeological Research.

Forte, M. and Siliotti, A. (eds) (1997) *Virtual Archaeology.* London, UK, Thames and Hudson.

Hodder, I. (1997) 'Always Momentary, Fluid and Flexible': Towards a Reflexive Excavation Methodology. *Antiquity* 71, 691–700.

Hodder, I. (1999) *The Archaeological Process.* Oxford, Blackwell.

Hodder, I. (ed.) (2000) *Towards Reflexive Method in Archaeology: The Example at Çatalhöyük by Members of the Çatalhöyük Teams. BIAA Monograph no. 28.* Cambridge, McDonald Institute for Archaeological Research.

Joyce, M. (1996) *Of Two Minds: Hypertext Pedagogy and Poetics.* Ann Arbor, Mich, University of Michigan Press.

Joyce, R. (2003) *The Languages of Archaeology.* Oxford, Blackwell.

Joyce, R. and Tringham, R. (2007) Feminist Adventures in Hypertext. *Journal of Archaeological Method and Theory* 14 (3: special issue: *Practicing Archaeology as a Feminist,* edited by A. Wylie and M. Conkey), 328–358.

Kansa, E. (2005) A Community Approach to Data Integration: Authorship and Building Meaningful Links Across Diverse Archaeological Data Sets. *Geosphere* 1, 97–109.

Landow, G. (1992) *Hypertext: The Convergence of Contemporary Critical Theory and Technology.* Baltimore, Md., Johns Hopkins University Press.

Lock, G. (2003) *Using Computers in Archaeology.* New York, Routledge.

MacDougall, D. (1998) *Transcultural Cinema.* Princeton, NJ, Princeton University Press.

Manovich, L. (2001) *The Language of New Media.* Cambridge, MA, MIT Press.

Okin, J. R. (2005) *The Information Revolution: The Not-for-dummies Guide to the History, Technology, and Use of the World Wide Web.* Winter Harbor, ME, IronBound Press.

Pavlu, I. (2000) *Life on a Neolithic Site.* Praha, Institute of Archaeology, CAS.

Richards, J. (2002) Digital Preservation and Access. *European Journal of Archaeology* 5, 343–366.

Shane, O. and Küçük, M. (2000) Presenting Çatalhöyük. In I. Hodder (ed.) *Towards Reflexive Method in Archaeology: The Example at Çatalhöyük by Members of the Çatalhöyük Teams,* 218–228. Cambridge, McDonald Institute for Archaeological Research.

Shanks, M. (1991) *Experiencing the Past: On the Character of Archaeology.* London, Routledge.

Shanks, M. (2007) Digital Media, Agile Design and the Politics of Archaeological Authorship. In T. Clack and M. Brittain (eds) *Archaeology and Media,* 273–289. Walnut Creek, CA, Left Coast Press.

Sontag, S. (1977) *On Photography.* New York, Delta Books.

Soudsky, B. and Pavlu, I. (1972) The Linear Pottery Culture Settlement Patterns of Central Europe. In P. Ucko, R. Tringham and G. Dimbleby (eds) *Man, Settlement, and Urbanism,* 317–328. London, Duckworth.

Stevanović, M. (2000) Visualizing and Vocalizing the Archaeological Archival Record: Narrative vs. Image. In I. Hodder (ed.) *Towards Reflexive Method in Archaeology: The Example at Çatalhöyük by Members of the Çatalhöyük Teams,* 235–238. Cambridge, UK, McDonald Institute for Archaeological Research.

Tringham, R. (1991a) Households with Faces: The Challenge of Gender in Prehistoric Architectural Remains. In J. Gero and M. Conkey (eds) *En-*

gendering Archaeology: Women and Prehistory, 93–131. Oxford, Basil Blackwell.

Tringham, R. (1991b) Men and Women in Prehistoric Architecture. *Traditional Dwellings and Settlements Review* III, 9–28.

Tringham, R. (1994) Engendered Places in Prehistory. *Gender, Place, and Culture* 1, 169–203.

Tringham, R. (1995) Archaeological Houses, Households, Housework and the Home. In D. Benjamin and D. Stea (eds) *The Home: Words, Interpretations, Meanings, and Environments*, 79–107. Aldershot, Avebury Press.

Tringham, R. (1996) Preliminary Report of the Excavation of the Eneolithic Tell of Podgoritsa, Bulgaria. *Berkeley Archaeology* 3, 7–9.

Tringham, R. (2004) Interweaving Digital Narratives with Dynamic Archaeological Databases for the Public Presentation of Cultural Heritage. In W. Börner and W. Stadtarcheologie (eds) *Enter the Past: The E-way into the Four Dimensions of Cultural heritage – CAA2003., Computer Applications and Quantitative Methods in Archaeology*, 196–200 (full version on accompanying CDROM). Oxford, UK, Archeopress (BAR International Series 1227).

Tringham, R. (in press a) Household through a Digital Lens. In C. Foster and B. Parker (eds) *Household Archaeology: New Perspectives from the Near East and Beyond*. New York, Eisenbrauns Publishing.

Tringham, R. (in press b) The Public Face of Archaeology at Çatalhöyük, Turkey. In R. Tringham and M. Stevanović (eds) *House Lives: Building, Inhabiting, Excavating a House at Çatalhöyük, Turkey. Reports from the Bach Area, Çatalhöyük, 1997–2003*. Los Angeles, CA: Cotesen Institute of Archaeology Publications, UCLA.

Tringham, R. and Ashley, M. (in press) Creating and Archiving the Media Database and Documentation of the Excavation. In R. Tringham and M. Stevanović (eds) *House Lives: Building, Inhabiting, Excavating a House at Çatalhöyük, Turkey. Reports from the Bach Area, Çatalhöyük, 1997–2003*. Los Angeles, CA: Cotesen Institute of Archaeology Publications, UCLA.

White, S. (2005) *A Brief History of Computing*. http://trillian.randomstuff.org.uk/~stephen/history/. Acessed: 04/01/2006.

Wittman, N., Tringham, R. and Ashley, M. (2007) Remixing Çatalhöyük. http://okapi.dreamhosters.co./remixing/mainpage.html. Accessed: 10/12/2009.

Wolle, A. and Tringham, R. (2000) Multiple Çatalhöyüks on the World Wide Web. In I. Hodder (ed.) *Towards Reflexive Method in Archaeology: The Example at Çatalhöyük by Members of the Çatalhöyük Teams*, 207–218. Cambridge, McDonald Institute for Archaeological Research.

5. Layers of meaning: Concealment, memory and secrecy in the British Early Bronze Age

Andrew Jones

Introduction

A number of features characterise mortuary rituals at the end of the Neolithic and the beginning of the Bronze Age in Britain (the period covering approximately 2200–1500 BC). These include the construction of barrows of layered earth and stone cairns of mounded rubble covering the dead; the burial of individuals as inhumations or cremations enclosed in grave cuts, stone cists, or coffins; and the deposition of artefacts in close association with the dead. Outside the mortuary sphere, but necessarily connected with it, this period of prehistory also witnesses the emergence of large scale hoards of artefacts, typically metalwork, typically deposited in watery places or buried beneath the ground.

We rarely reflect upon why each of these elements occurs together at the same period of prehistory. In this paper I will argue that these distinct practices are intimately connected to a fundamental change in the materiality of mortuary practices and in the understanding of the relationship between the living and the dead. I suggest that during the Late Neolithic/Early Bronze Age mortuary practices were primarily concerned with ideas of concealment and containment as a means of maintaining public secrecy and orchestrating remembrance. I argue that acts of concealment, covering, layering, discard and breakage are replete with meaning during this period in British prehistory. Layering is rich with memory, but also relates to protective practices and to the need for secrecy. Why this is so, and why this should come about during this period of British prehistory is the subject of this paper.

Layers, memories and protection

The significance of acts of concealment and destruction are evident in Michael Taussig's book *Defacement* (1999). Taussig is concerned to discuss a series of practices he describes as the 'labour of the negative'; including defacement, destruction, concealment and sacrifice. For Taussig, each of these activities is creative of sacred power, as things or people are *desecrated* they rupture or alter the surface appearance of everyday life. It is the relationship between depth and surface that is crucial here; it is the act of rupturing or sacrificing, thereby revealing that which is concealed which brings the relation between surface and depth into dramatic focus. These kinds of activities less reveal hidden secrets than reveal the social significance of secrecy. These acts, Taussig argues, reveal the importance of the public secret – 'that which is generally known, but which can rarely be articulated'. These practices are a web of activities that help articulate the relationship between depth and surface and aid the negotiation of the relationship between public secrets (knowing what not to know) and public knowledge. The possession of the knowledge of public secrets, as much as public knowledge, is a route to social power. I believe that the significance of secrecy and its relationship to power is something which can illuminate our understanding of a series of cultural practices during the Early Bronze Age, including the deposition of metalwork and the treatment of the body during mortuary ritual.

One subject that is absent from Taussig's account of the negotiation of public secrecy is that of memory. How are the acts of concealment, sacrifice and defacement remembered? How significant are the material forms that these activities take? A number of Taussig's case studies draw on the drama of revelation and concealment, masking and unmasking that take place in initiation rituals. Here the material accoutrements of ritual – masks, face and body paint – are critical to the sensory appreciation of the public secret. The materiality of ritual therefore helps to convey or impress itself upon memory. Taussig charts many acts of defacement from the destruction of dollar bills or the American flag to the deliberate defilement of a statue of the Queen and Prince Phillip outside the Australian Parliament in Canberra. Each of these events pivot upon the dramatic and spectacular destruction of material objects held to be sacrosanct. Again I argue it is both the material medium and its dramatic destruction which is crucial to the formation of memory. As we are well aware from other ethnographic and historical contexts the destruction or deliberate forgetting of artefacts forms a critical space for remembrance (Forty and Küchler 1999).

If we are to talk of acts of destruction, sacrifice and concealment we need to counterbalance this with an examination of those contexts in which objects do in fact retain their integrity. In discussing this we need to consider why some objects are destroyed, while others are treated with care prior to being concealed, and in what kinds of contexts these acts take place. Here a critical topic of discussion is containment and protection. In this regard I find Alfred Gell's discussion of apotropaic (or protective) practices in relation to the anthropology of art particularly illuminating (Gell 1998).

Gell's major emphasis lies in explaining the seductive power of art. He is particularly keen to understand how art objects mediate social agency. One central plank of his argument relates to the way in which decoratively complex surfaces attract or repel the viewer. Fields of repetitive or complex pattern create a cognitively powerful effect lending surfaces with an apotropaic function.

Decoration is therefore a component of a social technology for attracting or 'enchanting' the viewer so making art objects both seductive

in their power over others, and protective in their power as they visually arrest the viewer. An example of the protective power of designs is the *Kolam*. *Kolam* designs are intricate sinuous loops produced by women in Tamiland, south India as threshold devices. They are produced on a daily basis in sand, rice powder or lime and their purpose is to ensnare demons and so protect the household from harm (Gell 1998, 84–86).

Of significance here is the integrity of the surfaces of objects, or the visual effect of a surface created by a pattern. Nevertheless, I believe Gell's notion of apotropaism need not be limited to decorated surfaces, but may be extended to undecorated surfaces especially where those surfaces exhibit complexity or repetition in other ways. As when surfaces are covered in multiple layers or wrappings or cover, contain or hide that which is contained within. Surfaces contained by complex wrappings or coverings also exhibit cognitive complexity. We only have to consider the protective role of complex wrapping in the mortuary practices of New Kingdom Egypt to realise the significance that wrappings or coverings play. As Meskell observes for New Kingdom Egypt: 'linen wrapping provided the body with a type of all-over amuletic protection' (Meskell and Joyce 2003, 133).

The properties of wrapped surfaces lead us to consider the mnemonic consequence of layering. Again drawing on New Kingdom Egypt the purpose of wrapping was to achieve the transubstantiation of the individual from subject to object. Mummification, wrappings and coffin and sarcophagi designs were intended to produce a mimetic likeness of the deceased thereby extending their being beyond the mortal plane (Meskell and Joyce 2003, 129–134). Layers and surfaces were here used to mnemonic effect, to produce a reminder of the deceased.

We have discussed the importance of the integrity of surfaces as a counterpoint to Taussig's overarching discussion of the significance of the rupture of surfaces. Importantly both accounts emphasise the seductive power of material culture. The complexity of decoration and layering is cognitively seductive as it ensnares the viewer, but equally the stripping away of surface is seductive as it enables the viewer to glimpse or articulate the public secret. In either event the material qualities of the surface and the act of stripping it away are critical to the formation of memory. In what follows it is the materiality of material culture that I want to stress. An analysis of this materiality in terms of social power will be discussed in the conclusion.

Layering and containment in the British Late Neolithic/Early Bronze Age

It is my contention that a series of Late Neolithic/ Early Bronze Age practices are linked by a novel emphasis upon layers and surfaces. I will review some of these ideas in the British Late Neolithic/ Early Bronze Age, and then focus on how they are performed in the regional contexts of North-western and Northeastern Scotland.

Let us begin with the human body. The burial of entire inhumations in a dug grave pit, stone cist, wooden coffin or on the ground surface has been viewed as one of the characteristic features of early beaker burial. Importantly the sealed nature of the deposit ensures that individual remains intact. In rare instances we observe the human body wrapped in cloth as at Deeping St. Nicholas, Lincolnshire (French 1994). Here a female inhumation aged between 20–30, accompanied by a string of four jet beads and a polished pigs tooth, was wrapped in a shroud and placed as a secondary burial into an earthen barrow.

In some regions of Scotland – at sites like Horsbrugh Castle Farm, Peebleshire (Petersen *et al.* 1974) and Sand Field, Orkney (Dalland 1999) – it seems that burials within stone cists are being opened and revisited. Likewise a number of grave deposits in the Yorkshire Wolds suggest similar practices of re-opening, with some graves containing multiple individuals (Petersen 1972). Despite this, the character of Late Neolithic/Early Bronze Age grave architecture is suggestive of a concern with containment.

On the face of it, cremation deposits seem to contrast with inhumations, but they too evoke the notion of containment and the integrity

of boundaries or surfaces. Many are placed in pits or ceramic containers. In fact the image of containment is heightened by the inversion of many urns over cremation deposits. The relatively intact nature of Early Bronze Age cremations is all the more striking if we compare them with the far more token cremation deposits of the Late Bronze Age (Brück 1995). In both cases it is important that the body remains intact and is enclosed either by the grave cut, pit, stone cist, coffin, or by a ceramic container.

The containment of the body by ceramic container leads us to consider the role of artefacts in the Late Neolithic/ Early Bronze Age. I argue that it is no accident that the emergence of grave goods occurs in tandem with a mortuary rite that emphasises the integrity of the body. Julian Thomas noted some time ago that the body acts as a canvas for the mapping of identity (Thomas 1991a). Artefacts are arranged around the body for this purpose. More than this – artefacts *enclose* the body. This is especially the case where we see items such as jet or amber necklaces encircling the body, or goldwork arranged around the body.

The principle of containment is expressed even more vividly when we examine pottery. As already noted pots such as food vessels, collared and cordoned urns are used to contain the cremated remains of the dead. Sometimes the enclosure of the body is taken to extremes as with the double collared urn burial – with one urn upended on the other recently excavated at Bradley Fen, Cambridgeshire (Mark Knight, person. comm.). A similar 'cocktail shaker' arrangement of food vessels was found at Anc's Hill, Staffordshire (Chitty 1929; Mullin 2001; 2003). With inhumations an emphasis is also placed upon the most vulnerable points around the body's surface – pots such as beakers and food vessels are arranged around the body's orifices. Gavin Lucas (1996) notes this for the Early Bronze Age of Yorkshire (see also Tuckwell 1975). It is also a feature of the beaker burials of Northeast Scotland (Shepherd 1986).

While decorated pottery is not unique to the Early Bronze Age, what is notable is the context in which it is found. Robin Boast's analysis of beakers from domestic and funerary contexts across Britain demonstrates the preponderance of the most complex decorated beakers in funerary contexts (Boast 1995). While food vessels and the various forms of urns are found in both decorated and undecorated forms, it is notable that these forms of pottery are predominately found in funerary contexts.

What is striking is that the same vocabulary of decorative motifs also occurs on items of adornment, such as jet necklaces, as well as on small metal objects such as razors. It would appear that it was important not only to deposit artefacts with the dead, but to place *decorated* artefacts with the dead. In some cases artefacts are used to contain additional elaborately decorated objects – this is true of the series of nested collared urns containing an exotic French Vase à Anse from Gallibury Down, Isle of Wight (Tomalin 1988). The principle of enclosure is also observed at Sudbrook, Lincolnshire. Here an enlarged inverted collared urn covered a miniature collared urn standing upright in a sandpit. Three collared urns then encircled the deposit (Allen and Hopkins 2000, 299–300). The phenomenon of nesting is also true of accessory cups, which are often deposited within collared or cordoned urns in Scotland and Ireland (Kavanagh 1977; Longworth 1984).

We have seen how the principles of containment and layering relate to artefacts and the treatment of the body. How do they relate to barrow architecture? In their earliest stages barrows and cairns often consist of a circular area demarcated by a fence, ditch or low stone wall. This area is a focus for burial deposits. As Barrett (1988; 1990; 1994) has argued for Amesbury G71 and Winterbourne Stoke Crossroads, Wiltshire and Long Crichel 5 and 7, Dorset (Barrett *et al.* 1991) the construction of barrows is a lengthy process with a repetitive accretion of layers of earth and chalk to infill the burial zone. The creation of the barrow is the outcome of this successive process of layering. In a similar way Bradley (1998) has recently drawn our attention to the gradual enclosure and infilling of stone circles in northern and western Britain as their role shifts to one of burial.

At this point it is worth pointing out that this process of concealing the contents of barrows and cairns is akin to the process of infilling chambered tombs (Thomas 1991b). I do not have space to address this issue in detail but it is worth noting that chronologically speaking it is precisely at the point when chambered tombs are enclosed with successive layers of earth or stone rubble – often containing Early Bronze Age burials – that the first barrows are constructed.

In each case what we observe is a concern with containment – creating a relatively impermeable boundary around a monument and a related concern with concealing or infilling this area with layers of earth or stone. Each layering or containment event was made with reference to that which had gone before, however it is crucial that the initial phases of monuments were circular bounded enclosures. While the eventual outcome may have varied at different sites – resulting in the various categories of barrows or variant circles – the principles involved in their creation remained similar – a process of containment and concealment.

In a similar sense, the formation of barrow cemeteries relates to a series of individual decisions. However as many authors have noted barrow cemeteries also exhibit regularity, both at the level of individual cemeteries and at the regional level. Just as the process of barrow creation involves the gradual containment and concealment of their contents, so too the formation of barrow cemeteries conceals and contains regions of landscape. Aaron Watson (2001) has noted how the cemeteries at Overton Hill and Winterbourne Stoke Crossroads, Wiltshire channel movement and create thresholds around landscapes containing the important Late Neolithic henges at Avebury and Stonehenge respectively. In effect, from the perspective of an observer situated within either Stonehenge or Avebury a 'visual envelope' is created by barrows surrounding these monuments (Cleal *et al.* 1995). Similarly, Ann and Peter Woodward (1996) have demonstrated that the barrow cemeteries in Dorset form an arc around the Later Neolithic sites at Mount Pleasant and Maumbury Rings situated in the Frome Valley.

I have argued that the surface of the human body was covered in a nested series of layers, with artefacts surrounding the corpse, or cremation, and with the architecture of the mound gradually enclosing the body in a series of successive layers. In some cases the cemeteries of mounds, in which the dead lay, enclosed and concealed regions of landscape.

Deposition and defacement during the British Late Neolithic and Early Bronze Age

The subject of deliberate and structured deposition during the Late Neolithic and Early Bronze Age is an important area of discussion (*e.g.* Bradley 1990; Needham 1988; Pollard 2001; Richards and Thomas 1984). The major point to note here is not only that objects are deposited in formal arrangements but that there are rules governing acts of deposition. For example, for the Early Bronze Age it is typical to find daggers deposited in grave assemblages, while flat axes are usually deposited in non-funerary contexts singly or as hoards (Barrett and Needham 1988; Needham 1988). Artefacts are often deposited in formal deposits in special places; either in prominent dry land locations such as mountain passes or beneath spectacular geological features, or they are deposited in wetland locations such as bogs or rivers (Bradley 1990; 2000, 47–63). Finally, artefacts often appear to be deliberately broken or smashed prior to deposition. For instance flat axes are often broken in two, shaft hole implements such as battle-axes and stone axe-hammers are often broken across their hafting holes, ceramics such as beakers may be deliberately smashed (Woodward 2000; 2002) in certain contexts. Furthermore objects of adornment such as jet or amber spacer plate necklaces may be fragmented prior to deposition (Jones 2002; 2005; Woodward 2002). Objects of gold are likewise often deliberately crushed prior to deposition. This is true of the gold *lanulae* (decorated crescentic necklaces) of Ireland which are often found deposited in a crushed or tangled state (Eogan 1994). In many ways these deliberate acts of destruction appear to be the antithesis of the acts of concealment and layering that we have discussed above. It is important

to point out however that many of the objects, which undergo acts of defacement or destruction prior to deposition, are subsequently concealed. They are either buried in special places or they are removed from circulation, whether permanently or temporarily (Needham 2001), by depositing them in inaccessible places such as rivers or bogs.

The close relationship between grave contexts and the deposition of artefacts as hoards has been discussed since the recognition of the significance of artefact deposition (see Bradley 1990, 191–203). Here I argue that the burial of objects and people beneath layers of earth or stone and the deposition of artefacts beneath the earth or the shimmering surface of lakes, rivers or bogs are two poles of the same form of activity. On one hand we have burials which create a tangible reminder in the form of earth and stone of the deceased. On the other hand we have acts which are concerned with removing objects from visible public view. Both culminate in acts of concealment, and in this they are linked, but the two have quite different social effects. Below I want to consider these activities in two regions of Late Neolithic/Early Bronze Age Scotland as a means of drawing out these distinctions.

Layers of meaning in the Late Neolithic and Early Bronze Age of Aberdeenshire and Argyll, Scotland

My argument has been general so far. I now want to focus on case studies from two different regions of Scotland: Aberdeenshire (Northeastern Scotland) and Argyllshire (Northwestern Scotland). I have compared these two regions in a previous work (Jones 2003).

In many ways there appears to be a superficial similarity between the two regions in terms of their archaeology. Both have stone circles dating to the Early Bronze Age, both have evidence for prehistoric rock art, both have extensive evidence for burial in stone lined cists or beneath round stone or earthen cairns or barrows. The major difference lies in the evidence for the deposition of metalwork. While Argyll has native deposits of copper, there are few deposits of metalwork. In contrast Aberdeenshire has plentiful evidence for

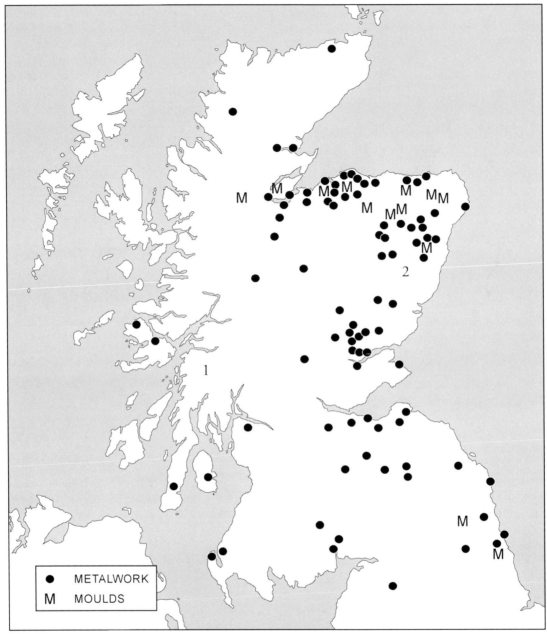

Figure 5.1 Map of Scotland illustrating the distribution of metalwork deposits and moulds. 1: Argyllshire; 2: Aberdeenshire (after Burgess and Schmidt 1981; Cowie 1988).

the deposition of both hoards and single finds of metal objects (Fig. 5.1).

These two regions are conjoined by networks of exchange although situated on opposite coasts of Scotland. Late Neolithic artefacts distinctive of Northeastern Scotland, such as carved stone balls, have been found in archaeological contexts in Mid-Argyll (RCAHMS 1988, 5). As noted above the

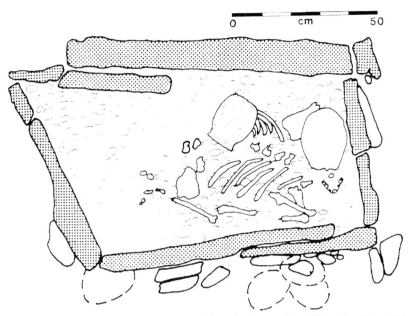

Figure 5.2 A typical Aberdeenshire cist burial accompanied by a beaker pot from Chapelden, Tore of Troup, Banff and Buchan district (after Greig et al. 1989).

high incidence of metalwork from Aberdeenshire distinguishes the region. Importantly a number of examples of this metalwork are likely to have come from Irish metal sources (Cowie 1988, 6). Argyllshire is a likely route of exchange from Ireland to other parts of Scotland and northern Britain.

Previously I have suggested that the two regions have distinctive memorial practices and that these offer different kinds of narrative platforms from which to form identity. In effect, due to the close relationship between the practice of remembrance and the formation of identities, what I have elsewhere termed 'technologies of remembrance' (Jones 2003), the identities formed in both regions are quite distinct. In Aberdeenshire the person relates themselves to the past through adherence to strict and formalised codes of behaviour, manifested in formal mortuary and metalwork deposits. In Argyllshire the person is more closely related to place and understands their place in the world spatially. Here I want to discuss these two regions as engaged in two related, but different, social strategies; strategies simultaneously meant to draw attention to the relationship between the living and

the dead and to shape remembrance. In each case I am keen to stress the significance of materiality in the performance of these social strategies.

Artefact deposition in Aberdeenshire

I want to focus in the main on the treatment of objects in Aberdeenshire, especially metalwork and ceramics. Here it is important to focus on the condition and context in which objects are deposited. The major classes of metalwork from Late Neolithic/Early Bronze Age Aberdeenshire include flat axes, halberds (a form of hafted dagger), spearheads, armlets. All of these are of copper or bronze. In addition there are rare examples of gold *lanulae* and necklaces fashioned from jet beads. Ceramics are mainly highly decorated beakers or food vessels.

Beaker pottery is deposited in two different kinds of context. Beakers are mainly found deposited in grave contexts. Beaker graves in Aberdeenshire are striking in their formality (Fig. 5.2). The body is placed in a flexed position in a stone cist (or box) and males and females are precisely oriented (Shepherd in Grieg *et al.* 1989). As is common with beaker burials throughout the British Isles, beaker burials in Northeast Scotland are composed of a well defined set of grave goods including the beaker, archer's wristguard and barbed and tanged arrowhead. In addition it is common to find flint artefacts or flakes, objects such as flint knives or scrapers in this context. There are patterns in the layout of these objects around the corpse. In particular beakers are typically found deposited behind or in front of the head or below the body near the bottom or feet.

A number of these beaker burials are found in small cemeteries, often located in prominent natural features such as knolls or glacial hillocks as at Buckie, Moray (Walker 1968); Lesmurdie, Cabrach (Robertson 1854); Leslie, Premnay (Callander 1912), Upper Boyndie, Tyrie (Low 1933) or Borrowstone, Newmills (Shepherd 1984; 1986). It is likely that these constitute small family groups (Shepherd 1986, 13). In the majority of cases however beaker burials are isolated. They are occasionally associated with earlier monuments as at Broomend of Crichie (Dalrymple 1855) where the beaker burials cluster around the monumental avenue leading to the henge. At Dalladies long barrow (Piggott 1972) and the ring mounds of Boghead (Burl 1984) and Midtown of Pitglassie (Shepherd 1996) sherds of beaker are inserted into the mound.

Occasionally beakers are deposited in other contexts. At the stone circle of Tomnaverie the sherds of two beakers were smashed against the ring cairn, while sherds of beaker are found at the stone circles of Loanhead of Daviot, Old Keig and Berrybrae (Burl 1979; 1995, 97). The act of breakage evinced at Tomnaverie is echoed at the beaker burial at Chapelden (Greig *et al.* 1989) where sherds from a second beaker appeared to have been deliberately deposited on the cover of a sealed cist. We seem to be picking up two kinds of act appropriate for the deposition of beakers. Either they are treated with great care and formality when they are deposited with the dead or they are deliberately smashed fragments and are inserted into earlier monuments. Fragmentation is also evident for other objects placed in burial contexts.

For example at Greenhowe, Pluscarden the end plates of a jet necklace were deposited with an adult inhumation, and at Hill of Roseisle sixty-four spacer plates were deposited with an inhumation (Shepherd 1985; Jones 2002, 167).

The deliberate destruction and deposition of artefacts is also a feature of the treatment of metalwork. As already noted, metalwork is mainly found as single finds or, occasionally, in the forms of hoard of artefacts. The provenance of many of these deposits is unclear but a number of the hoards of objects were deposited in special places. Cowie (1988, 20) notes a hoard of six axes from a stone cairn at Durris, and a hoard of 7–8 axes from a barrow at Hill of Fortrie, Inverkeithney. In addition he discusses the striking deposition of two axes from the Pass of Ballater placed into a cleft in the rocky scree of this foreboding place (Cowie 1988, 19). The extensive hoard from the Hill of Finglenny, Rhynie was deposited beneath a large stone overlooking the Late Neolithic henge at Wormy Hillock. Probably the most remarkable hoard comes from Colleonard Farm, Banff (Fig. 5.3). A hoard of seven axes was deposited within a food vessel. The axes were packed into the vessel with their blades uppermost; two flat slabs then protected the deposit.

Many of the axes in the Colleonard hoard as well as the Hill of Finglenny find are broken or damaged. The Colleonard hoard exhibits a variability of states of wear. All of the axes appear worn including the two axes decorated with 'raindrop' motifs. A further two axe fragments are present in the hoard. The Hill of Finglenny hoard includes eight axes, at least two of these axes have been deliberately snapped across the blade, and a further two fragments of axe are also present. Wear is also a feature of other artefacts found in hoards, such as the four halberds found at Auchingoul, Inverkeithny, Banff (Cowie 1988, 5).

Wear is present more generally on artefacts from the region. A survey of all metalwork for the region (data from inventories in Burgess and Schmidt 1981; Cowie 1988) suggest that 64% of all metalwork is damaged or fragmented prior to deposition. Some objects seem to suffer higher incidences of damage than others, of the

FINGLENNY

COLLEONARD FARM

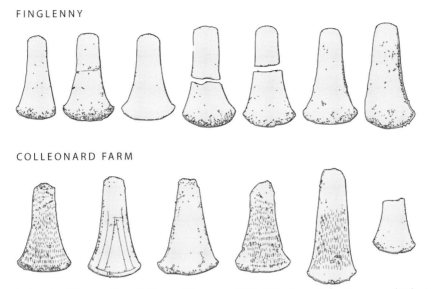

Figure 5.3 the hoards of flat axes from Colleonard Farm and Hill of Finglenny (after Burgess and Schmidt 1981).

few halberds and daggers from the region all are damaged. For axes the incidence of damage appears to be lower, with around 39 per cent fragmented or damaged. These differences in patterns of fragmentation are likely to relate in part to the different networks of exchange artefacts are caught up in; we should expect different artefacts to have biographies of different duration (Woodward 2002).

The high incidence of metalwork deposits, along with their often spectacular manner of destruction is a prominent feature of the Early Bronze Age of North-eastern Scotland. I argue that this destruction and deposition of metalwork and, to a lesser extent beakers and jet necklace, is an important social strategy of display. That artefacts were employed as objects of display is underlined by the high incidence of bronzes coated in tin from this region (Kinnes *et al.* 1979; Needham and Kinnes 1981), this technological development would have invested bronze with an unusual, and characteristic, colour and sheen.

Such display often draws on and blurs with the formality and display involved in laying out and dressing the corpse for burial. Indeed as we have seen the Colleonard Farm hoard draws directly on the grammar of contemporary funerary practice for

its significance. Likewise the unusual deposit of two bronze axes and a halberd from Sluie, Moray deposited in a cist (Cowie 1988, 18) metaphorically signifies human burial. Furthermore the grammar of burial is implied in the burial of the two hoards of axes at Durris and Hill of Fortrie in cairns or barrows. More generally this grammar is implicated in the sequence of activity surrounding the deposition of artefacts; they are collected together, then broken, then deposited beneath the ground. The real differences lie in the relationship between artefacts associated with the corpse and those that are deposited in non-funerary contexts. In funerary contexts artefacts are generally deposited complete, outside this context they are more often broken prior to burial. In both contexts I would argue that artefacts act as surrogates for the human body. In funerary contexts artefacts surround the corpse and the corpse is remembered through the medium of a regular assemblage of artefacts. The dead were effectively transubstantiated in the form of objects.

The integrity of objects accompanying the corpse is important to convey both a sense of personhood and to protect the corpse. However inside and outside funerary contexts we also observe fragmented artefacts. I have suggested elsewhere (Jones 2002) that the fragmentation of objects in and around funerary sites is a powerful act in which the deceased is remembered through the transaction of fragments of artefacts. This is especially true where components of objects such as jet necklaces are deposited while the living retains the rest of the artefact (Jones 2002).

The notion of artefacts as surrogates for, or metaphors of, the human body may be brought into focus when artefacts like metalwork are exchanged and transacted between the living (Barrett and Needham 1988; Cowie 1988). The deposition of metalwork therefore draws on the formulae of contemporary burial practices while its destruction severs the social ties that its transaction helped to create.

Both acts, the spectacular destruction of metal objects and the deposition of grave goods, impress themselves upon memory. In the first instance the colour of objects, their biographies or exchange histories and their breakage or defacement act as vehicles for remembrance. In the second instance the colour or decoration of objects and their formalised display around the corpse achieve the same function.

In this section I have emphasised funerary contexts and hoard as strategies for orchestrating remembrance. I have said less about monuments. This is not because monuments are absent in Northeast Scotland. Indeed the region is known for its Recumbent Stone Circles. These are evidently used for the cremation of individuals and the deposition of fragments of material culture. However they do not serve as focuses for the deposition of the dead or for artefact hoards until much later in the Bronze Age. Likewise, I have said little about contemporary rock art. In this region rock art tends to be executed in the vicinity of stone circles and is less extensive in the surrounding landscape. By way of contrast I now want to examine a region in Northwest Scotland where monumentality and rock art play a critical part in strategies of remembrance.

Layers of meaning in the Kilmartin Valley, Argyll

In discussing the archaeology of Northwest

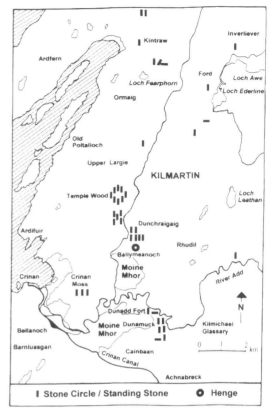

Figure 5.4 Map of Kilmartin Glen indicating the position of major monuments.

Scotland I want to focus a lot more closely on a well known prehistoric landscape: the Kilmartin valley, Mid-Argyll (Fig. 5.4) as a comparison to the commemorative practices of Northeast Scotland. I have chosen to focus on this region, as it is the subject of an ongoing field project.

The steep-sided, flat-bottomed valley of Kilmartin has a remarkable concentration of prehistoric monuments, including chambered cairns, cairns, cists, timber circles, stone circles, henges, standing stones and rock art. The Late Neolithic/Early Bronze Age sees a marked increase in monument building associated with reworking the landscape. During the Late Neolithic the henge at Ballymeanoch was built, as were the timber circles at Temple Wood and the timber circle and timber alignment at Upper Largie. During the

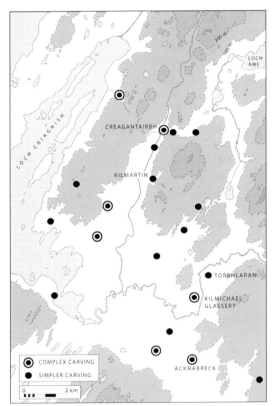

Figure 5.5 Map of Kilmartin Glen indicating the location of rock art sites.

Figure 5.6 Axe motifs at Nether Largie, Kilmartin Glen, Argyll.

Early Bronze Age a number of Neolithic features become the focus of burial – beaker burials in cists are inserted into Ballymeanoch henge and Temple Wood (Scott 1989). Probably the most spectacular process of reworking relates to the Nether Largie south chambered tomb. Here a series of beaker burials and a cremation were inserted into the compartments of the tomb and the tomb was sealed with successive layers of pebbles. The outer cairn was also the focus for two later cist burials, one with a food vessel (Henshall 1963).

Nether Largie is also the focal point for a linear cairn cemetery, which begins in the hills to the north with the impressive hilltop cairn at Carnasserie, and ends some miles to the south with the cists at Rowanfield. A further cemetery complex occurs around Ballymeanoch. Both Ballymeanoch and Nether Largie also have impressive stone rows.

Linear cist cemeteries, clustered in two groups in Upper Largie and Poltalloch are located on hill terraces.

Rock art is a feature of the archaeology of Kilmartin (Morris 1977). The most complex rock art sites are found in upland locations at the junction between valleys (Fig. 5.5), or at entry points into the main valley (Bradley 1997, 120–123). Less complex sites are found on the lower terraces of the valley overlooking monument complexes at Baluachraig, Nether Largie and Glennan. A number of monuments are also decorated, including Temple Wood stone circle with its double spiral, the series of cup and ring marks on the Ballymeanoch, Nether Largie and Torbhlaren standing stones and the series of axe motifs on cist slabs from Ri Cruin and Nether Largie North (Fig. 5.6). Geometric designs are found on cists at Cairnbaan, Barloisnoch and Badden (Campbell *et al.* 1960; Jones 2001; RCAHMS 1988).

How are these various features related to the mortuary process? Can we observe a sequence of activity? As a general observation the monuments in the Kilmartin valley are made up of both linear cist cemeteries and linear cemeteries of cist burials beneath cairns. Both cists and cairns contain food vessels. This suggests that the two forms of mortuary architecture are part of the same tradition; a tradition, which begins with the construction of cists and in certain cases, is finalised by the burial of cists beneath cairns. In addition, the cists are constructed with an unusual grooved technique. I have argued elsewhere (Jones 2001) that these are designed so as to be almost freestanding prior to burial beneath cairns, thereby providing access to the cist after burial takes place.

Support for this interpretation comes from Canon Greenwell who excavated the Kilmartin Glebe cairn. The re-interpretation of Greenwell's excavation by the Royal Commission ([1988] 1999, 28–29) suggests a two-phase construction with the earlier phase represented by a boulder ring and slab-built cist and the later by a further boulder-built cist and cairn enlargement. A similar sequence occurs at the cairns of Nether Largie Mid and North.

Indeed cist slabs themselves may have had a long life history prior to burial. At Nether Largie North the cist slab decorated with axe motifs and cup marks has at least four phases of superimposition (Bradley 1993, 91–93). As Bradley notes this slab is likely to have once been a free standing menhir, possibly part of a stone setting beneath the monument. The act of burying what had once been visible resonates with the excavation sequence at the nearby Temple Wood stone circle, where the cists in the southern circle were gradually encompassed within the monument (Bradley 1998; Scott 1989).

I want to think about the processes of containment and concealment in relation to art, artefacts and monuments. Art plays a significant role here. Curvilinear cup and ring motifs are found in open-air locations in the surrounding landscape. They are also found on prominent standing stones. A quite different vocabulary is found on artefacts placed with the dead (Simpson and Thawley 1972). Late Neolithic/Early Bronze Age ceramics such as beakers and food vessels possess complex linear and geometric motifs, as do spectacular objects such as the jet necklaces buried with inhumations at Kilmartin Glebe and Poltalloch. Stone cist slabs have similar geometric designs or they are carved with representational motifs such as axes. Cist slabs surround the cremated or inhumed body and where those cist slabs are decorated, decoration faces inward towards the corpse. In many cases they are enclosed by images, whether on pots, jet

necklaces or cist slabs. Images placed with the dead are different to those publicly visible on standing stones or on rock art. It seems likely that – as with the examples of Nether Largie North and Ri Cruin carved with images of flat axes – stones are recarved with hidden motifs before they are buried (Bradley 1993, 91–93; Jones 2001). In Kilmartin we begin to see the tremendous power and significance of the principles of concealment and enclosure, and these principles are made all the more obvious as they are marked out by images.

We can think of the features of the landscape as having undergone a series of distinct biographical stages. Artefacts that were once visible, worn or used are now buried with the dead in stone enclosures or cists. These sites and things are periodically revisited, and are commemorated by the construction of cairns or the erection of stone alignments. There is a subtle interplay then between what is hidden, and what is visible as the linear cairn cemeteries and stone alignments create a visible sense of order as they channel movement through the valley. However monuments are also placed in precise landscape positions so as to be effectively enclosed and overlooked by the rock art on the valley sides, which they often reference through decoration. Indeed the threshold to different zones in this landscape is marked by art.

How are we to think of these processes of concealment and containment? Art is used to define thresholds and directs the subject to highly visible monument complexes. Within monuments it circumscribes the dead. Art in the landscape marks out areas of significance which are then revealed by movement through the landscape. There is a similar relationship between secrecy and revelation with art within monuments; the art encircles the dead, as do the successive layers of earth and stone surrounding them. Art also signals the presence of something to be commemorated or remembered. The two forms of art in Kilmartin are meaningfully linked, the hidden art relates to protection and secrecy, while the open-air art draws attention to the significance of the monuments in which this hidden art lies. Kilmartin is unusual because images play such an important role in defining the relationship between the visible and the concealed.

In terms of the deposition of metalwork Argyll is remarkably sparse; very few metal objects have been found for the Late Neolithic/Early Bronze Age. Possibly the most spectacular objects are the two bronze armlets deposited in a cist with an extended inhumation along with a jet necklace at Loch Melfort, Lorn (RCAHMS 1975, 15). A number of flat axes have been found, such as those at Glenforsa, Mull, but nothing to match the hoards from the Northeast. Daggers are also deposited, as at Salen and Callachally, Mull where they accompanied beaker inhumations (RCAHMS 1980, 15).

The material practices of secrecy: Containment, concealment and deposition

I have argued above that there is an equivalence between the containment and concealment of the dead and the destruction and burial of artefacts like metalwork. This was brought to the foreground by comparing the practices of burial and metalwork deposition in two regions of Late Neolithic/Early Bronze Age Scotland. Metalwork obviously flowed through the Northwest; it is commemorated in rock art. It was 'concealed' or removed from public view by being exchanged. By contrast, in the Northeast it was concealed by being destroyed and buried. In the Northeast metalwork was treated in an analogous fashion to human bones, being deposited in pots, cists or barrows. In many ways the burial of metalwork substituted for the far less spectacular burial of the body in funerary contexts in the Northeast. By contrast, in Northwest Scotland the construction of monuments and the execution of rock art were of greater significance.

The wider significance of the practices of concealment and containment is captured in Taussig's phrase that 'secrecy magnifies reality'. That which conceals also reveals. Containing or concealing the dead either with layers of stone or earth, or through the execution of images also draws attention to their significance. Layers and images protect the dead, but they must be made visible to do this. In memorial terms, the act of

forgetting through burial creates a trace to be remembered. Equally the spectacular defacement or breakage of artefacts, especially metalwork, both destroys the object while simultaneously drawing attention to its power as a medium for the creation of social relations. The subsequent burial of bronzes likewise offers a space for remembrance, and in many cases burial occurs in a prominent natural feature. I believe that apotropaic and commemorative practices are linked by the materiality of the layer and surface, the dead are protected by layers, but through the gradual accretion of layers they are made visible and become objects for remembrance.

Why do we observe such an interest in secrecy, destruction, deposition, concealment and commemoration during the Early Bronze Age? In order to answer this we need to consider the sources of symbolic power during this period. The control of metal supply and circulation has long been considered a critical source of social power in the Bronze Age (Barrett and Needham 1988; Bradley 1990; Rowlands 1980). The manipulation of supply through increasingly spectacular acts of deposition was here seen to be central. In a similar sense the placing and the construction of the identity of the corpse at the graveside is seen to be critical to how the burial will be read in terms of the genealogies of the living (Barrett 1994, 123–127; Garwood 1991).

The ability to control the dead and the living in this way arises from the drama of the mortuary rite, which seeks to orchestrate remembrance by displaying the dead and then burying them beneath the earth (Jones 2005). In some cases, this process is aided by the spectacular deposition of coloured or decorated artefacts or through the cremation of the corpse. In exactly the same way the drama of artefact deposition is the locus for power, both over the control of remembrance and the supply of metal itself. Notwithstanding the possibility that some metal artefacts may have been retrieved after deposition (Needham 2001), it is surely the act of breaking and depositing them in the first place that is critical here.

It is the sequence of this event, the moment of highly visible revelation, followed by layering the corpse with artefacts and earth that supplies the dead with their magical force and makes them such a potent resource for the living. It is the *image* of the dead, and the *image* of artefacts being deposited that are critical to the efficacy and successful completion of funerary ritual or artefact deposition. It is for this reason that objects are laid out with formality around the corpse or in the hoard assemblage. It is also for this reason that the distinction between the realms of the living and the dead were so clearly demarcated by rock art in the Kilmartin region. Artefacts and the dead are transformed by deposition from physical traces to memory. It is the formality and display bound up in this transformation that ensures their survival in the memories of the living. It is not only the exercise of power through the manipulation of funerary ritual or artefact deposition, but the social power created by the containment of the results of these events which is critical. By drawing attention not only to the events of burial, but to the material and visible results of the events, whether as prominent barrow or cairn, or significant landscape feature, social power is maintained by the management of secrecy.

Bibliography

Allen, C. and Hopkins, D. (2000) Bronze Age Accessory Cups from Lincolnshire: Early Bronze Age Pot? *Proceedings of the Prehistoric Society* 66, 297–317.

Barrett, J. C. (1988) The Living, the Dead and the Ancestors: Neolithic and Early Bronze Age Mortuary Practices. In J. C. Barrett and I. A. Kinnes, (eds) *The Archaeology of Context in the Neolithic and Bronze Age: Recent Trends*, 30–41. Sheffield, Department of Archaeology and Prehistory, University of Sheffield.

Barrett, J. C. (1990) The Monumentality of Death; the Character of Early Bronze Age Mortuary Mounds in Southern Britain. *World Archaeology* 22, 179–189.

Barrett, J. C. (1994) *Fragments from Antiquity: An Archaeology of Social Life in Britain, 2900–1200 BC.* Oxford, Blackwell.

Barrett, J. C., Bradley, R. and Green, M. (1991) *Landscape, Monuments and Society: the Prehistory of Cranbourne Chase*. Cambridge, Cambridge University Press.

Barrett, J. C. and Needham, S. P. (1988) Production,

Circulation and Exchange: Problems in the Interpretation of Bronze Age Bronzework. In J. C. Barrett and I. A. Kinnes (eds) *The Archaeology of Context in the Neolithic and Bronze Age: Recent Trends*, 127–140. Sheffield, Department of Archaeology and Prehistory, University of Sheffield.

Bradley, R. (1990) *The Passage of Arms*. Cambridge, Cambridge University Press.

Bradley, R. (1993) *Altering the Earth: The Origins of Monuments in Britain and Continental Europe.* Edinburgh, Society of Antiquaries of Scotland.

Bradley, R. (1997) *Rock Art and the Prehistory of Atlantic Europe: Signing the Land.* London, Routledge.

Bradley, R. (1998) *The Significance of Monuments.* London, Routledge.

Bradley, R. (2000) *An Archaeology of Natural Places.* London, Routledge.

Brück, J. (1995) A Place for the Dead: The Role of Human Remains in the Late Bronze Age. *Proceedings of the Prehistoric Society* 61, 245–277.

Burgess, C. and Schmidt, P. K. (1981) *The Axes of Scotland and Northern England.* Munich, Beck'sche Verlagsbuchhandlung. Prahistoriche Bronzefunde Series: Abteilung IX, band 7.

Burl, H. A. W. (1979) *Rings of Stone.* New Haven, Yale University Press.

Burl, H. A. W. (1984) Report on Excavation of a Neolithic Mound at Boghead, Speymouth Forest, Fochabers, Moray 1972 and 1974. *Proceedings of the Society of Antiquaries of Scotland* 114, 35–73.

Burl, H. A. W. (1995) *A Guide to the Stone Circles of Britain, Ireland and Brittany.* New Haven, Yale University Press.

Callander, J. G. (1912) Notice of the Discovery of Two Drinking-Cup Urns in a Short Cist at Mains of Leslie, Aberdeenshire. *Proceedings of the Society of Antiquaries of Scotland* 46, 344–348.

Campbell, M., Scott, J. and Piggott, S. (1960) The Badden Cist Slab. *Proceedings of the Society of Antiquaries of Scotland* 94, 46–61.

Cleal, R., Walker, K. and Montague, R. (1995) *Stonehenge in its Landscape: Twentieth Century Excavations.* London, English Heritage.

Chitty, L. (1929) Twin Food Vessels Preserved at Aqualate Hall, Staffordshire. *Antiquaries Journal* 9, 137–140.

Cowie, T. (1988) *Magic Metal: Early Metalworkers in the North-East.* Aberdeen, Anthropological Museum, University of Aberdeen.

Dalland, M. (1999) Sand Fiold: The Excavation of an Exceptional Cist in Orkney. *Proceedings of the Prehistoric Society* 65, 373–415.

Dalrymple, W. (1855) Notes of the Excavation of a Tumulus, at Auchleven, in the Parish of Premnay and District of Garioch, Aberdeenshire. *Proceedings of the Society of Antiquaries of Scotland* 1, 431–432.

Eogan, G. (1994) *The Accomplished Art*. Oxford, Oxbow.

French, C. (1994) *Excavation of the Deeping St. Nicholas Barrow Complex*. Lincoln, Lincolnshire Archaeological Heritage Report Series 1.

Forty, A. and Küchler, S. (1999) *The Art of Forgetting*. Oxford, Berg.

Garwood, P. (1991) Ritual Tradition and the Reconstruction of Society. In P. Garwood, D. Jennings, R. Skeates and J. Toms (eds) *Sacred and Profane*: *Proceedings of a Conference on Archaeology, Ritual and Religion, Oxford 1989*, 10–32. Oxford, Oxbow.

Gell, A. (1998) *Art and Agency: an Anthropological Theory*. Oxford, Clarendon.

Greig, M. K., Greig, C., Shepherd, A. N. and Shpeherd, I. A. G. (1989) A Beaker Cist from Chapelden, Tore of Troup, Aberdour, Banff and Buchan District, with a Note on the Orientation of Beaker Burials in Northeast Scotland. *Proceedings of the Society of Antiquaries of Scotland* 119, 73–81.

Henshall, A. (1963) *The Chambered Tombs of Scotland*: *Volume 1*. Edinburgh, Edinburgh University Press.

Jones, A. (2001) Enduring Images? Image Production and Memory in Earlier Bronze Age Scotland. In J. Brück (ed.) *Bronze Age Landscapes: Tradition and Transformation*, 217–228. Oxford, Oxbow.

Jones, A. (2002) A Biography of Colour: Colour, material Histories and Personhood in the Early Bronze Age of Britain and Ireland. In A. Jones and G. MacGregor (eds) *Colouring the Past: the Significance of Colour in Archaeological Research*, 159–174. Oxford, Berg.

Jones, A. (2003) Technologies of Remembrance: Memory, Materiality and Identity in Early Bronze Age Scotland. In H. Williams (ed.) *Archaeologies of Remembrance: Death and Memory in Past Societies*, 65–88. New York, Kluwer Plenum.

Jones, A. (2005) Matter and Memory: Colour, Remembrance and the Neolithic/Bronze Age transition. In E. DeMarrais, C. Gosden and C. Renfrew (eds) *Rethinking Materiality: the Engagement of Mind with the Material World*, 167–178. Cambridge, McDonald Institute for Archaeological Research.

Kavanagh, R. (1977) Pygmy Cups in Ireland. *Journal of the Royal Society of Antiquaries of Ireland* 107, 61–95.

Kinnes, I. A., Craddock, P.T ., Needham, S. and Lang, J. (1979) Tin-Plating in the Early Bronze Age: The Barton Stacey Axe. *Antiquity* 53, 141–143.

Longworth, I. (1984) *Collared Urns of the Bronze Age in Great Britain and Ireland*. Cambridge, Cambridge University Press.

Low, A. (1933) Two Short Cists at Upper Boyndlie, Tyrie, Aberdeenshire. *Proceedings of the Society of Antiquaries of Scotland* 67, 176–186.

Lucas, G. (1996) Of Death and Debt: A History of the Body in Neolithic and Bronze Age Yorkshire. *Journal of European Archaeology* 4, 99–118.

Meskell, L. and Joyce, R. A. (2003) *Embodied Lives: Figuring Ancient Maya and Egyptian Experience*. London, Routledge.

Morris, R. (1977) *The Prehistoric Rock Art of Argyll*. Poole, Dolphin Press.

Mullin, D. (2001) Remembering, Forgetting and the Invention of Tradition: Burial and Natural Places in the English Early Bronze Age. *Antiquity* 75, 533–537.

Mullin, D. (2003) *The Bronze Age Landscape of the Northern English Midlands*. Oxford, Archaeopress.

Needham, S. P. (1988) Selective Deposition in the British Early Bronze Age. *World Archaeology* 20, 229–248.

Needham, S. P. (2001) When Expediency Broaches Ritual Intention: The Flow of Metal Between Systemic and Buried Domains. *Journal of the Royal Anthropological Institute* 7, 275–298.

Needham, S. P. and Kinnes, I. A. (1981) Tinned Axes Again. *Antiquity* 55, 133–134.

Petersen, F. (1972) Traditions of Multiple Burial in Later Neolithic and Early Bronze Age England. *Antiquaries Journal* 129, 22–55.

Petersen, F., Shepherd, I. A. G. and Tuckwell, A. N. (1974) A Short Cist at Horsburgh Farm, Peebleshire. *Proceedings of the Society of Antiquaries of Scotland* 105, 43–62.

Piggott, S. (1972) Excavation of the Dalladies Long Barrow, Fettercairn, Kincardineshire. *Proceedings of the Society of Antiquaries of Scotland* 104, 23–47.

Pollard, J. (2001) The Aesthetics of Depositional Practice. *World Archaeology* 33 (2), 315–333.

RCAHMS (1975) *Argyll Volume 2: Lorn*. Edinburgh, HMSO.

RCAHMS (1980) *Argyll Vol 4: Mull, Tiree, Coll and North Argyll*. Edinburgh, HMSO.

RCAHMS (1988) *Argyll Volume 6: Mid-Argyll and Cowal*. Edinburgh, HMSO.

Richards, C. and Thomas, J. (1984) Ritual Activity and Structured Deposition in Later Neolithic Wessex. In

R. Bradley and J. Gardiner (eds) *Neolithic Studies*, 189–218. Oxford, British Archaeological Reports.

Robertson, A. (1854) Notes of the Discovery of Stone Cists at Lesmurdie, Banffshire, Containing Primitive Urns. *Proceedings of the Society of Antiquaries of Scotland* 1, 205–211.

Rowlands, M. (1980) Kinship, Alliance and Exchange in the European Bronze Age. In J. C. Barrett and R. Bradley (eds) *Settlement and Society in the British Later Bronze Age,* 15–55. Oxford, British Archaeological Reports.

Scott, J. (1989) The Stone Circles at Temple Wood, Kilmartin, Argyll. *Glasgow Archaeological Journal* 15, 53–124.

Shepherd, I. A. G (1985) Jet and Amber. In D. V. Clarke, A. Foxon and T. Cowie (eds) *Symbols of Power in the Age of Stonehenge*, 204–216. Edinburgh, HMSO.

Shepherd, I. A. G (1986) *Powerful Pots: Beakers in North-East Prehistory.* Aberdeen, Anthropological Museum, University of Aberdeen.

Shepherd, A. N. (1996) A Neolithic Ring-Mound at Midtown of Pitglassie, Auchterless, Aberdeenshire. *Proceedings of the Society of Antiquaries of Scotland* 126, 17–52.

Simpson, D. and Thawley, J. (1972) Single Grave Art in Britain. *Scottish Archaeological Forum* 4, 81–104.

Taussig, M. (1999) *Defacement: Public Secrecy and the Labor of the Negative.* Stanford, Stanford University Press.

Thomas, J. (1991a) Reading the Body: Beaker Funerary Practice in Britain. In P. Garwood, D. Jennings, R. Skeates and J. Toms (eds) *Sacred and Profane: Proceedings of a Conference on Archaeology, Ritual and Religion, Oxford 1989*, 33–42. Oxford, Oxbow.

Thomas, J. (1991b) *Re-thinking the Neolithic*. Cambridge, Cambridge University Press.

Tomalin, D. (1988) Armorican Vases à Anses and their Occurrence in Southern Britain. *Proceedings of the Prehistoric Society* 54, 203–221.

Tuckwell, A.N. (1975) Patterns of Burial Orientation in the Round Barrows of East Yorkshire. *Bulletin of the Institute of Archaeology University of London* 12, 95–123.

Walker, I. C. (1968) Beakers from Easter Gollachy, near Buckie, Banffshire. *Proceedings of the Society of Antiquaries of Scotland* 100, 188–190.

Watson, A. (2001) Round Barrows in a Circular World: Monumentalising Landscapes in Early Bronze Age Wessex. In J. Brück (ed.) *Bronze Age Landscapes: Tradition and Transformation*, 205–216. Oxford, Oxbow.

Woodward, A. and Woodward, P. (1996) The Topography of Some Barrow Cemeteries in Bronze Age Wessex. *Proceedings of the Prehistoric Society* 62, 275–291.

Woodward, A. (2000) *British Barrows: A matter of Life and Death.* Stroud, Tempus.

Woodward, A. (2002) Beads and Beakers: Heirlooms and Relics in the British Early Bronze Age. *Antiquity* 76, 1040–1047.

6. Constructing the warrior: Death, memory, and the art of warfare

Bryan Hanks

Death is not an event in life: we do not live to experience death. If we take eternity to mean not infinite temporal duration but timelessness, then eternal life belongs to those who live in the present.

(Wittgenstein 1961, 147)

Introduction

There has been an increasing interest in exploring the social aspects of late prehistoric warriors in Eurasia. While some scholars have focused more on the ranking and prestige connected with political authority (*e.g.* Earle 1987; Kristiansen 1998; Kristiansen and Larsson 2005; Shennan 1986) others have emphasised the fluid nature of identity and ethnicity and the wide range of variability in their material expressions. Such approaches have shifted towards theoretical archaeologies, which explore the nuances of the socially constructed body, object materiality, and the significance of funerary rites and monuments as loci for the construction and negotiation of individual and community identities (Arnold 2001; Babić 2002; Dietler 1994; Jones 1997; Wells 2001).

However, the role of memory also has become a vibrant topic of discussion recently among archaeologists, as reflected in the increasing number of conference sessions and edited volumes devoted to this issue (*e.g.* Van Dyke and Alcock 2003; Williams 2003). Many scholars have turned to Connerton's (1989) influential work, which made a useful distinction between two types of memory practices. The first, *embodied* or *incorporated* memory, highlights bodily action and commemorative performance (1989, 7). The second, *inscribed* practices, emphasises the physical nature of texts, monuments, and other material objects as receptacles of information and memory (1989, 73). Connerton's categorisation has been further extended by a number of scholars focusing on the significance of these forms of memory practice for structuring cultural transmission and its relationship to material culture – particularly with regard to non-literate societies (Küchler 1987; Rowlands 1993; Whitehouse 1992).

Goody (2000, 27) has argued that there is a fundamental difference in how memory works within 'oral traditions', or non-literate societies, and that both performance and mnemonic devices play a crucial role in recalling and structuring cultural knowledge. This emphasis on material culture and memory situates archaeological study in a unique position for understanding both long-term cultural continuity and change within prehistoric societies. For example, while past ritual actions connected with embodied and mnemonic practices may be difficult to reconstruct archaeologically, the remnants of these activities are often well represented within archaeological contexts. As Van Dyke and Alcock have suggested, archaeologists '…possess four broad, overlapping categories of materially accessible media through which social memories are commonly constructed and observed: ritual behaviors, narratives, objects and representations, and places' (2003, 4). Within this area of study over the past several years, it is particularly the connection between death, burial, and monumentality that has gripped the attention of archaeological inquiry (Barrett 1990; 1994; Mizoguchi 1993; Williams 2003, 5). While the role of memory through commemorative practices of the living is clearly an important arena of interpretation within mortuary studies, this chapter sets out to examine in more detail the relationship between memory, life history, and the construction of personhood.

It has been suggested that memory is more closely situated within the social body rather than within the individual (Halbwachs 1992). While this is an important perspective, as it emphasises the *social* framework of memory rather than treating it simply as a psychological phenomenon (Williams 2003, 6), it can be argued that it also de-emphasises the importance of memory in the construction of *self*. In recent years, many cognitive theorists have suggested that individual or autobiographical memory is an essential element in the formation of self-identity. As Wang and Conway state, 'instead of defining the self as a mental (the soul) or physical (the body) substance, many contemporary theorists (*e.g.* Conway 1990; Ochs and Capps 1996) conceive of the self as developed, expressed, and reconstructed through narrative creations of the past with temporal and causal dimensions' (2006, 10). This places the role of memory well within the complex fabric of self-identity negotiation and connects with the cultural and physical transformations undertaken throughout an individual's life-time (Fowler 2004, 38–39). Through this on-going 'biographical narrative', the concept of embodiment, including the corpus of physical elements aggregated through the materiality of the body, form a vital component in the continual construction and renegotiation of the individual (Fowler 2002; 2004; Strathern 1988).

This theoretical view can be linked with recent more nuanced approaches to the bioarchaeology of the human body, which emphasise lifecycles, age transitions, and gender negotiation (Gilchrist 2000; 2004; Robb 1997; 2002; Sofaer 2006). In order to more productively investigate the

role of memory in the ontological construction of individuals, it therefore becomes necessary to comprehend more fully the connection between materiality, memory, and bodily experience. This paper aims to examine these important issues as they relate to the emerging socio-historical category of *warriorhood* in the Eurasian steppe Early Iron Age – a period characterised by dynamic social, technological, and ritual transformations.

De-constructing the warrior

Several works in recent years have specifically investigated the material, technological and social aspects of prehistoric warfare in Eurasia (Carmen and Harding 1999; Gilchrist 1999; Kristiansen and Larsson 2005; Osgood *et al.* 2000). One of the most important theoretical discussions regarding this is the 1995 paper by Paul Treherne entitled, 'The Warrior's Beauty: the Masculine Body and Self-Identity in Bronze-Age Europe'. Treherne raises a number of important questions about the material aspects of warrior identity and lifestyle and also their significance in death, burial and commemoration events. Treherne's article highlights death and the construction of social memory through the articulation of the symbolic and aesthetic *beauty* of the warrior during the process of burial. Through the postmortem treatment and conspicuous display of the corpse a fixed image of the warrior individual is inscribed within the memory of the living participants. It is precisely through this memory negotiation and reaffirmation that the deceased individual attains a form of immortality. As Treherne states, 'the culmination of a beautiful death in funerary rites fixes a place for the deceased both in the landscape and the minds of others and as such is one way to obviate the horror and anonymity of death's threshold' (1995, 123). In this way, both life and death are integral elements within the construction of warriorhood and through the process of burial it is possible to transmute the social grief, fear, and finitude associated with death. A similar point, relating to death as described in the Homeric epics, is offered by Vernant when he suggests that, 'death is not a simple demise, a privation of life;

it is a transformation of which the corpse is both the instrument and the object, a transmutation of the subject that functions in and through the body' (1991, 68).

At the very core of these perceptions of transcendence and commemoration lies the subjectivity of the social body, which is constructed throughout the life history of the individual and is therefore conditioned through both individual agency and the cultural norms and attitudes of the society. Treherne argues persuasively for the significance of *masculinity* and *beauty* as key social themes within the construction of a warrior ethos and the bodily aesthetics connected with a lifestyle linked to warfare and violence (1995, 129). As he suggests, the warrior's male symbolism was constituted through a set of themes and behaviors that became 'naturalised' through repeated association and use: '*warfare* seen in weaponry, *alcohol* seen in drinking vessels, *riding/driving* seen in horse harness/ wheeled vehicles, and to a lesser degree *bodily ornamentation*', such as tweezers, razors and combs (1995, 108). While this approach does provide an important vocabulary for recognising the construction of warriorhood through a particular type of lifestyle, it nevertheless has been criticised both for its lack of historicity regarding the 'warrior' category and for failing to consider the trajectory of warrior identity as it changes throughout an individual's lifetime. As Gilchrist has suggested, distinct age grade transitions – such as puberty and old age – can be crucial stages in the development of identity and are therefore significant life events in the *bodily experience* of warriors (Gilchrist 1999, 66; 2004, 144). Such life stages and identity formation also frequently have important changing material correlates in the form of body modification (*e.g.* scarification, tattooing, etc.), dress, adornment, weaponry, and other material symbolism.

Recent approaches to the study of late pre-historic rock art in Europe have focused on the relationship of such material referents in the construction of masculinity and 'maleness'. Yates' study of Bronze Age rock art in Sweden examined how signs of masculine identity are mapped, or written, onto the body rather than being derived solely from biological sex attributes (1993, 67). In this study, he argues that the perception of masculinity is mediated through potent imagery such as weaponry, erect phalluses, exaggerated calf muscles, and antlers. Drawing particularly on the ethnographic case study of the Sambia of New Guinea, which illustrates how maleness is achieved by young initiates through the ingestion of semen from older males, Yates argues that societal categories of maleness and masculinity are not biologically determined but are rather culturally constructed through the potency of specific material elements (1993, 50).

The symbolism used to denote masculinity in Bronze Age rock art, and its connection with a warrior ethos, thus supersedes a strictly male/female dichotomy to infer a masculine/non-masculine form of identity (Gilchrist 1999, 74). Such an approach emphasises how identities are formed through socially expressive power, in this case metonymic masculinity, and mediated through the efficacy of material culture. This strongly suggests that the construction of warriorhood should be understood as a complex negotiation between identity construction, bodily experience and memory, and symbolic material elements connected with a particular lifestyle of violence and aggression experienced throughout an individual's lifetime.

Warfare in the Eurasian steppe

The rise of warrior activities in the Eurasian steppe region has been frequently linked with archery and the use of the horse. While debate still surrounds the interpretation of evidence for the earliest domestication of horses, the archaeological record suggests that chariot technology preceded the widespread use of horses in mounted warfare. Renfrew (1998) has suggested that these two horizons, the chariot and the horseman, represent distinctive fields of social expression, which he labels 'cognitive constellations'. Similar to Treherne's argument regarding naturalised symbols, Renfrew's constellations denote important techno-cultural transitions and symbolism and ideology connected to specific forms of social practice in warfare. One can therefore envision the transition from the use of the chariot in the Bronze Age, perhaps linked with elite dominated prestige networks, to the emergence of warfare on horseback as the creation of a new social environment focused on individual mobility.

The relationship between new forms of technology and new styles of warfare also brought about changes in cult practices and funerary rituality, all of which helped to reinforce new lifestyles and social institutions based around the effectiveness of mounted combat. These important social changes are reflected by changing patterns in the treatment of the dead in many regions of the steppe during the transition from the Late Bronze Age to Early Iron Age, which dates approximately to the first centuries of the first millennium BC. Mortuary practices at this time emphasise the construction of elaborate and highly visible tombs, often with individual inhumations, which signaled the importance of creating a lasting memory of deceased individuals within both the landscape and in the minds of the social community (Hanks 2003a; 2003b). The construction of complex burial mounds, conspicuous consumption through animal sacrifice (mainly horse, cattle and sheep/goat), and the placement of anthropomorphic stone markers, embodied the warrior ethos and sustained the memory of the individual through the prestige and aesthetics of the warrior horseman lifestyle (Hanks 2000; 2001).

Conventional interpretations of these monuments have been concerned with understanding them as a reflection of elite rank and status (Davis-Kimball *et al.* 1995; Bokovenko 1996; Koryakova 1996). While this is certainly an important view, it often over-emphasises the significance of larger social structures at the expense of understanding the complex negotiation of individual identities and their meaning in the context of social institutions such as warfare. For example, the most commonly used term to describe Early Iron Age warriors is that of the *Scythian Triad,* which has been defined as a funerary package made up of three specific material categories: 1) weaponry items, 2) horse riding equipment, 3) and objects decorated in the Animal Style art pattern. The triad package also has

been interpreted as representing widespread ethnic and cultural unity connected with the origins and migration of the Scythians. Unfortunately, such interpretations have plagued understandings of the complexity of diffusion associated with ritual practices and material culture stretching from the North Pontic steppe to the Altai mountain region in Western Siberia.

Yablonsky and Bashilov have addressed this problem through a series of papers in recent years (Yablonsky 2000; 2002; Bashilov and Yablonsky 2000) and have argued that the triad concept continues to be used simply because there is a lack of a better theoretical framework in which to explain both the geographically widespread distribution of the triad elements and their localised variability. Returning to the theoretical discussion introduced at the beginning of this chapter, it may be useful to consider the triad package as part of a much broader social and material transition connected with the emergence of new forms of identity and warfare practices in the Early Iron Age. In this way, several distinct lines of material evidence can be recognised that appear to have an important role in changing perceptions of warrior identity and lifestyle: 1) the creation of large elaborate funerary complexes, 2) wide-spread use of the horse and related weaponry for mounted warfare, 3) new forms of artistic style and animal symbolism, and 4) changing perceptions of body materiality and identity.

Death, commemoration, and monumentality

While the kurgan (tumulus) form of burial has a long history in the steppe region, dating back to the Eneolithic period, it reaches its most elaborate and widespread expression in the first half of the first millennium BC. Large-scale complexes, constructed variously from stone, wood, and soil, represent new ways of commemoration and unprecedented levels of communal effort.

Some of the earliest evidence for these activities has come to light in recent years through field research programs in Mongolia (see Wright 2007 for good overview). Unique stone constructions

Figure 6.1 Plan of khirigsuur Urt Bulagyn from central Mongolia illustrating central stone mound, rectangular 'fence', and surrounding peripheral stone mounds (after Allard and Erdenebaatar 1995, 552).

called *khirigsuurs* have been excavated and dated to the final centuries of the second millennium BC and the Final Bronze Age (Allard and Erdenebaatar 2005; Erdenebaatar 2004). While khirigsuurs vary in size, the main elements of these sites include a central circular mound of stones, a surrounding square or circular 'fence' delineated by surface stones, and small peripheral satellite mounds that typically contain burnt animal bone deposits (Fig. 6.1). Stone pathways, standing anthropomorphic stones (known conventionally as *deer stones*), and smaller slab burials are also commonly associated with these sites and may represent different phases of construction and/or diachronic cultural use. Excavations at several khirigsuurs have revealed evidence of human remains in addition to complex deposits of sacrificed horses – including crania, neck vertebrae and limb bone elements – as well as other domestic animal species (Allard and Erdenebaatar 2005).

It seems likely that khirigsuurs had an important mortuary function, although the nature of their layout and the seemingly complex nature of ritual activities carried out at the sites suggest that their construction played a significant role in the development of new ceremonial activities (Erdenebaatar 2004, 190). The widespread use of 'fences', perhaps as symbolic boundaries, and stone pathways to delineate and structure khirigsuur ritual space seems to suggest that mortuary events and other ritual activities at these sites took on a highly institutionalised form of practice with site composition and layout closely adhered to (Wright 2007). Although there are a number of questions still surrounding the exact construction characteristics and use of khirigsuurs, their appearance at the end of the second millennium BC is highly significant in that they precede the first large scale Iron Age mortuary sites of Arzhan I and Arzhan II in Tuva (Altai Mountains) and the so-called 'royal' Scythian tombs of the Black Sea region.

The massive Arzhan I tomb, which has been dated from the 9th to 8th centuries BC, was excavated by Soviet archaeologists Gryaznov and Mannai-ool from 1971–1974 (Bokovenko 1995a; 1995b; 1996; 2004; Gryaznov 1980; Mallory *et al.* 2003; see Rolle 1989 for good description). The site yielded an incredible array of human remains including a male and female in the central burial vault and a further 15 individuals surrounding them. Even though Arzhan was heavily looted in antiquity, it still produced some of the earliest evidence of animal style art. Moreover, the sheer size of the complex (120 meters in diameter and height of 4 meters), its composite radial construction of wooden beams and stone covering, and immense sacrifice of approximately 160 horses, exemplify the significant socio-political organisation possible at this time. In fact, it has been suggested that the scale of communal work at Arzhan, and the wide variation in the types of bronze bits included with the sacrificed horses (24 different types of bridles), point to a collective funerary project by individual groups from outside the local region (Bokovenko 1995a, 265–271). Such large scale efforts may represent the burial of a very important leader of an early tribal confederation in the Western Siberian region (Bokovenko 2004, 23).

More recently, the discovery and excavation of the richly furnished Arzhan II tomb, which was not looted and dates to the 7th to 6th centuries BC, is also strongly indicative of the scale of wealth and social power attained by elite individuals in the Altai Mountains region (Chugnov *et al.* 2004). Such massive tombs, analogous in scale not in form, are also seen by the 5th–4th centuries BC in the North Pontic steppe (Reeder 1999; Rolle 1989; Rostovtzeff 1922). These well-known mortuary complexes reflect significant cultural changes and socio-political interactions between Greek colonies on the northern coast of the Black Sea and indigenous steppe groups known traditionally as Scythians. The widespread appearance of these funerary complexes signaled the emergence of new institutions of social power and commemoration. Over the period of just a few centuries, the socio-political effectiveness of mounted warfare stretched from Mongolia in the east to the present day territory of the Ukrainian steppe in the west. While such funerary complexes clearly reflect new institutions of political power and social commemoration, what evidence exists for a more detailed understanding of warriorhood at this time? The best evidence for the material nature of the warrior lifestyle is in the form of rock art, anthropomorphic standing stones, and well-preserved human remains recovered from frozen tombs. An examination of this evidence suggests that warriorhood at this time represented a highly complex form of identity negotiation.

Art agency and embodiment

Petroglyphs and pictographs represent some of the earliest visual imagery to be found in the steppe region (Rozwadowski 2004). While some rock art panels predate the second millennium BC, it is particularly during the Bronze and Iron Ages that rock art becomes most pronounced. Depictions of domestic and wild animal species, weaponry, wheeled vehicles, and anthropomorphic figures dominate the compositions. In addition to rock art, some of the earliest recognisable forms of warrior embodiment are anthropomorphic menhirs. Over 700 of these standing stones, called deer or stag stones, are dispersed throughout the steppe zone with the majority found in Mongolia,

Figure 6.2 Plan and sketch view of deer stone concentration and circular stone mounds from Ushkiin-Uver, Mongolia (after Novgorodova 1989, 204).

the Lake Baikal region, and the Sayan-Altai Mountains (Bayarsaikhan 2005; Fitzhugh *et al.* 2005; Volkov 2004). The absolute dating of the deer stones, like other forms of rock art, has been problematic, although it is generally accepted that their initial emergence occurred in the Late Bronze Age at approximately 1500 BC and intensified in the first centuries of the first millennium BC at the dawn of the Early Iron Age. Scholarly study of deer stones has a long history and they have been tied to a number of theories regarding the emergence and spread of early Indo-Iranian mythology, cosmology, and Eurasian animal style art (Baldick 2000; Jettmar 1967; Gryaznov 1984; Rudenko and Rudenko 1949; Rudenko 1960; Volkov 1967; 1981).

The exact pattern of ornamentation on the deer stones varies widely but common themes include the incorporation of deer and other animals (*e.g.* horses, leopards, boars, etc.), weaponry, disc shaped objects and other geometric patterns, and in some instances human physical features (Fig. 6.2). In most cases, the abstract anthropomorphic nature of the stones is achieved through the vertical division of the stone into three separate zones – with a neckline/necklace and belt line used as boundaries. The earliest deer stones are believed to date to the Late Bronze Age and approximately 1500 BC, although they have most often been associated with the Early Iron Age 'nomadic' cultures of the first millennium BC. A number of scholars have argued that the animal imagery, particularly the stag motif, represents a deep cultural history in Siberian shamanism. Jacobson (1993; 2002) has suggested that the deer image is an indigenous and archaic symbol with strong cosmological significance stretching back to the Neolithic in West Siberia. The use of deer symbolism, as she argues, has had strong cultural continuity well into the Iron Age but its original visual and mythic energy was lost through various historical transitions and the fluidity of its use.

Recent research on animal style and its relationship to Western Siberian shamanism and cosmology has provided a meaningful theory for the origins and meaning of early steppe religion and art. As Jacobson has suggested in several publications, over the course of time various elements persist but cultural meanings change through generations of social practice. This is an important point of view, especially when considering the role of embodiment and materiality connected with new forms of social practice and identity construction. Such changes would have particular potency when considering the role of social memory and mnemonic practices. For example, while great debate surrounds the origins, diffusion, and meaning of animal style, far less attention has been placed on understanding its actual role within newly emerging social contexts of warfare in the Late Bronze Age and the widespread adoption of mounted warfare by the Iron Age. One exception to this would be the theory put forward by Gryaznov, who proposed that deer stones exhibiting the 'wrapping around' style of decorative motifs represented the body painting and/or tattooing of individual warriors, such as the famous Pazyryk corpses from the Altai (Gryaznov 1984; Jettmar 1994). A practice that Gryaznov theorised was originally inscribed on round wooden poles or tree trunks (1984, 81).

Gryaznov's inspiration for this idea came from the well-preserved human remains recovered from frozen tombs in the Altai Mountains dating to the 3rd to 5th centuries BC. These tombs are representative of the Pazyryk culture of which numerous tumuli have been documented (Bokovenko 1995b; Gryaznov 1950; Rudenko 1970; Rolle 1989). Six of the largest barrows, the so-called 'royal tombs', were excavated during the Soviet period. The first tomb was opened by Gryaznov himself in 1929 and 5 additional tombs were excavated by Rudenko from 1947 to 1949. These mortuary complexes yielded over one thousand organic remains, including human corpses, horse carcasses, objects created from wood and leather, and various textiles. The unique state of preservation was the result of natural permafrost conditions. However, of all the exquisite organic remains recovered from the Pazyryk tombs, it is the corpse of the male individual recovered from Barrow 2, and the tattoos covering much of his body, that have captured the attention of many scholars.

It is apparent from the physical analysis of this individual, a male in his 60s, that he suffered an extremely violent end by being bludgeoned in the head with an axe-like instrument. He also had been scalped, with his skin torn from ear to ear backwards to the neckline. Even though he had met a very cruel fate, his body was handled with the utmost care during funerary preparations and final interment. Like many of the other Pazyryk corpses, his entrails and musculature had been removed through long slits made in the arms, legs, back, and thorax. In fact, even though his scalp had been taken, the remainder of his hair had been neatly shaven and two small leather bags, one containing a lock of hair and the other fingernail clippings, were included with him. One of the most fascinating aspects of treatment was the placement of a false beard (with straps for attachment) under the head of the male in barrow 2 during interment (Rudenko 1970, 105). This is a particularly interesting fact, since he was of a Mongoloid phenotype and would have had very little facial hair in life. Such behavior indicates complex attitudes about the potency of facial hair and the significance of this symbolism in life and death.

The tattoos of the Barrow 2 male depict a variety of mythological beings such as stags with eagle heads, winged tigers, figures of mountain

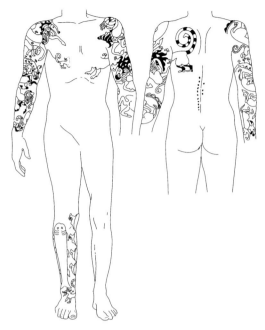

Figure 6.3 Tattooing on male from Barrow 2 at Pazyryk (after Rudenko 1970, 109).

Figure 6.4 Line drawing of horse head-dress from Barrow 2 at Pazyryk (after Rudenko 1970, 182).

goats, a beast of prey with an eagle head, and a large fish design on the lower right leg (Fig. 6.3). There are also lines of dots along the spine of the lower back and on the right leg, which may have been a form of medicinal treatment. A particularly important aspect of the tattoos is that they appear to have been applied in the man's youth – as there was discoloration of the muscle tissue but not of the fat layer between the muscle and skin. Rudenko surmised that the fat layer would have accumulated in the man's adult years and therefore the tattoos must have been applied when he was younger (Rudenko 1970, 112–113). Moreover, it is unlikely that the tattoos would normally have been visible, as the clothing found with the Pazyryk corpses was made up of close-fitting shirts, breeches, kaftans, shoes and stockings. This suggests that the tattooing was perhaps conducted as part of a *rite de passage* during adolescence or at various times during early adulthood to mark specific events.

In addition to the human bodies recovered at Pazyryk, sacrificed horses were included with richly ornamented harnesses, saddles, and other equipment (see Gryaznov 1950, Rudenko 1970, and Rolle 1989 for detailed description). One of the most intriguing elements of the horse gear is the richly designed masks and headdresses, of which there are several types ranging from stylised deer and elk antlers to various combinations of animals. For example, one headdress recovered from Barrow 2 illustrates the complexity of associated imagery. It comprises an elaborate metamorphic composition of the head of a deer with a ram's head above and a dove perched on the ram's horns (Fig. 6.4).

In addition to the masks and headdresses, the harness trappings of the horses are also well preserved and exhibit a stunning array of ornamentation and artistic style. While some have argued that the elaborate horse furnishings were used specifically for the funeral, Rudenko notes that many of the items show evidence of repair. This suggests that the equipment may have been an important element in social display and performance at other times. What is certainly clear from the elaboration of the horses and their accompanying equipment is that they represented one of the primary elements for the conspicuous display and performance of individuals and that the aggregation and composition of various animal elements provided an extremely potent media for such activities.

Since the discovery and excavation of the original Pazyryk tombs, other sites such as Bashadar, Tuekta, Berel, Ak-Alkha, and a tomb containing a female in the Ukok Plateau, have significantly added to the corpus of well preserved organic remains recovered from Early Iron Age sites in the Sayan-Altai mountains region (Polosmak 1992; 1994; 1998). Overall, this art displays an amazing variety of zoomorphic representation, with one of the main compositions being the *predator-prey* type. The general form of this artistic expression draws on the motifs of the stag, felines, birds, the juxtaposition of planes, and the various mixing or hybridisation of different animals. It has been suggested that these themes originated from external sources in Central Asia, the Near East, and Mesopotamia where analogous motifs such as griffins, lions, and other carnivores attacking herbivores were common in iconography. As Rudenko notes, it is especially the predator-prey motif that scholars have suggested may relate to the 'blood-thirstiness, remoteness, ferocity or sensitivity' of warriors (1970, 288). Although Rudenko himself did not strongly support these ideas, it is necessary to think more critically about the meaning and use of artistic elements and other objects within the context of Early Iron Age social practices. It is also necessary to address how specific forms of materiality, combining traditional motifs with new hybrid forms of intentionality, were connected to social memory and the construction of individual and corporate identities.

Bricolage and the warrior

In this next section, it is important to bring a number of the elements discussed within the chapter together in order to form a more coherent theory for the construction of Early Iron Age warriorhood identity. At the beginning of the paper, it was suggested that through important

elements of body materiality, social memory, and biographical stages, the construction of person-hood is mediated. Such a perspective offers an important way of thinking more critically about the way in which individuals in these societies achieved warriorhood through the utilisation of specific material, technological, and social referents.

In light of the emergence of mounted steppe warriors by the early first millennium BC, it was argued that the elaborate funerary monuments, effectiveness of mounted warfare, and changing perceptions of the social body provided the setting for a new institution of warfare practices. It was also suggested that the primary nexus of meaning for this was the social body and the material elements that constitute it. Through the Iron Age case studies discussed above, it is possible to focus in more detail on three main issues: the social context of warfare, the significance of tattooing, and the agency of visual metaphor and tension through the medium of animal style art. In order to understand how these themes come together and form a new system of meaning and intention it is useful to consider the concept of *bricolage*, which was first employed by Lévi-Strauss as a way of understanding myth making in non-literate societies (1966).

Following Lévi-Strauss, the *bricoleur*, or agent, creates new meaning by combining symbols or elements that may individually come from very different contexts of meaning. Such action may not have a pre-planned outcome but rather is achieved through a process of aggregation of culturally available symbols and material elements (1966, 21). In more recent years, the concept of bricolage has been further developed as a way of theorising how new patterns of meaning emerge through processes of social practice.

Michel de Certeau has taken this to mean a sort of 'arts of making' whereby various elements of ritual action, material objects, and everyday routine articulate through human practice to produce a bricolage (Dant 1999, 71; de Certeau 1984, xii–xviii). While this view sets the concept of bricolage in a rather abstract plane of human practice, somewhat similar to *habitus* in not being actively constructed through specific forms of knowledge or institutionalised structures, I prefer to think of bricolage as a category of practice by which individuals and/or subgroups within a culture actively and fluidly develop a technology of meaning and representation. In this way, bricolage and bricoleur provide a conceptual foundation for understanding changes in ritual practice, myth making, artistic metaphor, and mnemonic meaning of material objects through the individual agency of choice and selection. This provides a way of understanding how symbolic traditions change over time and how the selective appropriation and contextualisation of different elements provides the setting for new cultural meanings. Such a perspective may offer a more nuanced way of understanding key transformations in the vibrant visual art and material culture of the Eurasian steppe Iron Age as such media factored importantly within changing perceptions of body identity within specific historical settings. Based on widespread ethnographic studies, it is well substantiated that a warrior lifestyle and ethos are strongly rooted in bodily identity and practice (*e.g.* tattooing and painting, rites de passage, scarification, masking, wearing of magic talismans, etc.), and in the materiality and potency of material culture (*e.g.* weaponry, defensive shields, maces and staffs of power, the application of artistic metaphors, etc.). In this next section, I would like to consider how these issues fit within the dynamic of warfare and within the cultivation of the warrior lifestyle as a category of social practice.

Warfare as social practice

A variety of ethnographic and anthropological studies have provided examples of the complexity of aggression and warfare between societies and the multitude of cultural responses to these activities (*e.g.* Ferguson and Whitehead 1992; Harrison 1993; Keeley 1996). What is clear from such anthropological study is that the individuals, events and deeds that contribute to the cultural prestige and status of warfare clearly form a significant part of societies with strong institutions of warriorhood. When considering these factors, particularly from

the point of view archaeological interpretation, it is all too easy to emphasise the status and prestige of this lifestyle and overlook the fact that warriorhood is something that must be cultivated from an early age. For example, it may be a rather simple act to pick up a bow or sword but it is entirely a different matter to use them effectively against an opponent in a time of crisis! Within traditional societies, individuals on the path to warriorhood often do so through prescribed social transitions or *rites de passage*.

In a case study focused on age grading and ethnicity among the Loikop (Samburu) in Africa, an interesting relationship between age grading, material culture in the form of spears and their stylistic variation, and a highly active pattern of identity negotiation is illustrated. The implications of this study are profound in that it highlights how Loikop age grades, based on three stages comprising *boys*, *warriors* and *elders* (each divided into younger and older components), are strongly reinforced through the creation of cohort collective identities (Larick 1985; 1986). As Larick describes, '… each cohort travels through the age grades creating different behavioral and material styles. Successive cohorts of warriors dress, speak, and dance in distinctive ways, and their material accoutrements also diverge markedly' (1986, 275). What is particularly interesting is the way in which cohorts draw on various elements of style taken from neighboring ethnic groups in order to configure the formal traits of their own representative material culture. This active pattern of stylistic appropriation and aggregation reflects a complex setting for identity negotiation. As Larick suggests, this is based on internal processes of socio-cultural innovation, which factor importantly into the creation of social differentiation within groups, and also the larger scale ethnic interactions that take place between groups (1986, 278).

The Loikop case study suggests two important aspects of warriorhood that may be useful when considering Eurasian steppe material patterns. The first is the significance of understanding warriorhood as a complex process of group and individual identity negotiation that often begins at an early age within societies. The second is that cross cultural interaction provides the setting for the adoption of external form and style characteristics in active processes of social differentiation and in the creation of new forms of material culture. These factors provide a meaningful social context for understanding both the movement of style between ethnic groups as well as the variation of material culture within and between groups. While such studies have regularly focused on clothing, adornment and weaponry, one of the most significant arenas of transformation in this process is the body and the way in which both self-identity and group ethnicity are mediated through its conditioning, modification, and adornment. For example, modification of the body through scarification, painting and tattooing forms a special category of social practice linked with the inscription of identity, biography, and memory (Gell 1993, 3–4; Kuwahara 2005, 17). While such evidence is rarely available to archaeologists, the Pazyryk case study discussed above provides a window into such practices for the Early Iron Age and therefore deserves a closer look.

Tattooing

The act of inscribing the skin in a permanent fashion is a strong statement regarding self-identity and social meaning (Kuwahara 2005; Thomas *et al.* 2005). While symbolism and artistic style form vital components of tattooing, the inscription of the skin also has a considerable temporal dimension. In this sense, tattooing can at once be individual and collective and represents a strong connection between the real or imagined past and the contemporary. As Kuwahara notes, 'tattooing marks the personal and collective past on the body' and therefore forms an important 'biography and history of the person' (2005, 17–18). In traditional societies, such inscriptions have particular significance during transitions in social stages, such as initiation rites into warrior cults, age grades, or other important events within an individual's life history. Another important element in tattooing is its symbolic and magical potency. For example, Gell's study (1993) of Polynesian tattooing emphasises its use both in very specific social contexts and in its unique ability

to exist at a level of plurality and ambiguity within the same society. While this seems contradictory, Gell's interpretation emphasises the role of individual agency in tattooing and its relationship to body signification and identity.

Such anthropological perspectives of tattooing suggest deep social and personal facets in the inscription practices revealed on the Pazyryk male from Barrow 2, discussed above. Available evidence indicates the tattooing was applied in the man's youth and covered much of his body. While a strong point was made of connecting his tattoos to the construction of warrior identity, it is clear that within these societies at this time body modification was not solely connected with males and aspects of warriorhood. The excavation of a well preserved female in the Ukok plateau of the Altai Republic (Russian Federation) also revealed evidence of tattooing on the shoulders, arms, and hands that closely resembles some of the designs on the Barrow 2 male (Polosmak 1994; 1998). This tattooing has routinely been interpreted as a sign of high social status among these peoples, however, the restricted nature of the tattooing (only 3 of the 8 recovered Pazyryk bodies) suggests a much closer connection with individual choice and life history (Polosmak 1998, 156). While few Iron Age corpses are recovered with the remarkable preservation of the frozen tombs in Siberia, other material evidence from Iron Age burials in the steppe region also appears to suggest complex practices linked to body painting and tattooing.

In several burials located in the southern Ural Mountains of the Russian Federation and Northern Kazakhstan combinations of coloured powder, bone pipes, *gryphaea* shells, and bronze mirrors are often recovered. In contrast to the Pazyryk frozen remains discussed above, the human remains recovered from these burial contexts typically yield only osseous materials. Chemical analyses of the minerals indicate that a wide variety of resources were used in the preparation of pigments, such as magnetite, realgar, quartz, azurite and malachite (Tairov and Bushmakin 2002). Such minerals would produce shades of red, green, blue, black and white. Analysis of mineral residues found on small stone altars, within shells, and in hollow bone tubes with pointed ends suggest that the pigments were used for a variety of practices including cosmetics, body painting, and tattooing (Tairov and Bushmakin 2001; 2002, 185–190). The inclusion of the items within burial contexts also suggests that these practices formed an important part of the materiality and identity of individuals even at death (Tairov and Bushmakin 2002, 190). In combination with the use of other material objects and animal style art, such practices formed an important medium for identity construction and display.

Art and intentionality

While the aesthetic nature of art and its use as a semiotic form of communication have been routinely emphasised, other approaches have emphasised the *active* and *fluid* social contexts in which art takes on meaning. One of the most important approaches to this in recent years has been the work undertaken by Gell on the connection between art and agency (1996; 1998). For example, Gell emphasises the '*agency, intention, causation, result,* and *transformation',* of art and views it as a, '… system of action, intended to change the world rather than encode symbolic propositions about it' (Gell 1998, 6, original emphasis). Moreover, Gell considers art and its application as a set of social practices linked through time and space. As such, he suggests that art should be seen not simply as an 'aggregate of fragments' with unknown social linkages, but rather as an important connective tissue entwining the materiality of the body with the potency of artistic metaphor and agency. As he states, '… a person and a person's mind are not confined to particular spatio-temporal coordinates, but consist of a spread of biographical events and memories of events, and a dispersed category of material objects, traces, and leavings, which can be attributed to a person and which, in aggregate, testify to agency and patienthood during a biographical career which may, indeed, prolong itself long after biological death' (Gell 1998, 222). While this view is situated at a rather abstract level, it nevertheless effectively emphasises the dynamic nature of art and suggests that meaning is constructed within

networks, specific material settings, and through individual memory and biography. This theoretical view situates art and its application within the conceptual domain of bricolage and bricoleur, as discussed above. With these concepts in mind, and returning again to the Pazyryk case study, the variety of animal style art themes and their application would seem to connect significantly with these perspectives on the socially active nature of art and its application.

In consideration of the Pazyryk burial remains, there are three main themes that appear to have special relevance when considering art agency: *context, metamorphosis and hybridism.* Regarding context, Parker Pearson has suggested that there is a structured logic to the placement of animal designs in the organisation of the Pazyryk tomb contents and in the application of motifs on certain material objects. As he points out, there appears to be an association with the application of the chimera/griffin creatures, and to a lesser extent certain bird motifs, with the human bodies in the inner chamber of the burials (1999, 66). Whereas, other motifs, particularly the 'predator-prey' figures of carnivores attacking herbivores, are more commonly associated with the horses and are situated in the outer chamber area. He also notes that the 'predator-prey' configuration is frequently applied to the saddles and saddle covers and therefore may have acted as an important 'symbolic interface' between the rider and the horse (1999, 67).

It is beyond the scope of this chapter to address the complexity of the Pazyryk materials in great detail, however, a detailed analysis of the motifs associated with the bridles, saddles and masks on the horses from Pazyryk, and a comparison with materials from other sites such as Tuekta, Berel, Bashadar, Katanda, and Ulandryk-Tashanta, has been undertaken by Jacobson (1993, 57–74). She specifically addresses the composition and ordering of predation and transformation themes around the axis of the horse and the use of animal style themes on headgear elements deposited with human remains. While Jacobson (1993, 69) seems to favour the idea that the horse masks and bridles were made for purposes of burial and the journey of the dead, since many of the items appear too fragile for everyday use, it is not absolutely certain that this was their primary purpose. The number of horses buried within the Pazyryk tombs and other sites and the variation of their accoutrements suggest that horses provided an important medium for social display in addition to being vital elements in the activities surrounding death and burial and the rite of passage from the world of the living to the dead (Fig. 6.5). While it is possible to discern patterns in the animal style art of the horse gear, as is well illustrated by Jacobson, a high degree of individual choice in the selection and use of specific motifs, metaphor, and intentionality also seems to have existed in their adornment. While it may be difficult to ascertain the specific meaning of the animal style masks and accoutrements associated with the horses, their use in combination with animal style felt covers draped over the log coffins, the tattooing of human skin, and the careful preparation of the human bodies during embalming all seem to relate to powerful conceptions of symbolic boundaries (Parker Pearson 1999, 64). The use of predation, metamorphosis, and hybridism also indicates vibrant and dynamic metaphors of action and intention.

Recent studies on the use of animal iconography in Iron Age Greece and temperate Europe have indicated that hybridism and metamorphic compositions provided an important medium for the creation of metaphoric tension and energy (Shanks 1993; Green 1997). Studies focusing on the use of zoomorphic themes in early Celtic art also have indicated that such motifs played a significant role in the display associated with warfare and were commonly associated with the decoration of horses and war-gear (Green 1992, 131). The use of hybrid imagery associated with creatures such as griffins and chimeras, which perhaps intentionally stimulate the ambiguity between wild and domestic, also provided an effective context for emphasising tension and conflict within artistic compositions (Shanks 1993, 380–381). Such perspectives on the active nature of art, and its role in the performance and display characteristics of warfare and warrior or

Figure 6.5 Line drawing of horse # 5 from Pazyryk kurgan 1 with mask and ornamented saddle (after Gryaznov 1950, 30).

elite identities, would appear to offer an important avenue for re-evaluating the rich collection of art objects recovered from Pazyryk and other Early Iron Age burials in the steppe region. Such studies have figured prominently in the interpretation of zoomorphic agency in a number of other prehistoric case studies from around the world (*e.g.* Borić 2005; Flannery and Marcus 1993; Girard 1977; Linares 1977; Ingold 2000).

Conclusion

Much of the literature on the Eurasian steppe Iron Age has been preoccupied with the death and burial events of this time. While mortuary data does indeed form much of the material evidence for this period, it is important that archaeologists not be misled into creating only archaeologies of *death* rather than archaeologies of *life*. As Fowler has recently stated in more general terms, the broader agenda of Post-Processual archaeology seems to have become synonymous with attempts to 'people the past' (2004, 5) and as a result much greater emphasis is being placed on conceptualising personhood and identity.

This chapter has attempted to draw on various

theoretical perspectives in order to consider more critically the concept of 'warriorhood' as a category of social practice rather than as a static marker of status within ranked societies. It has been suggested that the major shift in social and material conditions connected with the Iron Age were intertwined within changing technological patterns of warfare, new forms of bodily identity, and new ritual practices linked to the death and social commemoration of warriors. Material patterns in the form of elaborate tombs, rock art, and anthropomorphic standing stones also provided important physical contexts for both inscribed and embodied memory practices surrounding the lifestyle of the warrior. Such elements provided a crucial material context for recalling individuals, events, and life histories within specific landscape settings as communities drew on elements of the past to redefine their place within the conditions of the present. Through new forms of structured rituality and commemorative display, the warrior lifestyle was imbued with meaning – ensuring that memory, materiality, and place figured prominently in both life and death.

Bibliography

Allard, F. and Erdenebaatar, D. (2005) Khirigsuurs, Ritual and Mobility in the Bronze Age of Mongolia. *Antiquity* 79, 547–563.

Arnold, B. (2001) The Limits of Agency in the Analysis of Elite Iron Age Celtic Burials. *Journal of Social Archaeology* 1(2), 210–224.

Babić, S. (2002) 'Princely Graves' of the Central Balkans – A Critical History Research. *European Journal of Archaeology* 5(1), 70–88.

Baldick, J. (2000) *Animal and Shaman: Ancient Religions of Central Asia*. London, I. B. Tauris and Company Ltd.

Barrett, J. (1990) The Monumentality of Death: The Character of Early Bronze Age Mortuary Mounds in Southern Britain. *World Archaeology* 22(2), 179–189.

Barrett, J. (1994) *Fragments from Antiquity*. Oxford, Blackwell.

Bashilov, V. and Yablonsky, L. (2000) Some Current Problems Concerning the History of Early Iron Age Eurasian steppe Nomadic Societies. In J. Davis-Kimball, E. M. Murphy, L. N. Koryakova and L. T.

Yablonsky (eds) *Kurgans, Ritual Sites and Settlements: Eurasian Bronze and Iron Age,* 9–12. Oxford, BAR International Series 890.

Bayarsaikhan, J. (2005) Shamanistic Elements in Mongolian Deer Stone Art. In W. Fitzhugh, J. Bayarsaikhan and P. Marsh (eds) *The Deer Stone Project: Anthropological Studies in Mongolia 2002–2004*, 41–53. Washington DC, Smithsonian Institution.

Bokovenko, N. A. (1995a) Tuva during the Scythian Period. In J. Davis-Kimball, V. A. Bashilov and L. T. Yablonsky (eds) *Nomads of the Eurasian Steppes in the Early Iron Age,* 265–281. Berkeley, Zinat Press.

Bokovenko, N. A. (1995b) Scythian Culture in the Altai Mountains. In J. Davis-Kimball, V. A. Bashilov and L. T. Yablonsky (eds) *Nomads of the Eurasian Steppes in the Early Iron Age*, 285–295. Berkeley, Zinat Press.

Bokovenko, N. A. (1996) Asian Influence on European Scythia. *Ancient Civilizations from Scythia to Siberia: An International Journal of Comparative Studies in History and Archaeology*, 3(1), 97–122.

Bokovenko, N. A. (2004) Migrations of Early Nomads of the Eurasian Steppe in a Context of Climatic Changes. In E. M. Scott, A. Yu. Alekseev and G. Zaitseva (eds) *Impact of the Environment on Human Migration in Eurasia,* 21–33. London, Kluwer Academic Publishers.

Borić, D. (2005) Body Metamorphosis and Animality: Volatile Bodies and Boulder Artworks from Lepenski Vir. *Cambridge Archaeological Journal* 15(1), 35–39.

Carmen, J. and Harding, A. (eds) (1999) *Ancient Warfare: Archaeological Perspectives*. Stroud, Sutton.

de Certeau, M. (1984) *The Practice of Everyday Life*. Berkeley, University of California Press.

Chugunov, K., Parzinger, H., and Nagler, A. (2004) Chronology and Cultural Affinity of the Kurgan Arzhan-2 Complex According to Archaeological Data. In E. Scott, A. Alekseev and G. Zaitseva (eds) *Impact of the Environment on Human Migration in Eurasia*. NATO Science Series, IV Earth and Environmental Sciences Vol. 42, 1–7. London, Kluwer Academic Publishers.

Connerton, P. (1989) *How Societies Remember*. Cambridge, Cambridge University Press.

Conway, M. (1990) *Autobiographical Memory: An Introduction*. Philadelphia, Open University Press.

Dant, T. (1999) *Material Culture in the Social World*. Philadelphia, Open University Press.

Davis-Kimball, J., Bashilov, V. and L. Yablonsky (eds)

(1995) *Nomads in the Eurasian Steppes in the Early Iron Age.* Berkeley, Zinat Press.

Davis-Kimball, J. (1998) Statuses of Eastern Early Iron Age Nomads. In M. Pearce and M. Tosi (eds) *Papers from the EAA Third Annual Meeting at Ravenna 1997 Volume I: Pre- and Protohistory,* 142–152. Oxford, BAR International Series 717.

Dietler, M. (1994) The Iron Age in Mediterranean France: Colonial Encounters, Entanglements, and Transformations. *Journal of World Prehistory* 11, 269–358.

Earle, T. (1987) *How Chiefs Come to Power. The Political Economy in Prehistory.* Stanford, Stanford University Press.

Erdenebaatar, D. (2004) Burial Materials Related to the History of the Bronze Age in the Territory of Mongolia. In K. Linduff (ed.) *Metallurgy in Ancient Eastern Eurasia from the Urals to the Yellow River,* 189–222. Lampeter, Edwin Mellen Press.

Ferguson, R. B. and Whitehead, N. L. (eds) (1992) *War in the Tribal Zone: Expanding States and Indigenous Warfare.* Santa Fe, School of American Research Press.

Fitzhugh, W., Bayarsaikhan, J. and Marsh, P. (eds) (2005) *The Deer Stone Project: Anthropological Studies in Mongolia 2002–2004.* Washington DC, Arctic Studies Center.

Flannery, K. V. and Marcus, J. (1993) Cognitive Archaeology. *Cambridge Archaeology Journal* 3, 260–270.

Fowler, C. (2002) Body Parts: Personhood and Materiality in the Manx Neolithic. In Y. Hamilakis, M. Pluciennik and S. Tarlow (eds) *Thinking through the Body: Archaeologies of Corporeality,* 47–69. London, Kluwer Academic.

Fowler, C. (2004) *The Archaeology of Personhood: An Anthropological Approach.* London, Routledge.

Gell, A. (1993) *Wrapping in Images: Tattooing in Polynesia.* Oxford, Clarendon Press.

Gell, A. (1996) Vogel's Net: Traps as Artworks and Artworks as Traps. *Journal of Material Culture* I/I, 15–38.

Gell, A. (1998) *Art and Agency: An Anthropological Theory.* Oxford, Clarendon Press.

Gilchrist, R. (1999) *Gender and Archaeology: Contesting the Past.* London, Routledge.

Gilchrist, R. (ed.) (2000) *Human Lifecyles.* London, Routledge (special issue of *World Archaeology* 31, 3).

Gilchrist, R. (2004) Archaeology and the Life Course: A Time and Age for Gender. In L. Meskell and R.

Preucel (eds) *A Companion to Social Archaeology,* 142–160. Oxford, Blackwell.

Girard, R. (1977) *Violence and the Sacred.* London, John Hopkins.

Goody, J. (2000) *The Power of the Written Tradition.* Washington, Smithsonian Institution Press.

Green, M. J. (1992) *Animals in Celtic Life and Myth.* London, Routledge.

Green, M. J. (1997) Images in Opposition: Polarity, Ambivalence and Liminality in Cult Representation. *Antiquity* 71, 898–911.

Gryaznov, M. P. (1950) *Pervyi Pazyrykskii Kurgan (The First Pazyryk Kurgan).* London, Cresset Press.

Gryaznov, M. P. (1969) *The Ancient Civilization of South Siberia.* London, Cresset Press.

Gryaznov, M. P. (1980) *Arzhan: tsarskiy kurgan ranneskifskogo vremeni (Arzhan: A Royal Kurgan of the Early Scythian Period).* Leningrad, Nauk.

Gryaznov, M. P. (1984) O monumental'nom iskusstve na zare skifo-sibirskikh kul'tur v stepnoi Azii (Regarding Monumental Art at the Beginning of the Scytho-Siberian Culture in the Asian Steppe). *Arkheologichiskii Sbornik* 25, 76–82.

Halbwachs, M. (1992) [1950] *On Collective Memory* (trans. L. A. Coser). Chicago, University of Chicago Press.

Hanks, B. K. (2000) Iron Age Nomadic Burials of the Eurasian Steppe: A Discussion Exploring Burial Ritual Complexity. In J. Davis-Kimball, E. M. Murphy, L. N. Koryakova and L. T. Yablonsky (eds) *Kurgans, Ritual Sites and Settlements: Eurasian Bronze and Iron Age,* 19–30. Oxford, BAR International Series 890.

Hanks, B. K. (2001) Kurgan Burials of the Eurasian Iron Age – Ideological Constructs and the Process of Rituality. In A. T. Smith and A. Brookes (eds) *Holy Ground: Theoretical Issues Relating to the Landscape and Material Culture of Ritual Space Objects,* 39–48. Oxford, BAR Series S956.

Hanks, B. K. (2003a) *Human-Animal Relationships in the Eurasian Steppe Iron Age: An Exploration into Social, Economic and Ideological Change.* Unpublished Ph.D. Thesis, Department of Archaeology, University of Cambridge.

Hanks, B. K. (2003b) The Eurasian Steppe 'Nomadic World' of the First Millennium BC: Inherent Problems within the Study of Iron Age Nomadic Groups. In K. Boyle, C. Renfrew and M. Levine (eds) *Ancient Interactions: East and West in Eurasia.* Cambridge, McDonald Institute Monographs, 183–197.

Harrison, S. (1993) *The Mask of War: Violence, Ritual, and the Self in Melanesia*. Manchester, Manchester University Press.

Ingold, T. (2000) *The Perception of the Environment: Essays on Livelihood, Dwelling and Skill*. London, Routledge.

Jacobson, E. (1983) Siberian Roots of the Scythians: Stag Image. *Journal of Asian History* 17, 68–120.

Jacobson, E. (1993) *The Deer Goddess of Ancient Siberia: A study in the Ecology of Belief*. Leiden, Brill.

Jacobson, E. (2002) Petroglyphs and the Qualification of Bronze Age Mortuary Archaeology. *Archaeology, Ethnology, and Anthropology of Eurasia* 3(11), 32–47.

Jettmar, K. (1967) *Art of the Steppes*. London, Crown Publishers.

Jettmar, K. (1994) Body-Painting and the Roots of the Scytho-Siberian Animal Style. In B. Genito (ed.) *The Archaeology of the Steppes: Methods and Strategies*, 3–15. Naples, Istituto Universitario Orientale.

Jones, S. (1997) *The Archaeology of Ethnicity: Constructing Identities in the Past and the Present*. London, Routledge.

Keeley, L. (1996) *War before Civilization: The Myth of the Peaceful Savage*. Oxford, Oxford University Press.

Koryakova, L. N. (1996) Social Trends in Temperate Eurasia during the Second and First Millennia BC. *Journal of European Archaeology* 4, 243–280.

Kristiansen, K. (1998) *Europe before History*. Cambridge, Cambridge University Press.

Kristiansen, K. and Larsson, T. (2005) *The Rise of Bronze Age Society: Travels Transmission and Transformations*. Cambridge, Cambridge University Press.

Küchler, S. (1987) Malangan: Art and Memory in a Melanesian Society. *Man* n.s. 22(2), 238–255.

Kuwahara, M. (2005) *Tattoo: An Anthropology*. Oxford, Berg.

Larick, R. (1985) Spears, Style and Ttime among Maa-Speaking Pastoralists. *Journal of Anthropological Archaeology* 4(1), 201–215.

Larick, R. (1986) Age Grading and Ethnicity in the Style of Loikop (Samburu) Spears. *World Archaeology* 18 (2), 269–283.

Lévi-Strauss, C. (1966) *The Savage Mind*. Chicago, University of Chicago Press.

Linares, O. (1977) *Ecology and the Arts in Ancient Panama: One the Development of Social Rank and Symbolism in the Central Provinces* (Studies in Pre-Columbian Art and Archaeology 17). Washington DC, Dumbarton Oaks.

Mallory, J., McCormac, F. G., Reimer, P. J. and

Marsadolov, L. S. (2003) The Date of Pazyryk. In K. Boyle, C. Renfrew and M. Levine (eds) *Ancient Interactions: East and West in Eurasia*, 183–197. Cambridge, McDonald Institute Monographs.

Mizoguchi, K. (1993) Time in the Reproduction of Mortuary Practices. *World Archaeology* 25(2), 223–235.

Novgorodova, E. (1989) *Drevnyaya Mongoliya (Ancient Mongolia)*. Moskva, Academiya Nauk.

Ochs, E. and Capps, L. (1996) Narrating the Self. *Annual Review of Anthropology* 25, 19–43.

Osgood, R., Monks, S. and Toms, J. (2000) *Bronze Age Warfare*. Gloucestershire, Sutton Publishing Limited.

Parker Pearson, M. (1999) *The Archaeology of Death and Burial*. Gloucestershire, Sutton Publishing Limited.

Polosmak, N. V. (1992) Excavations of a Rich Burial of the Pazyryk Culture. *Altaica* 1, 35–42.

Polosmak, N. V. (1994) *Griffins Watching Over Gold (the Ak-Alakha Kurgans) [Steregyshchie zoloto grify (ak-alakhinskie kurgany)]*. Novosibirsk, Academiya Nauk.

Polosmak, N. V. (1998) The Burial of a Noble Pazyryk Woman. *Ancient Civilizations from Scythia to Siberia*, Vol. 5, 125–163.

Reeder, E. (1999) *Scythian Gold: Treasures from Ancient Ukraine*. New York (NY), Harry N. Abrams, Inc.

Renfrew, C. (1998) All the King's Horses. In S. Mithen (ed.) *Creativity in Human Evolution and Prehistory*, 260–284. London, Routledge.

Robb, J. (1997) Violence and Gender in Early Italy. In D. Frayer and D. Martin (eds) *Troubled Times: Osteological and Archaeological Evidence of Violence*, 108–141. New York, Gordon and Breach.

Robb, J. (2002) Time and Biography: Osteobiography of the Italian Neolithic Lifespan. In Y. Hamilakis, M. Pluciennik and S. Tarlow (eds) *Thinking through the Body: Archaeologies of Corporeality*. London, Kluwer Academic.

Rolle, R. (1989) *The World of the Scythians*. Los Angeles, University of California Press.

Rostovtzeff, M. (1922) *Iranians and Greeks in Southern Russia*. Oxford, Clarendon Press.

Rozwadowski, A. (2004) *Symbols through Time: Interpreting the Rock Art of Central Asia*. Pozan, Insitute of Eastern Studies.

Rowlands, M. (1993) The Role of Memory in the Transmission of Culture. *World Archaeology* 25(2), 141–151.

Rudenko, S. I. (1960) *Kultura naselenia tsentrsknogo*

Altaya v skifskie vremya (The Culture of the Central Altai Population during the Scythian Period). Moskva-Leningrad, Academiya Nauk.

Rudenko, S. I. (1970) *The Frozen Tombs of Siberia.* London, Dent.

Rudenko, S. I. and Rudenko, S. M. (1949*) Iskusstvo skifov Altaya (Altai Scythian Art).* Moskva, Academiya Nauk.

Shanks, C. (1993) Style and the Design of a Perfume Jar from an Archaic Greek City State. *Journal of European Archaeology* 1, 77–106.

Shennan, S. (1986) Central Europe in the Third Millennium BC: An Evolutionary Trajectory for the Beginning of the European Bronze Age. *Journal of Anthropological Archaeology* 5, 115–146.

Sofaer, J. R. (2006) *The Body as Material Culture: a Theoretical Osteoarchaeology.* Cambridge, Cambridge University Press.

Strathern, M. (1988) *The Gender of the Gift: Problems with Women and Problems with Society in Melanesia.* Berkeley, University of California Press.

Tairov, A. and Bushmakin, A. (2001) Mineral'nye Poroshki ez Kurganov Uzhnogo Urala i Severnogo Kazakhstana i ikh Vozmozhnoe Ispol'zovanie (Mineral Powders from Barrow Mounds of the Southern Urals and North Kazakhstan and their Possible Function). *Rossiiskaya Arkheologiya* 1, 66–75.

Tairov, A. and Bushmakin, A. (2002) The Composition, Function and Significance of the Mineral Paints from the Kurgan Burial Mounds of the South Urals and North Kazakhstan. In A. Jones and G. MacGregor (eds) *Colouring the Past: The Significance of Colour in Archaeological Research,* 175–193. Oxford, Berg.

Thomas, N., Cole, A. and Douglas, B. (eds) (2005) *Tattoo: Bodies, Art, and Exchange in the Pacific and the West.* Durham, Duke University Press.

Treherne, P. (1995) The Warrior's Beauty: The Masculine Body and Self-Identity in Bronze Age Europe. *Journal of European Archaeology* 3(1), 105–144.

Van Dyke, R. and Alcock, S. (eds) (2003) *Archaeologies of Memory.* Oxford, Blackwell.

Van Dyke, R. and Alcock, S. (2003) Archaeologies of Memory: An Introduction. In R. Van Dyke and S. Alcock (eds) *Archaeologies of Memory,* 8–13. Oxford, Blackwell.

Vernant, J. P. (1991) *Mortals and Immortals: Collected Essays* (edited by F. Zeitlin). Princeton, Princeton University Press.

Volkov, V. (1967) *Bronzovyi i Zheleznyi vek severnoi Mongolii (Bronze and Iron Ages in Northern Mongolia).* Studia Archaeologica Instituti Historiae Academiae Scientarium Republicae Populi Mongoli V, (1). Ulaanbaatar, Academiya Nauk.

Volkov, V. (1981) *Olennyie Kamni Mongolii (Deer Stones of Mongolia).* Ulaanbaatar, Academiya Nauk.

Volkov, V. (2004) Olennye Kamni Mongol'skogo Altaya (Deer Stone of the Mongolian Altai). In A. Gei (ed.) *Pamyatniki Arkheologii i Drevnego Iskusstva Evrazii (Eurasian Archaeological Monuments and Ancient Art).* Moscow, Academiya Nauk.

Wells, P. (2001) *Beyond Celts, Germans and Scythians.* London, Duckworth.

Wang, Q. and Conway, M. (2006) Autobigraphical Memory, Self, and Culture. In L-G. Nilsson and N. Ohta (eds) *Memory and Society: Psychological Perspectives,* 9–27. New York, Psychology Press.

Whitehouse, H. (1992) Memorable Religions: Transmission, Codification and Change in Divergent Melanesian contexts. *Man* n.s. 27(4), 777–799.

Williams, H. (ed.) (2003) *Archaeologies of Remembrance: Death and Memory in Past Societies.* New York, Kluwer Academic.

Wittgenstein, L. (1961) *Tractatus Logico-Philosophicus* (trans. D. Pears and B. McGuinness). New York, Humanities Press.

Wright, J. (2007) Organizational Principles of Khirigsuur Monuments in the Lower Egiin Gol Valley, Mongolia. *Journal of Anthropological Archaeology* 26, 350–365.

Yablonsky, L. T. (2000) 'Scythian Triad' and 'Scythian World'. In J. Davis-Kimball, E. M. Murphy, L. N. Koryakova and L. T. Yablonsky (eds) *Kurgans, Ritual Sites and Settlements: Eurasian Bronze and Iron Age,* 3–8. Oxford, BAR International Series 890.

Yablonsky, L. T. (2002) Archaeological Mythology and Some Real Problems of the Current Archaeology. In K. Jones-Bley and G. B. Zdanovich (eds) *Complex Societies of Central Eurasia from the Third to the First Millennia BC: Regional Specifics in the Light of Global Models,* 82–94. Washington D.C., Institute for the Study of Man.

Yates, T. (1993) Frameworks for an Archaeology of the Body. In C. Tilley (ed.) *Interpretive Archaeology,* 31–72. Oxford, Berg.

7. Memory and microhistory of an empire: Domestic contexts in Roman Amheida, Egypt

Anna Boozer

As this wave from memories flows in, the city soaks it up like a sponge and expands. ... The city, however, does not tell its past, but contains it like the lines of a hand written in the corners of streets, the gratings of windows, the banisters of steps, the antennae of the lightening rods, the poles of the flags, every segment marked in turn with scratches, indentations, scrolls.

(Calvino 1972, 11)

People foolishly imagine that the broad generalities of social phenomena afford an excellent opportunity to penetrate further into the human soul; they ought, on the contrary, to realize that it is by plumbing the depths of a single personality that they might have a chance of understanding those phenomena.

(Proust 1993, 450)

Introduction

Within an imperial framework, individuals and groups invoke memories of the past to denote both their social identity and their placement within the empire. An examination of quotidian mnemonic processes offers an opportunity for us to explore the ways in which local peoples negotiated, influenced, and responded to imperial social climates. The Roman Empire provides a salient framework for exploring memory because it was the iconic ancient empire, inscribing its control over a vast range of territories and peoples, each with its own distinct history and identity. The present work explores two Roman Egyptian houses as touchstones for the complex post-conquest conditions that intertwined memory, identity, and empire.

Roman domestic spaces provide an ideal nucleus for exploring identities and memories because the Roman house served as a vessel for the cultural identity and memory practices of its inhabitants. Although Roman houses differed architecturally to varying degrees across the Empire, they retained a similar cultural role. The material residues of these houses provide a compelling visual and architectural construct of the inhabitants' identity in Roman society because they served as a nexus for reflecting and forging both domestic life and public careers. As the material embodiment of the self, the Roman house signified social and ancestral status to visitors, thereby enabling the inhabitants to affirm or eschew a Roman identity (Hales 2003). Domestic wall paintings, in particular, served as essential ciphers of identities (both of the owner and the visitor) because they often included vignettes that necessitated a classical education. In order to assemble narratives from these paintings, viewers required familiarity with historical events, classical training, and creativity. Individuals outside of this cultural sphere may have had a host of responses to traditionally Roman works that would have been influenced by their ethnicity, gender, age, and so on. The process of assembling narratives from domestic wall paintings was creative and displayed one's placement with respect to Roman culture and education (Bergmann 1994). As such, the narratives deployed in such domestic decoration were deeply embroiled in identity politics, memory practices, and the Roman Empire.

This chapter contextually analyses two houses from Roman Egypt in order to draw attention to the significance of mnemonic practices within the daily lives of individuals who lived within an imperial framework. I first explore imperial frameworks as fertile arenas in which memory practices reinforced signifiers of individual and community identities. I then turn to domestic contexts, which are critical zones for exploring how individuals drew upon memories when performing their daily lives. I then examine two Roman Egyptian domestic contexts from Amheida (ancient Trimithis) in the Dakhleh Oasis, Egypt. One house was high status and displayed a Roman-Greek heritage in wall paintings, texts, and material culture, while the other house displayed a subdued, hybrid Roman-Greek-Egyptian heritage in the material culture. I offer specific examples of memory and identity from these domestic contexts and the implications these signatures would have when viewed within the greater social fabric of imperial consolidation.

Conceptions of Memory

Most theoretical expositions of social memory follow the usage originated by Maurice Halbwachs, a sociologist, who contended that memory must be understood as a social phenomenon. Halbwachs also founded the concept of collective memory, which denotes a group's shared, constructed, or inherited memory (Halbwachs 1992 [1925]). Subsequent scholarship augmented the concept of a group identity separate from individual memory and described the exploitation of social memory to create and reinforce a sense of individual and community identity (Basso 1996; Blake 1998).

Given the significance of identity within memory practices, it is worth delving into the concept in greater detail. The concept 'identity' expresses the ways in which individuals and groups differentiate themselves in their social relations with other individuals and groups (Jenkins 1996, 4). Identity positioning functions on two different planes: on one hand the greater social milieu defines identities by formal associations and categories; on the other hand, the single subjective

agent experiences many shifting facets of identity throughout the life span (Meskell 2001, 189). Social categories of identity are generally enduring and regenerative while an individual identity includes facets that can be fleeting, fragmented, and contextually contingent. Both individual and group identities comprise multiple influences such as heritage, genealogy, ethnicity, gender, age, economic class, and so forth. Because identities are multiply constructed and maintained they are fluid and contextually dependent and should be considered with reference to an individual's perceived sameness or exclusion and opposition to these multifarious influences.

The multiplicity and permeability of identities produce real challenges for archaeologists, even in contexts that are reinforced by contemporary written sources. The most accessible means of assessing identity archaeologically is through exploring mechanisms of identity construction and maintenance. These mechanisms loosely tether facets of identities to historically understood trajectories and take the form of social, material and memorial practices. A study of memory promises a fruitful approach towards understanding how identities are socially created and maintained. Indeed, memory infuses social meanings into the past, present, and future (Connerton 1989; Fentress and Wickham 1994 [1992]; Fagan 1996; Lovell 1998). Memories of heritage – be they real or mythical – are particularly potent forces in the collective imagination of identity.

Within archaeology, Van Dyke and Alcock describe four converging categories for exploring social memory transmission: ritual behavior, narratives, representations, and places (Van Dyke and Alcock 2003, 4–5). These categories of memory are intertwined and mutually reinforcing. The current work engages the last two categories of material memories (representations and places) in an exploration of identity politics. Paintings and other representational media may commemorate past events, such as mythic narratives, and thereby aid the memory process. Material displays of past identities serve as reminders of the past invoked by the present and as incentives that shape the future (Lovell 1998, 14–15). A single synchronic image can stimulate a host of memories, reforming and coalescing their diversity and contradictions, thereby positioning the past in the present and creating collective images in the present. Places associated with past events or attachments serve as significant vectors for exploring memory because they evoke a spectrum of emotions and memories ranging from mundane, everyday activities to monuments or sites of violence.

Memory and imperialism

When imposing forces control the present and future, evocation of the past infuses new meanings into places, representations, social identities, and traditions. Rearticulation of this past represents more than mere cultural archaism and nostalgia, it also offers imperial agents and local individuals an arena for social and political expression (Alcock 2001). The construction of the past could do much to symbolically smooth over social divisions, creating a sense of community identity (Basso 1996; Alcock 2002) or, alternatively, promote more restricted and selective identities (Bodnar 1994; Johnson 1995; Bohlin 1998). Within empires, rulers deployed the past in claims of universality and legitimacy, often creatively selecting and transforming both recent and deep pasts (Sinopoli 2003). Likewise, the influence of local areas should not be underestimated since the activities of local and non-elite actors often provoked changes in imperial structure, agendas, and approaches (Deagan 2001).

Since memory performed such an active role in empire building and maintenance one would expect that it would attract scholars of ancient Egypt, a geographical area that was occupied by both conqueror and conquered during its long, interleaved history. Egyptology, however, has provided only a few studies of memory (McDowell 1992; Montserrat and Meskell 1997; McDowell 1999; Richards 1999; Baines and Lacovara 2002; Meskell 2003) and has yet to produce any that address how different groups constructed memories with the framework of empire.

The present work explores memory during the period in which Rome conquered Egypt, although

this conquest was not the first time that this ancient civilization had been occupied. Egypt's long and layered history of foreign domination had potent implications for memory practices under the Romans. When Cambyses conquered Egypt in 525 BC, the Persians were the first outsiders to incorporate Egypt within a larger imperial power structure. The Persians did not settle in Egypt and relied on hegemonic imperial practices rather than on territorial integration. Signs of a Persian presence can be found in the temples they dedicated and the water works they constructed, particularly in the oasis region.

The Persians lost Egypt to Alexander the Great in 332 BC. After Alexander's death, the Ptolemaic Dynasty ruled Egypt for nearly 300 years and, unlike their Persian forerunners, focused largely on the development of Egypt. Part of this development included a policy of settling foreign soldiers on the land and creating numerous Greek settlements, particularly in Alexandria and the Fayum region. In order for individuals to advance in society, Egyptians often took on Greek names, learned to write in Greek, and familiarised themselves with Greek culture (Bowman 1986, 122–123). Meanwhile, the Greeks disdained Egyptians as lesser beings with a disorderly nature and a plethora of disreputable traits.

Egypt again became a province within a greater empire following the Roman conquest in 30 BC. By the time the Romans arrived there was a powerful Greek overlay in place, particularly in the forms of government administration and legal systems as well as linguistically, socially, and materially in certain geographic locales. Relatively few Romans immigrated to Egypt in comparison to the many thousands of Greeks that went to Egypt under Ptolemaic rule. This distinction was partially a function of the Roman policy that did not promote immigration to Egypt because of a concern that it might be used for political opposition (Lewis 1983, 16).

Various groups responded to the new social conditions of Roman rule differently. Local interests, social status, ethnicity and other vectors of identity influenced peoples' social choices and opportunities. Although households of different status levels may have had competing interests, they also had strong community-oriented tendencies. The pressures of Roman rule may have united different status groups in social cohesion against foreign occupation, while other households may have taken advantage of and supported the regime as a means of increasing their own wealth and social position. Still others may have regarded this new regime with indifference and ambivalence. Individuals, communities, and ethnic groups often articulated their alliances through citations of historical and mythological events from the past. Hellenism, in particular, offered a salient means of symbolising alliances with Roman rule. The Greek/Egyptian dichotomy created under the Ptolemies fostered aspirations to Hellenism and local elites, regardless of their ethnic heritage, relied upon Greek cultural symbols in order to promote their status (Lewis 1983, 39). Opportunism during the Roman Period thus involved a complex negotiation of ethnic categories that directly intertwined memory and identity. Remembering the past signified past group identities and distinguished, fashioned, and potentially transformed current connections between individuals and their relationship to society. In this context, representations of the past affected both individuality and the interactions between individuals and groups within society. The radiating influence of Hellenism in the Roman imagination reveals how the configurations of meaning, memory, and identity that defined a Greek heritage were reinscribed on an imperial Roman stage.

Memory and domestic contexts

In Roman Egypt, houses are iconic of these complex post-conquest social conditions. Across the Empire, Roman houses differed architecturally to varying degrees but they retained a similar cultural role. The upper class Roman house served as a nexus that reflected and shaped domestic life and the public careers of individuals. The material residues of these houses provide a compelling visual and architectural construct of the inhabitants' identity in Roman society. The Roman house,

as the material embodiment of the self, could be seen as an affirmation of the inhabitant's Roman identity as well as signifying social and ancestral status to visitors (Hales 2003).

Representational media, such as wall paintings and decoration, provided clues to viewers about the identity and status of the inhabitants. The process of assembling narratives from domestic wall paintings was creative and displayed one's placement with respect to Roman culture and education (Bergmann 1994). In order to unwind the social signifiers within the vignettes, it was essential that viewers have a familiarity with historical events and popular classical works as well as a penchant for creativity. Individuals outside of this classically educated cultural sphere must have had a host of responses to traditionally Roman works and these responses would have varied depending on diverse vectors of identity, such as their ethnicity, gender, age and so on. As such, the narratives deployed in such domestic decoration were deeply embroiled in identity politics, memory practices, and Roman imperialism.

In order to understand the way in which individuals made use of memory in the Roman Empire, I suggest that we draw attention to the place where these memories occurred, teasing out the local specificities and peculiarities that we must gloss over when we employ macroscale models. In so doing, I employ a microhistorical perspective. Microhistories are useful during certain phases of historical research because they underscore the initiative and capacity that historical agents have for mediating circumstances marked by ambiguity (Ricoeur 2004, 187). This approach is particularly suited for assessing facets of identity since an individual's identity is fluid and contextually dependent. By investigating individuals and small groups, microhistorians are able to ascribe a range of potential characteristics to bounded social and historical milieus (Cerutti 1990; Ginzburg 1993; Gribaudi, Levi *et al.* 1998).

By examining individuals, families, or small groups within their social fabric, we become aware of variants that macroscale analyses flatten out in quantitative approaches. Macroscale analyses, which examine the force of structural constraints exerted over a long time span, are not abrogated by microscale analyses. Rather the macroscale provides the contextual frame for situating and interpreting the array of options accessible and engaged by agents on the microscale. Ultimately, meticulous and broadly applicable histories require variations in scale. The principle inherent in variation in scale is that different scales do not simply generate more dense data about interconnections, but rather they bring to light new connections that were imperceptible in the macrohistorical scale (Ricoeur 2004, 210). Small-scale investigations can indicate innovative directions for future research on the macroscale through the production of novel data. Over time, the aggregates of these studies can provide nuanced and quantitatively viable histories.

Postprocessual archaeology has long attempted to access 'individuals' in the past, that is, to locate and theorise individual agents regardless of how representative these individuals were within their socio-temporal framework (Morris 1993; Bailey 1994; Meskell 1994; Hodder 2000). However, in the process of teasing out much needed theorisations of individuals, the larger cultural matrix has often been left by the wayside. By contrast, a microhistory explores characteristics of social strata for specific social periods through individuals and small groups. Culture reins in the historical and social variability of these individuals, by offering the individual 'a horizon of latent possibilities – a flexible and invisible cage in which he can exercise his own conditioned liberty' (Ginzburg 1993, xxi). The vocabulary that culture provides individuals is at their disposal to articulate their own social variability within their cultural matrix. These microhistories enable us to understand reciprocal cultural exchanges between the dominant social classes and the subordinate social classes (Bakhtin 1965).

Houses, in particular, provide a glimpse into intimate spaces and how individuals materially expressed memories and cultural exchanges. As Bachelard saliently explicated, houses embody our memories, our selves and uncertain, spectral pre-histories (Bachelard 1994, 47). They tug against concrete perceptions and touch upon imagination,

memories, and dreams. The materiality of the house itself can embody continuity of origin (Tringham 2000), or it can serve as a vessel for relics from the past in the form of objects and narratives (Gillespie 2000, 12–13). The house embodies memories of individuals and the specificity of personal histories localised spatially. It provides a sense of continuity and even a sense of origins beyond the lived experience of any of the inhabitants. Memories of individuals, collective memories, and deep pasts converge and reside within the household vessel.

The Roman house provides an evocative example of the home as a *locus* that reflected and shaped the cultural identity of its inhabitants. It was the setting for domestic life as well as the public careers of upper-class individuals and therefore served as a visual and architectural construct of the inhabitants' identity in Roman society (Mazzoleni 1993, 292; Hales 2003, 2). The Roman house, as an extension of the self, affirmed the inhabitant's Roman identity and signalled social and genealogical status to visitors. It was not ethnicity so much as a mastery of Roman culture that shaped an individuals' ambitions and abilities to achieve those ambitions within the Roman Empire (Woolf 2003, 13). Citations of the past were deeply embroiled in domestic identity constructions (Thébert 1987, 407) because adept references to historical and mythological events conveyed an individual's identity and mastery of Roman culture. Commemorating the past through representational media imbued inhabitants with a sense of deep history and transmitted a specific heritage to visitors. In the context of empire, such narratives highlighted the potentially divergent histories of imperialist and local agents while shaping future trajectories and agendas.

Roman Egyptian houses and households have been notoriously under-studied (Bailey 1990; van Minnen 1994; Bagnall 2001; Alston 2002, 45–52), although a few studies do exist (Husselman 1979; Hobson 1985; Bowman 1986, 146–150; Alston 1997). The neglect of these houses is unfortunate since the subtle and everyday aspects of remembering offer fertile grounds for exploration and Egypt offers some of the best-preserved Roman houses available to us. Indeed, Egyptian domestic contexts from all periods have often been left by the wayside in favour of mortuary and religious contexts. Although there are studies of memory that claim to access Egyptian household contexts (Meskell 2003), they primarily consider ancestral busts and mortuary contexts rather than objects from everyday life. These studies have informed the present work, but I would like to redirect our focus from the mortuary sphere to the domestic, where there is much to learn about the memories and identities of the living.

Amheida (Ancient Trimthis)

The following paragraphs examine two domestic contexts from Amheida (ancient Trimithis), an important city in the Dakhleh Oasis on the periphery of Roman Egypt (Fig. 7.1). Amheida today is remarkably well preserved (Fig. 7.2). It has a long occupational history, and it reached its greatest extent under Roman rule (1st to 4th centuries AD). This historical trajectory offers an excellent example of a locality that developed during a period of social, religious, economic, and political change under the Empire. Preliminary research suggests that the first house retained signatures of both the local past as well as a mythical Greek past that was more in line with the constructed heritage of its conquerors. The second house, discussed in less detail, shows a more complicated fusion between Greek and local memories.

The New York University Amheida Project (directed by Roger Bagnall, Paola Davoli, and Olaf Kaper) has identified and mapped four different sectors of the urban site: Area 1 is both domestic and industrial, Area 2 has vaulted and domed structures that are elaborately painted, Area 3 has an impressive pyramid that is surrounded by vaulted tombs, and Area 4 is a temple mound (Fig. 7.2). Amheida was one of the most important towns in the Dakhleh Oasis during the Roman and Byzantine centuries. Documentary sources indicate that it became a city by the fourth century and was treated on the same level as the neighbouring city, Mothis and the more distant

Hibis in the Khargeh Oasis (Wagner 1987, 191). The substantial above ground remains and surface pottery scattered across the urban center represent dates ranging from Pharaonic to Late Antique periods and the surrounding environs contain evidence of prehistoric lithic scatters, an Old Kingdom site and several cemeteries. Late Antique ruins dominate the visible site surface today.

The historical trajectory of Amheida complements that of the greater Dakhleh Oasis. In the 1970s and 1980s, The Dakhleh Oasis Project surveyed the entire Dakhleh Oasis, revealing a moderate resident population in Dakhleh – a total of forty-nine sites – throughout the Pharaonic period (Churcher and Mills 1995). By contrast, an excess of two hundred sites represents the Roman and Byzantine centuries of occupation. A recent re-evaluation of the Dakhleh ceramics seriation suggests that there are more Ptolemaic sites than originally accounted for in this initial survey, yet it remains clear that the Roman Period is represented in greater numbers than any other period until the present day. The reasons for this enormous expansion in population cannot be found in documentary sources but it is clear that, before the present day, the oasis population expanded to its greatest extent during the Roman Period.

Greek memories in Roman Egypt: A microhistory

Our first house at Amheida is situated in Area 2, an area of the site that, from the surface, appears to have a dense concentration of structures decorated with painted and molded plaster (Fig. 7.2). Immediately south of this house, and sharing a wall, lies another house of similar design and dimensions. Adjacent to the house in the north there is a large open area surrounded by walls and filled with refuse that was used for some unknown function. West of this domestic area, on the highest point of the site, lie the remains of a sandstone temple dedicated to Thoth of Set-wah. This temple has been completely dismantled over time, although the features and cartouches that survive suggest that it was active into the Roman Period (Davoli and Kaper 2005). Southeast of

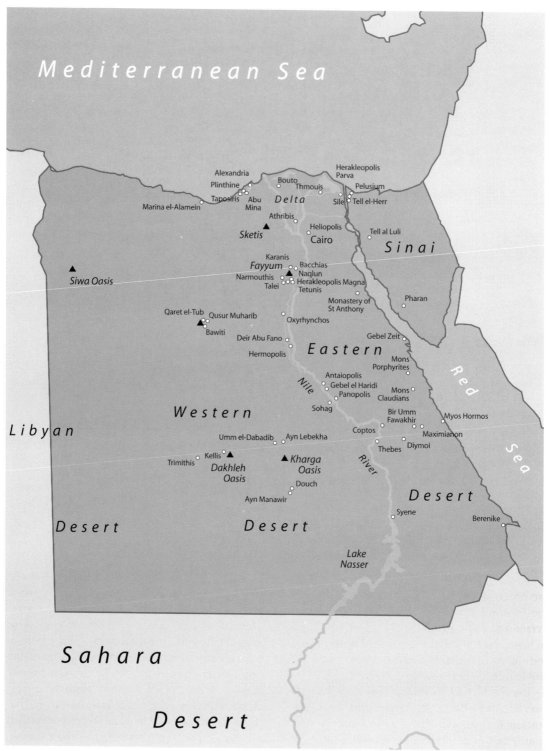

Figure 7.1 Map of Egypt.

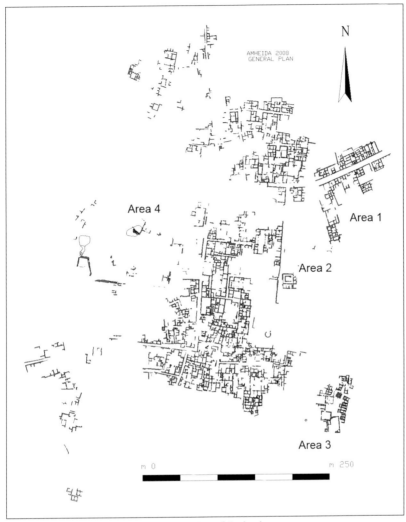

Figure 7.2 Map of Amheida.

the house the terrain flattens out and provides the location for tombs and a Roman Period pyramid that dominates the vista. These principal architectural features complemented by stark sand and an escarpment to the north comprised the visible urban environment of the house.

The Dakhleh Oasis Project took a preliminary look at Amheida in 1979, clearing the upper portion of two walls from a structure in Area 2, an area of the site that has a concentration of vaulted and painted structures. In so doing they found paintings with Greek mythological figures (Leahy 1980; Mills 1980). These figures were reburied until formal excavations commenced in 2004. At this time, the excavation of this structure is largely complete. Preliminary results from the recent excavations suggest that the structure was a mud-brick, late Roman house dating to the end of the third century with abandonment in the middle of the fourth century. Its basic layout consists of a central room with decorated rooms to the west and south, utilitarian rooms to the north, and

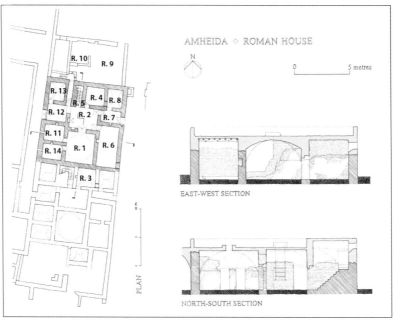

Figure 7.3 Plan of House, Area 2.1.

additional undecorated rooms to the east (Figs 7.3 and 7.4).

Many of the architectural features of this house are typical of local domestic architecture from the Roman Period as can be seen by comparison with recent work by the Dakhleh Oasis Project at Ismant el-Kharab (ancient Kellis), a town located east of Amheida in Dakhleh. Results from these excavations indicate that Roman Dakhleh domestic architecture typically consists of a single-storey structure with barrel vaulted roofs. A staircase provided access to the roof, which was often used as additional work and storage space. Within the house, there was typically a central area surrounded by living and work spaces, a feature signifying more Romanised houses. Walls were mud-plastered and often contained strips of whitewash along rear walls, around doorways, and wall niches (Hope, Kaper *et al.* 1989; Knudstad and Frey 1999). Presumably this whitewash provided illumination of these dark spaces, particularly when lamps were placed in the niches.

The house at Amheida contained decorative features that currently have no contemporary

parallels in the Dakhleh Oasis; Greek mythological wall paintings. We should be cautious in stating that this decoration is of a singular programme since much research remains to be done at Amheida itself as well as other houses further afield. For example, this structure may have been part of a planned *insula*, which contained at least one house of similar layout and dimensions.

As an assemblage, the material culture suggest that the major period of occupation was sometime between the late 3rd through the middle of the 4th century AD. The latest datable coins and *ostraka* that we have date to the reign of Constantius II, which gives us a *terminus ante quem* for the occupation of the house. The ceramic assemblage from the house is similar to fourth century domestic assemblages from nearby Ismant el-Kharab, with many multi-functional vessels represented in the most common local fabric (Dunsmore 2002; Pyke 2005).

The house could be entered from a room on its eastern end, which was doubtless the main entrance into the functional areas of the house (Fig. 7.3, R7). It provided direct access to a central room

AMHEIDA ◇ ROMAN HOUSE

AXONOMETRIC FROM NORTH-EAST

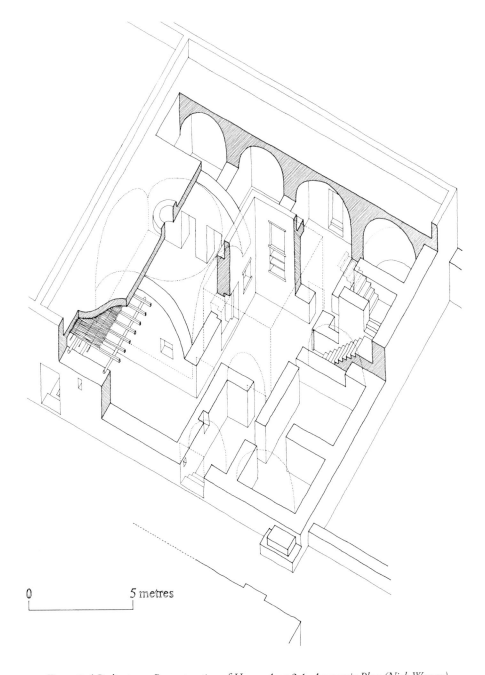

0   5 metres

Figure 7.4 Preliminary Reconstruction of House, Area 2.1: Axonomic Plan (Nick Warner).

and a utilitarian room to the north. The entrance itself was a simple, rectangular room with mud plaster walls. It was devoid of decoration with the exception of a small, arched niche with ornamental moulding along one of the walls.

Room 2, accessible from the eastern entrance, functioned as the central axis point within the house (Fig. 7.3, R2). It was necessary to walk through room 2 in order to manoeuvre through the house. It could be entered from a total of six doorways, including a staircase to the roof as well as the eastern entrance. There were several episodes of floor replastering and repair, which suggests heavy usage. As a central nexus for the house, individuals in the household probably used this space throughout the day for transit throughout the house as well as tasks that required more light than the other rooms would have afforded. The walls were covered in mud plaster and were completely replastered at least twice. The first layer of plaster shows traces of red pigment, suggesting that the walls were at least partially painted. The second coating consists of coarse mud plaster. The walls have two large niches with shelves for the storage of *ostraka* (a class of written artefacts using broken pottery as a material), other small, portable objects, and a large pot that was mortared into the corner of one of the niches. The *ostraka* from this room provide crucial hints about the identity of the inhabitants and will be discussed in greater detail below.

Two rooms, located in the northern part of the house, were used for utilitarian purposes, such as the storage and preparation of food (Fig. 7.3, R4, R8). The two rooms were once connected, but the door connecting them was plastered over at a later stage. Both rooms had low subdividing walls that created storage spaces. One of these rooms contained a hearth while the eastern room contained instruments for grinding. Both rooms were covered in grey-brown mud plaster with straw inclusions and the eastern room had a whitewash band running along the north wall of the room and partially along the eastern and western walls. The quality of the floors in these rooms was poor and both yielded high numbers of objects, including jar stoppers, animal bones, coins, and *ostraka*. We

also found oasis polished ware vessels that were local imitations of *terra sigillata*, a prestige ceramic that was used throughout the Roman Empire. These ceramics were not utilitarian but rather were employed to impress visitors and cultivate a chosen identity.

The courtyard gave access to an elongated room (Fig. 7.3, R6). This room was unusually large and was once covered with a flat roof, as could be seen by the presence of several decayed beams and mud plaster with palm rib impressions. The presence of a flat roof in a house containing vaults occurs on occasion in the Dakhleh Oasis (Hope 1987; Hope 1988). At Kellis, better-preserved examples reveal that these flat roofs were constructed with palm ribs, tied together as bundles, supported by beams of palm, and then covered with mud plaster and possibly bricks. These Kellis roofs seemed to have been used as storage spaces since numerous pottery vessels and papyri were associated with the roof collapse (Hope 1988). It is possible that the room from the Amheida house served a similar function. The west wall of the room possesses a niche that was once shelved. Grey-brown mud plaster covers the walls and white plaster bands surround both the doorway and the niche. Few artefacts were recovered from the room so it is not possible to determine the function.

Four unexcavated vaulted rooms form the west wing of the structure (Fig. 7.3, R11, R12, R13, R14). Test trenches were excavated in these rooms to determine the presence of painted plaster and what conservation effort would be necessary for the wall paintings when they are excavated. In the course of this preliminary testing it was found that three rooms were completely whitewashed and painted with various motifs that appear consistent with Roman wallpaper style wall painting (Wallace-Hadrill 1994, 23). At this time very little can be said about these paintings since the test trenches were terminated at the top of these paintings. However, one of these rooms displayed the presence of both geometric and figurative motifs in the upper registers of the paintings. No objects from secure contexts were recovered in these rooms because they have not been fully excavated.

In addition to these presumed living spaces there was a large painted room, accessible from room 2 (Fig. 7.3, R1). These paintings are currently unique in the history of Roman wall painting because they represent Homeric mythologies at such a late date. Although preliminary interpretations have been offered (Leahy 1980; Mills 1980), they await substantive study by art historians. However, preliminary dating of these paintings and contextualisation of their placement can be presented at this time.

Some of the scenes from the walls of the painted room are still *in situ* and it is possible to reconstruct some of the upper registers with fragments found from the remains of collapsed wall debris. From *in situ* paintings and fragments, it is clear that the arrangement of the paintings followed a simple plan, with figural scenes positioned above geometric designs representing stonework. Although the wall paintings display the hand of a skilled artist, the materials used were of poor quality, which caused the original paintings to deteriorate during the occupation of the house. The occupants had the paintings repaired in at least two episodes and there is some indication that they may have altered the original motifs slightly in places (Whitehouse 2005). As more structures are excavated at Amheida, it would be useful to compare the quality of materials used to determine if they co-occur with other architectural and socio-economic attributes.

The room originally had a domed roof, supported in the corners by four pendentives, the triangular segments that allowed the rectangular plan of the walls to support the circular shape of the dome. The entire interior surface of the walls, the pendentives and the dome were covered with whitewash and selectively decorated. Fragments collected from the collapsed dome reveal that it was partially decorated, with the central portion holding a colorful geometric design. The pendentives were painted with figures of nude winged female figures with outstretched arms holding a floral wreath in their hands that reached from one figure to the next. Some parallels to these figures, as well as the architecture, can be found in a mortuary context, the tomb of Petosiris at al-Muzawwaqa

in the Dakhleh Oasis, although it is notable that these tombs are more strongly Egyptian in design. The Petosiris tomb has similar figures supporting the heavens amid an interesting melding of Greek, Roman, and traditional Egyptian mortuary motifs (Osing 1982; Whitehouse 1998).

Beginning with painting on the northern wall, which divides the painted room from the courtyard, there are several recognisable mythological scenes. To the left of the door leading to the courtyard, Perseus holds the head of Medusa, while he rescues Andromeda from a diminutive sea monster. This scene is distinguished from all other scenes because it has a pale yellow background rather than the white background used for the other painted scenes in this room. All of the scenes have light coloured backgrounds, which were traditionally used during the Late Antique Period in areas that admitted little natural light (St. Clair 2002, 245). Below Perseus and Andromeda is an unconnected and less sophisticatedly painted sub-zone that consists of two panels. The left panel depicts a servant in a decorated tunic standing beside wine jars in a rack and the right panel shows a nude child lounging on a bolster. Helen Whitehouse suggests that this child is a representation of Harpocrates and that it originally featured a snake that was subsequently obscured by a later addition of cherub-like wings (Whitehouse 2005). To the right of the door leading to the courtyard, Eurycleia washes Odysseus' feet while he reclines on an elevated stool covered in sheepskin (Fig. 7.5). A noble woman, presumably Penelope, sits to the right of these figures and looks off into the distance rather than at Odysseus. It is the occasion of his homecoming and the moment where the nurse first recognises his concealed identity. Although the story is well known, the painting is unique in Egypt (Jackson 2002, 295, note 116). An occasion of homecoming raises tempting questions about the homeland of the occupants of this house and why this particular moment in the story of Odysseus was chosen.

The eastern wall of the same room is divided into two horizontal registers containing smaller painted figures than those found on the other walls. Between the two figured scenes, a grey band labels the figures in the scenes in Greek. Beneath

Figure 7.5 Room 1, North Wall, Eurycleia washes Odysseus' feet.

Figure 7.6 Room 1, East Wall, Polis.

these registers there is an additional geometric zone. Only the lower portion of the upper register and the geometric zone survive *in situ*. A possible temple is represented on the left with four columns and an architrave and the city walls below. To the right of the images of public architecture, a woman labelled as *Polis*, gestures toward the temple with her right hand and holds a golden sceptre in her left (Fig. 7.6). The depiction of public architecture was not uncommon in Roman domestic wall paintings and may have been employed as an analogy to the control the *paterfamilias* had over his own world that, in turn, was represented as high status (Hales 2003, 128–129, 144–145). Lisa Montagno Leahy, in one of the few articles published on the paintings, posits that the figure of *Polis* represents Amheida itself (Leahy 1980, 354), which suggests that the inhabitants included Amheida within the trajectory of Greek and Roman heritage displayed on the walls. Indeed, the personification of cities was a common practice in the Greek and Roman worlds. On the same register of this eastern wall, Aphrodite and Ares are caught in the act of adultery (Fig. 7.7). Hephaistos uses an invisible net of chains to hold them while a group of inquisitive male gods steals a look as the drama unfolds.

The west wall of the room is only partially preserved. Like the east wall it is divided into horizontal registers by a black register line and only the lower register survives *in situ*. Individual scenes

on the lower register seem to be subdivided by a vertical black line. Beneath the scenes a geometric zone appears again, just as it did on the eastern wall. The figured scene portrays a family at dinner (Fig. 7.8). Four figures, three adult males and a woman, recline on a couch and listen to the music provided by a figure to their left. A smaller figure, a male child, stands next to the musician. It is tempting to view these figures as the family that inhabited this particular house but there are no means of verifying such conjectures. Three large detached blocks from this wall display mythological material comparable to myths encountered on other walls in this same room. These scenes include Orpheus charming the animals with his lyre; a chariot scene featuring a male figure in military dress standing beside a female figure at ease; and a group of figures, including a woman, restraining another figure, who wields a sword. Despite the incomplete state of these blocks, many related fragments have been identified amongst the smaller detached pieces,

Figure 7.7 Room 1, East Wall, Gods and Aphrodite.

Figure 7.8 Room 1, West Wall, Family at Dinner.

and reassembly should aid specific identification of the myths recounted in these images (Whitehouse 2005).

The south wall of the room is the most poorly preserved wall of the painted room. It contained a large niche that may be partially responsible for the collapse. To the right of this niche there remains *in situ* only a horse's head above a reclining woman wearing a turban. The details of this figure recall scenes in which an emperor rides in victory above prostrate barbarians however the *in situ* paintings and the associated fragments cannot yet verify such an identification (Whitehouse 2005).

The use of representational media to commemorate past events is one of the most accessible means for archaeologists to retrieve memory. Wall paintings are particularly helpful media for understanding memory because the social behaviours that accompany them have a long history of study in the Roman context. As Bettina Bergmann has argued, educated Romans learned proper attitudes for approaching the narratives displayed in decorated houses. The entire process of manoeuvring through the house involved a creative association between the scenes displayed and memories of mythologies from the Greek and Roman past (Bergmann 1994, 226). Mastery of Roman culture, regardless of one's origin, was an important component of patronage and privilege. Being or becoming Roman entailed a participation in a cultural system that was composed of material culture, habit, and social *mores* common to the

empire (Woolf 2003, 238–249). Furthermore, knowledge of mythology became an effective status marker that unified the elite across the Roman Empire (Cameron 2004, 218).

The visitors and inhabitants of this house would have interpreted the deployment of Greek mythological scenes within the context of the Roman Empire, even if some visitors did not understand specific cultural references because they were missing from their own educational repertoire. The material manifestations of narrative anchored memories and bestowed them with tangible and long lasting associative aspects within their contexts of usage and display. For example, Edward Said has demonstrated that narratives are significant components to the intertwining of culture and imperialism. Narratives within imperial or colonial contexts enable the expression of identity and expound the existence of divergent histories for colonists or colonised peoples (Said 1993, xii). Material indices of narrative, in particular, enable palpable and residually potent memories both within the initial context of their creation and in the long-term.

The Amheidan wall paintings recount a large number of Homeric myths and the painter of these scenes rendered iconic moments that emphasised the textual component of myths, rather than the ways these myths were traditionally represented in art at this time. This choice to emphasise the text links the individual identities of the inhabitants into historically understood categories and provides a potent representation of a classical identity. Elite efforts to carry on the Roman tradition throughout the empire symbolised their participation in the greater Empire and buttressed their prestige locally (Thébert 1987, 329). Since Homer was the cornerstone of a proper Greek education, the scenes at Amheida not only cite a deep mythological past but they also emphatically declare that the occupants possessed the education and creativity associated with elite members of the Roman Empire. Within an imperial context, such memories take on great significance because they maintain a particular lifestyle and embody a set of cultural *mores* (Said 1993, 66). Through the citation of both recent and deep mythological pasts, these wall paintings promoted a sense of continuity between the past and a civic identity at Amheida. Furthermore, the representation of *Polis* tempts an interpretation of these paintings as a declaration that Amheida itself, a *polis*, was a descendent of its classical civic ancestors. Along with this *polis*, the household inherited its proper social position as part and parcel of this Roman social context.

It is unclear who would have had access to these paintings and at what times. Glimpses of these paintings would have been possible from most rooms in the house yet it is unlikely that everyone would be provided admittance. Indeed, the privilege of viewing the paintings may have been a subconscious marker of status within the household, as was often the case in Roman houses. Romans often used decoration in order to underscore differences in social distinctions. Sometimes the decoration itself mattered less than the contrast between decorative types or between the presence or absence of decoration (Wallace-Hadrill 1994, 47). The individuals who visited and occupied this space may have viewed the room differently depending upon divergent vectors of their identity, be it age, sex, ethnicity, or even class.

These ostentatious displays of Roman traditions are complemented by other strands of evidence. For example, all but one of the *ostraka* were written in Greek and a few identify a city councilor named Serenos, who was probably one of the owners of

this house (Bagnall and Ruffini 2004). In addition to these letters, a large number of *ostraka* refer to businesses related to wells, which have always been the real measure of wealth and importance in the oasis (Giddy 1987; Mills 1998). These texts affirm that the owner of the house was probably of an elite status with a margin of control over local civic affairs (Bagnall and Ruffini 2004). Since the man who commissioned the decoration of his house typically held the decisive role of determining the themes and perhaps even the way they were carried out (Thébert 1987, 393), it is likely that these paintings were commissioned and planned by Serenos or one of his ancestors. Furthermore, all of the names represented in the *ostraka* have strong Greco-Roman associations, affirming that individuals with Greco-Roman public personae comprised Serenos' social realm. A more mundane affirmation of an elite, Romanised identity can be found in the presence of oasis polished ware ceramics. This house thus manifests a confluence of heritage displays in a high-status house.

There was a general lack of material left behind, suggesting that the departure from the house was slow and planned. The occupants most likely removed valuable and personal items at this time and therefore there is little that remains with which to reconstruct the lives of individual inhabitants beyond that of an elite male, Serenos, and the associated status of his role in society. As of yet, we have not recovered identities of other individuals inhabiting the house and we have only scant yet tantalising hints of the identities of potential visitors to the house from the *ostraka*. We are left with questions regarding who else would have inhabited this space and how their interpretations would have shifted during the course of their own life spans and in reflection of their gender, status, and ethnicity.

The representational media in this house enhance our understanding of the individuals that occupied this space since they commemorate Greek and Roman heritage through mythology. The citation of this heritage links the identities of individuals in this house to historically understood categories of ethnicity where Hellenism was vital for inclusion in the upper echelons of society.

Serenos's presentation of Hellenism would have enhanced his social position and was possibly even the standard for individuals of a similar placement in society. This microhistory catalyses questions that may help guide future work on the houses at Amheida, Roman Egypt, and beyond.

Indeed, this close examination of Serenos's house helps highlight possible interpretations for incomplete material from other houses at Amheida. For example, a thick fragment of wall-plaster with a heading in large letters and four lines of Greek poetry was found on the surface of an elaborate, potentially domestic structure north of the one currently under excavation (Bagnall 2005). This fragment probably originates from the same structure as the fragments of a metrical text discovered at Amheida prior to excavations at the site (Wagner 1976). These fragmentary texts have Homeric associations and appear to have been part of the wall decoration of this house. Signifiers of a classical education may prove to be an important theme at Amheida among wealthier inhabitants. Poetry has been found elsewhere in Dakhleh, suggesting that a Greek education may have been an important component of daily life in Roman Dakhleh. The means of expressing a classical education may vary – be it through texts, paintings, architectural signatures, or portable artefacts – but its potential omnipresence is notable, particularly the emphasis on Homer.

Hybrid memories in Roman Egypt: A microhistory

Another excavated house from Amheida provides some effective facets of contrast with the previous house, particularly with respect to the proposed intersection between status and heritage mnemotics. This second house is from Area 1, in the northern portion of the site, where there is a concentration of industrial and vernacular domestic architecture (Fig. 7.2). With dimensions of 11×11 meters, this second house is much smaller than Serenos' house and is approximately square in plan view (Fig. 7.9). Although the building itself was considerably eroded by the strong sand-laden wind in this portion of the site, the material culture

and botanical remains were preserved to a higher degree than the house in Area 2. The ceramics and associated texts suggest that the second house might be of a slightly earlier date than Serenos' house, with an occupation falling largely in the mid to late 3rd century AD.

This house offers a more complicated association with memory and heritage than our previous house. The general architectural layout draws upon a Romanised model, with a central courtyard through which individuals accessed most of the rooms. Aside from the architectural layout of the house, the inhabitants did not present a clear preference for either a Roman or an Egyptian ethnicity. The occupants may have had either an ambivalent view towards ethnic heritage or a mixed heritage. For example we recovered a number of objects associated with traditional Egyptian practices, such as an amulet of the Egyptian god Bes, who was a protector of children, childbirth and women. Another faience amulet represents a hybrid animal of an Egyptian nature and also probably had an apotropaic function. Emmer wheat glumes that we recovered also point towards an Egyptian heritage since Egyptians traditionally consumed this type of wheat during the Pharaonic periods but it has been virtually unattested, until now, during the Roman Period (Walter 2005). This uncommon usage of traditional foods suggests that at least some of the inhabitants in this house were Egyptian.

The material culture from this house was not uncomplicatedly Egyptian, however, since we have recovered a number of objects that drew upon Greek and Roman traditions. For example, we recovered a statue fragment that emulates Greek design standards. The body is nude and rendered naturalistically in conformity with Greek and Hellenistic ideals rather than Egyptian or even Roman traditions, both of which favoured clothed male bodies. Unlike the previous house, there were no ceramics from this house that imitated the high-status ceramics used within the greater Roman Empire. Simple, coarse vessels with practical uses for cooking and storage were favoured here (Pyke 2005).

These individuals were not poor by any means as

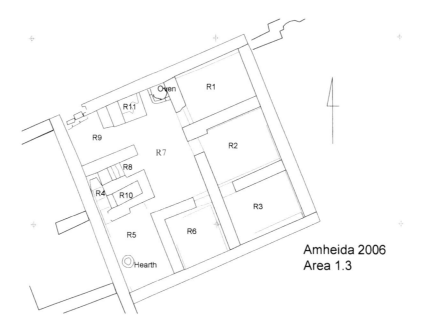

Figure 7.9 Plan of House, Area 1.3.

we can see from a few of the other objects that we have recovered. For example, we recovered a gold glass bead that must have derived from Alexandria since it was made with typical Alexandrene techniques. We found other modest jewelry as well, including several simple bronze rings, which could have been used in economic transactions as well as for adorning the body.

We catch a few glimpses of this family's daily occupations through the textual residues of their everyday lives. The *ostraka* from this house show a prevalent use of Greek and make it clear that the occupants were involved in trade of some kind and possibly even lower level estate management, perhaps for an individual such as Serenos, who lived in the previous house (Ruffini forthcoming). Beneath the floors of this structure we found demotic texts that suggest that there was once a native Egyptian settlement located nearby. Although these texts cannot illuminate the identities of the inhabitants of this house they may reveal a deep past for this family as indigenous occupants of the region.

Unlike Serenos' house, this house displayed its

heritage in ambivalent and muted ways, picking and choosing aspects of Greek, Roman, and Egyptian culture. We find a family transitioning into a mixed heritage between multiple traditions and we gain insight into how ordinary people experienced and remembered the tangled social changes brought about by Roman rule.

Conclusion

Memory and heritage are critical components of identity formation and continuance. Within the context of empire, the display of heritage reinforces and informs connections between individuals and their relationship to society. Our two Roman Egyptian houses provide illustrative microhistories of the post-conquest conditions that intertwined memory, identity, and empire. The first house examined here provides us with the image of Serenos that he wanted to display; an elite male with an element of control over local civic affairs, a definite signature of Hellenism and a penchant for Homer. The *ostraka*, architecture, and material culture affirm this identity emphatically.

Our second house showed a family that migrated slowly and intricately to a fusion between Egyptian, Greek, and Roman traditions with different family members choosing different signatures, potentially at different times. Importantly, traditional Egyptian practices could be found most potently in the common goods in everyday life, such as protective amulets and food remains. By contrast, we find that more grandiose objects tended to be Greek or Roman, such as architecture and statuettes. These divergent microhistories expose a protracted process of remembering the past that proves much more complicated than what we can describe with binary categories such as resistance and compliance or Romanised and un-Romanised.

These incremental changes, aggregated over numerous families, create a pixilated image of how individuals remembered the past within an imperial system. Close studies of these memories will help us understand who crafts these memories, how, where, and why. Comparisons between additional microhistories will illuminate the Roman Empire as a complicated, multifaceted force of social change in individual lives, rather than a seamless whole.

Acknowledgements

I would especially like to thank Roger Bagnall and Paola Davoli for their invaluable suggestions. Thanks also to Dušan Borić, Liz Mazucci, Giovanni Ruffini and Lindsay Weiss for reading and commenting upon earlier drafts.

Bibliography

Alcock, S. (2001) The Reconfiguration of Memory in the Eastern Roman Empire. In S. E. Alcock, T. N. D'Altroy, K. D. Morrison and C. M. Sinopoli (eds) *Empires,* 323–350. Cambridge, Cambridge University Press.

Alcock, S. (2002) *Archaeologies of the Greek Past: Landscape, Monuments, and Memories.* Cambridge, Cambridge University Press.

Alston, R. (1997) Houses and households in Roman Egypt. In R. Laurence and A. Wallace-Hadrill (eds) *Domestic Space in the Roman World: Pompeii and beyond,* 25–39. Portsmouth, RI, JRS Suppl. 22.

Alston, R. (2002) *The City in Roman and Byzantine Egypt.* New York, Routledge.

Bachelard, G. (1994) *The Poetics of Space: The Classic Look At How We Experience Intimate Places.* Boston, Beacon Press.

Bagnall, R. S. (2001) Archaeological Work on Hellenistic and Roman Egypt, 1995–2000. *American Journal of Archaeology* 105, 227–243.

Bagnall, R. S. (2005) Textual Finds. In R. S. Bagnall (ed.) *Amheida Project 2005,* 69–70. New York, Columbia University.

Bagnall, R. S. and G. R. Ruffini (2004) Civic Life in Fourth-Century Trimithis: Two Ostraka from the 2004 Excavations. *Zeitschrift für Papyrologie und Epigraphik* 149, 143–152.

Bailey, D. M. (1990) Classical Architecture in Roman Egypt. In M. Henning (ed.) *Architecture and Architectural Sculpture in the Roman Empire,* 121–137. Oxford, Oxford University Committee for Archaeology.

Bailey, D. W. (1994) Reading Prehistoric Figurines as Individuals. *World Archaeology* 25(3), 321–331.

Baines, J. and Lacovara, P. (2002) Burial and the Dead in Ancient Egyptian Society: Respect, Formalism, Neglect. *Journal of Social Archaeology* 1(2), 5–35.

Bakhtin, M. (1965) Introduction. *Rabelais and his World,* 1–58. Cambridge, Massachusetts, MIT Press.

Basso, K. (1996) Wisdom Sits in Places. In K. Basso and S. Feld (eds) *Senses of Place,* 105–149. Santa Fe, SAR Press.

Bergmann, B. (1994) The Roman House as Memory Theater: The House of the Tragic Poet in Pompeii. *The Art Bulletin* 76(2), 225–256.

Blake, E. (1998) Sardinia's Nuraghi: Four Millennia of Becoming. *World Archaeology* 30(1), 59–71.

Bodnar, J. (1994) Public Memory in an American City: Commemoration in Cleveland. In J. R. Gillis (ed.) *Commemorations: The Politics of National Identity,* 74–89. Princeton, NJ, Princeton University Press.

Bohlin, A. (1998) The Politics of Locality: Memories of District Six in Cape Town. In N. Lovell (ed.) *Locality and Belonging,* 168–188. London, Routledge.

Bowman, A. K. (1986) *Egypt after the Pharaohs 332 BC–AD 642.* Hong Kong, University of California Press.

Calvino, I. (1972) *Invisible Cities.* New York, Harcourt, Inc.

Cameron, A. (2004) *Greek Mythography in the Roman World.* Oxford, Oxford University Press.

Cerutti, S. (1990) *La ville et les métiers: naissance d'un langage corporatif (Turin, 17e–18e siècle).* Paris,

Editions de Lécole des hautes études en sciences sociales.

Churcher, C. S. and Mills, A. J. (1995) *Reports from the Survey of the Dakhleh Oasis: 1977–1987*. Oxford, Oxbow Monograph.

Connerton, P. (1989) *How Societes Remember*. Cambridge, Cambridge University Press.

Davoli, P. and Kaper, O. (2005) Area 4.1. In R. S. Bagnall *Excavations at Amheida*, 4–10. http://www.amheida.org, Columbia University.

Deagan, K. (2001) Dynamics of Imperial Adjustment in Spanish America. In S. E. Alcock, T. N. D'Altroy, K. D. Morrison and C. M. Sinopoli (eds) *Empires: Perspectives from Archaeology and History*, 179–194. Cambridge, Cambridge University Press.

Dunsmore, A. (2002) Ceramics from Ismant el-Kharab. In C. Hope and G. E. Bowen (eds) *Dakhleh Oasis Project: Preliminary Reports on the 1994–1995 to 1998–1999 Field Seasons*, 11. Oxford, Oxbow.

Fagan, B. (1996) The Arrogant Archaeologist. In K. D. Vitelli (ed.) *Archaeological Ethics*, 238–243. Walnut Creek, Altamira Press.

Fentress, J. and Wickham, C. (1994 [1992]) *Social Memory: New Perspectives on the Past*. Oxford, Blackwell.

Giddy, L. L. (1987) *Egyptian Oases*. Wiltshire, England, Aris and Phillips Ltd.

Gillespie, S. D. (2000) Beyond Kinship: An Introduction. In R. A. Joyce and S. D. Gillespie (eds) *Beyond Kinship: Social and Material Reproduction in House Societies*, 1–21. Philadelphia, University of Pennsylvania Press.

Ginzburg, C. (1993) *The Cheese and the Worms*. Baltimore, Johns Hopkins University Press.

Gribaudi, M., Levi, G. *et al.* (1998) *Mikrogeschichte, Makrogeschichte: komplementär oder inkommensurabel?* Göttingen, Wallstein Verlag.

Halbwachs, M. (1992 [1925]) *On Collective Memory*. Chicago, University of Chicago Press.

Hales, S. (2003) *The Roman House and Social Identity*. Cambridge, Cambridge University Press.

Hobson, D. W. (1985) House and Household in Roman Egypt. *Yale Classical Studies* 28, 211–229.

Hodder, I. (2000) Agency and individuals in Long-Term Process. In M. Dobres and J. Robb (eds) *Agency in Archaeology*, 21–33. London, Routledge.

Hope, C. (1987) The Dakhleh Oasis Project: Ismant el-Kharab 1988–1990. *Journal for the Society for the Study of Egyptian Antiquities* XVII, 157–176.

Hope, C. (1988) Three Seasons of Excavation at Ismant el-Gharab in Dakhleh Oasis, Egypt. *Mediterranean Archaeology* I, 160–78.

Hope, C., Kaper, O. *et al.* (1989) Dakhleh Oasis Project: Ismant el-Kharab 1991–92. *Journal for the Society for the Study of Egyptian Antiquities* XIX, 1–22.

Husselman, E. M. (1979) *Karanis. Excavations of the University of Michigan in Egypt 1928–1935: Topography and Architecture*. Ann Arbor, University of Michigan.

Jackson, R. B. (2002) *At Empire's Edge: Exploring Egypt's Roman Frontier*. New Haven, CT, Yale University Press.

Jenkins, R. (1996) *Social Identity*. London, Routledge.

Johnson, N. (1995) Cast in Stone: Monuments, Geography and Nationalism. *Environment and Planning: Society and Space* 13, 52–65.

Knudstad, J. E. and Frey, R. A. (1999) Kellis: The Architectural Survey of the Romano-Byzantine Town at Ismant el-Kharab. In C. S. Churcher and A. J. Mills (eds) *Reports from the Survey of the Dakhleh Oasis in the Western Desert of Egypt 1977–87*, 189–214. Oxford, Oxford Monograph.

Leahy, L. M. (1980) Dakhleh Oasis Project: The Roman Wall-Paintings from Amheida. *Journal for the Society for the Study of Egyptian Antiquities* 10.

Lewis, N. (1983) *Life in Egypt under Roman Rule*. Oxford, Clarendon Press.

Lovell, N. (1998) Introduction: Belonging in Need of Emplacement? In N. Lovell (ed.) *Locality and Belonging*, 1–24. London, Routledge.

Mazzoleni, D. (1993) The City and the Imaginary. In E. Carter, J. Donald and J. Squires (eds) *Space and Place: Theories of Identity and Location*, 285–301. London, Lawrence & Wishart.

McDowell, A. G. (1992) Awareness of the Past in Deir el-Medina. In R. J. Demarée and A. Egberts *Village Voices*, 95–109. Leiden, Centre of Non-Western Studies.

McDowell, A. G. (1999) *Village Life in Ancient Egypt: Laundry Lists and Love Songs*. Oxford, Oxford University Press.

Meskell, L. M. (1994) Dying Young: The Experience of Death at Deir el Medina. *Archaeological Review from Cambridge* 13(2), 35–45.

Meskell, L. M. (2001) Archaeologies of Identity. In I. Hodder (ed.) *Archaeological Theory: Breaking the Boundaries*, 186–213. Cambridge, Polity.

Meskell, L. M. (2003) Memory's Materiality: Ancestral Presence, Commemorative Practice and Disjunctive Locales. In R. M. Van Dyke and S. E. Alcock (eds) *Archaeologies of Memory*, 34–55. Oxford, Blackwell.

Mills, A. J. (1980) Lively Paintings: Roman Frescoes in the Dakhleh Oasis. *Rotunda* 13, 19–25.

Mills, A. J. (1998) A Note on a New Old Kingdom Site in the Dakhleh Oasis. *The Journal of the Society for the Study of Egyptian Antiquities* 25, 61–65.

Montserrat, D. and Meskell, L. M. (1997) Mortuary Archaeology and Religious Landscape at Graeco-Roman Deir el Medina. *Journal of Egyptian Archaeology* 84, 179–198.

Morris, C. (1993) Hands Up for the Individual! The Role of Attribution Studies in Aegean Prehistory. *Cambridge Archaeological Journal* 3(1), 41–66.

Osing, J. *et al.* (1982) *Denkmaler der Oase Dachla aus dem Nachlass von Ahmed Fakhry.* Mainz am Rhein, Phillip von Zabern.

Proust, M. (1993) *The Guermantes Way.* New York, Modern Library.

Pyke, G. (2005) Pottery. *Amheida Project Field Reports.* http://www.amheida.org.

Richards, J. (1999) Conceptual Landscapes of the Egyptian Nile Valley. In W. Ashmore and A. B. Knapp (eds) *Archaeologies of Landscape: Contemporary Perspectives*, 83–100. Oxford, Blackwell.

Ricoeur, P. (2004) *Memory, History, Forgetting.* Chicago, University of Chicago Press.

Ruffini, G. R. (forthcoming) Ostraka from Area 1.3. In A. Boozer (ed.) *Reports from the Columbia University Excavations at Amheida, Egypt: A Roman Period Domestic Context.*

Said, E. (1993) *Culture and Imperialism.* New York, Vintage.

Sinopoli, C. M. (2003) Echoes of Empire: Vijayanagara and Historical Memory, Vijayanagara as Historical Memory. In R. M. Van Dyke and S. E. Alcock (eds) *Archaeologies of Memory*, 17–33. Oxford, Blackwell.

St. Clair, A. (2002) Late Antique Transitions: A Decorated Room on the Palatine in its Late Roman Context. *Memoirs of The American Academy in Rome* 47, 229–258.

Thébert, Y. (1987) Private Life and Domestic Architecture in Roman Africa. In P. Veyne (ed.) *A History of Private Life: From Pagan Rome to Byzantium*, 313–409. Cambridge, Massachusetts, Belknap Press of Harvard University Press. I.

Tringham, R. (2000) The Continuous House: A View from the Deep Past. In R. A. Joyce and S. D. Gillespie (eds) *Beyond Kinship: Social and Material Reproduction in House Societies*, 115–134. Philadelphia, University of Pennsylvania Press.

Van Dyke, R. M. and S. E. Alcock (2003) Archaeologies of Memory: An Introduction. In R. M. Van Dyke and S. E. Alcock (eds) *Archaeologies of Memory*, 1–13. Oxford, Blackwell Publishing.

van Minnen, P. (1994) House-to-House Enquiries; An Interdisciplinary Approach to Roman Karanis. *Zeitschrift für Papyrologie und Epigraphik* 100, 227–251.

Wagner, G. (1976) Inscriptions et graffiti grecs inedits de la Grande Oasis (Rapport preliminaire. Kargeh et Dakhleh, mars et juin 1975). *Bulletin de l'Institut Francais d'Archeologie Orientale* 76, 283–288.

Wagner, G. (1987) *Les Oasis d'Egypt.* Cairo, Institut Français d'Archéologie Orientale du Caire.

Wallace-Hadrill, A. (1994) *Houses and Society in Pompeii and Herculaneum.* Princeton, NJ, Princeton University Press.

Walter, J. (2005) Archaeobotany. *Amheida Project Field Reports*, from http://www.amheida.org.

Whitehouse, H. (1998) Roman in Life, Egyptian in Death: The Painted Tomb of Petosiris in the Dakhleh Oasis. In O. Kaper (ed.) *Life on the Fringe: Living in the Southern Egyptian Deserts during the Roman and Early-Byzantine Periods*, 253–270. Leiden, Research School SNWS.

Whitehouse, H. (2005) Wall-paintings of Area 2.1, Room 1. *Amheida Project Field Reports*, from http://www.amheida.org.

Woolf, G. (2003) *Becoming Roman: The Origins of Provincial Civilization in Gual.* Cambridge, Cambridge University Press.

8. The depiction of time
on the Arch of Constantine

Adam Gutteridge

Visiting the Arch of Constantine (Fig. 8.1) can sometimes be a splendidly chaotic affair. The historical topography that so obviously influenced the original choice of its location – bounded by the Colosseum to the east, the Palatine to the west, and the Forum to the northwest – continues to affect and shape its reception in the present. Almost seventeen centuries ago, its proximity to these monumental centres would have influenced the ways in which it was perceived by its viewers, who understood it as a part of the sacred topography of the Eternal City. Today, its location brings tides of tourists and visitors, who hurriedly flow by it to get from the Colosseum to the Forum and back again, viewing it as but one stop in the monumental map of Ancient Rome. More monumental memories continue to be exhumed and displayed from the ground around it, with the exposure of the area around the base of the Meta Sudans directly to the north of the structure. Today the Arch is encircled by a skirt of tall metal railings, prohibiting any close contact with the monument; the railings are themselves often surrounded by the blankets of street traders, laden with imitation designer handbags and ersatz Ray-Bans. Depending on the quality of the fakery on offer and the sunniness of the day, often more people come to the railings to browse the merchandise than to peer at the past. The general feeling is that (unlike much of the adjacent forum, perhaps) this is a monumental space that continues to live in the present, instead of existing as an oddly-frozen, cosmetically-scoured topographic tableau. It accrues more moments, amidst the buskers and the traders, finding a living space inside the present city, and although partitioned, it continues to interact with the modern world going on around it. As will be further explored below, the monument itself is an intentional collision between times, designed to fuse together images of the past and images of the present, with occasionally jarring effect. Standing beside it today, one sees other, more whimsical temporal 'collisions': the men dressed as gladiators and centurions, hawking their image round the Colosseum for tourists' snapshots, can be glimpsed smoking a cigarette, talking on a mobile phone.

Introduction

The Arch of Constantine was dedicated by the Senate of Rome, in celebration of the tenth year of the Emperor Constantine's rule. Constantine had been acclaimed Emperor on the occasion of the death of his father, Constantius I, in AD 306 at York. At that time the Roman Empire was ruled by a collegiate system of Imperial government, with four emperors holding power together. The system of succession in this tetrarchy was non-hereditary, and Constantine's attempt to become a member of the ruling Imperial college following the sudden

Figure 8.1 The Arch of Constantine, Rome, north face.

death of his father amounted to a usurpation of legitimate authority, and indeed, it precipitated a protracted civil war amongst the Empire's rulers. Constantine himself was able to cross the Channel, and establish an Imperial court in the city of Trier for some years, whilst he strengthened his powerbase. His main rival for supreme rule in the western half of the empire was another usurper named Maxentius, who like Constantine, had claimed power because his father had been one of the legitimate Emperors. The centre of Maxentius' power was the city of Rome itself, and the struggle between the two rulers to claim sovereignty of the western Empire eventually led Constantine and his army to march south and invade Italy. The decisive battle took place at the Milvian Bridge outside Rome in AD 312, where Maxentius was defeated and killed, and Constantine was able to enter the capital of the Empire as its sole ruler in the west. History has accorded especial significance to this battle, as contemporary observers later recorded that prior to its commencement, Constantine had experienced some form of religious epiphany. This event came to be understood as a conversion to the Christian faith, at that time a relatively minor cult. Constantine was the first openly Christian Emperor, and in the aftermath of his victory in AD 312 he brought an end to the zealous, if sporadic, bouts of institutional persecution directed against the Church.

The Arch of Constantine

The monument dedicated to Constantine by the Senate in honour of his decennalian celebrations was a triple-bayed arch, which employed both figurative and non-figurative *spolia* throughout its structure. In its earliest and strictest definition, both the word and the concept of *spolia* substantially predate the world of Late Antiquity. Understood very specifically, they referred to the booty of war: spoils which the victorious forces plundered from the vanquished armies and their cities, in order that they might be displayed as the material symbols of victory (Bassett 1991, 92; Flower 2000; Kinney 1997, 120–123; 2001, 138). This kind of triumphal action was still comprehensible in the later empire, but what archaeologists and historians mean when they use the term widens greatly during this period. Principally it has come to mean architectural components of older buildings that are reused in later constructions. Naturally, this is not an activity which was practiced solely in the later empire, as the alteration and reuse of older buildings was hardly unheard of in the earlier classical world. Yet what is clear is that such architectural activities increase from the later third century onwards, specifically in the public monumental sphere, and although it continued to be a characteristic response to the built material heritage of Roman culture long into the Renaissance and beyond, this style of construction might certainly be said to have something characteristically late antique about it, existing as a definite part of the period's cultural and material lexicon. *Spolia* play an increasingly visible and prominent role in architecture of the period (especially in buildings characterised as both public and imperial), and our historical sources have also preserved a range of opinions about it, from the vernacular to the official (Coates-Stephens 2003; Kunderewicz 1971). However, it has been suggested that such a rise in evidence during the later empire is connected as much to the changing uses to which *spolia* are being put, as an actual increase in the practice itself: whilst such reuse of architectural elements may have been as common in the earlier Empire, it was for the main unobtrusive and often invisible (*i.e.*

structurally interior, rather than exterior), and in contrast, many of the primary examples of late antique monumental spoliation are not only visible and exterior, but are intentionally designed to be so (Kinney 1997, 124–125; Ward-Perkins 1999, 225–226). It is this change in the deployment of reused materials that is therefore significant, and the specific movement of reused materials into the visible realm of architectural expression is a fundamental change in architectural practice. The repatching of porticoes at the Colosseum in Rome sometime in the first half of the third century seems to mark a watershed in this change, as the first surviving example of obviously apparent *spolia* mixed with new material, fully in view (Kinney 1997, 125). Neither was the Arch of Constantine the first Imperial arch in Rome to explicitly display spoliated reliefs: the surviving fragments of the monument known as the Arcus Novus (De Maria 1988, 197–203, 312–314; Kleiner 1992, 409–413; Laubscher 1976; Torelli 1993), probably dedicated to Diocletian and Maximian in AD 293 (for this disputed date, see Buttrey 1983 and Chastagnol 1987), reveal a structure clad with ancient reliefs, some of which had been retouched before being incorporated into the new monument's fabric.

The Arch of Constantine, and use that it makes of spoliated material in its sculptural programme, is a comprehensively studied subject in the field of late antique art and architecture (see most recently, Elsner 2000 on its use of *spolia*; Holloway 2004, 19–54 for a general survey; Pensabene and Panella 1999 on its archaeology; Wilson Jones 2000 on the its architecture). The monument reuses figurative reliefs and statues from at least three older Imperial monuments (for the best illustration of Arch's arrangement of *spolia*, see Elsner 1998, 188, fig. 126): eight relief panels forming four scenes, plus eight free-standing statues, from a monument of Trajan celebrating victory in his Dacian campaigns (Leander Toutai 1987); eight tondi featuring scenes of hunting and sacrifice from a Hadrianic monument (Turcan 1991); and eight reliefs from a monument of Marcus Aurelius (Angelicoussis 1984; Ryberg 1967, 28–76). It has been recently suggested that the monument's reuse of older forms

also extends to a fourth structure, as the overall architectural composition of the Arch (triple-bayed with eight columns) was a direct and intentional emulation of the Arch of Severus (Wilson Jones 2000, 66, 70; a suggestion also made by Brilliant 1984, 122). The older pieces of figurative art were augmented by a number of new carvings from the time of Constantine (L'Orange and Von Gerkan 1939): pedestals at the bases of the eight columns on the long sides of the monument; the spandrels of all three arches themselves; two tondi on the shorter sides depicting scenes of mythic cosmology; and a lengthy frieze which wrapped itself around the entire structure and narrated the story of Constantine's journey to, victorious battle for, and post-conquest deeds in, the city of Rome (it has been intimated that the pedestals and the frieze itself may also be *spolia*, originally from the workshops of Maxentius, Knudsen 1989; 1990). It should be pointed out that whilst the fourth century work was new in the sense that it was likely carved specifically for the Arch, recent work on the structure has shown that individually, every single element of the Arch's structure, from its eight free-standing columns to the individual blocks of stone themselves, have all been reused (Pensabene and Panella 1993–1994, 174–283; 1999, also refuting the earlier suggestion that the Arch's entire structure was Hadrianic in origin, Melucco Vaccaro and Ferroni 1993–1994). The two long sides of the monument also boasted identical inscriptions, announcing the nature of the monument and describing, with some vaguely religious terminology, the victory of the Emperor to which it had been dedicated. The Arch's epigraphy also included acknowledgements of his decennalian vows, in abbreviated form, on both of the long sides of the Arch's façade.

One of the principal unanswered questions concerning these spoliated pieces is their location and status prior to reuse in the Arch. Such a question should be, and indeed has been (*e.g.* Kinney 1997, 127–128), asked of spoliated material in general, although the evidence that is available to answer this question is exceedingly slim. What evidence there is, however, appears to suggest a form of coordinated management system for the collection and subsequent reuse of older monumental elements, rather than a strategy of more haphazard pilfering. It has been pointed out, for example, that some of the reliefs reused as *spolia* on the Arco di Portogallo in Rome appear to have been damaged by fire prior to their reincorporation into the Arch's fabric, possibly suggesting that the destruction of their original monument in some form of disastrous event may have prompted their salvage and subsequent reuse (Kinney 1997, 146). Similarly, capitals which are reused in three of Rome's late antique churches – S. Sabina, S. Stefano Rotondo, and S. Maria Maggiore – all appear to share the same incised graffito marking, which is perhaps indicative of a specific collection and/or storage event, in which they existed as a group together (Coates-Stephens 2003, 341 n. 1). Such archaeological evidence is lacking from the *spolia* that are reused in the Arch of Constantine (although it has been argued that the general size and nature of the monumental elements that were reused–specifically the Trajanic frieze–suggested that their original location lay somewhere other than the city of Rome, Holloway 1985), but those analyses of the monument that stress its internal coherence have suggested something similar. It has been argued that the precision of the monument's architectural planning shows that the specific elements chosen for reuse were neither random choices, nor purely accidental inclusions, and instead must have been the result of specific decisions; therefore it is most likely that they were selected from a warehoused stockpile of resources awaiting the late antique architects, who made such selections in line with a master plan (Wilson Jones 2000, 65). Excavations of the Capitolium in the North African town of Sabratha revealed that subsequent to the earthquake of 365, the shell of the building was apparently used to store what were considered reusable architectural elements of those buildings destroyed in the disaster (Kenrick 1986, 114; for storage and deposits of marble in Ostia, and evidence from Rome, see Pensabene 2000). Similarly, a papyrus has survived which appears to be a quasi-official inventory of all the columns in a particular town, along with their dimensions and their state of repair, which may represent a survey of materials available for potential reuse (Lukaszewicz 1979). It is significant, however, in the case of the Arch of Constantine that the spoliated monuments were specifically Imperial constructions. Slightly later legislation in the Theodosian Code suggests that private citizens were *de facto* prohibited from using *spolia* in their own personal constructions (*e.g. CTh* 15.1.19, passed in AD 376, and directed towards those in Rome who should ensure that any new buildings were completed '…without bringing together old buildings, without digging up the foundations of noble buildings, without obtaining renovated stones from the public, without tearing away pieces of marble by the mutilation of despoiled buildings'). Thus it was the action of reusing the past, as much as any message involved, which marked the Arch out as a significant and State-sponsored construction, built by the exercise of Imperial prerogative (this approach to *spolia* had a long heritage in Medieval Rome, and popes later found it efficacious to use *spolia* in church building, in order to emphasise their power over ancient public monuments, Kinney 1986, 390). Although it is not clear to what extent the monuments were stored or curated prior to their phase of reuse, or whether they were reused as *spolia* immediately subsequent to their collection, it is clear, however, that the fragments were not casually foraged, and that intentional strategies of collection were in place.

Recutting and rewriting: Image and word

This brief study offers an exploration of how *time itself* was depicted through the monument's iconographical programme (for further context of this issue, see Gutteridge 2006). Perhaps the most immediately obvious collision between the present and the past is the overt treatment of *spolia* on the monument. These are *spolia* which have been altered in a significant way, in order to manipulate and recalibrate the past's traces and ensure that they interacted with the monumental present in a particular fashion. In the case of the Arch of Constantine, wherever the reused sculpture depicted an emperor in front of its *mise-en-scène*, his likeness has been altered in order that the individual depicted might resemble Constantine, (or on two occasions, an Imperial companion). The head of Trajan is recut on both of the scenes in the Arch's interior passageway, on Slab I (Trajan's *adventus*/Constantine as *liberator urbis*) and Slab V (Trajan charging/Constantine as *fundator quietis*) (Leander Toutai 1987, 91–95). A number of the Imperial heads on the Hadrianic tondos are either badly weathered or broken off entirely, but those surviving today bear the image of Constantine and either Constantius I or Licinius I (Evers 1991, 786–793; L'Orange and Von Gerkan 1939, 165–169). The Constantinian heads that replaced the features of Marcus Aurelius seem to have been entirely lost, and those currently attached to the Arch are the relics of a restoration project undertaken by Clement XII in 1732; there is some dispute over whether these replacements were intended to portray Constantine, or are instead likenesses of Trajan (Angelicoussis 1984, 142; Elsner 2000, 163 n. 23; Gradara 1918; Stuart Jones 1905, 251–252). Apart from this recutting of the heads, there seems to be little else which has been done to the monumental *spolia*, perhaps aside from some limited drilling and reshaping on the Trajanic frieze (Hannestad 1994, 86–96).

This recutting of the older Imperial portraiture to the recognisable face of Constantine (who appears as the very embodiment of the 'young ruler'-type, replicating the vigour and quasi-divine *numen* of the ancient Alexander, *cf.* Bruun 1976, 122–3; Harrison 1967; Wright 1987), firstly implicates the stance of the present towards that which has passed, and secondly suggests certain styles of imagining time itself. Firstly, the ability of Constantine to appear and reappear throughout the monumental rhythms of the Arch's decorative sculpture, wearing the guises of a variety of his predecessors (or, perhaps, having them appear in the guise of Constantine), creates the image of a past which is subject to not only re-imagination, but also manipulation. Apart from the facially 'cosmetic' changes, no attempt is made to update the styles of the older statuary, to try and hide the revisionist's hand (on this clash of styles, see Elsner 1998, 19). Not only can the emperor of the

present manage to refigure the past in order that he might be able to appropriate the victories and images of his forebears, but such action is overt and acceptable. Secondly, by presenting this array of instants occurring in the monument's now, events which had been originally separated in the flow of time (the battles of Trajan, the victory celebrations of Marcus Aurelius, the *ingressus* of Constantine) are condensed (Elsner 2000, 163–165). They all appear to be happening simultaneously on the monument itself, colliding into the static present, and the boundaries of the past which might have prevented them from running into each other, have been elided. One might be reminded of the curious saying of Damascius, reported by Simplicius: 'Similarly to space preventing the parts of separate bodies from being contiguous, time prevents the events of the Trojan War from being confounded with the events of the Peloponnesian War, and in an individual it prevents confounding the state of a new-born with that of a youth' (quoted in Pines and Sambursky 1971, 65). On the Arch of Constantine, such time is missing, and the events of Trajan's Dacian campaign have become confounded with the battle at the Milvian Bridge. Such collision is perhaps most pronounced in the assemblage of sculptural moments at the northern end of the monument's eastern face. Here, as the Emperor Constantine stands to address the crowds from a rostrum in the Roman forum after his victory outside the city, he is flanked by statues of the long-dead emperors Hadrian and Marcus Aurelius (L'Orange and Von Gerkan 1939, 82–84). Not only do the modified figures of both of these men appear throughout the monument as a whole, but immediately above the head of the statue depicting the petrified and deified Hadrian, his living body, albeit with his facial features changed, offers sacrifices to Apollo (Fig. 8.2). For Elsner, Kinney, and Wilson Jones, the real innovation of the Arch of Constantine was that it sought to end the association of such recutting of Imperial portraiture with the concept of *damnatio*, instead brokering a reverence of the past through the disfigurement of it (Elsner 2000, 173–175; Kinney 1997, 143; Wilson Jones 2000, 70). Such a conceptual erasure of the past had long been

Figure 8.2 Oratio of Constantine (below) and recut Hadrianic tondo featuring sacrifice to Apollo (above), Arch of Constantine, Rome, north face, eastern side.

possible via a variety of rescripts and *damnationes*, something in which the Senate and Constantine himself had participated with the renaming and rededication of a basilica built by Maxentius (Curran 2000, 79–82; Peirce 1989, 403–405). Yet modification of *spolia* on the Arch is far from such uniform erasure of the past, and therein lays its importance. The alteration of an event's specific participant (such as the hunting Emperor becoming Constantine rather than Hadrian), whilst retaining its context, illustrates an image of historical time as a mosaic of instants which can be reproduced with different participants, and then displayed as time-less fragments in a constant present. These fragments become self-contained instants, loosed from their own context, and replaced into singular timeframe, so that Hadrian sacrifices to Apollo, in the same 'time' as he sits as a statue in the forum.

The cultural image of time during the period may be further enlightened by this ambiguous stance towards the historical past to which the monument makes reference. Such an approach has often been taken by scholars who sought to discern whether or not the monument was Christian in any way, or whether instead it undermined rather than reinforced the narratives of Constantine's conversion written by Eusebius and Lactantius. The issue of whether or not Constantine was a Christian in AD 315 (or indeed, in AD 312) is a comprehensively entangled affair, and one which is unlikely to achieve any absolute resolution (for recent studies of the nature of Constantine's 'conversion'-event of AD 312, see Barnes 1985; Curran 1996, 68–71; Errington 1988, 309–310; Straub 1967; some earlier work that addressed this question remains relevant, including Alföldi 1948, 16–35; Baynes 1972, 6–11; Jones 1949, 79–102). Although there is not the slightest hint of explicit Christianity in any form on the monument itself, scholars have often been drawn to the ecumenical phraseology of the main inscription, found on both of the Arch's longer sides (*CIL* VI.1139). In this sparse epigraphic brevarium of Constantine's victorious campaign, his victory is prompted: '… QVOD INSTINCTV DIVINITATIS MENTIS MAGNITVDINE…', *at the instigation of the divinity, in the greatness of his mind*; the loose ambiguity of the *instinctu divinitas* has been seen, in the words of Wilson Jones, as being '…all things to all comers' (Wilson Jones 2000, 70). It has even been suggested that the *mentis magnitudine* may have something of a Christian ring to it, referring to the divine mind inspiring Constantine, rather than the mind of the Emperor himself (Bowersock 1986, 302–303). If we are to believe the accounts of Eusebius and Lactantius, then Constantine was indeed driven towards his victory by a divine power, and this power that lit the skies of his sight and mind was the Christian God (his religious epiphany was accompanied by some kind of vision, which supposedly prompted his conversion; for recent interpretations see DiMaio *et al.* 1988; Nicholson 2000; Weiss 2003). Yet the monument, dedicated by a still-pagan Senate three years later, was highly unlikely to overtly reference whatever

Christian *anecdota* were in currency at the time, and even less likely to advertise any wavering apostasy in the Imperial religious tradition. Thus it may be that the inscription's interpretation is intentionally nebulous, making use of a shadowy yet powerful and benevolent Divinity which is neither traditionally pagan nor innovatively Christian. A similar interpretation has also been made of the panegyric offered to Constantine in AD 313 at Trier, stressing that the rhetor's use of a parallel phraseology to describe Constantine's divine inspiration during his victorious campaign against Maxentius is also intentionally ambiguous, determined to avoid giving offence to either pagans or Christians by describing the emperor's patron 'divinity' in a neutral way (Odahl 1990). Such ambiguity is perhaps also played out in the reshaping of the Hadrianic tondi, which in their entirety would have comprised scenes of the emperor participating in both hunts and their attendant sacrificial rites. These appear to have been manipulated in order that Constantine appears as the hunting emperor four times, while his companion (either his father Constantius I, or his co-regent Licinius I) takes the main part of the Imperial pagan pietist (Wilson Jones 2000, 70–72; for details of the tondi's composition and recutting, see L'Orange and Von Gerkan 1939, 165–169), sacrificing to the pagan gods twice, and leaving Constantine to offer sacrifice possibly only once (the fourth tondo, the scene with Silvanus, is badly damaged). Thus, although the new Constantinian frieze lacks an explicit scene of the newly-arrived emperor offering thanksgiving sacrifices in Rome, he is associated with the recut Trajanic scenes of acceptable piety, and shares the actual pagan duties with an associate.

Overall, it appears perfectly plausible that whilst there is nothing overtly Christian about the Arch's iconographic programme or its interpretive retelling of history, in its careful wording of Constantine's victory and its apparently careful avoidance of a scene in which he sacrifices to the pagan gods in the present (and perhaps only once in the retouched and elided 'past'), the monument courts ambiguity through vagueness and silence. There is no need to go as far as to say that the

Arch of Constantine is constructed as a specifically 'post-structuralist'-style monument, where there is no 'truth' in the historical record, but its stance towards the events of the recent past is determinedly intended to allow for numerous interpretations. If one viewed the monument as a pagan, there would be little to offend the sensibilities, with an Emperor explicitly claiming the trans-temporal patronage of pious and virtuous Imperial archetypes. Conversely, for the Christian minority, or those with a vaguely syncretistic bent to their devotions (and Christian or not, Constantine was surely one of these), the partial exclusion of sacrifice and the inclusion of a *divinitas* would have prompted a different interpretation of the structure. There is even an argument, advanced by Peirce, in which the monument might be read as a thanksgiving to the god Sol Invictus (Peirce 1989, 406–407). If history already exists in fragments, as events which are available for salvage and reclamation, recutting and manipulation, and as this is the case with the identities and faces of emperors long since dead, then such an exegetic generosity might to extend to events of the recent past. One is allowed, as a viewer, to make of the monument what one will, and as the monument is essentially a material synecdoche for the historical events which it represents, then these events themselves become implicitly available to interpretation. This anagrammatic past becomes capable of assembly and reassembly by different observers with their variety of stances.

With the acknowledgement that this fragmentary past had been the subject of a specific rather than random harvest, another level of temporality becomes evident in the monument. By making a monument out of fragments that have fallen into decay, the relationship between the monumental past, present, and future is immediately thrown into some ambiguity. Imperial monuments – and most especially those that are meant to proclaim a triumph – are intended by their Imperial sponsors and designated architects to have a ferociously tenacious hold on a city's landscape over time. Monuments are built in order that they may live on, and the salvage of such memorials and their manipulation has a significant bearing on the expected perpetuity of the present. Although Kinney has argued that one of the innovative features of the specific Imperial reuse of monuments, such as that seen on the Arch of Constantine, is of a kind of *renovatio* of memory, rather than its *damnatio* (Kinney 1997, 143–146), there may well be an added level of complexity. For these are not the nameless cabal of silent columns with which Constantine peopled the nave of the Lateran basilica (for the use of *spolia* in the Lateran, see Lindros Wohl 2001, 87–91); instead, they are specific and hallowed names of emperors gone by. It has also been argued that this emphasis on identity and personality has the effect of stressing what might be termed a 'continuity of doing', where the actions of all emperors combine around the face of Constantine, collapsing the differences between them, and the concept of the 'Emperor' become a thing, rather than a person (Elsner 1998, 81; 2000, 158, 165). Brilliant has gone further, and argued that this spoliate collection of 'types' on the Arch, using trans-temporal (and therefore generic) scenes of Imperial virtue, rather than specific mimetic depictions of Constantine's own past, is intended to subvert linear causal time and instead express the teleological inevitability of Constantine's triumph by showing that all of the past, in its entirety, led up to the Emperor's victory (Brilliant 1970, 78).

By reusing fragments from their monuments which have otherwise fallen into oblivion, and recutting old triumphs, Imperial memory itself is subject to an overwrite. Indeed, Carruthers has argued that this kind overwriting is the only possible way in which cultural forgetting can occur. In her terminology, such 'monumental crowding', the imposition of new patterns of building over existing memories succeeds where total demolition/oblivion fails, by cacophonously blocking out a memorial's message, rather than simply leaving a memory-gap (Carruthers 1998, 54–56). Explicitly, the Arch of Constantine celebrates commemoration, in its materialisation of the events of 312, but implicitly it must acknowledge its own potential futility. If the monuments of Trajan, Hadrian, and Marcus Aurelius have fallen into fragments, and their names erased by the passage of time, then Constantine's

Arch itself must acknowledge that the same may well happen to it one day. The seeds of its own admitted mortality are sown in its design. To make a memorial out of the obliterated fragments of other memorials is to provoke an increased understanding of the nature of oblivion.

The image of the future and temporal elision

In its fullness, the monument binds these fragments of the past together with intimations of both future temporality, and also a purer, cosmic time. The future appears in two main guises on the Arch (although there is perhaps a third appearance: a recent interpretation of the Arch's main inscription suggests that by Late Antiquity, '*instinctu divinitas*' had come to mean a specifically supernatural prompting from divine authority which involved a measure of foreknowledge, divinatory power, and prophetic understanding of the future (Jones Hall 1998)). The first principal depiction of the future is the promise which is offered in the paired scenes of *oratio* and *liberalitas*: the Imperial pledge of a peace and prosperity that was yet to come (Brilliant 1984, 121; Peirce 1989, 415). After overcoming the tyrant and his faction, Constantine addresses the assembled populace at the omphalos of Empire, as the bringer of peace and the conqueror of factionalism; in the next scene, he distributes the bounty of this peace to the phalanx of people below, illustrating the promises that the future would bestow. This is the extension into the future of triumph over the tyrant, affirmed by the main inscription, and the illustration that the Emperor's might is not restricted to a control over the vagaries of the battlefield alone. The second appearance of the future comes in the form of the lesser inscriptions which appear above the monument's pair of flanking arches. On the monument's northern face, the epigraphy promises 'VOTIS X...VOTIS XX', *as I vowed for ten years, so I vow for twenty*, and the southern face similarly offered its own tidings for the future: 'SIC X...SIC XX', *so ten, so twenty*. Also appearing on the *spolia* incorporated into the Arcus Novus (*CIL* VI.31385), the dedication of monument featuring such vows was common during Imperial anniversary celebrations, as was the minting of a coinage issue featuring a variation on the legend (see Mattingley 1950; 1951 for the numismatic evidence); although it has been argued that the form of the words on the Arch of Constantine would be more suitable for the Imperial vicennalia of AD 325–326 (Richardson 1975, 78, this suggestion was decisively refuted by Buttrey 1983). Again, as with the scenes featuring the Emperor offering social and material prosperity in the Constantinian frieze, these vows also reflect a promise and a control over the times that were yet to come. They also offer a sense of temporal replication, one which is common in all the vows which are made in this formula: so as the last ten years have been, the next ten will be so too; just as I vowed ten years ago, so I vow again. If the dedication of an Arch made from the fragments of the past suggests an attitude towards *renovatio* and the attempt to dissolve the distinction between the past and the future, such epigraphic promise equally suggests the attempt to do the same with the distinction between the present and the future. It attempts to tell the viewers of Rome that the future and the present will be made of the same times, the same promises, the same eras, just as the past appears peopled by the Emperor of the present.

The final level of temporal elision comes on the shorter sides of the monument, those which face east towards the Colosseum and west towards the Palatine and the Forum. Here, included above the sections of the narrative frieze were two newly carved roundels. That on the west shows the chariot of Luna, drawn by two horses, above the scene of the *profectio* of Constantine's army, whilst that on the east portrays the quadriga of Sol, set above the victorious *ingressus* into Rome. Both cosmic personifications vault over a personified Oceanus, both are accompanied by winged attendants, and both probably held globes in their hands (L'Orange and Von Gerkan 1939, 162–166; for the suggestion that the descending Luna symbolises Maxentius' fall and the ascending Sol represents the dawn of a new Constantinian era, see Brilliant 1984, 122–123, and for the cosmic sympathy between the ascending Sol and the *adventus* of Constantine

as symbolic of the semi-divine light vested in the imperial personage, see MacCormack 1972, 731–733). The form and the inclusion of these two panels hints at a final temporal level: cosmic time, and its synchronisation with the more historical and human events with which it is depicted. The levels all come to meet on these shorter sides of the Arch's structure, where the recut events of Trajan's Dacian wars chime not only with the narrative of Constantine's victorious campaign, but also with the divine time of the two Constantinian tondos. Such synchronicity is more pronounced on the eastern side of the Arch's programme, on the shorter side facing the Flavian amphitheatre. Here, on the uppermost register, the pose of the horse, charging towards the right from out of a crowd of military trumpeters in the Trajanic frieze (figures designated 40 and 41 on Slab IV, Leander Toutai 1987, 20–21), is replicated by the quadriga of Sol as it vaults Oceanus (L'Orange and Von Gerkan 1939, taf. 38a), and is matched by the three rearing horses in the centre of the Constantinian *ingressus* frieze below (Fig. 8.3) (the recent analysis of the Arch's architectural composition by Wilson Jones (2000) has stressed that the entire structure of the monument has been comprehensively planned and rigorously designed, and that none of the compositions or placements of sculpture are likely to have been either accidental or incidental). The replication of this pose from the past, the present, and the realm of cosmic time, draws clear and purposeful links between the three scenes and thus further elides the chronological boundaries between them. This level of cosmic sympathy between different planes of time suggests that they are co-incidental, rather than exclusive or separate, that the past, the present, and the ever are simultaneous.

Conclusion: The image of transtemporality

Pierce has labelled the Arch's ability to compare elements of the past and the present on equal terms as '…trans-historical…' (Peirce 1989, 416; *cf.* 'This deliberate reuse of the past…collapses temporal distinctions' [Brilliant 1984, 122]). However, as

Figure 8.3 Arch of Constantine, Rome, east face (arrows added).

frieze, do not appear to follow any particular sequence, and instead have been interpreted as stationary 'icons' which depict the idealised qualities of the Emperor, rather than any specific sequential narrative (Elsner 2000, 165). Thus, the actual design of the monument encompasses the opposition between icon and frieze, and therefore between moment and narrative. But there is a greater sense of the ways in which the Arch breaks down the boundaries between categories of distinct times, and instead creates a temporality where boundaries are both conceptually and materially erased. The boundaries that might have been expected to separate the distinct temporal realms of past, present, future, and the transcendental time of the spheres, are loosened and dissolved in the Arch of Constantine, so that with this erosion of boundaries, there is a sense that a distinct monumental aesthetic of time emerges. The transmissibility of the past–the simple linear continuity offered by an aetiological approach to the built landscape–has been replaced by its citability (*cf.* Arendt 1992, 43). This spoliation at once has to recognise the destructive power of the present over the past, and at the same time, its ability to save, restore, and change it. Yet it can only do this by saving fragments and renovating what little it has, and literally moving objects out of time's linear flow, transcending decay and meshing temporal horizons. A linear temporal tradition puts the past in order, specifically a chronological order which 'reads' the built and material landscape through the universal translator of the unidirectional arrow of time. A culture which collects, restores, overtly spoliates, and selectively curates its past creates a different 'order' which although not chaotic, is nevertheless based on the individuality of each object and their intrinsic (though multiple) meanings, and therefore fully idiosyncratic because each object has a unique reason for its place in the order. Beyond this order, however, it also works to create a material map of time, one that cannot be 'read' as unidirectional or linear, but which is instead a patchwork, collage, bricolage, of moments and memories, some past and some present (and some, perhaps, referring to the future) which are

has been suggested above, the evidence instead points toward a monument that is fully trans-*temporal*. Much has been made of the nature of the narrative form of the Constantinian frieze, and the play which it makes between notions of stasis and of movement (*e.g.* Elsner 2000, 165–169; Peirce 1989, 414–415). Recent history is retold as Constantine marches around Italy and the Arch, coating the monument with a unidirectional narrative journey through his campaign. Yet the frieze depicts this temporal progression in a series of extremely static tableaux: six scenes which are visually separated from each other, a number of which have rigidity and an almost petrified immobility as their primary stylistic feature. Similarly motionless instants are depicted in the spoliated scenes, which unlike the Constantinian from their contexts untimely ripped, and forged into a non-Euclidean landscape. These spoliated fragments of vanished buildings or the recut heads of dead emperors cannot ever be entirely divorced from their original context, because they will never become fully unhooked from their origins, yet those origins have themselves become loosed from the linear progression of events, to become recombined into different processions, non-linear, or even simultaneous. This means that although events and their material manifestations are moved, shuffled, and relocated in the spatial and temporal landscape, they are never fully out-of-time, as it is impossible for any object to stand outside this level of significance; instead, the movement, reshaping, or cleansing of objects constitutes a complete relocation in the landscape of time, moving them out of linear sequence. Thus, it is an asequentiality, rather than an atemporality, which is created by spoliated masonry, recut faces, and mobile material moments from the past.

Coda

The concepts of spolia *and spoliation seem to me one of the more suitable metaphors for how we 'do' archaeology. At the very least, resemblances between the bricolage monumental narrative produced by late antique masons, and the tales about the past produced by ourselves, deserve some remark. The Arch of Constantine has dutifully done what was asked of it, and survived the ever-rising tides of oblivion. It stands as an almost-memorial to an almost-truth: things survive, and what survives of them (or indeed, of us), can be made to tell a story. This is still an almost-truth, still ambiguous, because we can never escape from the fact that if that solid masonry moment of Constantine has made that journey to us, the pieces of which it is made, the original monuments that were fragmented and splintered, have not. The Arch, its façade marbled with the past, prized and preserved individual instants of lost stories, collating the scattered elements and reusing them to people its own monumental narrative. As archaeologists, we are ever aware that what we can glimpse and hold of the past societies we try to understand is but an infinitesimal fraction of what once was. It is our principal goal to try and create*

meaningful accounts of the past from the odd remnants that chance has allowed us. These inchoate fragments, huddled survivors of omnivorous entropy, must be fashioned and tooled to speak both convincingly and unanimously of the past they left behind. We shape them, these fragments shored against ruin, graft and overlap them, making them fit into our designs and schemes, individual elements of other stories we know to be lost but made to speak our minds for us. But we still need to believe in the Arch's almost-truth. If we found that we were afloat on a true sea of oblivion, and that we saw no spires piercing the surface of the water from the drowned cities below, then we would be truly lost on oceans of amnesia. But we know that some things do survive, have survived, and that whilst they are but grains of sand, and that death has undone so many, we strive to bring the pieces back together, to recombine them and make them tell the stories that we want to hear. In archaeology, this spoliation, this perpetual juggling between the past and the present and the desire to create memorials (that are intended to survive us as our scholarly epitaphs), is commonplace and everyday. The repetitive rhythmic movement between the past and the present, the removal of individual instants from their embedded layers of context, the shuffling of our kaleidoscopic attempts to combine different pasts to speak to the present, and our refusal to let these fragments fall away silently from the future, all play a role in the ways in which we create and interpret our cacophonous spoliated memorials to the archaeological past.

Acknowledgements

This is a heavily-revised version of the paper that I read to the conference at Columbia University, and contains elements of my PhD research, *Time and culture in Late Antiquity* (Cambridge University, 2005), which was funded by an AHRB studentship. I am very grateful both to the AHRB, and to Churchill College, Cambridge, for making my attendance at the conference possible. I also happily acknowledge other debts: to Dušan Borić, for the invitation to speak, and for making me feel so welcome; to Kim Bowes, for advice and encouragement; to Cornelius Holtorf, for two years my research advisor in Cambridge, who has always offered me his valuable guidance and insight; and to my parents, who first gave me the opportunity to visit Rome, and have thus provided me with a whole set of memories that I continue to excavate.

Bibliography

Alföldi, A. (1948) *The Conversion of Constantine and Pagan Rome*. Oxford, Clarendon.

Angelicoussis, E. (1984) The Panel Reliefs of Marcus Aurelius. *Mitteilungen des Deutschen Archaeologischen Instituts Roemische Abteilung* 91, 141–205.

Arendt, H. (1992) Introduction. In W. Benjamin, *Illuminations*, 6–58. London, Fontana.

Barnes, T. (1985) The Conversion of Constantine. *Classical Views* 29, 371–391.

Bassett, S. (1991) The Antiquities in the Hippodrome of Constantinople. *Dumbarton Oaks Papers* 45, 87–96.

Baynes, N. (1972) *Constantine the Great and the Christian Church*. London, Oxford University Press.

Bowersock, G. (1986) From Emperor to Bishop: The Self-Conscious Transformation of Political Power in the Fourth Century A.D. *Classical Philology* 81, 298–307.

Brilliant, R. (1970) Temporal Aspects in Late Roman Art. *L'arte* 10, 64–87.

Brilliant, R. (1984) *Visual Narratives: Storytelling in Etruscan and Roman Art*. Ithaca, Cornell University Press.

Bruun, P. (1976) Notes on the Transmission of Imperial Images in Late Antiquity. In E. Curaverunt *et al.* (eds) *Studia Romana in Hororem Petri Krarup, Septuagenarii*, 122–131. Odense, Odense University Press.

Buttrey, T. (1983) The Dates of the Arches of 'Diocletian' and Constantine. *Historia* 32, 375–383.

Carruthers, M. (1998) *The Craft of Thought: Meditation, Rhetoric, and the Making of Images, 400–1200*. Cambridge, Cambridge University Press.

Chastagnol, A. (1987) Aspects Concrets et Cadre Topographique des Fêtes Décennales des Empereurs à Rome. In *L'Urbs: Espace Ubain et Histoire*, 491–507. Rome, École Française de Rome.

Coates-Stephens, R. (2003) Attitudes to Spolia in Some Late Antique Texts. In L. Lavan and W. Bowden (eds) *Theory and Practice in Late Antique Archaeology*, 341–358. Leiden, Brill.

Curran, J. (1996) Constantine and the Ancient Cults of Rome: The Legal Evidence. *Greece and Rome* 43, 68–80.

Curran, J. (2000) *Pagan City and Christian Capital: Rome in the Fourth Century*. Oxford, Oxford University Press.

De Maria, S. (1988) *Gli Archi Onorari di Roma e dell'Italia Romana*. Rome, Bretschneider.

DiMaio, M. *et al.* (1988) *Ambiguitas Constantiana*: the *caeleste signum dei* of Constantine the Great. *Byzantion* 58, 333–360.

Elsner, J. (1998) *Imperial Art and Christian Triumph*. Oxford, Oxford University Press.

Elsner, J. (2000) From the Culture of *Spolia* to the Cult of Relics: The Arch of Constantine and the Genesis of Late Antique forms. *Papers of the British School at Rome* 68, 149–184.

Errington, R. (1988) Constantine and the Pagans. *Greek, Roman and Byzantine Studies* 29, 309–318.

Evers, C. (1991) Remarques sur l'Iconographie de Constantin: À Propos du Remploi de Portraits des 'Bonnes Empereurs'. *Mélanges de l'École Française de Rome: Antiquité* 103, 785–806.

Flower, H. (2000) The Tradition of the *Spolia Optima*: M. Claudius Marcellus and Augustus. *Classical Antiquity* 19, 34–64.

Gradara, C. (1918) Restauri Settecenteschi Fatti all'Arco di Constantino. *Bullettino della Commissione Archeologica Communale di Roma* 46, 161–164.

Gutteridge, A. (2006) Some Aspects of Social and Cultural Time in Late Antiquity. In W. Bowden, A. Gutteridge and C. Machado (eds) *Social and Political Life in Late Antiquity*, 569–601. Leiden, Brill.

Hannestad, N. (1994) *Tradition in Late Antique Sculpture: Conservation-Modernization-Production*. Aarhus, Aarhus University Press.

Harrison, E. (1967) The Constantinian Portrait. *Dumbarton Oaks Papers* 21, 79–96.

Holloway, R. R. (1985) The Spolia of the Arch of Constantine. *Numismatica e Antichità Classiche* 14, 261–273.

Holloway, R. R. (2004) *Constantine and Rome*. New Haven, Yale University Press.

Jones, A. H. M. (1949) *Constantine and the Conversion of Europe*. London, English Universities Press.

Jones Hall, L. (1998) Cicero's *instinctu divino* and Constantine's *instinctu divinitas*: The Evidence of the Arch of Constantine for the Senatorial View of the 'Vision' of Constantine. *Journal of Early Christian Studies* 6, 647–671.

Kenrick, P. (1986) *Exacavations at Sabratha 1948–1951*. London, Journal of Roman Studies Monograph 2.

Kinney, D. (1986) *Spolia* from the Baths of Caracalla at Sta. Maria in Travestere. *Art Bulletin* 68, 379–397.

Kinney, D. (1997) *Spolia, damnatio,* and *renovatio memoriae. Memoirs of the American Academy in Rome* 42, 117–149.

Kinney, D. (2001) Roman Architectural *Spoila. Proceedings of the American Philosophical Society* 145, 138–161.

Kleiner, D. (1992) *Roman Sculpture.* New Haven, Yale University Press.

Knudsen, S. (1989) Spolia: The So-Called Historical Frieze on the Arch of Constantine. *American Journal of Archaeology* 93, 267–268.

Knudsen, S. (1990) Spolia: The Pedestal Reliefs on the Arch of Constantine. *American Journal of Archaeology* 94, 313–314.

Kunderewicz, C. (1971) La Protection des Monuments d'Architecture Antique dans le Code Theodosien. In A. Giuffré (ed.) *Studi in Onore di Edoardo Volterra volume IV,* 137–153. Rome, Facoltà di Giurisprudenza dell'Università di Roma.

Laubscher, H. (1976) *Arcus Novus und Arcus Claudii, Zwei Triumphbögen an der Via Lata in Rom.* Göttingen, Vandenhoeck & Ruprecht.

Leander Toutai, A.-M. (1987) *The Great Trajanic Frieze: The Study of a Monument and the Mechanics of Message Transmission in Roman Art.* Stockholm, Svenska Institutet i Rom.

Lindros Wohl, B. (2001) Constantine's Use of Spolia. In J. Fleischer, J. Lund and M. Nielsen (eds) *Late Antiquity: Art in Context,* 85–115. Copenhagen, Museum Tusculanum.

L'Orange, H. and Von Gerkan, A. (1939) *Der Spätäntiken Bildschmuck des Konstantinsbogen.* Berlin, Walter de Gruyter.

Lukaszewicz, A. (1979) Some Remarks on P.Lond III 755 and the Problem of Building Materials in the Fourth Century A.D. *Archeologia* 30, 115–118.

MacCormack, S. (1972) Change and Continuity in Late Antiquity: The Ceremony of *Adventus. Historia* 21, 721–752.

Mattingly, H. (1950) The Imperial 'Vota'. *Proceedings of the British Academy* 36, 155–195.

Mattingly, H. (1951) The Imperial 'Vota' (Second Part). *Proceedings of the British Academy* 37, 219–268.

Melucco Vaccaro, A. and Ferroni, A. (1993–94) Chi Construì l'Arco di Constantino? Un Interrogativo Ancora Attuale. *Atti della Pontificia Accademia di Archeologia: Rendiconti* 66, 1–60.

Nicholson, O. (2000) Constantine's Vision of the Cross. *Vigiliae Christianae* 53, 304–323.

Odahl, C. (1990) A Pagan's Reaction to Constantine's Conversion: Religious References in the Trier Panegyric of AD313. *The Ancient World* 21, 45–63.

Peirce, P. (1989) The Arch of Constantine: Propaganda and Ideology in Late Roman Art. *Art History* 12, 387–418.

Pensabene, P. (2000) Reimpiego e Depositi di Marmi a Roma e a Ostia. In S. Ensoli and E. L. Rocca (eds) *Aurea Roma: dall Città Pagan alla Città Cristiana,* 341–350. Rome, Bretschneider.

Pensabene, P. and Panella, C. (1993–94) Reimpigio e Progettazionr Architectonica nei Monumenti Tardo-Antichi di Roma. *Atti della Pontificia Accademia di Archeologia: Rendiconti* 66, 111–283.

Pensabene, P. and Panella, C. (eds) (1999) *Arco di Constantino tra Archeologia e Archeometria.* Rome, Bretschneider.

Pines, S. and Sambursky, S. (1971) *The Concept of Time in Late Neoplatonism: Texts with Translations, Introduction and Notes.* Jerusalem, Israel Academy of Sciences and Humanities.

Richardson, L. (1975) The Date and Program of the Arch of Constantine. *Archeologia Classica* 27, 72–78.

Ryberg, I. (1967) *Panel Reliefs of Marcus Aurelius.* New York, Archaeological Institute of America.

Straub, J. (1967) Constantine as KOINOS EPISKOPOS: Tradition and Innovation in the Representation of the First Christian Emperor's Majesty. *Dumbarton Oaks Papers* 21, 35–55.

Stuart Jones, H. (1905) Notes on Roman Historical Sculpture. *Papers of the British School at Rome* 3, 213–271.

Torelli, M. (1993) Arcus Novus. In E. M. Steinby (ed.) *Lexicon Topographicum Urbis Romae: volume I,* 101–102. Rome, Quasar.

Turcan, R. (1991) Les *tondi* d'Hadrien sur l'Arc de Constantin. *Académie des Inscriptions & Belles-Lettres: Comptes Rendus,* 53–80.

Ward-Perkins, B. (1999) Re-using the Architectural Legacy of the Past, *entre Ideologie et Pragmatisme.* In G. Brogiolo and B. Ward-Perkins (eds) *The Idea and Ideal of the Town between Late Antiquity and the Early Middle Ages,* 225–244. Leiden, Brill.

Weiss, P. (2003) The Vision of Constantine. *Journal of Roman Archaeology* 16, 237–259.

Wilson Jones, M. (2000) Genesis and Mimesis: The Design of the Arch of Constantine in Rome. *Journal of the Society of Architectural Historians* 59, 50–77.

Wright, D. (1987) The True Face of Constantine the Great. *Dumbarton Oaks Papers* 41, 493–507.

9. Archaeology and memory on the Western Front

Paola Filippucci

Archaeology and the Western Front

The debris and devastation of the First World War in Belgium and France were quite rapidly removed and repaired during the early 1920s (see Clout 1996). The remains of trenches, shell-holes, dugouts and other installations were filled up with other debris and covered with a shallow layer of topsoil so that where possible cultivation and habitation could be restored. Only in the vicinity of memorials or monuments sometimes remains of the battlefield were preserved and conserved (see Gough 2004). Elsewhere, hasty burial and removal has helped to preserve wartime remains and war-shaped landscapes (see Saunders 2002). Excavations to retrieve Great War remains have occurred on the Western Front since the 1920s, by those looking for memorabilia and souvenirs for collecting or selling. This sort of excavation continues today although it has been declared illegal in the various countries concerned (see Saunders 2002, 104). Typically, collectors and so-called 'looters' are digging for artefacts and portable remains and in the process overlook or even destroy structures or features that they encounter. A very different approach is taken by archaeologists, who have recently begun to take an interest in Great War remains (see AGG 1999; Boura 1997; Price 2004; Saunders 2002; Schofield *et al.* 2002). Remains and sites are excavated by scientific archaeological methods: that is, rather than simply digging holes to find things, systematic excavation pays attention to and records every detail of context and stratification and positions objects within them.

Great War archaeology is gathering momentum in Britain and to a lesser extent in France, where only very recently such remains were reclassified as 'archaeological' so that now excavations require a permit from the archaeological authorities (*cf.* Saunders 2002). Great War archaeology is thus an emergent discipline that concerns sites and remains that are 'recent' by comparison with the traditional object of archaeology, and may be considered 'contemporary' in the sense that they refer to a time that is just beyond the horizon of living memory and, as such, can still elicit emotion in the present day (see *e.g.* Boura 1997; Gouletquer 1997; Saunders 2002; *cf.* Buchli and Lucas 2001). This has led some to propose that such archaeology has not only a scientific agenda but also a memorial function, that it is a 'memory-making activity' (Saunders 2002, 107; *cf.* Boura 1997; Price 2004).

In practice, too, the archaeology of Great War remains on the Western Front takes place in an emphatically memorial landscape: since the war, innumerable monuments, memorials, ossuaries and cemeteries were built in the former 'battlefields' of Belgium and France by the various countries touched by the conflict, forming a vast 'landscape of remembrance' stretching from the North Sea to the Alps (see Roze 1999). Since the war these constructions have embodied national narratives about the war and its significance, and also hosted and partly structured the way in which successive generations have related to the war and, especially, to the massive losses it caused in families and communities, making the Western Front an immense site of mourning and memory (see Winter 1995). Can the present-day work of archaeologists be seen as part of this and if so, how? In what follows I will try to answer this question by analysing the case of an excavation of a segment of Western Front battlefield next to a major memorial monument site, enabling a comparison between monumental and archaeological ways of approaching the war period. My data will be drawn from participant observation of the excavation and from an exhibition recently organised by the excavation team concerning their activities.

Digging the trenches

The excavation that I will discuss was conducted in 2005 by No Man's Land, a British-based but international team that includes professional and academic archaeologists and some non-archaeologists such as, among others, a museum curator, a library curator, a policeman, an army operative, an IT consultant (see http://www. redtwo.plus.com/nml/). All are united by a passionate interest in the First World War and in the last few years they have conducted a series of excavations of war sites in different parts of the Western Front, sometimes in co-operation with local archaeologists and archaeological services. The excavations have been funded by a variety of sources, including in the case that I will discuss, by a television company filming a documentary series on the Great War (broadcast in UK on Channel 5 in September/October 2006, with the title 'Trench Detectives'). The stated aim of this group is to develop, consolidate and gain recognition for 'battlefield archaeology' as a branch of archaeology and as an antidote to what they see as the indiscriminate excavation and looting of World War I sites by amateurs and collectors and traders of military memorabilia. Their aim, in the words of a team member, is to do good archaeological work within the context of the Great War, both in battlefield and other war-related sites. A panel of a recent exhibition dedicated to this team's work (*Finding the Fallen*, National Army Museum, London from 11–11–2005 to 26–3–2006, see www.national-army-museum.ac.uk) describes their aims as the

'systematic [archaeological] examination of the Western Front'. As explained in the exhibition, the application of the skills and techniques of modern archaeology to Great War remains can help, firstly, to integrate a documentary record that is said to be incomplete or contradictory especially where and when the fighting was most intense. Secondly, archaeology can help to document dimensions of the war experience overlooked by official documentation, notably the mundane and messy detail of soldiers' daily lives, from the shape of latrines to the structure of trenches: 'whatever military manuals show, real trenches were always different'. Archaeology 'can show the reality of life and death with an immediacy that other sources do not achieve'. Last but not least, through its attention to detail and context of each find and its advanced techniques for identification and reconstruction, archaeology can sometimes contribute to the identification of recovered human remains: 'personal items [...] can provide a direct link to an individual soldier in the Great War'. Indeed, as the exhibition illustrated, since its inception the team has not only retrieved several bodies, but has also succeeded in identifying some of them that could be reburied not only with full military honours but also with a name and, in one case, in the presence of their descendants.

These various aims animated the excavation in which I participated in 2005. At the site we excavated, Beaumont Hamel, located in the Northern/British sector of the Western Front, we uncovered stretches of second-line trenches that the material evidence suggested were successively utilised by French and British/Allied forces between 1915 and 1918. The walls of the trenches conserved remains of telecommunication wires. A dugout (a small square 'room' of corrugated iron held up by angle irons) was also found. The finds within it suggested that while it finished its 'life' as a latrine, at one stage the dugout had been an advanced medical post, catering for soldiers just before and just after they went up to the first line and into action.

More broadly the site saw action on July 1st, 1916 (Battle of the Somme), one of the major events of the 'British' and Allied war. Indeed the excavation trench was in full sight of one of the main war memorials built by one of the Allied nations, who suffered high losses in the vicinity in 1916. As well as a monument, this memorial contains the remains of trenches in its precinct, now covered over by grass (*cf.* Gough 2004). The excavation uncovered parts of the same trench system located outside the memorial precinct. The layout of the trenches both in the memorial and beyond can be known fairly accurately from maps and aerial photographs made at different points in the war. However the excavation provided evidence of use, reuse and modification that could be dated with some accuracy through artefactual evidence, providing a more detailed and fine-grained narrative about a particular, 'local' stretch of the front.

On the excavation this sort of 'archaeological narrative' (as one of the excavators called it) was contrasted by the team with the narrative looked for by the television company. The aim of this last was not simply that of revealing the 'human angle' on the war, but also of establishing a direct, personal contact with specific individuals through artefacts (badges, personal items) or physical remains. The TV company's agenda to some extent drove this excavation (for instance by leading to the opening of a new trench when the first one did not yield any clear traces of individual presences). At the same time it was also in tension with the excavators' commitment to 'doing things properly', that is to carefully and accurately record the remains within the time permitted and analyse the development and findings of the excavation as a complex whole including sequences of structures, features and finds. The tension between these two agendas surfaced in part through jokes about the need to 'find bodies' or about what specific finds might mean: so for instance when a round from a .38 pistol was found someone recalled that the poet Robert Graves had owned a .38 when he was at the front: 'let's tell the TV guys it's Graves's gun'.

More generally, around and through archaeology this team also presented its aims as opposed to what some of its members described as a sentimentalised view of the First World War, attributed to those individuals and associations who rely on history but also on literature and so tend to have a tragic view centred on soldier's deaths and on mourning (a view summarised by a team member as 'Futility and all that', by reference to Wilfred Owen's poem of that title). Instead, as another team member put it to me, 'all there is to know about the war is that we went there, we fought and we died, we won the war'. This speaker is a founder member of this group and it may be suggested that he might see archaeology as contributing to this unsentimental, rather matter-of-fact approach to this event.

Matter-of-fact knowledge of the First World War was amassed on the excavation through the well-established archaeological routines of painstaking attention to detail and rigorous, careful observation, description and recording of every detail of soils, layers, features and finds including some very familiar objects: so before identifying something as a tin of corned beef, it is carefully recorded and described as a 'rectangular, heavily rusted iron object with sides of thin sheet metal'. One effect of this approach was to neutralise at least for a time the potential emotive charge of some of the things recovered: by the time fragments of human bone or ammunition rounds were been bagged and tagged, located within numbered contexts, counted and dated to produce lists like the one below, their poignancy was, temporarily at least, lessened.

Context 27:
> Residual French rounds, latest dated April–June 1914.
> British .303 include ×1 1911; ×2 1914; ×12 1915; ×4 1916
> ×87 illegible.

Context 38:
> Residual French rounds, latest Jul–Sept. 1914.
> British .303 include ×2 1914; ×13 1915
> ×98 illegible.

As this list suggests, the level of precision by which finds can be classified and identified in this context (within a month or even 'within a few minutes' as I was told, for certain sorts of evidence) is exponentially greater than in earlier periods. Many in the group mentioned this as the key attraction of First World War archaeology, and gave the example

Figure 9.1 View of the excavation: beyond a fence is the Beaumont Hamel Newfoundland Park, with the Newfoundland Regiment memorial monument (right).

of when a historian in the group had managed to identify the exact gun emplacement from where the shell was shot that had produced a shell-hole they had recently excavated.

A taste for precision may be linked with a commitment to archaeological rigour and accuracy but also I think implies a bid to find a way 'in' to the war past. So for instance a historian in the group told me that 'the best moment in my life as a historian' came when he found on an army list the name of a soldier whose body the group had excavated and identified. Everyone else spoke passionately about this case as well as of other bodies found and identified by the group, and of how they had managed to track down the soldier's family and had attended his funeral and burial. Detail, in this case, led to a deeply emotional and personal connection with the war past and to carrying out some very personal acts of care and mourning. The identification and proper burial of human remains, as already mentioned, is a key aspect of battlefield archaeology for this team: so also a team member mentioned his desire to create a special unit devoted to the proper disposal of human remains still recovered all over the Western Front, that are often improperly handled or treated (at the very least through the loss of artefacts that may enable identifications) by those who dig the battlefields in search of memorabilia. Other group members said more generally that what attracts

them to First World War archaeology is the fact that one can feel 'more involved' than if one were excavating ancient Romans 'because there are members of my family, whom I have known, who have lived this': because this past is linked to our present directly through an unbroken chain of personal links, known not only intellectually but also in an embodied and affective way, through family and kinship.

In practice both on and off site the excavators at once applied an archaeological methodology that takes an impersonal, external, dispassionate approach to sites and finds, 'distancing' them (*cf.* Buchli and Lucas 2001, 9), and said and did things that created or suggested emotion-laden closeness and even a sort of identification with the soldiers. First and foremost there was the weather, cold and wet for much of the time so that the excavation trench was turned into a freezing quagmire of sticky, icy mud. Though this is common in excavations in Northern Europe, in this setting through jokes and comments we were continually reminded of iconic Western Front imagery of cold, muddy, wet and frozen troops. This same link was drawn in the exhibition, in which the comment that 'the struggle with the weather in many sectors of the front [...] could be as difficult as that with the enemy' was illustrated not only with a photograph of a British soldier thigh deep in mud, but also with an inset of 'one of the NML team failing to bail rainwater out of the excavation at Serre'. The image of troops beset by the cold was evoked when to warm up someone passed around some rum, commenting that this was what British troops in the war had drunk against the cold.

A sense of connection and, even, identification may have been facilitated and lent authenticity by the evocative power of place (*cf.* Schofield *et al.* 2002, 4): there we were, cold and muddy working in archaeological trenches that are also 'the' trenches, digging like 'they' did in the same sticky clay, using tools the design of which, as someone reminded us, dates back to the First World War. Such comments blurred the boundary between past and present and it seemed only half a joke when someone, who by mistake had over-excavated a trench floor, was told that it didn't matter because 'it's still real Western Front clay' so the over-excavated surface is still 'real' Western Front trench. So too when I filled some modern sandbags with soil to revett the spoilheap, the joke was that I am doing 'ethnoarchaeology'; in practice the boundary between past and present blurred as the soil I used to fill the bags was spoil from the excavation of the remains of a layer of sandbags from 1916.

A sense of direct connection with the war past was strong (and certainly most 'real') in relation to unexploded ordnance about which we were warned in the preliminary briefing ('don't hit anything too hard!'), so that when on the first day suddenly the dig filled with a chemical smell many of us looked up in alarm till it became clear that it was someone using a can of spray paint. Later, when suspected gas canisters were uncovered, we had to evacuate the site and stay upwind as the team's two members trained at ordnance disposal suited up and put on masks and worked for a nerve-wracking hour till they emerged sweaty and exhausted to report that the containers were fortunately empty. At such moments (as I expect when human remains are found) the war felt very close and present.

At the preliminary briefing we were also told that the excavation, in sight of an important and much-visited memorial, is 'a sacred site to many people' and therefore while on site we should behave accordingly, without making too many jokes about dead bodies (as I am told, black humour helps to cope with the emotion and distress of finding a body). However during the excavation people did joke, often irreverently as when a latrine bucket was found and someone was photographed sitting on it, trousers down; or when the two suited up for ordnance disposal staged a pretend kiss through their gas masks.

In spite of the irreverence, both on and off site there was also utmost respect for the soldiers who had fought the war and, especially, the fallen. It may be suggested that this was expressed implicitly in and by the very attention given to the meanest detail of soldiers' lives (and deaths), from the narrowness of trenches to the basic sanitation to the amount of unexploded (*i.e.* faulty) ordnance, to the pitiful remains of shattered bone evoking

Figure 9.2 Modern sandbags (top left) are filled with sandbag contents from the Great War (the layers visible in the far section of the trench). The tool inside the trench is a modern entrenching tool the design of which, its owner points out, was first used in the Great War.

the brutality of weapons. This attention is imposed by the archaeological method but was elaborated on through comments and discussions on and off site that also contributed to an unsentimental discourse about the troops as people who had a tough job to do and did it. Respect is also expressed explicitly when, as I was told, on one occasion rum was drunk ceremonially and poured onto a trench where human remains were found; or when on and off site people sing First World War songs or when, on the last night of the excavation, someone proposed a toast 'to the Fallen', described as 'them out there for whom we do this'. These words suggest that, while the excavators oppose their own approach to the Great War to that of

TV crews (too sensationalist) or amateurs (too sentimental), they see their work as a scientific enterprise that however also fulfils an obligation towards the fallen. In this respect, their archaeology may be seen as a form of tribute to the dead and so also, therefore, as a form of commemoration, an act of memory.

Monuments and memory

Anthropological approaches to 'memory' regard it not (or not only) as an individual and cognitive act of recollection of the past, but as a social act, consisting of the imaginative reconstruction of past events in light of social and contemporary concerns and preoccupations (*e.g.* Portelli 1991). Remembering in this sense is a form of social dialogue (or sometimes argument) through which relationships are made and unmade (see *e.g.* Halbwachs 1980; *cf.* Yanagisako 1985). As a social act, 'memory' also has a strong moral dimension; it is a form of moral practice (Lambek 1998). To remember is to engage with the past, often to express a social commitment or pledge towards certain others, for instance as a witness (Lambek 1996, 243–244; *cf.* Portelli 1999, 15; 1991).

The moral aspect of memory was particularly explicit and central in the case of the First World War. As with all wars, 'remembering' the Great War entailed first and foremost mourning and commemorating its victims and this from the start was presented in public (and often in private) contexts as a matter of fulfilling a 'duty' to the fallen, of repaying a 'debt' towards them (*cf.* Audoin-Rouzeau and Becker 2000, 175*ff.*; Osborne 2001, 67; Winter 1995, 15*ff.*; Winter and Sivan 1999). The immediate survivors and mourners embodied their bid to remember in monuments, memorials and cemeteries (see Sherman 1999; Winter 1995). As Winter has brilliantly demonstrated, these structures not only provided sites for mourning, but also simultaneously for affirming and reconstructing social and moral ties that had been rent by the conflict: ties with the dead but also with other survivors, with whom a form of 'kinship' came to be felt, based on shared suffering and a shared

sense of obligation towards the dead and each other (1995, 24, 29*ff.*; 1999; see also Audoin-Rouzeau and Becker 2002, 203*ff.*).

For Winter, the social and moral function of Western Front memorial sites faded with the demise of the generations of immediate survivors and mourners (Winter and Sivan 1999, 10). However, these sites have continued and continue to be visited and to elicit the interest of successive generations and so, arguably, to structure how the war is remembered (see *e.g.* Saunders 1999). An example is the memorial site at Beaumont Hamel, which overlooks the excavation that I have discussed above, a 'memorial park' that encloses several monuments and cemeteries and a stretch of the battlefield with remains of the same trench system uncovered in the excavation. As in present-day 'heritage' sites, there are guided tours and a Visitors' Centre; however ceremonies and commemorations are still held periodically at this site and at the entrance a sign reminds visitors to 'behave respectfully' and more specifically not to 'hunt, cycle, have picnics, shout, climb the monuments', introduce dogs or vehicles or any kind. This concept is reiterated (less prosaically) in the opening lines of a poem engraved on a bronze plaque that greets visitors as they enter the memorial precinct:

'Tread softly here! Go reverently and slow!
And with bowed head, and heart abased strive hard
To grasp the future gain in the sore loss!
For not one foot of this dank sod but drank
Its surfeit of the blood of gallant men.'

As a recent study has shown, this site has today a triple function: as a 'sacred' space, as a 'dramaturgical' space, and as a 'temporal' space, evoking for visitors a particular day in the war, in which most of the regiment commemorated here was wiped out (Gough 2004, 248). These three aspects are intertwined: as Gough shows, the narrative of events and the reading of battlefield topography presented at the site are partial and selective, sacrificing historical complexity to the bid of illustrating and commemorating the wartime bravery and sacrifice of the regiment to whom the site is dedicated (Gough 2004, 250–251).

The site also selectively presents the past in the sense that the remains of the battlefield that it encloses have been significantly modified, ostensibly the better to conserve them. Trenches and detritus that had originally been visible has now been covered over by grass and visitors are invited to examine the reconstructions of trenches and other features. The grass cover smoothes the contours of the old battlefield and gives the site a sense of order and of being a 'timeless, unviolated, preindustrial' surface: since the Great War neatly cut grass has been perceived as a healing cover over the scarred land and also, by extension, the bodies and souls of dead and living (Gough 2004, 247, 251–252). In the same allusive vein the various monuments contained in the precinct refer to the death of soldiers indirectly (*cf.* King 2001): so some of the fallen are represented by an animal, emblem of their regiment, surrounded by rocks and trees that evoke their homeland; others are represented by a soldier standing proudly in his regimental garb; yet another memorial, constructed over a shell-hole where soldiers had been buried, consists of a circle of headstones surrounding a cross, the so-called 'cross of sacrifice'.

'Sacrifice' is a concept used across the memorial to refer to the soldiers' deaths, presented as acts of 'giving': 'To the glory of God and in perpetual remembrance of those officers and men of the Newfoundland forces who gave their lives by land and sea in the Great War' reads the plaque on the main monument listing 800 names of soldiers 'with no known grave'. Like all giving, this too calls for a return (Mauss 1990 [1929]), a concept made explicit in the poem already mentioned:

> '[Its surfeit of the blood of gallant men.]
> Who for their faith their hope – for life and liberty
> Here made the sacrifice – here gave their lives
> And gave right willingly – for you and me.
> [...]
> On this grim cratered ridge they gave their all
> And giving won.
> [...]
> Our hearts go out to them in boundless gratitude.
> [...] [God] has repaid their sacrifice – and we – ?
> God help us if we fail to pay our debt
> In fullest full and all unstintingly!'

This poem also states that men died then 'for you and me' and therefore directly addresses and also interpellates today's visitors: 'and we – ? God help us if we fail to pay our debt'. The poem draws a direct and explicit link between past and present that, through the concepts of sacrifice and debt, is configured as a loop of duty and obligation if not reciprocity. The poem, and arguably the whole memorial, poses a question to the future, positioning visitors as survivors or successors. By evoking the enormity of the sacrifice, the poem also intimates that the debt is inextinguishable, so that the question is, arguably, an open question: 'and we – ?'.

A future-oriented perspective on the death of soldiers is typical of war memorials and monuments. Since the Great War, monuments have assisted with the mourning process by giving a higher meaning to soldiers' deaths (Rowlands 2001). This is achieved (or attempted) partly by framing those deaths within a long-term temporal perspective, that of a gift to or sacrifice for future generations who must reciprocate by 'remembering', that is keeping alive not only the memory of individual fallen but also the ideals that animated the sacrifice in the first place (see King 2001, 156; *cf.* Rowlands 2001). The poem cited above presents this last as an open question: as mentioned, this could refer to the fact that the debt is so great as to be ultimately inextinguishable. So, monuments and memorials structure the way in which we remember the war by positioning us in relation to it as survivors, who must (and can only) contemplate the fate of its victims and feel thankful and perhaps guilty: indeed, as Audoin-Rouzeau and Becker put it, the Great War is 'a paradigm case' for thinking about 'the weight of the dead on the living' (2000, 1). How does this compare with archaeology's approach to the war past?

Archaeology and memory

As my ethnography shows, the archaeologists' attitude is one of respect and admiration for the soldiers, and a bid to honour their suffering and mourn the fallen animates their activity, that, as indicated, includes efforts to identify any human remains so as to give them a proper burial. On all these counts they participate in the culture of remembrance materialised by monuments, memorial sites and cemeteries. However, in and through the excavation the No Man's Land team archaeologists also take an approach to and perspective on the war past alternative to that suggested by monuments.

Although the memorial precinct is separated from the excavation by a simple fence and they contain remains of a single trench system, the mood on each site is different. In the memorial precinct, as I have shown, the mood is reverential, with mourning and commemoration emphatically presented as matters of the utmost seriousness. Not so on the excavation: on site, for instance, we eat and drink, shout, sing, make irreverent jokes and introduce vehicles (a mechanical digger to remove the topsoil). On site, the war past is first and foremost an object of observation and analysis rather than reverential contemplation. As already discussed, archaeology is taken to the First World War remains as a professional practice that enables the retrieval and detailed recording of finds that, once analysed both in relation to each other and to other available documentation, help to piece together a picture or narrative of the past that aims to be historically accurate. This is the primary and driving aim of excavation.

At the same time, archaeological excavation leads to touch objects and to occupy spaces that people in the past (in this case the soldiers) had touched or occupied. Whether or not this is openly acknowledged, what is acquired through excavating, alongside quantified, precise, abstracted knowledge of artefacts and layers, is embodied, practical knowledge of things and places (*cf.* Bourdieu 1977). This sort of sensuous, embodied knowledge can be tapped for its power to evoke (*cf.* Connerton 1989): indeed in the case of the excavation I have discussed it seems to play on the imagination of excavators who, mainly through jokes, express feelings of empathy and even identification. These feelings are also hinted at in video footage presented in the NAM exhibition, showing excavators expressing their emotion at finding certain objects: 'I never

thought I would be able to hold one of these'. The exhibition also made such experience available to visitors by inviting them to handle fragments of shell-casing, presumably to test at first hand their weight and roughness. In the exhibition the evocative dimension of physical objects was also acknowledged in a comment attached to a display of personal objects of soldiers: 'when examining these objects, it takes only a little imagination to be transported back 90 years, to the scene as a group of pals share out some sweets or cigarettes from home [...]'. So, too, commenting on the excavation, one of the archaeologists suggested that its finds could be used to design a tour that would take visitors up from the road towards the second line and then on to the first line and into the German lines: by this, they would retrace the soldiers' actual footsteps as they mounted on the line in 1916 and thereby 'visit a battlefield' as opposed to 'only look at the memorial site'. As these comments suggest, archaeology is thought to have the potential to transport people 'into' the past: that is, not only to piece together an image of the past that is historically accurate, and so also historically contextualised; but also, fleetingly, to provide a viewpoint that is *in* the event as it occurs. In other words, to construct an 'archaeological narrative' of an event is also arguably to remove temporal perspective: to bypass, for an instant, historical context and see an event with the eyes of participants rather than of posterity.

In the specific case of the First World War remains, the means offered by archaeology to imaginatively 'enter' the past may be contrasted with the way in which monuments and memorials position the living as posterity, survivors and successors. Clearly, even by taking us 'into' the war past archaeology cannot change the incontrovertible fact that it is not us but others who have suffered, fought and died: however, it can perhaps provide an alternative approach to the question of how to repay those who died 'for us'.

As Buchli and Lucas discuss (2001), excavation and especially recording translate 'an everyday perceptual language into an archaeological one' (Buchli and Lucas 2001, 9). What they mean is that in archaeology material reality is quantified, classified, positioned within a grid of quantifiable space-time: so in the excavation that I have described, ordnance is counted and classified according to type and date, a corned beef can is described in terms of its shape and texture, the fragment of a human rib bone is put into a numbered bag and taken away with other finds from the same context. This helps to extricate objects and spaces from present-day classifications and understandings and also from imaginative and emotional associations and attachments (in this case, the horror of killing, the pitiful last meal, the torn flesh). By this, objects are made available for interpretation as part of an 'other' time, 'the past' in relation to 'the present' that the archaeologist occupies.

Through archaeological treatment objects, and the past, are made 'other' also in another sense. Through its focus on the intimate, minute detail of things and layers, archaeology makes visible that which in objects was (and is) not necessarily invested with significance of meaning. This not only defamiliarises objects but also arguably makes visible the 'thing-ness' (for lack of a better word) of things, that is their inertia, their existence and endurance separately from social and cultural relevance or meaning (*cf.* Fletcher 2002). This helps to realise that the past 'really happened' but also that it is 'past', irredeemably gone and irretrievably in/of another time: it shows that while things can endure, the past (or aspects of it) resist incorporation into later times. Through this realisation, the past is allowed to stand separately from and so, arguably, to interrupt the present.

It is this last aspect which in my view gives archaeology its potential as a memorial act different from and arguably opposed to that mediated by monuments. Put bluntly, the monument invites us to contemplate the soldiers' lives through the prism of their death: through the excavation, we are able to regard soldiers' deaths in relation to their lives and experiences while in uniform. The two sites position us differently in relation to the same past: as we contemplate the monument, we look at the war as survivors, invited to feel guilty for not knowing how to repay those who died 'for us'. The excavation by contrast enables archaeologists

to touch the messy reality of lives in the war and to create a narrative from 'within' the event rather than after it. Still inevitably spectators, archaeologists of the First World War (and arguably their audiences) can nevertheless move between reverential remembrance, scientific detachment and imaginative empathy or perhaps even identification. Moreover, in relation and through archaeology the three aspects interact in a particular way: by showing the mundane, messy, brutal or also banal detail of the wartime past archaeology provides an image of the soldiers' lives and deaths that not only helps to imaginatively 'enter' the war past but also questions the sublimated representation of soldiers' pain associated with monuments and memorials (see King 2001; Rowlands 2001). As such the archaeological image is pitted against the bid of memorials to recuperate symbolically the fate of soldiers by investing it with meaning as 'sacrifice' (*cf.* Jay 1999, 239). The 'archaeological narrative' by contrast brings the war past into the present as a reality that to some extent resists incorporation, troubling and disturbing us.

In a way, archaeology can be seen as an agent of a 'refusal to mourn' the Great War that is quite materially and literally expressed in and by the act of excavating and uncovering buried portions of the apocalyptic war-scapes of the Western Front, reversing their 'smoothing over' in the name not only of reconstruction but also of consolation, embodied by monuments and memorials (see Jay 2001, 227–230; also Gough 2004; King 2001; Rowlands 2001). If this is so, then Great War archaeology 'makes memory' not so much or not only because it creates more detailed and accurate accounts of the war, but because, by countering efforts to sublimate the soldiers' suffering, it refreshes the pain and with it, arguably, the power of that past to engage us emotionally and morally (*cf.* Lambek 1996; Laqueur 1996).

Conclusions: Archaeology, the Great War and memory

Since starting ethnographic research along the Western Front, I have noticed that many people express surprise when I mention that remains of

trenches, shell-holes, tunnels and other installations from the time of the Great War still exist
in the region. This reaction concerns remains that
are only ninety years old and is puzzling if it is
considered that the survival of much older remains
is accepted and taken for granted by most people,
familiar with archaeology and its potential to
discover the past. The relative 'invisibility' of Great
War remains, at odds with their chronological
location, may be due to the massive visibility of
the many monuments, memorials and cemeteries
that punctuate the landscape of the former Western
Front and arguably dominate the imagination of
its visitors. In light of the discussion above, this
may be rephrased to say that what dominates the
imagination of post-war generations (including
ours) is the symbolic time-space materialised and
structured by monuments, that as indicated is
shaped by notions of giving, posterity, debt, and
a duty to reciprocate tying past and future into a
loop. It is this time-space that contains (in both
senses of the word) the war and its suffering and
may contribute to make people feel that the war,
though relatively close chronologically, is *elsewhere*
than in physical remains. By finding remains of
1914–1918 in the ground of present-day France,
archaeology instead turns the war past, so far
imagined mainly through monuments and verbal
texts, into 'a buried physical reality' (Barkan
1999, 20–21). By this, archaeology may create
'new imaginative possibilities' (Barkan 1999, 25)
for those who contemplate the war past in the
present. Specifically, as revealed and presented
through archaeology such remains locate the war
into a time-space that could perhaps be termed
'chronological', no less symbolically constructed
than that mediated by monuments (see *e.g.* Gell
1992; Lucas 2005), but that places the wartime
and its posterity in a shared dimension (*cf.* Barkan
1999, 25). That is, by uncovering and focusing
our attention onto the physical remains of the
Great War, archaeology makes us feel that the war
inhabits our same time-space and through this, as
my ethnography seems to suggest, it opens a new
imaginative highway towards that past, that makes
us able to go 'back' there to witness the fate of
soldiers in all its bare mundane matter-of-factness

and brutality, refreshing the pain of it and with it
our ability to engage with it on a moral plane.

The impulse to re-imagine the Great War now
may stem from a 'paradox' in current perceptions
of the Great War identified by Audoin-Rouzeau
and Becker (2000, 10). They note a recent
revival of interest in the First World War in the
public culture of many of the former belligerent
countries, manifested in a proliferation of films,
fiction, non-fiction, exhibitions, the creation of
museums and initiatives of valorisation of former
battlefield sites (see also Winter 2000). This in
their view was triggered by the commemoration
of the eightieth anniversary of the end of the war
in 1998 but more profoundly caused on the one
hand by developments in the international political
scene that have made the war feel close and actual,
notably the re-emergence of nationalistic conflict
(that in Bosnia brought Sarajevo back in the news)
(Audoin-Rouzeau and Becker 2000, 10). On
the other hand, the former belligerent countries
may suffer from 'unfinished mourning', resulting
from the effort in belligerent countries to repress
grieving in order to enable physical and moral
reconstruction and to idealise and honour the
fallen that leads to a return of the negated pain of
bereavement among later generations (2000, 9,
224, and *passim* 203–225).

The 'paradox' is that in spite of this newly
felt closeness, the ideals and symbols that moved
the war's contemporaries now feel irretrievably
alien and incomprehensible, so that 'it is as if we
wished to understand the Great War more than
ever before, without being sure of ever having
the means to do so' (Audoin-Rouzeau and Becker
2000, 10–11). Transposing this to memorial sites
it could be argued that, today, we are still (or
once again) moved by what happened so that the
monuments and memorials of the First World
War have the power to interpellate us: however we
cannot respond in the terms that they set, through
notions like piety, duty, sacrifice and honour. This
may elicit new ways to remember the war including
that offered by archaeology, that without resolving
the paradox may offer an alternative way to morally
and imaginatively connect with the war past and
so, in other words, to remember it.

Archaeology's way of 'remembering' the war, that emphasises the matter-of-factness of the past, may finally address a more general aspect of the current proliferation of representations of the Great War. For Huyssen (2003) a 'boundless desire for narratives of the past, for re-creations, re-readings, re-productions' (Huyssen 2003, 5) in many contemporary societies addresses the 'fundamental need of modern societies to live in extended forms of temporality' (Huyssen 2003, 25). This is undermined by current technology that tends to compress temporal and spatial horizons and 'increasingly voids temporality and collapses space' (Huyssen 2003, 4–6; see also Hartog 2003). In this context public and private memorial acts proliferate as 'survival strategies' to regain 'a strong temporal and spatial grounding of life and the imagination' (Huyssen 2003, 6). In practice photography, film, recorded sound and the Internet, a boom in historical scholarship and its diffusion through an 'ever more voracious museal culture' make the past, including that of the Great War, 'part of the present in ways simply unimaginable in earlier centuries' (Huyssen 2003, 3; *cf.* Fabiansson 2004). However, the proliferation of images of the past in the present further weakens temporal boundaries and, especially, threatens 'the stability of the past in its pastness' (Huyssen 2003, 3). Arguably, archaeology has the power to evoke such irreducible 'pastness'.

Today's archaeologists draw on modern media in creating and disseminating images of the pasts that they unearth, from computer simulations and reconstructions of structures and finds to the making of documentaries for television as in the case of the team discussed in this paper. At the same time, like the archaeologists whose work I have discussed, they ground their knowledge of the past on a scientific practice that, as also discussed, by highlighting the inertia or 'thing-ness' of things also establishes the past as having a reality that is partially independent of subsequent interpretations. So, arguably, archaeology has the ability to restore, however fleetingly, a sense of the irreducible distance between past and present, reviving the 'constitutive tension' between them that for Huyssen is fundamental in continuing to imagine time as articulated into a present and especially a future (Huyssen 2003, 10). This leads to venture in conclusion that archaeology may 'make memory' today as one of the 'survival strategies' by which we seek to keep hold on to the weight of the past, ballast for our conceptions of present and future.

Acknowledgements

I wish to thank No Man's Land for welcoming me to the group and for putting up with my questioning and my anthropological beady eye. I also wish to thank Martin Brown more particularly for his feedback and suggestions on an earlier draft of this paper. Many thanks also to Jane Gilbert for invaluable discussions, and to participants to the symposium 'Archaeological Anthropology' (Cambridge, May 2005) where this paper was first presented.

Bibliography

AGG (1999) L'Archéologie et la Grande Guerre. *14–18 Aujourd'hui, Today, Heute*, Dossier no. 2.

Audoin-Rouzeau, S. and Becker, A. (2000) *1914–1918 Understanding the Great War.* London, Profile Books.

Barkan, L. (1999) *Unearthing the Past.* New Haven and London, Yale University Press.

Boura, F. (1997) Le Poids des Morts ou Comment s'en Débarasser. *Les Nouvelles de l'Archéologie*, 70, 15–17.

Bourdieu, P. (1977) *Outline of a Theory of Practice.* Cambridge, Cambridge University Press.

Buchli, V. and Lucas, G. (eds) (2001) *Archaeologies of the Contemporary Past.* London, Routledge.

Clout, H. (1996) *After the Ruins.* Exeter, University of Exeter Press.

Connerton, P. (1989) *How Societies Remember.* Cambridge, Cambridge University Press.

Fabiansson, N. (2004) The Internet and the Great War: The Impact on the Making and Meaning of Great War History. In N. J. Saunders (ed.) *Matters of Conflict,* 166–178. London, Routledge.

Fletcher, R. (2002) The Hammering of Society: Non-Correspondence and Modernity. In J. Schofield, W. G. Johnson and C. M. Beck (eds) *Matériel Culture,* 303–311. London, Routledge.

Gell, A. (1997) *The Anthropology of Time*. Oxford, Berg.

Gough, P. (2004) Sites in the Imagination: The Beaumont Hamel Newfoundland Memorial on the Somme. *Cultural Geographies* 11, 235–258.

Gouletquer, P. (1997) Les Implications Théoriques de l'Affaire Alain-Fournier. *Les Nouvelles de l'Archéologie* 70, 19–21.

Halbwachs, M. (1980) *The Collective Memory*. New York, Harper and Row.

Hartog, F. (2003) *Régimes d'Historicité*. Paris, Seuil.

Huyssen, A. (2001) *Presents Pasts*. Stanford, Stanford University Press.

Jay, M. (1999) Against Consolation: Walter Benjamin and the Refusal to Mourn. In J. Winter and E. Sivan (eds) *War and Remembrance in the Twentieth Century*, 221–239. Cambridge, Cambridge University Press.

King, A. (2001) Remembering and Forgetting in Public Memorials of the Great War. In A. Forty and S. Küchler (eds) *The Art of Forgetting*, 147–169. Oxford, Berg.

Lambek, M. (1996) The Past Imperfect: Remembering as Moral Practice. In P. Antze and M. Lambek (eds) *Tense Past*, 235–254. London, Routledge.

Laqueur, T. (1996) The Past's Past. *London Review of Books* 19 September, 3–7.

Lucas, G. (2005) *The Archaeology of Time*. London, Routledge.

Mauss, M. (1990 [1929]) *The Gift*. London, Routledge.

Osborne, B. (2001) In the Shadows of Monuments: The British League for the Reconstruction of the Devastated Areas of France. *International Journal of Heritage Studies*, 7, 59–82.

Portelli, A. (1991) *The Life of Luigi Trastulli and Other Stories*. New York, State University of New York Press.

Portelli, A. (1999) *L'Ordine è giá Stato Eseguito*. Rome, Donzelli.

Price, J. (2004) The Ocean Villas Project: Archaeology in the Service of European Remembrance. In N. J. Saunders (ed.) *Matters of Conflict* 179–191. London, Routledge.

Rowlands, M. (2001) Remembering to Forget: Sublimation as Sacrifice in War Memorials. In A. Forty and S. Küchler (eds) *The Art of Forgetting*, 129–145. Oxford, Berg.

Roze, A. (1999) *Fields of Memory*. London, Seven Dials, Cassell & Co.

Saunders, N. J. (1999) Matter and Memory in the Landscapes of Conflict: The Western Front 1914–1999. In B. Bender and M. Winer (eds) *Movement, Exile and Place*, 37–53. Oxford, Berg.

Saunders, N. J. (2002) Excavating Memories: Archaeology and the Great War, 1914–2001. *Antiquity* 76, 101–108.

Schofield, J., Johnson, W. G. and Beck, C. M. (eds) (2002) *Matériel Culture*. London, Routledge.

Sherman, D. J. (1999) *The Construction of Memory in Inter-War France*. Chicago, The University of Chicago Press.

Winter, J. (1995) *Sites of Memory, Sites of Mourning*. Cambridge, Cambridge University Press.

Winter, J. (2000) Public History and the 'Historical' Project, 1986–1998. In M. Demossier and J. Picard (eds) *Recollections of France*, 52–67. Oxford, Beghahn.

Winter, J. and Sivan, E. (eds) (1999) *War and Remembrance in the Twentieth Century*. Cambridge, Cambridge University Press.

Yanagisako, S. (1985) *Transforming the Past*. Stanford, Stanford University Press.

10. *Terra incognita*: The material world in international criminal courts

Lindsay Weiss

Introduction

At this very moment, the International Criminal Tribunal for the former Yugoslavia, or ICTY, sits in a kind of global nowhere – a place of no state sovereignty – though it is located in a building formerly occupied by a bank in a quiet neighbourhood in The Hague. Slobodan Milošević and others have been tried here on a set of charges with which the world is now well familiar, but what is not familiar to the global audience is the context of this trial and the specifics of its day to day organisation. At its most obvious, this process is the imagining, institutionalising and legitimising of a set of global legal institutions – the global courtroom ritual. The tradition of the international court continues to attempt to establish its authority, and, for this reason, it is especially interesting, and worth further study, that we are witnessing the emergence of a new kind of history production. This form of history-making is one that uses legal and quasi-legal institutions like the ICTY (or truth commissions, as in South Africa) to validate a particular historical reading. The construction of this historical form rests upon the enforcement of international conventions of justice, and it therefore comes to read the particular charges and crimes through these conventions. The widespread common sense about such legal entities is that they are constructed to deal with a particular and unique variety of legal transgression – cases in which what has happened so supersedes the moral legitimacy of any single state to deal with it that a new institution must be formed.

This new institution, in turn, derives its administrative mechanisms from an eclectic sampling of international courtroom protocols and a collaboration of legal systems and diverse legal practitioners. Within this unfolding process, the collection of evidence, witness testimony and other courtroom habits gravitate towards a practice which conveys the strongest sense of global impartiality and 'traditional' protocol in the face of an international mandate. This would seem to disable the potential of materiality (that is, the precise material form the crime takes, its local landscapes and landmarks) to inform the daily courtroom proceedings of The Hague's international tribunals. Following an archaeological perspective, I will be concerned to investigate the phenomenon of the international courtroom as it presents the opportunity to articulate a heightened legal and political disposition towards the realm of materiality (Meskell 1998). As such, I will be primarily concerned with the peculiar history of courtroom moments in which material objects and landscape have been given consideration in international criminal tribunals. These instances, which I will discuss below, are arguably examples in which the particular object or landscape exceeds a merely *functional* role as evidence, to the extent that its introduction into the courtroom's activities come to shatter the analytical passivity with which objects are typically 'thought' (Baudrillard 2003, 5). I discuss the potential for material objects and devastated landscapes not just as corroborative testimony but as providing, even within the existing legal framework, an anchoring from which discourse on even the most private, ephemeral or unspeakable violations can be brought more effectively into the sphere of international judgment and witnessing. In this context, the question could be raised that dealings with the material or landscape aspects of crimes is perhaps more appropriate to truth and reconciliation committees, especially as there has already been one established for war crimes in Bosnia-Herzegovina. The problem with this is the explicit emphasis on reconstruction or construction of a nation-state. Such enterprises, while useful for the resolution of collective traumas and inter-group mediations, address issues of criminality in a subsidiary manner to international tribunals. In this sense, and because I believe that the material culture is so explicitly linked to the criminal aspects of crimes against humanity, I feel that they are more appropriately addressed in the context of the prosecution of the most important agents in a hearing of mass genocide or crimes against humanity (Bass 2002).

Materiality and international tribunals

International criminal courts in their modern form date to the closure of the Second World War with the trials by the victorious powers at the International Military Tribunal at Nuremberg (upon which the form and procedure of the contemporary International Criminal Tribunals are importantly modelled), but these new courts, instead, follow a mandate established by the United Nations. In all of these international courts, material objects and sites have, of necessity, constituted the evidence upon which the tribunals' proceedings consider the veracity of witness testimony. It is, however, a role that is, historically, almost always subsidiary to the text of witness accounts. Indeed, the conditions have been such that 'the material evidence and particularly the testimony of material evidence took second place to eyewitness or confessional information' (Buchli and Lucas 2001, 121). Interestingly, when there has been a foregrounding of materiality in the courtroom – and in such cases it has almost always been in regard to images of the landscape – it has been attendant only to cases of the greatest or unprecedented large-scale crimes. While for many lawyers in particular, this foregrounding of materiality within the courtroom in unique circumstances might seem to stretch

too far the established limits of traditional textual and oral legal discourse, I would like to suggest that this misses a more profound relationship at work between these large-scale crimes and material evidence. In fact, a new way of thinking about crime has the potential to be forged, and, because the discipline of archaeology has always been concerned to understand the material testimony to events long past and particularly for events that leave little or no textual records, it may be uniquely well placed to be an important site for recognising that the import of material witness may require a methodological move to the realm of material inquiry. Though still comparatively quite young, the emergence of the international criminal courts (such as the International Criminal Tribunals for the former Yugoslavia established in 1991 and Rwanda, established in 1994) will doubtlessly come to assume their own historicity – their own tradition (Hobsbawm and Ranger 1992), and I suggest that a more archaeologically inclined sensibility towards the material contours of the locales, landscapes and material clues and objects that imbricate within the criminal proceedings would provide legal discourse the ability to more adequately accommodate the parameters of large-scale criminal projects that continue to inhabit material landscapes. Because the function of these international tribunals is as much about legitimating historical narratives as it is about prosecuting criminals at large, there is an obligation to take serious account of the importance of the material aspects and settings for the collective memories and traumas of survivors.

The Nuremberg Trial

It is often true that the most startling and revealing moments of a trial arise from the presentation, in opening statements or testimonies, of materials or images of landscapes that somehow speak more effectively to the atrocity under examination than words could. Perhaps the first and most effective example of this is the famous showing of the film called *Nazi Concentration Camps* (directed by George Stevens) during the opening statement for the prosecution at the Nuremberg trials – one

Fig. 10.1 The court looks on as a film is screened as evidence during the trial of Adolf Eichmann (Courtesy of USHMM and The Israel Government Press Office).

of the first times filmic evidence was submitted within a juridical setting (Fig. 10.1). As Douglas describes in *Memories of Judgment*:

> The camera shows the scar of the building upon the blackened earth surrounded by dirty snow, and then draws close, examining the brittle remains of burnt corpses…which captures not the active commission of atrocities but the wounds they leave behind–upon the earth, the dead, and the survivors. (Douglas 2001, 23)

The film was not discussed after the screening. Unusually, the court adjourned without any words, 'the spectators were so disturbed that the presiding judges retired without a word and without announcing as usual the time set for the next session' (Douglas 2001, 23). The question then arises: how does such imagery bear upon the oral and documentary evidence that has already established the occurrence of such events. What are the limitations brought upon legal discourse by the exclusion of the spaces and places left by the crimes? Where precisely does imagery of this sort leave its radical imprint?

More recently, at the ICTY, a video of killings associated with the 1995 Srebrenica Massacre, shown by prosecutors at the Milošević trial on June 1st, 2005, evoked a similar sense of discursive rupture, with powerful repercussions both in the courtroom and beyond. As Nataša Kandić, a human rights activist from Belgrade's

Humanitarian Law Fund put it, 'Everything burst, the whole bubble of hiding evidence and denying crimes within the 10 minutes it took to broadcast the video' (Kratovac 2005).

Large-scale crimes and the radical imprint

Before addressing these questions, it is important to delineate how precisely the landscape or material world has had its most acute legal relevance in international criminal proceedings. The 1949 Geneva Conventions stipulate that civilian property as well as cultural property should be protected except in the case of imperative military necessity. That is to say, the material world ought to be protected insofar as it is collectively or privately owned or indispensable to the survival of a community – unless these very things or buildings are being used for military action. Unfortunately, however, the category of landscape (as it comes thus to be conceived under the jurisdiction of international tribunals) is also a category that may pre-emptively marginalise other objects or landscapes – often simply by virtue of their purported cultural or historical irrelevance. This may occur even when it is precisely these material sites and objects which might carry the greatest potential to deepen our understanding of, or in some cases provide the only medium for a proper understanding of, a particular crime. It can be the case that these emotive and useful vessels for remembering and profoundly conceptualising the residual nature of crimes against humanity fall to the wayside when they are considered inadequate to the bureaucratic requirement of belonging to such categories as private property or cultural monuments. However, the scope and scale of genocidal regimes would appear to usher into the world a crime that would seem to exist without historical precedent, which Hannah Arendt describes as occurring when 'a criminal guilt oversteps and shatters any and all legal systems' (cited in: Douglas 2001, 39). Within such a new criminality, whose parameters have yet to be satisfactorily named by a set of laws, I would argue that a vacuum is created into which even the most everyday objects and items of the landscape become inscribed with traumatic reminders of surveillance, loss, death, ethnocide and instability. This is because these objects and places are not only inscribed by their violent histories, but they actively enter into a dialectical relationship with those people they have affected and therefore become not only relics of history (or equipment in the Heideggerian sense) but rather something that bridges 'existential and the empirical' time – and thus can perhaps most successfully speak to the relationship between the historical crime and its victims (Ricoeur 1984, 124).

All of this would suggest that the legalistic exclusion or de-prioritisation of the presence or image of such objects, places and landscapes inherently cripples the ability of prosecutors, witnesses and defendants to speak most effectively to the materially situated relationship between the perpetrator and victim. To return to the case study of the ICTY, it would seem entirely within the legitimate legal jurisdiction of these new trial chambers to engage materiality more profoundly. It is established that each trial chamber of the ICTY will 'admit any evidence which it deems to have probative value' (ICTY Rule 8(c)), unless there is a specific reason to question its reliability (ICTY Rule 95)' (Murphy 1999, 80). This paper will set as its goal, then, a sort of descriptive genealogy of the probative value of materiality – with particular attention to the ways in which the incorporation and engagement of the material aspects of large-scale crimes translates an experience of the crime that is more effective than documents and oral testimony. As archaeologists have long understood, the narrative efficacy of materiality is not necessarily proportionate with the objects' or landscape's comprehension within the more prominent categories of monuments, archives and documents. This is particularly the case when the criminal element was the same authority compiling and monumentalising such historical institutions. In such instances, the investigator often finds that 'the most valuable traces are the ones that were not intended for our information' (Ricoeur 1984, 117). In this regard, in the same way that the archive functions to conceal the court's (and the historian's) reliance on memory ('the womb of

history': Ricoeur 2004, 87), so the narrow category delineated for evidence 'proper' attempts to conceal the court's dependence on a larger, much less determinate and ever-changing landscape.

Archaeologists have long considered the mutually constitutive relationship between the landscape and its occupants. Their investigative methodology often relies on the absence of written evidence or testimonial, and, therefore, the discipline has formulated a sophisticated treatment of the landscape in order to better articulate the phenomenal experience of the material world. An important recent example is Tim Ingold's notion of the *temporality* of the landscape. It examines the landscape as operating in a more embodied and dialectical relationship with people (1993). Importantly, Ingold's work, and that of others who operate within the archaeological medium, seeks to discard the kind of Cartesian optic in which the landscape seems to dwell either 'out there' or as being condensable into one synchronic moment (Bender 2001; Byrne 2003; Preucel and Meskell 2004). Ingold (1993) traces his project as being comparable to Bordieu's attempts to restore to anthropological study (using Mauss' study of the gift exchange) the constant foregrounding of the diachronic. Bourdieu's point is that the reductionist context of synchronic models for such practices as gift exchange, elides the most crucial element – the temporal. Ingold attempts to restore just such a temporality to discussions of the landscape, arguing that any cartographic approach, or any approach attempting a 'view from nowhere' can only imagine the landscape as being 'inscribed' by its inhabitants, rather than exploring the very incorporation of the landscape by its inhabitants. When the landscape can be seen as being 'neither…identical to nature, nor…on the side of humanity *against* nature' and instead be envisioned as intrinsic to human existence, Ingold concludes that 'it is *with* us, not against us, but it is no less real for that' (Ingold 1993, 154).

I would like to develop even further this notion of the landscape as being 'with us' by extending this notion to a different sort of landscape, one of conflict and violence, in which the landscape might also potentially be 'with them', so to speak. In so doing, this topoanalysis shifts from the traditional phenomenological analysis of more felicitous sorts of lived spaces (*e.g.* Bachelard 1969) to one which will consider the implications of power and constraint on the lived landscape – focusing on sites referred to by Foucault as 'heterotopias' (Foucault 1986). It is in the context of political tensions and conflicts, then, that I would like to consider the landscape – particularly as it participates in crimes that certain communities perpetrate upon others. To this purpose, consideration of the landscape becomes something other than the consideration of a visual image or a material *a priori* to the events that occurred within it. 'To perceive the landscape is therefore to carry out an act of remembrance, and remembering is not so much an act of calling up an internal image, stored in the mind, as of engaging perceptually with an environment that is itself pregnant with the past' (Ingold 1993, 153).

Eichmann in Jerusalem

I would like to begin by drawing from some historical examples that exemplify this point. During the famous trial of Eichmann in Jerusalem, one of the testimonies was that of Rivka Yoselewska in which she described crawling out of the mass grave where her would-be executioners had left her for dead. Somehow, she had been left alone, and she notes that she had paused to look back on the earth that was covering parts of what was intended to be her own mass grave. As she recounted, 'blood was spouting. Nowadays, when I pass a water fountain I can still see the blood spouting from the grave. The earth rose and heaved' (Douglas 2001, 173). Her terrible and perpetually unresolved relationship with this event describes with dreadful detail the most intimate ways in which the past is so often insinuated into the everyday materiality of the present. A water fountain becomes an instrument of horror, an agent that incessantly re-incorporates the crime into the woman's daily walks – a fact that cannot have eluded the machinations of the perpetrators of those crimes. It is precisely in this sense that the landscape may be 'with us', as Ingold suggests, but perhaps 'with us' to destructive and damaging

ends. As Alfred Gell might have it, the every day water fountain becomes the index that perpetually links the original violent act perpetrated upon the witness – repeatedly and unpredictably eliciting a re-enactment of the crime itself, and, hence, in an important sense we can trace this back to the systematic and persistent effects of the 'evil artist' (Gell 1994, 65). Thus, widening the realm of acceptable evidence of mass crimes against humanity is a project that a judicial body – particularly one sensitive to its own precarious existence within the imaginary terrain of the global, might find immensely useful.

When a crime becomes large-scale, to speak of the crime as having taken place once, with an imagined fixity in time and place, is inadequate – inadequate to expressing, for example, the spatio-temporal span of cultural genocide or the filling of mass graves. Yet, it is not about expanding the protective scope of laws or customs of war to more buildings and heritage sites; rather, it is about a *criminal* consideration – and stems from the perpetrator's ability to insinuate the crime into the very homes, cafes, streams, roads, forests, and even drinking wells of the victims. As such, we cannot think of the landscape as instantaneously regaining its neutrality with the cessation of war crimes; instead, the victim's perception of the landscape has likely become ineradicably charged with a history of violence. In other words, the mutually constituting identity of the victims and the landscape do not occur without the constant interpolation of history. 'The past is hidden somewhere outside the reach, beyond the realm of intellect, in some material object (in the sensation which that material object will give us) which we do no suspect' (Proust 1981, 57–58).

Seremetakis discusses the unevenness with which regional narratives unfold over the landscape (Seremetakis 1994). Like Benjamin and Bloch, she emphasises that changes in society do not descend upon the landscape as a seamless event, but rather occur unevenly, leaving residual 'dark stones' that interrupt the totality of time-narratives:

> There are expressions of non-synchronicity which become material encounters with cultural absence and possibility. There are islands of historicity,

discontinuous punctures, that render the imperceptible perceptible as they produce marked moments – tidal pools where an experiential cosmos can be mapped out in miniature (Seremetakis 1994, 12).

Seremetakis chooses to emphasise the constant possibility of re-capitulation through these 'dark stones' and implies that there is some form of creative potential to be unlocked – a 'liberation from political grids' (Seremetakis 1994, 13). But the case may also be that in precisely these material repositories for micro-practices – these sites of everyday trajectories that slip beneath the panoptic gaze – *negative* possibility may also lie in wait for the unsuspecting victim. In these places and material objects, not only is there the potential for positive re-enactments of every day histories but also the potential for the deep and traumatic reminder of what might have been but is unalterably lost, an ambush of negative nostalgia that awaits the victim at every stoppage. This is not merely an exaggerated awareness of the absence, but a terrible longing for what cannot be any longer and for what has been irrevocably stopped, and this is perhaps a different kind of stillness than the one that Seremetakis describes. It is not simply the inversion of presence, but, as with the necktie of deceased loved one, certain objects can serve to heighten the presence of absence – and instigate longing for what is unalterably absent (Ash 1996). The abjection becomes something that the landscape and material world revolve around – drawing its inhabitants into similar orbits of horror. Julia Kristeva (1982), speaks of the relationship these objects continue to impose on their observer (Fig. 10.2):

> … in the dark halls of the museum that is now what remains of Auschwitz, I see a heap of children's shoes, or something like that, something I have already seen elsewhere, under a Christmas tree … The abjection of the Nazi crime reaches its apex when death, which, in any case, kills me, interferes with what, in my living universe, is supposed to save me from death: childhood, science, among other things (Kristeva 1982, 4).

For Kristeva, the empty shoes, despite their museumisation, have inscribed upon them the

Fig. 10.2 The shoes of prisoners killed by Croatian ustashe militia at the Gradina execution site near the Jasenovac concentration camp in World War II (Courtesy of USHMM).

power of horror which continues to radiate the machinations of the perpetrators well past the calendrical span of time that can adequately demarcate the passing of the crimes themselves. A remarkable illustration of just how radically this same specific negative object of the shoes can speak to can be found in the testimony of Adolf Berman at the Eichmann trial. After his testimony, Berman removed a pair of children's shoes that he had previously removed from the tens of thousands that were strewn on the ground among skulls and bones.

> It was a stunning moment, in terms of the shoes' power to conjure the single missing child and of the power of a single object to stand for the slaughter of the innocents. Yet it was also Bauman's position in the story that explains why the sight of the shoes emerged as one of the most moving moments of the trial. For one felt that Bauman had been carrying the shoes around in his well-worn briefcase since the day he discovered them … only now had he finally been supplied an occasion for placing his terrible memento on display on a world stage. By permitting Bauman to display his shoes in a manner that transformed this artifact of loss into evidence of criminality, the trial provided a degree of closure to the traumatic memories that Bauman had been carrying around since the war's closure (Douglas 1994, 162).

So too, both of these moments eerily evoke the absence from the Milošević trial of a very similar

Fig. 10.3 A memorial wreath on the site of a mass grave in the Ebensee concentration camp (Courtesy of USHMM).

material testimony. We know, though it is not one of the crimes which Milošević is charged with at the ICTY and thus the court will never see the evidence, that, in October 2000, Milošević's secret police (the Special Operations Unit – JSO) abducted and killed a former ally, the former Serbian President Ivan Stambolić, in the forests of Fruška Gora after he had gone for a run outside of his house in Belgrade that day. Due to the heavy media coverage of the events, the television images and newspaper photographs of the gruesome discovery of his quicklime grave quickly became etched in the minds of the Serbian public. As described in *The London Independent*, each turn of the excavators shovel revealed his running shoes, bits of bone, and pieces of clothing – harrowing and precise visual articulations of the force with which the end of his life had been planned and concealed (Zimonjić 2003).

Materiality and the historical crime

The immense potential objects and landscapes carry to perpetrate their historicity (Fig. 10.3) extends well beyond any understanding of material evidence to be gained from the arid parameters of the Geneva Conventions (Osiel 2000). It is so

profound that even those who cannot bear first-hand witness to the crimes themselves recognise the radical possibility of explicit testimony of the objects themselves. Unlike the paradigm of legal precedent, which foregrounds those aspects of witness accounts that fall within the known terrain of prosecutable criminal act, the materiality that surrounds the crime reminds the court of that which does not yield to this limited set of signifiers. The materiality points to another mode of comprehending the historical crime. As Arendt states:

> [c]omprehension does not mean denying the outrageous, deducing the unprecedented from precedents, or explaining phenomena by such analogies and generalities that the impact of reality and the shock of experience are no longer felt. It means, rather, examining and bearing consciously the burden which our century has placed on us – neither denying its existence nor submitting meekly to its weight. Comprehension, in short, means the unpremeditated, attentive facing up to, and resisting of, reality – whatever it may be. (Arendt 1966, xxvi)

These material spaces and objects come to function much like Latour's 'actants'. In the context of a massive criminal initiative, they do not merely represent, symbolise, or objectify the desire to eliminate or eject a people; instead, they actually constitute the means to surgically remove a cultural group, polluting or usurping even their most banal links with that land – whether historically, monumentally, ritualistically, and often avoiding the articulation of as much in words. As Latour says, 'the very notion of discipline is impracticable without steel, without the wood of the door, without the bolt of the locks' (Latour 2000). In the case of large-scale ethnocidal projects, these material resources provide the means for circumventing the textual (and consequently incriminating) modes of terrorising and eliminating groups, and, by erasing the textual archives of a group, these physical modalities come to have an even stronger disciplinary claim. 'The Serb action of destroying all written documentation of Kosovar Albanians is an interesting case in point; the systematic policy to erase all documents, physical and electronic,

190 *Lindsay Weiss*

Fig. 10.4 The International Criminal Tribunal for the former Yugoslavia rents its space in a former insurance company building (Courtesy Paul O'Hanlon).

that can testify to the existence of an ethnic group…' (Buchli and Lucas 2001, 122). This kind of project, which seeks to sever a people's connection with their *place* in the world, can be construed as genocidal, and it explicitly implicates the landscape itself as an instrument of terror. The project can be seen as one that imposes a certain prohibition on sites and lands that are directed against a particular group – a sort of prohibition which functions no less powerfully than the traditional sorts of prohibitions that dominate abstract space. As Lefebvre states, 'it is impossible to say how often one pauses uncomfortably for a moment on some threshold – the entrance to a church, office or 'public' building, or the point of access to a 'foreign' place – while passively, and usually 'unconsciously' accepting a prohibition of some kind. Most such prohibitions are invisible' (Lefebvre 1991, 319). In this project, to the extent that the landscape and even its most banal markers are employed as a genocidal device and to the extent that the intended victims experience it as such, these places develop a social agency that is intimately entangled with the agency of the criminal and that forces upon the most intimate and traditional landmarks and landscapes of the targeted population a series of prohibitions that continue to exact an invisible toll. As Slobodan Milošević stated in cross-examining of a witness:

Q: All right. Can I infer, on the basis of what you've been claiming, that the security forces did not attack KLA [Kosovo Liberation Army] strongholds that they left them alone and then they went out to burn peaceful villages, to kill the livestock and damage these *places*? Is that what you are claiming, Mr. Crosland?
A. That's exactly what I'm saying, Mr. Milošević …
(ICTY, 8021, italics added)

The International Criminal Tribunal for the Former Yugoslavia and Milošević

The indictments brought against Milošević for the regions of Kosovo, Bosnia-Herzegovina and Croatia, were introduced before the ICTY (Fig. 10.4) by senior trial attorney Mr. Nice on February 12th with descriptions of the 'medieval savagery and the calculated cruelty' that the prosecution set out to prove had so exceeded the bounds of legitimate warfare. For the crimes committed in Kosovo, Mr. Nice gave an account of what happened at Kozica in 1998, where fifty women had gathered together for safety, and, under the false assumption that they were going to be taken by soldiers to a mosque for shelter, were instead taken to a house, which was then tied up with wire to lock them inside. A mother and her 20-year-old daughter were separated during the events, and the mother, who escaped, returned later to search the area for her daughter. The body of the daughter was subsequently found by international aid workers (with those of the seven other women who were the last to be taken from the house) at the bottom of three different wells – into which they had been thrown 'probably alive and after who knows quite what had happened to them' (ICTY, 13).

On subsequent visits to The Hague, I attended the Milošević trial, for a few weeks in July of 2002 and again during July of 2003. One of the witnesses I was present for was that of a Dr. Baccard, who reviewed many of the autopsy reports for the ICTY. On one of the days I was in attendance, he dealt with Milošević's attempt to deconstruct the reports that were conducted on the bodies of the victims taken from the wells. The unpleasant details of Baccard's task were striking, but perhaps more disturbing, on that day, was the emphasis and presentation of the crime and the relevant evidence as it was presented by the accused. Although this was not made available to those in attendance in the gallery, the judges were provided photos of the corpses on that day, and, in fact, all of the cross-examination conducted by Milošević revolved entirely around the state of the corpses – in terms of whether or not assault of any nature was actually determinable from the evidence. In his cross-examination of the medical expert, Milošević proposed alternative explanations for the state of the corpses:

> Q: But do you exclude the possibility, for example, of this kind: That the victim wanted to hide herself, that she jumped over the edge and that while she was jumping over these rough edges, these abrasions were caused, as you call them, on the inner side of her upper thigh and that, later on, she drowned; that nobody threw her there into the well. Would that be a theoretical possibility, plausible? (ICTY, 8056).

The implications of this hypothetical scenario are obviously profoundly disturbing in a number of ways. The materiality of the crime seems to be left to the suggestive commentary of Milošević himself, who seemed to be actually garnering the elements of the landscape to his defence. The wells became the unwilling recipients of these women's suicides, the water handily serving to dissolve the trace of the crime before the bodies could be recovered. Milošević's cross-examination refuses to discuss the death of these women outside of the context of their prolonged immersion in water, emphasising their decay, using terms such as 'hemolysis of erythrocytes' in order to elevate the authority of the process. He repeatedly insisted '[n]one of the drowned women had any traces which would indicate that they fought against someone or that they were thrown forcibly or were injured…' (ICTY, 8064), despite the disagreement of expert witness Dr. Baccard. Milošević, in the absence of any efficacious use of the environment by the prosecution, mythologises the landscape of the crime and creates a scenario in which the ephemeral quality of the forensic traces comes to constitute an almost exonerative function. Indeed, it seemed that it was the landscape itself that was

cross-examining Dr. Baccard, when in reality the prosecution could have had it the other way around, as I will discuss.

Now of course, the landscape was far from a neutral space, and in many ways it could quite effectively be thought of as the crystallisation of the horror that was occurring. 'Through the actions of snipers, civilians were shot in their homes as they watched television, drank coffee or prayed, shot outside their homes as they crossed the street, cleared rubbish, collected wood for heat, or fetched water, as they rode in buses or on trams' (ICTY, 132). This description of Sarajevo during the 1992 siege rings true for the inhabitants of Kozica and others across the landscape, for whom actions of every day life suddenly had become a ritual of potential annihilation. No part of the landscape, it would seem, was devoid of snipers or incapable of housing one's death. The terrorising of the landscape served both the more prosaic function of persuading targeted ethnic groups to leave the land, but, more fundamentally, such an experience resets the existential terms by which the terrorised remain upon the land. As Taussig has written, '[w]hat distinguishes a culture of terror is that the epistemological, ontological, and otherwise purely philosophical problem of reality-and-illusion, certainty-and-doubt, becomes infinitely more than a 'merely' philosophical problem. It becomes a high-powered tool for domination and a principal medium of political practice' (Taussig 1984, 492). Kemal Hadžić tried to capture in his photographs the existential implications of this. He describes the altering of the relationship between oneself and the landscape: '[t]he buildings and material objects carried a new energy. That is because at any second they could explode and kill. Like an egg that can hatch, except it brought danger and death' (Douglas 2001, 152).

Returning to the cross examination of Dr. Baccard, the clinical facts were that the corpses were in such an advanced state of degeneration that the evidence could be arguably construed as pointing either way. Milošević focused upon the evidence within the parameters of decay, of progressive evidentiary obscurity. We are instilled with the sense that the bodies were retrieved too late and, hence, that they no longer could cohesively bear witness to their own destruction, and somewhere in this process is the eradication of the ephemeral crime itself. The algorithm of a successful genocide requires just such an elimination of the landscape in evidentiary discussions. These wells themselves, so strangely absent from the courtroom discussions, wherever they may exist in the landscape of Kozica (of course they continue to exist, even if filled), are testimonies to the historical crime: their terrible emptiness now, their abandoned water. It is imperative to understand the full after effect of how such a crime might come to resonate within the daily life of a resident of Kozica, where there is no major water distribution system and where wells thus represent primary water sources on the landscape. This defilement is not only for the immediate family members of the victims but also for those for whom such wells, roads, gardens or other such ordinary everyday landmarks have been given the imprimatur of the terrorising criminal, as their presence continues the culture of terror in 'rumor and fantasy' and memory. 'These sites of memory cannot be maintained at a distance, divorced from the embodied persons who feel the troubling proximity of physical deaths as well as the persistent physicalities of the dead. If we are to acknowledge the perceived agency of material domains in contemporary experiences of these memories, then the embodiment of persons as enmeshed in sites of memory must be recognised' (Hallam and Hockey 2001, 127).

None of these considerations seemed to enter within the courtroom discussion of the crime, neither in the dramatic opening statements of the prosecution, nor in the testimonies of the witnesses. Understandably, if the landscape is tacitly assumed by the language of the court to be either 'out there' or 'in the mind' of the victims, then it becomes impossible to speak about the terrorising dialectic that exists between people and their landscape within a formally legal register. Even without the vocabulary of a 'humanistic geography' (Cosgrow 1989, 171), I would argue that the materiality of the mass crime and its landscape function as a significant trace – one that speaks effectively to the actions and events disseminated throughout the

court's discourse. The presiding judge of the trial chamber, Judge May, had previously established that 'we have rules which allow documents to be produced on the grounds that they largely speak for themselves' (ICTY, 9883). The possibility of material objects and landscapes being allowed to speak for themselves is very essential if light is to be brought to bear on the full implications of these crimes. How, for example, are the sites of these wells woven into contemporary rumour, or even muted through secrecy? Looking beyond the particular communities they effect, situated within a wider matrix of similar landscapes of devastation, the wells might arguably contribute to an understanding of the nature of the greater mass crimes that were occurring, in the sense that they serve to map out '[t]he precise patterns of repression [as it] varied from one region to another' (Doretti and Fondebrider 2001, 138).

Conclusion

The criminal proceedings of international tribunals in general cannot be romanticised as having more powers than any other historically constituted court, and '[n]o one should entertain the illusion that the relative success of the ICTY…has somehow exorcised the spectre of genocide and other massive crimes from out midst' (Akhavan 2001, 31). Moreover, there is no simple sense in which sites of terror on the landscape are easily resolved or redeemed merely by their formal recognition within criminal proceedings. It is important, however, (in spite of the disintegration of the memories of survivors and the moments in which their testimonies seems to exceed any logical legal function) to recognise what has long gone unstated within the context of courts, although it is something that has long been examined and teased out of the material landscape within archaeological practice, that there is a profound tenacity inherent in certain objects, markers and monuments in the landscape – a tenacity tending towards the continual recapitulation of the intentions and agendas of power. This is, simply, the founding logic of a materially-situated historical practice, and yet, this understanding offers a profound and underutilised resource for getting at something which can, at present, only tacitly and inarticulately be invoked within the terms of most contemporary global courtroom proceedings. Given the rather intrinsic problematic of asserting a global space of law – and the inherent conflict such a transcendental invocation of rights produces as it intercalates with the question of particular landscapes and objects, which fall within the juridical domain of other nation-states, it would be somewhat impossible to expect such courts to create new laws based upon these existential realities. It is important, nonetheless, to remember that the landscape of the survivor is a very different place, a place that, in no small sense, becomes a perpetuation of the dialogue between the perpetrator of the crime and the victims. As the psychiatrist Stevan Weine has suggested, '[m]emories can be triggered by a sight, a smell, a sound, or a feeling…[they] can take over the survivor, hurling them out of their involvement in a current situation and dropping them back into the abyss' (Weine 1999, 77). Thus, restoring some sense of the mundane and everyday embodiments of life in a landscape will be necessary if there is to be more than a token sense of justice for the victims of large-scale crimes such as genocide. It is the precise dimensions and parameters of such giant crimes – the crimes that have fallen under the gaze of the emergent international criminal system since the Holocaust – that can be best clarified with the profound juridical consideration of how deeply materiality is imbricated within the lifecycle of these crimes. Finally, it will be in their consideration of the mutually constitutive relationship between a people and their landscape that, to some extent, the courts will be reminded of their responsibilities to deal with the real dimensions of horror – not only for those already 'disappeared' by this process, but for those for whom every day holds the possibility of re-entry.

Bibliography

Akhavan, P. (2001) Beyond Impunity: Can International Criminal Justice Prevent Future Atrocities? *American Journal of International Law* 95(1), 7–31.

Arendt, H. (1966) *The Origins of Totalitarianism*. New York, Harvest Press.

Ash, J. (1996) Memory and Objects. In P. Kirkham (ed.) *The Gendered Object*, 219–224. Manchester, Manchester University Press.

Bachelard, G. (1969) *The Poetics of Space*. Boston, Beacon Press.

Bass, G. J. (2002) *Stay the Hand of Vengeance: The Politics of War Crimes Tribunals*. Princeton, Princeton University Press.

Baudrillard, J. (2003) *Passwords*. New York, Verso.

Bender, B. (2001) Landscapes-on-the-move. *Journal of Social Archaeology* 1, 75–89.

Bettig, R. V. (1996) *Copyrighting Culture: The Political Economy of Intellectual Property*. Boulder, CO., Westview Press.

Buchli, V. and G. Lucas (2001) Bodies of Evidence. In V. Buchli and G. Lucas (eds) *Archaeologies of the Contemporary Past*, 121–125. New York, Routledge.

Byrne, D. (2003) Nervous Landscapes: Race and Space in Australia, *Journal of Social Archaeology* 3(2), 169–193.

Cosgrove, D. (1989) Geography is Everywhere: Culture and Symbolism in Human Landscapes. In D. Gregory and R. Walford (eds) *Horizons in Human Geography*, 118–135. Basingstoke, Macmillan.

Dinur, Y. (1961) Transcript for the court proceedings from the trial of Adolf Eichmann. District Court of Jerusalem: session 68: 57621. http://www.nizkor.org/hweb/people/e/eichmann-adolf/transcripts/Session-068-01.html.

Doretti, M. and Fondebrider, L. (2001) Science and Human Rights: Truth, Justice, Reparation and Reconciliation, a Long Way in Third World Countries. In V. Buchli and G. Lucas (eds) *Archaeologies of the Contemporary Past*, 138–157. New York, Routledge.

Douglas, L. (2001) *The Memory of Judgment: Making Law and History in the Trials of the Holocaust*. New Haven, Yale University Press.

Foucault, M. (1986) Of Other Spaces. In N. Mirzoeff (ed.) *The Visual Culture Reader*, 237–244. London, Routledge.

Gell, A. (1994) *Art and Agency: An Anthropological Theory*. New York, Berg Publishers.

Hallam, E. and Hockey, J. (2001) *Death, Memory and Material Culture*. New York, Berg Publishers.

Handler, R (2003) Cultural Property and Culture Theory. *Journal of Social Archaeology* 3(2), 353–365.

Hobsbawm, E. and Ranger, T. (1992) *The Invention of Tradition*. Cambridge, Cambridge University Press.

ICTY, International Criminal Tribunal for the Former Yugoslavia (2002) *Transcripts of The Prosecutor of the Tribunal v. Slobodan Milošević*, The Hague: ICTY. http://www.un.org/icty/cases/indictindex-e.htm

Ingold, T. (1993) The Temporality of the Landscape. *World Archaeology* 93(1), 57–97.

Kratovac, K. (2005) Bosnian Execution Video Shakes Families. ABC News International. June 3rd.

Kristeva, J. (1982) *Powers of Horror: An Essay on Abjection*. New York, Columbia University Press.

Latour, B. (1988) *The Pasteurization of France*. Cambridge, MA, Harvard University Press.

Latour, B. (2000) The Berlin Key or How to Do Words With Things. In P. M. Graves-Brown (ed.) *Matter, Materiality and Modern Culture*, 10–21. New York, Routledge.

Law, J. and Hassard, J. (1999) *Actor Network Theory and After*. Boston, Blackwell Publishers.

Lefebvre, H. (1991) *The Production of Space*. Oxford, Blackwell.

Meskell, L. (1998) *Archaeology Under Fire: Nationalism, Politics and Heritage in the Eastern Mediterranean and Middle East*. London, Routledge.

Murphy, S. D. (1999) Progress and Jurisprudence of the International Criminal Tribunal for the Former Yugoslavia. *American Journal of International Law* 93(1), 57–59.

Osiel, M. (2000) *Mass Atrocity, Collective Memory and the Law*. New Brunswick, Transaction Publishers.

Preucel, R. and Meskell, L. (2004) Places. In R. Preucel and L. Meskell (eds) *Companion to Social Archaeology*, 215–229. Malden, MA., Blackwell.

Proust, M. (1981) *Remembrance of Things Past: Swann's Way* (trans. C. K. Scott Moncrieff). London, Chatto & Windus.

Ricoeur, P. (1984) *Time and Narrative I*. Chicago, University of Chicago Press.

Ricoeur, P. (2004) *Memory, History, Forgetting*. Chicago, University of Chicago Press.

Rowlands, M. (2002) Heritage and Cultural Property. In V. A. Buchli (ed.) *The Material Culture Reader*, 105–114. New York, Berg.

Seremetakis, C. N. (1994) *The Senses Still: Perception and Memory as Material Culture in Modernity*. Boulder, CO., Westview Press.

Strathern, M. (2002) Emergent Relations. In M. Biagioli and P. Galiston (eds) *Scientific Authorship: Credit and Intellectual Property in Science*, 165–194. London, Routledge.

Taussig, M. (1984) Space and Ethnic Distinctions: Culture of Terror – Space of Death. Roger Casement's Putumayo Report and the Explanation of Torture. *Comparative Studies in Society and History* 26(3): 467–497.

Weine, S. M. (1999) *When History is a Nightmare: Lives and Memories of Ethnic Cleansing in Bosnia-Herzegovina*. New Brunswick, Rutgers University Press.

Zimonjić, Vesna Perić (2003) Milošević's Wife Defiant over Murder Warrant. *The London Independent* March 31st.

11. YugoMuseum:
Memory, nostalgia, irony

Mrdjan Bajić

Observer

Have you ever wished that you could make an enormously voluminous collection of objects that together had absorbed the meaning of the epoch in which you lived? And then, to group these objects according to your decision, to your will or whim, with the conviction that, grouped in just this way, they render with more truth and blatancy their meaning and significance into the field of obviousness; creating a profile of the 'fabric' of historical facts and layers – of which they give evidence – thereby revealing the malignancy of the era. Yugomuseum is the result of such a wish. Yugomuseum was conceived in Belgrade, a pathetic remnant of the blown-out Yugoslavia, a country whose corpse, in the moment of its collapse, was renounced with scorn and disgust by nearly everyone. The shadow of the 'prison of peoples' and the 'paradise of self-management' continued posthumously to produce an identity that, with the prefix 'ex', was affixed with unreasonable ferocity to its former inhabitants. This identity is ever-present in the lives of the people: in dreams, with the reading of morning papers, when they leave this region forever, when they come back, when they meet new people, and especially when they meet each other and mingle again. Personal identity, gained with great anguish, remains overshadowed by territorial and national identity. Overshadowed by images of uncanny events. Overshadowed by memories – which no one wanted anymore. And by objects – which no one cared for anymore, objects with a surplus of meaning. These fragments, both burdening and insignificant, pompous and bizarre,

are like pieces of wrapping styrofoam: no matter how vigorously you wave, they neglect to fly away from a new coat. I ask: can these fragments be assembled and arranged in a particular fashion so that they create a new kind of wrapping? A kind that spurs a greater understanding of our previously shallow and in a way, empty, common memory, thus allowing us to reassess our past?

Observer (second time)*

The Past is never absent from the Present. History is not the exclusive terrain of historians, who can be likened to divers. They dive in, discover something, classify it, name it and leave it on the shelf, so that it may be forgotten. However, non-divers (*i.e.* ordinary people) never run out of oxygen and are never eaten by sharks, nor do they experience any other hazards that hinder their interactions with history. These non-divers dress up nicely and go to a gallery or, better still, to a museum where they observe the exhibits from a safe distance and then later if they have enough time, discuss what they saw. But 'Art' is not what we see displayed in a museum in the same way that history is not the exclusive subject of historians. Art is never absent from the Present either, a present which constantly sends us more and more unavoidable and terrifying bills, whether one finds oneself in ex-Yugoslavia or any other place in the world, but especially in ex-Yugoslavia, and with a particular intensity. The fact that the billing in this country continues to pile up in such ghastly, bloody and rapid forms is just a minor peculiarity. Here, the systems and means of avoiding their payment are more than essential, but the unbearable truths will not disappear if we simply stop paying attention to them.

Many people asked me whether I was *really* going to create *YU Museum*. One simple fact was intentionally overlooked when this question was posed: *YU Museum* already *really* exists. So I tried to prove its existence to everyone, including myself. This museum does not need halls and walls; you do not need to purchase a ticket to gain admission. You move about in it at no cost every day, whether you want to or not, whether you can accept the fact that your identity has been built in a reality that repeats itself endlessly or not: 'There has never been neither war nor trauma; Goli otok (Bare Island) has never existed; communists have never executed anyone; chetniks and ustashes have never slaughtered the innocent; the Karadjordjevićs were great democrats; the Serbian Orthodox Church despises secular wealth; Milošević is not guilty of war crimes because there have been no war crimes at all; Koštunica is a nationalist but a moderate one; the Karićs are capable businessmen, etc.' The aim of Yugomuseum (using the tissue of historical facts and a large number of artefacts as materials for shaping this non-existent museum space into a real physical thing) is to question the idea that a museum is a place where art is stocked, when it can rather be understood as somewhere in which we live everyday, as well as to show that the attempts to construct this museum are themselves a process of creating art. A museum created by our diving ventures into our own history (with a bit of nostalgia and cynicism added to ease digestion), with its exhibits that once stood neatly, quietly, ignored on shelves, is going to cost us dearly.

Presenter

Dear visitors, let us commence our tour of the museum: Welcome to Yugomuseum. Yugomuseum, the project created between 1998 and 2002, is situated in Slavija Square, the biggest, most traffic congested and surely the most unusual square in Belgrade, the capital of Serbia, former Yugoslavia. Slavija square is the business centre of the city that was never truly realised, a square that is the site of many intersections, where the layers of various historical epochs and ideological messages stand mixed together, layers which continue to change and interweave. Here are some examples of these layers:

- A monument, in the spirit of social-realism, from the 1950s, of Dimitrije Tucović: the true leader of the Labour Movement from the beginning of the twentieth century, who, on the eve of the First World War, in the Parliament – by the necessity of his convictions – voted against war credits, and later, became – by the necessity of his emotions – a volunteer soldier and was killed in the same war.
- The Temple of St. Sava, the largest Orthodox Church: its construction began at the opening of the last century in the Kingdom of Yugoslavia and was restarted some eighty years later, in the late 1980s, as a proof of the revival of Orthodoxy.
- Hotel Slavija: made of glass and aluminium, a miracle of socialist modernism, and next to it:
- Hotel Slavija Two: made of brass and stone, a miracle of post-socialist postmodernism.
- The still unfinished Central Bank of the former Yugoslavia: too large for present needs.
- Opposite, a Hole: a building site that has existed for sixty years. In the 1990s, during the time of the rise of false banks, it was decided to build another false bank here, and a false building site materialised for the false pyramidal Dafiment Bank.
- All around, street sellers and dealers of foreign currency during the 1990s.
- Small shops selling traditional hamburgers and pljeskavice from the same period.
- The first McDonald's restaurant in Eastern Europe: opened in 1988, a symbol of the economic development interrupted by Milošević's devastating war economy in the 1990s.
- Well-known benches: from which thousands of citizens of Belgrade, exactly one half of the university-educated population, left for the airport by bus.

This is the location where the promotion of Yugomuseum was announced in August of 1999, in the atmosphere of reconstruction, after the NATO bombardment. Yugomuseum was announced with the erection of a scaffold and billboard in Slavija Square. A twenty-seven-metre-high monument was to be constructed here: a creation of media misinformation, depicting a

Figure 11.1

Figure 11.2

sickle and hammer crossed with the IBM logo. Behind this monument, a huge museum would be created, simultaneously an underground shelter, where the bizarre objects, irradiated by the historical importance of the events impressed in them from the seventy-year history of Yugoslavia, would be exhibited.

At that first moment, confusion was the first reaction – but then competent authorities urgently took the billboard and construction materials away, long before the legally obtained license for its erection expired.

In 1999, at the very beginning, great interest in the Museum arose through e-mail activity. Images of the exhibits, with explanatory subtitles, found their way to art lovers – who usually forwarded them to their friends – thus creating long chains of house collections.

Let us take a closer look at a random sampling of twelve of the Yugomuseum exhibits, which have been ordered chronologically, according to the historical sequence of the events they represent. They have been selected to determine the temporal, ideological, geographical, moral and sentimental boundaries of the Yugomuseum project.

*041: **The Banovinas.** 400×600×900cm, 2001. (Fig. 11.1)

Iron; soil; the uniform of the heir to the Austro-Hungarian throne, Franz Ferdinand, murdered in Sarajevo in 1914; the bronze equestrian sculpture of King Alexander Karadjordjević the Unifier, crowned in 1919 after the First World War, becoming the king of the united Kingdom of Serbs, Croats and Slovenians; various flowers growing on

the territory of banovinas – the first administrative region of the Kingdom of Yugoslavia. *Donated by the Illyrian Movement.*

*033: **Dynasty.** 500×500×500cm; 2001. (Fig. 11.2)

King Alexander Obrenović and Queen Draga, murdered and cut into twenty-six pieces; the suitcase of King Peter the First Karadjordjević, in which he brought his entire belongings upon his coming to power in Serbia; the decree announcing the January 6th Dictatorship; the car in which King Alexander Karadjordjević was assassinated in Marseilles; the fountain pen prince regent Pavle Karadjordjević used to sign the Tripartite Treaty with Germany; the gold bars taken to London in 1941; the uniform King Peter the Second Karadjordjević wore at his marriage in London 1942; the lump of native soil prince Alexander Karadjordjević kissed upon his return to Yugoslavia in the Nineties; the White Palace; wood. *Donated by the Crown Council.*

*040: **Parade.** 900×600×1200cm, 2001. (Fig. 11.3)

Wood; cardboard; youth, workers and the honest intelligentsia; a hammer and sickle, woven from red carnations; the inscription: 'Brotherhood and Unity'; the coat of arms of Socialist Federal Republic of Yugoslavia and its republics on the movable platform which was a part of the 1st of May Parade in 1957. *Donated by Bagat.*

*017: **Dinar.** 200×30×18cm, 1999. (Fig. 11.4)

Aluminium; iron; a banknote with one zero (0) from the time of the Economic Reform in the

Figure 11.3

Figure 11.5

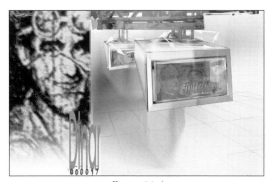

Figure 11.4

Figure 11.6

Sixties, displaying the figure of Alija Sirotanović, a famous miner, shock worker and a hero of the socialist era; a banknote with eleven zeros (00000000000) from the period of the highest inflation ever recorded (1993), with the figure of J. J. Zmaj, the celebrated Serbian poet from the epoch of Romanticism; armed guards. *Donated by IMF.*

*018: **Cordon**. 350×350×2500cm, 1999. (Fig. 11.5)

Parts from the Smederevo Steelworks, which was never profitable; a piece of asphalt from Surčin Airport; eighty-eight elite guards welcoming Comrade Tito at Surčin Airport after his visit to Kim Il Sung and the fraternal Republic of North Korea; a red carpet; a sound recording of Korean girls singing the song 'Comrade Tito, to Thee We Swear' in the language at that time called, *Serbo-Croatian. Donated by the 25th of May Museum.*

*044: **1968**. 140×80×80cm, 2001. (Fig. 11.6)

Student demonstrations in 1968; the flag of 'Red University – Karl Marx'; the accordion that played when 'Kozara kolo' was danced; tear gas; sound recording: the actor Stevo Žigon reciting Robespierre's speech at the Jacobin club from *Danton's Death*: 'Our eyes were open. We saw the enemy preparing and rising but we did not give the signal for alarm. We let the people itself to...' *Donated by Student Cultural Centre.*

*010: **Suit**. 240×120×80cm, 1999. (Fig. 11.7)

Aluminium; glass; neon; the suit President Slobodan Milošević wore when he saw Kosovo for the last time in the summer of 1998; film clip: people in Kosovo Polje, 1986; sound recording of the historical sentence: 'No one is allowed to beat these people!'; iron. *Donated by the Republic of Serbia.*

*026: **Shoes**. 140×60×120cm, 1999. (Fig. 11.8)

Shoes worn by President Milošević while

Figure 11.7

Figure 11.9

Figure 11.8

Figure 11.10

signing the Dayton Agreement; shoes worn by President Clinton while applauding the signatories of the Dayton Agreement; a Bosnian medieval bogomils tombstone with lines from the Bible and the Koran, inscribed with Cyrillic, Latin and Arab letters – cut in two pieces. *Donated by SFOR.*

*028: **Hat.** 300×400×300cm, 1999. (Fig. 11.9)

Glass; depleted uranium; hologram projection of the Statue of Liberty; wood; elephant feet; the hat with a crocodile skin ribbon and the brooch in the shape of a butterfly worn by Dr. Madeleine Albright during her first visit to the American peace keeping units in the New Multi-ethnic, Multi-confessional, Multi-cultural and Multi-radioactive Kosovo. *Donated by the UN.*

*031: **The Power Shovel.** 280×280×450cm, 2000. (Fig. 11.10)

The power shovel that levelled the entrance to the Radio and Television of Serbia Building

during the anti-Milošević revolution on October 5th 2000. *Donated by Dragoljub Milanović, director of the RTS national television.*

*052: **Helicopter.** (Video), 56 sec, 2001 (Fig. 11.11)

The famous chopper with its famous passenger to The Hague. *Donated by Dr. Zoran Djindjić.*

*050: **The Refrigeration Truck.** 2000×2000× 2000cm, 2001 (Fig. 11.12)

Water from the Danube; the refrigeration truck with its horrible load. *Donator unknown.*

This represents only a small part of the large Yugomuseum collection, which also consists of: Triglav Mountain; the pontoon bridge over the Neretva River; Lovćen's chapel; Ferhadija mosque; the lathe from Tito's workshop on Brioni Island; the Central Committee of the Communist Party of Yugoslavia building; the hologram projection of Jovanka Broz, Tito's wife; the model of Rambouillet castle; the eclipse of the sun over Belgrade on

Figure 11.11

Figure 11.12

August 11th, 1999; the grass on which, on May 4th, 1980, at the moment of the announcement of Tito's death, football players and fans of Hajduk (Croatian football team) and Red Star (Serbian football team), cried together; the typewriter on which the *SANU* (Serbian Academy of Arts and Sciences) Memorandum was typed; the flower from the coiffure of Professor Dr. Mira Marković, Milošević's wife; a sledge-hammer from Jasenovac concentration camp; a rock from Goli otok island; a fragment of the invisible (Stealth) plane F-117, taken down during 1999 NATO bombardment of Serbia; a piece of the floor on which the victorious game at the European Basketball Championships in 1997 was played; a rusty spoon, with which Professor Dr. Vojislav Šešelj threatened the Croats in 1991; the barbed wire surrounding Omarska concentration camp in Bosnia; the rifle with which Comrade Tito shot lions in non-aligned African countries; eight Meštrović caryatids from the Unknown Hero monument on Avala Mountain; a scale model of the 1993 siege of Sarajevo; the chocolate portraits of the chiefs of delegations at the first Summit of non-aligned countries; fifty-four TV sets with all the channels available on the territory of Federal Republic of Yugoslavia; young pioneers; the ethnic map of Croatia before and after Tudjman's reign; the projects from a competition for antifascist monuments in Lukovdo, Prilep, Ada, Kragujevac, Ljubljana, Valjevo and other places all over the former Yugoslavia – now partly or completely destroyed; the wooden stand with wax figures of the 209 members of delegations from 127 countries present at the funeral of J. B.

Tito on May 8th 1980, in Belgrade; Dobrica Ćosić (cryogenically frozen?) for the benefit of future generations; Vojislav Koštunica with rifle, cats and the Constitution; the complete belongings of the Karić family acquired in the Nineties; the book 'To Serbian People Through Dungeon Window' by orthodox bishop Nikolaj Velimirović; etc. etc. …

The first complete presentation of the exhibits comprising the Yugomuseum collection was at the Centre for the Cultural Decontamination in Belgrade during August and September 2001, marking the second anniversary of the Museum. Yugomuseum was subsequently displayed at the São Paolo biannual (2002), Kunsthale Project Space in Vienna (2003), and also presented to various audiences on many other occasions.

Until the final construction of Yugomuseum, the exhibits are preserved in *Yugomuseum Depot*, accessible via the Web at www.yugomuzej.com and various gallery presentations of select Museum segments.

Like any serious museum, in addition to the permanent collection, Yugomuseum includes: a Library, Archives, Storerooms, a Museum shop (where one can find a wide variety of objects: unique small sculptures, photographs, prints, posters and objects for everyday use, such as pillows, ashtrays, coffee sets, dining sets, T-shirts, glasses, tablecloths, nightgowns, bed linen, mats, etc.), and even a room for developing the creativity of children. This room is called 'the Games' and had in fact been conceived and carried out much earlier than the museum, but eventually became part of Yugomuseum. The Games is a group of iron tables on which groups of sculptures, toys, and objects are chaotically thrown:

(Photo boxes) – with digitally mastered, and reprinted photos of children from the 1960s: my own, my friends and members of my family;

(Skins) – Children's pyjamas, of red wool, knitted by my sister whose three grand children are living abroad;

(Red angels) – with red pioneer's scarf around their necks;

(Daddy's gift) – set of toys: tanks, airplanes, pistols, knives and bombs – daddy's gift for a successful boys growing-up;

(Mad Jovica) – combination of Mickey Mouse and a cheap and popular toy from the 1960s, which due to the lead in its base, doesn't matter how much pushed or thrown always gets the vertical position;

(Tears) – made from transparent polyester;

Each group of objects covers one segment of the complex chain in the growth of a child into 'a healthy and socially desirable youth'.

The commercial aspects of the museum are also considered as Yugomuseum is a self-financed organisation independent from both state and non-governmental funds.

The continued growth of the Museum is expected, due to the constant inflow of the surplus of history, but to complete the museum collection as much as possible, it should, by all means, include the following:

the bust of Dimitrije Tucović; all the books written about self-management; the taxi which took Dobrica Ćosić to become the first president of the third Yugoslavia; Tito's Blue Train; the Plastic Jesus from the film *Plastic Jesus*; the army uniform Richard Burton wore in the film *Sutjeska*; the cannon fired by Sergey Bondarscuk in the film *Neretva*; the cannon fired by Edvard Limonov at Sarajevo; the cannons fired in honor of the 1974 Constitution; the spoon from the story 'Spoon' by Antonije Isaković; the knife from the novel 'Knife' by Vuk Drašković; a fork from the presidential ship 'Galeb'; the tray M.T. banged on in February 1997 during the civil protests; RTS (Serbian Broadcasting network) news of unlimited duration; the New RTS news of unlimited duration; the advertisement 'When I say the truth

I mean *Politika*'; the unknown grave of Draža Mihajlović, *chetnik* leader from the Second World War; the gun king Aleksandar Karadjordjević was killed with; the royal gold returned from London; the paintings stolen from the Federal Assembly during the civil protests in October 2000; NATO spokesman Jamey Shea's platform fetched from Brussels; shoulder blade of the ox consumed at Pale; Milovan Djilas's war gun; the morals by Bora Ćosić and Sonja Biserko; all party membership booklets of the Communist Party of Yugoslavia; all the photos of all the people passing by in the Yugoslav Assembly and crying along Ljubljana-Belgrade railroad in 1980 when Tito died; all the hunting trophies from the villa in Karadjordjevo; a log from the 'Log Revolution'; yogurt from the 'Yogurt Revolution'; the exact list of the victims in the Jasenovac concentration camp; the exact list of the civil and military victims during NATO air raids; the exact list of the victims in the Goli Otok camp; the exact map showing mass graves in Kosovo; the exact map of locations enriched with depleted uranium; signs with the slogans: 'Better war than Treaty' from 1941, 'Trieste is ours' from 1945, 'Czechoslovakia is our homeland' from 1938, 'Solidarnosc' from 1980, 'Slobo-Slobodo' from 1989, 'Slobo go away' from 2000; the manuscripts from the Middle Ages saved from the monastery Dečani, Kosovo; the manuscripts from the Middle Ages saved from the monastery Krupa, Croatia; the sandals Buba Morina was wearing in 1989 when she went to the celebration of the 600th anniversary of the lost Kosovo battle; the tractor on which the Jovanović family left Kosovo forever in 1999; the fountain pen Dragiša Cvetković signed the Tripartite Treaty with; the fountain pen the military and technical agreement between NATO and the Yugoslav Army was signed with; the pencil Mira Marković wrote her diaries with; the uniform Marko Milošević president's son was wearing when he was not defending his homeland during the NATO bombing in 1999; Stane Dolanc's tie; the gun and the military cap Ratko Mladić gave as a present to Wesley Clark; the exact minutes report of the talks between Josip Broz Tito and Aleksandar Ranković immediately before the Fourth Plenum; the exact minutes report of the talks between Richard Holbrook and Slobodan Milošević in Dayton and Belgrade; ballot boxes from various periods; the magnetron for the never-finished accelerator in Vinča; the law on nationalisation; telegrams of support from various periods to various leaders; the popular bus in which the citizens of Babušnica returned from the contra-rally in Belgrade; the medical report from Kolubara and the Bor basin on lung diseases; future medical reports on cancer rates in Pančevo; confiscated wheat; goods from Slovenia which were intentionally not purchased; the White Book; Dark Wave; Red Devils; KGPT Šećerana; the referendum for Montenegrin secession, live; the mansion of Željko Ražnatović Arkan open to the public; the Central Prison; the Zemun Gang; the complete armament of the Special Unit from Kula; the Hague indictment against Vojislav Šešelj that he could not understand because it was written in Croatian; the monument to emperor Dušan, which was illegally erected by the Justice Minister, Vladan Batić; the building of TV Pink; the future session of the Yugoslav Assembly with the participation of Serbian, Albanian and Montenegrin deputies, live; etc, etc.

Thank you for visiting Yugomuseum.

Participant

Yugomuseum did not originate as a precise and premeditated project – it was literally configured and 'built' both by the time in which it emerged, and by some kind of permanent hopelessness. Hopelessness, which arose from the continuous, lasting (for several years!) and intense overflow of history into everyday life, to the degree that it completely suffocated the individual and his/her privacy, revoking every other perception of reality, except the one that goes through the prism of political and social context. This project emerged, not because art must enter the field of the political, but because the individual in such times of turmoil certainly has no right to be silent. To be silent as the individual, to pretend that one does not understand the context of political and social situations in which one functions, is a rather sad and miserable thing. Much sadder and

more pitiful, however, is the risk of turning to pamphletism.

The possibility to invent – in the time of the 'culture of lies' – even a bigger lie, and to speak about it like it is a self-evident truth – seemed to me a very good way to depict and copy that epoch.

It also seemed to me that, to invent one's own institution, exaggerated and pretentious as it is, in times when almost all other (renowned and prominent) 'real' institutions are in fact rotten and disgustingly repulsive, is a meaningful and sensible reaction, if not something like sweet revenge.

Further, it made sense to 'populate' this invented institution with invented, virtual sculptures, (for how reasonable it would be, in elementary conditions of a 'bare life', especially during the bombardment of Belgrade, to try to make real sculptures in the world of obvious decay of material reality).

And furthermore, I chose to objectify this personal premeditation.

Due to a lively e-mail communication, a multitude of until then unknown people took part in the realisation of the Yugomuseum project, with their suggestions, reactions, photo-contributions, essays and comments. An exchange occurred which was much more alive then the one you get at so-called *real* exhibitions and something was made with the help of those who usually only watch. A sudden and salvationist escape from loneliness and exclusion was obtained when they did not refuse to be a part of the shouting crowd.

Thus, in some way, the restrain of the rampant common memory that you share with other people around you and the use of the 'tissue' of historical facts as the material in establishing an imaginary institution appeared to me as a good way to mock the large and horrifying history. Through the use of irony this reality composed of one-sided ideological interpretations and empty nationalistic phrases was finally decentralised.

The intention was not to judge historical figures and events, and particularly not to condemn the memories, but to drive ourselves – through the means of a visual vocabulary, with direct visual or face-to-face confronting – to encounter the uncanny, unbearable segments from our past, which we did or didn't understand at the time, and which took place either completely out of our control or with our mute assent that resulted from our inactivity. No matter what, these are the layers that belong to us, or if you will, these are the layers to which we belong. For intentional oblivion cannot cut off the layers of memory. Fortunately so, because any kind of memory is better than the emptiness of amnesia.

(In any case, this observer, speaker, and participant, didn't know how to do it in any other way.)

Note

* A part of this subtext under the title of 'Observer (second time)' is an extract from the interview given to Lidija Merinik (Dr. L. Merenik, 'One Man Band', Remont art magazine 3/4, Beograd, 2001). The part under the title of 'Presenter' is the text which was read along with a slide projection on Yugomuseum as series of lecture-performances/presentations from 1999 to 2003: Budapest (Hotel Gelert), Strasbourg (Universite des Sciences Humaines), Pančevo (PIJS), Budapest (Central European University), Beograd (Alternativna akademska obrazovna mreža), Berlin (Shaubinne), Karlsruhe (ZKM), Novi Sad (Akademija likovnih umetnosti), Beograd (Škola za savremenu umetnost), Albany (University at Albany), New York (Columbia University), New York (New York Institute for Technology), Kruševac (Narodni muzej) and Vienna (Wiener Festwochen).

12. Memory, melancholy and materiality

Victor Buchli

Memory requires a certain degree of iterability both material and discursive in order to sustain it. It is this iterability that presences the absence of a loved one, the nation, home, or ones subjectivity or sexuality. From Foucault we know the importance of the iterative structures both materially and discursively that sustains subjectivities through various disciplines, such as the trained sinews of the soldiers body that remind him that he is no longer a peasant but a well trained disciplined soldier. However, when this iterability fails, both materially and discursively then there is a crisis of being.

The recent significance of the immaterial (see Rowlands 2005; Miller 2005) and its problems represent some serious challenges to the way we understand material culture and its material and discursive iterablity. Pierre Nora has asserted that a society without memory frantically preserves everything. What Nora (1989) describes here is a shift in material and discursive intra-actions (see Barad 2003) that sustain memory; a shift from *milieux de memoire* sustained by doxic assumptions and close knit communal oral traditions to *lieux de memoire* (places of memory) which are essentially remains of where one might say *milieux de memoire* took place and are therefore preserved. This might also be seen as change of memory technologies from earlier predominantly discursive ones changing into something more material. The rapid changes of nineteenth, twentieth and twenty-first century life means modern memory work as a result 'relies on the materiality of the trace, the immediacy of the recording, the visibility of the image' – as Nora has stated (Nora 1989,13),

which is really what the work of material culture studies has been since the nineteenth century to precisely facilitate such memory work in light of rapid industrialisation and colonial expansion. It has been from its beginning the melancholic attempt (Shanks 1992) to grasp, materialise and bring into being that which has been already lost – and thereby deny that loss. It is an active form of resistance to the march of history – it is in Freudian terms, a refusal to mourn; a refusal to acknowledge the loss and move on and it is instead a pathological melancholic denial of this obvious loss, desperately attempting to hang on to something which is no longer there. There is probably no aspect of material culture studies or archaeology, which is not subject to this melancholic yearning. Eng and Kazanian (2003) have suggested that this melancholic denial of the march of history which is the march of the Victor is fundamentally a radical denial of the dominance of historical power whatever form it takes on. Thus one can say material culture studies and archaeology have always been described by this radical dimension. However, this radical melancholic work has been characterised by a certain materiality to realise its work: the fragment, the souvenir, the artefact of material culture in all its variously constituted materiality. In this respect we should not forget the historically contingent nature of material culture itself and its object of study. Within a Foucauldian framework materiality can be seen as having been marshalled to create disciplines and subjectivities that empower as well as disempower. This is where material culture and archaeology as areas of cultural work have emerged.

However, the disciplining effects of materiality have been considerably attenuated – rendered increasingly ineffectual by changes in the materiality of late capitalist experience as evidenced by recent Critical Legal work on actuarial practices (Simon 1988). These studies have suggested a shift away from the exertion of power from those based on the disciplining effects of the material world. This is a shift from attempts to affect the materiality of the world – discipline it, shape it, incarcerate it, etc. but instead rather to manage it. This is what the sociologist Nicholas Rose refers to as the emergence of governance at a distance (Rose 1998) within late-capitalist neo-liberal societies. Power is not exerted materially but actuarially through the ephemeral aggregates of actuarial tables or the emergence of the 'psy' disciplines (such as psychology, etc.) described by Rose which create self-responsibilising, self-managing subjects that can be regulated from afar. Simon's characterisation of the social effects of actuarial practices suggests a form of social life that is attenuated, diffuse and incoherent. It only comes into a situated coherence in the form of aggregates based on diverse and contingent qualities – nothing that might inhere in something or someone we might describe as a subject based on a meaningful population or individual lived experience. As Simon states 'Actuarial practices can mobilize segments of the population and form majorities that have no patterns of shared experience or structures of association and no basis for understanding themselves as motivated by a common cause' (Simon 1988, 793). Simon is describing here an attenuation of moral density that shapes social life, from traditional status groups (Simon 1988, 793) to aggregates. In short fragmented subjects are forged according to formal criteria foreign to any lived experience (after all what does it really mean to be a member of the actuarial aggregate: male non-smoker with a drivers license in a 94151 area code, of which I am one?). Yet it is increasingly through such aggregates that juridical and actuarial power is being exercised, rather than any readily felt or identifiable lived subject position. This suggests that aggregates are formed according to the requirements of dominant

powers: juridical, actuarial etc. However, they also erupt and coalesce in the form of class action suits to exert power collectively at the grass roots level amongst the disempowered. These are highly attenuated coherences, however. Increasingly these situated mercurial coherences emerge as quickly as they disappear in the negotiation of social life and power. Thus there is a loss of any meaningful coherent subjectivity, sacrificed with the exertion of power through highly attenuated and ontologically barren aggregates. A coherent fixed, palpable and essential subjectivity is lost within these circumstances. Simon argues that legal responses to this state of affairs have been mired in a refusal of the dissipation of the individual relying on rights oriented legal remedies focused on the Liberal notion of an abstract individual rather than on group strategies such as affirmative action (Simon 1988, 785) which might be more effective under these circumstances.

I would like to suggest that this melancholic preoccupation with the mercurial properties of social life is not just the preoccupation of archaeologists and other like-minded people but characteristic of our state of affairs in general. Within such an unstable, constantly shifting setting everything is archived, desperately saved – every one is a historian (Nora 1989), constantly archiving their lives, as evidenced by the rise of popular genealogy and the unprecedented degree of documentation, through video, digital photography, and other technologies. Consider for instance the hidden video archive of any individual's life that, when required by the powers that be, can be collected and presented in the instance of any missing person whose last hours can be summoned by police and security cctv footage. An otherwise anonymous life instantly becomes public spectacle.

However like Luria's patient we must forget in order to be healthy (Forty 1999). This forgetfulness is of course provided for by the sheer superfluity of information that envelopes us obscuring so much, unless the powers that be force it to erupt to the surface as in the cctv footage of someone's last known movements. But this also makes the task of constituting memory, materialising it problematic and consistently unstable. Necessary forgetfulness, however, comes at the ontological price of a tragic lightness of being described by Lipovetsky whereby '... it allows more individual freedom, but it generates greater malaise of living [...] which renders us increasingly problematic to ourselves and others' (Lipovetsky 1994, 241). This 'tragic lightness' can be exploited as suggested in recent critiques of actuarial practices and social control. But if there is a lesson to be drawn from Foucault all power is at once enabling and disabling – it is probably up to us as students of material culture to understand this ephemerality and the 'tragic lightness' of our circumstances better – to at once understand its disabling effects but more importantly its enabling ones. Thus the potential of this iterative failure raises some important issues if we are to consider the role of memory and the increasing prevalence of the immaterial in late capitalist life. The ephemerality of capital, financial transactions, the impact of new actuarial practices privileging management over the material effects of traditional Foucauldian disciplines all call our traditional approaches towards materiality and memory into question.

The increasing failure of material practices to sustain iterability makes this increasingly problematic (such as the uncertain fate of digitised information, photos, etc. and the ephemeral and changing media for information storage.) We are in a situation where we are no longer able to presence that which is absent yet are achingly and knowingly aware of that absence of something that is no longer and can no longer be. This suggests a material and mnemonic state of affairs that is characterised by a profound melancholy in the technical sense of Freud's original conceptualisation. Our connection to the world socially and materially is increasingly melancholic. In a sense the process of mourning and the role that traditional materiality plays to facilitate it – by reincorporating that which is absenced into the present and part of our world is thwarted. This melancholic state of affairs inhibits this incorporation within our material and discursive iterative structures. For the simple reason that absences cannot be effectively re-iterated materially or discursively and thereby reincorporated, hence our constant failure to recover the past. Melancholy

resists containment. It is always excessive and always resisting incorporation, whereas proper non-pathological mourning contains this excess, resolves it and moves on.

Take for example the disappeared of the Argentine military dictatorship (Buchli and Lucas 2001). It was the melancholic mourning over that which cannot be presenced, the remains of lost sons and daughters by the Mothers of Argentina, that challenged the political order, calling the government and its past to accountability and facilitated by the presencing of the disappeared by forensic archaeologists. However, once the presencing has occurred, their remains found, the materiality of the disappeared is able to be sustained and thus effectively materially and discursively re-iterated, through ritual mourning practices. This challenge, however, then subsides, mourning takes over, and the absences, now presences, are able to be materially and discursively integrated within prevailing social practices through public rituals of mourning and burial. Thus reconciliation and reincorporation can occur. Order has been challenged and affected, but now it has been restabilised. This is why museums and their artefacts are said to be the enemies of memory permanently ossifying it, forcing us to forget. Similarly, one can consider the melancholic images and artefacts associated with a miscarriage – a person that was to be, a potential presence, absent, but without the public means to mourn and incorporate within social rituals of mourning and burial associated with socially viable kin. If the child never was, how can it be mourned? Yet it was there and the melancholic artefacts associated with such mourning constantly assert that absent presence that never was (Layne 2000).

However, increasingly the materialities in which we are engaged are not able to function in such a way. Thus I would argue we might be moving to a state of affairs that is increasingly melancholic as a consequence of its increasing immateriality, despite the fleeting nature of the ephemerality of social life and its political promise described by Lipovetsky (1994). Presencing is extremely problematic under the conditions of immateriality – memory which presencing enables is highly unstable. As recent actuarial practices suggest, the strategic essentialisms upon which marginalised groups, ethnic and sexual are able to cohere as political subjects become increasingly problematic. The body and its subjectivities are not only difficult to sustain politically within these actuarial regimes but are difficult to cohere conceptually as our post-structuralist critiques suggest.

Hallam and Hockey (2001) have argued that the ephemerality of material life in late capitalist societies so cogently noted by Appadurai (1986) seems to produce desires for permanence to counteract these forces – this is the melancholic work of the various forms of material culture studies which constitute this materiality. They argue that it is no accident that memorial technologies and communal memory is such an important focus of the work of social scientists. However, rather than see this as a battle that we are constantly doomed to lose, because it is inevitably unstable and ephemeral we might see this as a terrain whereupon the critical empirical work of archaeologists and others can use this melancholic impulse and its excesses to challenge the status quo through its incessant re-imaginings and 'eruptive' materialisations – being eruptive they function abjectively within the remains of the forgotten, rejected and wasted: this is after all the dirt of the dirt archaeologist – that challenges the boundaries and structures of social life. As Mary Douglas (1993) noted, this has a 'composting' effect, reintegrating the abject and facilitating social regeneration. What seems to be happening now is that this process is accelerated, and widely dispersed – the tragic lightness of Lipovetsky (1994) and the technologies of materialisation that material culture studies and archaeology serve are more attenuated, and immaterial. Thus how we work and what we do under such circumstances require a reappraisal or maybe just a slight shift in perspective as suggested by Coloredo-Mansfield (2003). Maybe we should begin to 'liquefy' rather than 'objectify' – that is study the changing states of materiality in which we are implicated – which dominant powers seem to be transforming and consider how they disempower as well as empower (Coloredo-Mansfield 2003).

It might be useful to consider the violations of boundaries that fluid immateriality entails: their dissipation, violating the outsides and insides that constitute materiality and durability through waste, decay, and seepage (see Edensor 2005 and DeSilvey 2006). These moments of seepage are not unlike Walter Benjamin's historical disruptions described by Eng and Kazanjian (2003). Like the ephemerality of fashion they keep open the possibility of continual renewal and challenge the settlements of the present such as the new hold actuarial and managerial practices have over us inhibiting coherence. This increasing inability to cohere that we are more and more susceptible to, suggests that this fluidity too can be used against the exercise of power. In which case we might be witnessing a new terrain of micropowers, whose fluidities can enable as easily as they can disable. The problem of memory under these increasing immaterial conditions at this historical moment might offer some insight as to how to work these processes against their inhibiting effects. Rather than bemoaning the material and semiological effects of late-capitalism, as many critics do, it might be more useful to see how they both empower and disempower, that is both enable and disable under current circumstances. That conventional Western ontology is in crisis is no reason not to try and understand these new forms that might be engendered and their enabling effects under the conditions of late capitalism.

The superfluity of information, means that as easily as it can evanesce so too can it easily concresce (to appropriate language from Alfred North Whitehead). As Rudi Coloredo-Mansfield suggested '[s]ome things we need to liquefy, not objectify' (Coloredo-Mansfield 2003). It might be said that it does not take too much to refocus and cause the eruptions in times of emergency described by Benjamin that challenge power (Eng and Kazanian 2003). Such an approach might help us move away from the seemingly fruitless debates of material culture as text at the expense of corporeal phenomenological understanding. There has been a tendency to analyse the textual and oral in distinction and at a remove from the material as though these aspects of materiality

Figure 12.1 Bernardo Bellotto, The ruins of the old Kreuzkirche in Dresden, 1765 (reproduced with permission from Kunsthaus in Zürich).

were in opposition. It might be more useful to move beyond debates of material culture as text and onto the more hybrid forms through which semiosis occurs and their particular material dimensions. We could see them as existing along a continuum of material and discursive intra-actions of social life – working in a more hybrid fashion to sustain social and material life (see Barad 2003) – in short address the processes of liquefaction and objectification.

That we require material things to perform the memory work that they do is because of the conditions of social life within late-capitalism – material things were not called upon to do such work in the past. As Nora notes oral traditions facilitated his *milieux des memoires* rather than the materially sustained *lieux des memoires* of the present. Materiality was configured and worked differently in our recent past as in other

ethnographic contexts and as surely as it was in the more remote past of traditional archaeology. Different technologies with different materialities have been in effect in the past, and the recent past as well as they are emerging into effect in the present. In terms of their enabling qualities, we might consider the work of the archaeology of the recent past whereby the archaeological act facilitates those 'eruptions' in the present within the superfluity of information in which we are enveloped and thereby challenge the settlements of the present (Buchli and Lucas 2001).

In light of this one might consider how this melancholic preoccupation with the fluidity of material form and its 'eruptive' abilities might function. I would like to consider this painting (Fig. 12.1) from the Kunsthaus in Zürich painted in 1765 by Bernardo Bellotto the nephew and student of Canaletto. In 1762 Belotto returned to

Dresden after the Prussians had occupied it during the Seven Years War. In the course of attempting to restore the damage caused by the Prussians to the Kreuzkirche (depicted here), its only remaining East Wall collapsed. This is the scene that Bellotto painted in all its empirically engorged, hyper real, ethnographic and forensic detail. This is not an Arcadian image of Classical ruins we normally encounter filled with picturesque peasants, but a precise account of daily life surrounding these ruins, with its workers, passersby, gawkers, and *trümmerfrauen* (rubble women) (Kunsthaus, Zürich, n.d.) employed to clear away the debris. However, we are instantly reminded here of other rubble women of another time following the Allied destruction of Dresden in 1945. In fact that destruction of 1945 is impossible not to think of when viewing this painting. Passersby observing it in the gallery of the Kunsthaus in Zürich today read the pictures description and repeat the word Dresden several times knowingly re-iterating the more recent destruction of the city. Even though we know that this destruction that we are viewing was perpetrated by the Prussians we are more emphatically – through our knowing repetition of the word 'Dresden' – indicting the Allied forces of 1945. This is a consequence and indictment unimaginable by Bellotto at the time he painted this in 1765 but nonetheless a challenge and indictment that this painting in its excruciating detailed and I would add 'critically empirically' way was emphatically designed by Bellotto to illicit. 1945 and 1765 are closely concatenated and in fact conflated. This repetition, this conflation, that the viewing of Bellotto's image of 1765 and 1945 suggests also brings to mind other concatenations when we see this image and say 'Dresden' and then consider other forms of 'urbicide' in 2003 (Graham 2003) in all their empirical detail, constantly erupting on our television and computer screens and in our mind's eye that challenge prevailing settlements of power and history.

It might be useful to note here the nature of empirical representation either in visual culture or language to reproduce as completely as possibly the physical detail of that which is observed with minimal deviance in the interpretive eye of the observer. Its hyper-detail possesses a certain promiscuous excess that enables its assimilation in radically different contexts (see Thomas 1997). It is a curious effect of this empirical tradition which collapses time. It always retains a haunting and challenging immediacy: such as the uncanny qualities of a Vermeer. This is not a reality effect, this is not a true documentation of things as they are, but it is a powerful sleight of hand that facilitates a merging of horizons that such an empiricism effects that with radical force produces an identification or an assimilation as Thomas notes. Such empiricism collapses time, challenges the boundaries of historically produced temporalities causing time and place to erupt and collapse into one another as the two Dresden's of 1945 and 1765 do here in the case of the Bellotto, indicting both the Allies of 1945 as well as the Prussians of 1765. This is the melancholic effect of our empirical traditions that archaeology and ethnography have produced so well and which I would suggest have even greater work to do under the conditions of ephemeral superfluity in which we live now. But it is important to note that such empiricism can work in the opposite way. Bellotto's views of Warsaw where he was court painter after Dresden, were then used to reconstruct Warsaw after the Nazi occupation of the Second World War. Interestingly in this case the critically empirical work of Belotto was used in an equally radical and unexpected way to conflate 18th century Warsaw and an imagined vision of post-war twentieth century Warsaw to radically undo the effect of war. It facilitated a reincorporation and denial of Nazi devastation, performing the opposite function of Bellotto's image of the Kreuzkirche – materially forgetting the devastation of the Second World War as a form of counter-iconoclasm as Forty describes (Forty 1999, 10) whereby 'the filling of a void, whose emptiness had exercised diverse collective memories, ends by excluding all but a single dominant one' (Forty 1999, 10). It is precisely these eruptions that archaeology facilitates that momentarily challenge dominant settlements and whose melancholic refusal to let go provides a constant challenge to the way things appear to be.

Our increasingly melancholic circumstances which mourn the loss of coherent subjectivities are also the circumstances whereby these melancholic impulses erupt to challenge the highly attenuated and 'thin' settlements about which power mercurially coheres in the present.

Bibliography

Appadurai, A. (1986) *The Social Life of Things: Commodities in Cultural Perspective*. Cambridge, Cambridge University Press.

Barad, K. (2003) Posthumanist Performativity: Toward an Understanding of How Matter Comes to Matter. *Signs: Journal of Women in Culture and Society* 28(3), 801–831.

Buchli, V. (2002) Introduction. In V. Buchli (ed.) *The Material Culture Reader*, 1–12. Oxford, Berg Publishers.

Buchli, V. and Lucas, G. (eds) (2001) *Archaeologies of the Contemporary Past*. London, Routledge.

Colloredo-Mansfield, R. (2003) Introduction: Matter Unbound. *Journal of Material Culture* 11(8), 273–284.

DeSilvey, C. (2006) Observed Decay. *Journal of Material Culture* 11(3), 318–338.

Douglas, M. (1993) *Purity and Danger*. London, Routledge.

Edensor, T. (2005) *Industrial Ruins*. Oxford, Berg Publishers.

Eng, D. L. and Kazanjian, D. (2003) *Loss*. Berkeley, University of California Press.

Forty, A. and Küchler, S. (1999) *The Art of Forgetting*. Oxford, Berg Publishers

Foucault, M. (1977) *Discipline and Punish*. New York, Pantheon.

Graham, S. (2003) Urbicide by the Jordan. *New Left Review* 19 (Jan/Feb).

Hallam, E and Hockey, J. (2001) *Death, Memory and Material Culture*. Oxford, Berg Publishers.

Layne, L. (2000) He Was a Real Baby with Baby Things. *Journal of Material Culture* 5, 321–345.

Lipovetsky, G. (1994) *The Empire of Fashion: Dressing Modern Democracy*. Princeton, Princeton University Press.

Miller, D. (ed.) (2005) *Materiality*. Durham N.C., Duke University Press.

Nora, P. (1989) Between Memory and History: *Les Lieux de Mémoire*. *Representations* 26 (Spring), 7–25.

Oliver, K. (ed.) (1997) *The Portable Kristeva*. New York, Columbia University Press

Rose, N. (1998) *Inventing our Selves: Psychology, Power and Personhood*. Cambridge, Cambridge University Press.

Rowlands, M. (2005) A Materialist Approach to Materiality. In D. Miller (ed.) *Materiality*, 72–87. Durham, N. C., Duke University Press

Shanks, M. (1992), *Experiencing the Past: On the Character of Archaeology*. London, Routledge.

Simon, J. (1988) The Ideological Effects of Actuarial Practices. *Law and Society Review* 22(4), 771–800.

Thomas, N. (1997) *In Oceania*. Durham, N.C., Duke University Press.

Whitehead, A. (1978) *Process and Reality: An Essay in Cosmology*. New York, The Free Press.